THE CHARACTER OF THE GOOD RULER

·THE·

CHARACTER

Of a GOOD

RULER.

As it was Recommended in a

SERMON

Preached before his Excellency the
GOVERNOUR, and the Honourable COUNSELLORS, and Assembly of the REPRESENTATIVES
of the Province of *Massachusetts-Bay*
in *NEW-ENGLAND*.

On *May* 30. 1694.

Which was the Day for Election of
COUNSELLORS for that Province.

By *Samuel Willard*, Teach.r of a
Church in *Boston*.

Boston Printed by *Benjamin Harris*, for
Michael Perry, under the *West-End*
of the *Town-House*. 1694.

HE CHARACTER
OF THE GOOD RULER

A Study of Puritan Political Ideas
in New England, 1630–1730

BY T. H. BREEN

Associate Professor of History at Northwestern University.

The Norton Library
W·W·NORTON & COMPANY·INC·
NEW YORK

FOR MY PARENTS

Books That Live
The Norton imprint on a book means that in the publisher's
estimation it is a book not for a single season but for the years.
W. W. Norton & Company, Inc.

Library of Congress Cataloging in Publication Data
Breen, T. H.
    The character of the good ruler.
    Reprint of the ed. published by Yale University
Press, New Haven.
    Bibliography: p.
    1. Leadership. 2. Puritans. 3. New England—
Politics and government—Colonial period, ca. 1600–1775.
I. Title.
JK54.B74   1974   320.5'0974   74-14788
ISBN 0-393-00747-2

Printed in the United States of America
1 2 3 4 5 6 7 8 9 0

CONTENTS

ACKNOWLEDGMENTS

This work has profited from the advice of many loyal friends. David Axeen, Stephen Foster, Richard Warch, Frederick Bode, Erik Midelfort, Leon Schulzinger, Thomas Hanlon, and Laurence Moore offered valuable suggestions and criticisms all along the way. To David Axeen I give special thanks for many patient and painstaking hours of proofreading. Sydney Ahlstrom, David Hall, and J. H. Hexter, all of the Yale University faculty, have helped me to understand Puritanism and have corrected me when I went astray. When I was revising the manuscript for publication, Robert Middlekauff of the University of California at Berkeley provided important advice. My greatest debt without question is to Professors Edmund S. Morgan and Franklin L. Baumer, both of whom expressed early faith in my work. No acknowledgment would be complete without thanking my wife, Susan, who assisted me throughout.

T. H. B.

New Haven, Connecticut
January 1970

INTRODUCTION

The Character of the Good Ruler examines the transformation of political ideas in a society often regarded as a model of stability. The seemingly static quality of the seventeenth- and early eighteenth-century election sermons could easily lead one to conclude that political theory had changed very little during New England's first hundred years.[1] Certainly, much of the rhetoric dealing with the character of the good ruler in Massachusetts and Connecticut appeared the same in 1730 as it had in 1630. Year after year, Congregational ministers counseled the voters to select pious leaders—men who would defend the church from any danger, be it apathy or heresy. The traditional language, drawing upon medieval concepts, urged the colonists to honor their civil rulers as God's vicegerents on earth. And no election sermon was complete without a reminder that the Lord had established a divine order in the universe, giving every person a specific place and calling.

Despite their static appearance, Puritan political ideas were not an unchanging or uniform body of thought. To treat them as such involves the colonial historian in interpretive difficulties. We know, for example, that the early decades of the seventeenth century were a religious age, a time when Puritans as well as their enemies believed that all aspects of man's society came under God's purview. It was a period when people thought that the business of government possessed divine significance. But by the middle of the eighteenth century, as we also know, many colonists suspected that the

1. See Richard L. Bushman, *From Puritan to Yankee: Character and the Social Order in Connecticut, 1690–1765* (Cambridge, Mass., 1967), pp. 3–21.

Lord had retreated from human affairs, having elected to operate from a distance as an impersonal force sustaining the universe. The men of Benjamin Franklin's generation naturally judged their rulers by standards which were different from those of John Winthrop's. Unfortunately, in many historical accounts, the intellectual progression from Winthrop to Franklin is unclear, and the student of colonial America is usually informed that sometime around 1700 the monolithic Puritan movement simply crumbled under its own theological weight, allowing New Englanders to entertain new, previously unwelcome, political ideas. The transition, however, from an age of religion to an age of reason was much more complex than this standard interpretation admits.

During the first half of the seventeenth century people tended to discuss the character of the good ruler in spiritual language. Governor Winthrop, for example, reminded his critics repeatedly that civil magistrates have their "authority from God, in way of an ordinance, such as hath the image of God eminently stamped upon it." Winthrop's opponents disagreed with him on many details, but they accepted his basic premise about the divine nature of magisterial office. By the end of the century the rhetoric of New England politics had changed; and, as this investigation demonstrates, the Glorious Revolution was the crucial event in the transformation of Puritan ideas about civil leadership. The colonists rebelled against their appointed English governor, Sir Edmund Andros, not because he was an Anglican or because he was ungodly, but because he threatened the citizens' liberties and property. In other words, after 1689 the good ruler in Massachusetts and Connecticut was first and foremost a defender of civil rights and only secondarily a defender of the Congregational faith. During the last decade of the century a group of ministers unwittingly revealed the process that had occurred by urging the people of Massachusetts to support the colony's new royal charter (1691) because it "secures Liberty and Property, the fairest Flowers of the Civil State." The following chapters trace the movement from godliness to property in the continuing debate about the character of the good ruler.

The failure to take account of the evolution of Puritan political ideas not only has made it difficult to explain long-range intellectual shifts, but also has obscured the political flexibility and originality of each generation. Throughout the seventeenth century, New Englanders argued among themselves about the proper characteristics of the good ruler; and at no time did they reach full agreement about what those attributes should be. During the early years, for example, Governor Winthrop fought with the deputies when they defined the magisterial office in a manner which he could not accept. In the 1670s and 1680s, Samuel Nowell, William Hubbard, and Increase Mather each advocated different types of rulers for the Bay Colony, even though all three were loyal members of the Congregational church. And finally, the Glorious Revolution sparked an intense debate in Massachusetts and Connecticut about the responsibilities of political leadership within New England. There was simply no single or uniform Puritan response to political questions. On the contrary, one finds a rich variety of responses, and each generation conducted its own dialogue about the character of the good ruler. Disagreement about political principles, therefore, was not in itself an indication that the children of the founders had deserted the harmonious ways of the first Puritans. In fact, the original settlers of New England seem to have had as much trouble as did their sons in working out the limitations of civil office.[2]

When Puritan writers—pamphleteers as well as clergymen—discussed the character of the good ruler, they were concerned with more than his personal attributes. They believed, of course, that wealth, breeding, and education were important elements to be weighed at election time and were prepared to bar from office individuals who did not possess such qualifications. But for New Englanders the topic also included an analysis of the magistrate's duties after the voters had selected him. What were the limits of his authority? What were the powers of the people in determining civil policies? Was he responsible to the freemen who had chosen him or only to God? Should the ruler punish heresy or support religious toleration?

2. For an excellent exchange of views about the flexibility within Puritan thought, see Edmund S. Morgan, "New England Puritanism: Another Approach," *William and Mary Quarterly*, 3d ser. 18 (1961): 236–42; Darrett B. Rutman, "God's Bridge Falling Down: Another Approach' to New England Puritanism Assayed," ibid. 19 (1962): 413–14; and Morgan, "Letter to the Editor," ibid., pp. 642–44.

What was the magistrate's relation to private property and English liberties? Perhaps the most important consideration for the Puritans who wrote about the character of the good ruler was the cause and justification of revolution.

In order to understand the transformation of Puritan political ideas, it was necessary to reconstruct in considerable detail the historical context in which changes took place. It is extremely difficult, of course, to establish the relationship between political theory and historical events. Sometimes notions about the character of the good ruler influenced the way civil leaders actually behaved in office. But more often, theory seemed to joggle along behind practice. Many situations arose during the first hundred years which forced New Englanders to modify their beliefs about political leadership. People in the first generation expressed ideas about delegated authority only after Winthrop's civil decisions had begun to seem arbitrary. At a later time the influx of Quakers and Baptists into the Bay Colony caused the Puritans to reconsider the ruler's religious responsibilities. And Governor Andros's high-handed seizure of private property brought forth yet another readjustment in political theory. In fact, New Englanders seemed most willing to discuss the abstract characteristics of the good ruler when they were confronted with a bad or unsatisfactory one in office.

The close study of political ideas in their historical context revealed that the rhetoric of the election sermons as well as other political pronouncements was not as traditional as it might have first appeared. The clergy who preached to the voters and to the members of the General Court at election time were fully aware of the immediate problems confronting the rulers of New England. More often than not they used the opportunity to comment upon these problems. Sometimes a minister would cite a biblical passage which he thought bore on the political situation at hand. Others revealed their opinions by omitting one of the usual elements from the election sermon. Some preachers placed special weight on points which they knew their audience would regard as relevant; others like the Reverend John Davenport, came right out and attacked policies wihch they believed were ruining New England.

Sometimes the lower house in Massachusetts chose the election speaker, sometimes the upper house.[3] But whatever the case, knowledge of the peculiar events surrounding an election give the "standard" rhetoric fresh meaning for the historian of political ideas. In the process of writing this book, the election sermons formed only a small part of my research. An understanding of the total political environment helped to reveal subtleties in newspapers, pamphlets, and journals that might otherwise have gone unnoticed.

I do not mean to suggest, of course, that I tried to read between the lines or to see elements that another person looking at the same document would not also have spotted. I disagree with the scholar of the American Revolution who recently urged historians to "dissolve the distinctions between the Revolutionaries' stated intentions and their supposedly hidden needs and desires."[4] Since I had no way of getting at the Puritans' "hidden desires," short of mass psychoanalysis, I was forced to rely on what they told me their desires were. In all cases I have assumed that the seventeenth-century clergymen, politicians, and pamphleteers meant what they said, no matter how outrageous their words might now appear.

There is always a danger in a book of this type of anticipating historical events, of interpreting political rhetoric in light of some impending revolution or political crisis unknown to the people of the time. For example, it would have been tempting in chapter 1, which contains a discussion of English ideas about the good ruler during the 1620s, to have speculated on the intellectual roots of the Civil War and the success of Oliver Cromwell. To have done so, however, would have been misleading, since I have not worked out the transformation of English Puritan ideas in the years after 1630. A far greater temptation was to regard the entire project as an investigation of the background of the American Revolution. Fortunately, John M. Murrin warned against this pitfall, explaining that historians who look ahead tend to see "the period [before the Revolution] in categories radically different from those invoked by contemporaries to explain themselves. By focusing only on signposts

3. See the Bibliographical Essay for a full discussion of the election sermon as a source for the political historian.

4. Gordon S. Wood, "Rhetoric and Reality in the American Revolution," *William and Mary Quarterly,* 3d ser. 23 (1966): 16.

pointing ahead, they avoid confusing their insight with other signs
and scenes closer at hand."[5] As much as possible, I have accepted this
advice and have viewed the political spokesmen of each generation
not as proto-Sons of Liberty or as Jacksonian democrats, but as
individuals caught up in the special problems of their own time. In
a short epilogue, I make some suggestions about the possible connections between seventeenth-century political ideas and the eighteenth-century theory that underlay the American Revolution. Even
here, however, I have attempted to analyze the subject on its own
terms without glancing ahead to see what happened to these ideas
during the course of the Revolution.

Because I wanted to emphasize the unique quality of political discussion within each generation, I have avoided using such
descriptive terms as "moderate," "conservative," "liberal," "democrat,"
and "aristocrat." These words create serious problems in a study that
deals with such a long period of time. Take "conservative" as an
example of the difficulties involved. Governor. Winthrop might be
called a conservative because he resisted the deputies' demands for
constitutional limitations on the magisterial office. During the 1670s,
and early 1680s, the Congregational clergy—especially the Jeremiahs
—might also be labeled as the conservative element in New England
politics. And at still a later date, one could make a case that Governor
Joseph Dudley was politically more conservative than were many of
his contemporaries. The problem is, of course, that there is not
necessarily any relationship or even similarity between the ideas of
Winthrop and the Jeremiahs, between Winthrop and Dudley, or
between Winthrop and any other "conservative" in the seventeenth
and eighteenth centuries. Each of the periods treated in the following
chapters had its own conservative, moderate, and liberal representatives, but they were conservative, moderate, and liberal only in relation
to each other and not to groups that came before or after.[6]

5. John M. Murrin, "The Myths of Colonial Democracy and Royal
Decline in Eighteenth-Century America: A Review Essay," *Cithara* 5
(1965): 54.

6. See Oscar Handlin and Mary Handlin, "Radicals and Conservatives in Massachusetts after Independence," *New England Quarterly*
17 (1944): 343–55; and T. H. Breen, "John Adams' Fight Against
Innovation in the New England Constitution: 1776," ibid. 40 (1967):
501–20.

The use of a term like "conservative" to describe seventeenth-century New Englanders raises another, even more complicated, interpretive problem. Many of the persons who appear in this study were conservative in one sphere of their lives and liberal in another. One colonial scholar has recently discovered that during the 1670s some of the Puritan civil leaders most firmly committed to keeping the Congregational Commonwealth free from England's influence were the very men who were most willing to tolerate Baptist meetings in Boston.[7] Clearly, in this example one has to qualify the word "conservative" to indicate whether one is referring to a religious or political characteristic. Other studies have also demonstrated the dangers involved in categorizing historical figures as either liberals or conservatives. In his investigation of the effects of the Great Awakening, Alan Heimert found that the ministers who preached undiluted Calvinism tended to support the American Revolution wholeheartedly, while those who accepted the new, more rational Arminian beliefs were less enthusiastic about the political radicalism of the 1760s.[8]

In order to escape some of the problems associated with the traditional terminology, I adopted new categories. In chapter 2, for example, I describe the political division of the 1630s and 1640s as a split between the *Delegated* and *Discretionary* forces. And in the last sections of the book, I discuss the controversy over the character of the good ruler in terms of *Court* and *Country*. These categories are not intended to suggest that there were organized political parties or factions in seventeenth-century New England. Rather I hoped that words like Delegated and Discretionary, Court and Country would reflect general attitudes about the nature of political leadership. Or, put another way, following the lead of Marvin Meyers, I tried to capture the various political persuasions within each generation.[9]

One term, however, appears throughout this study—"Puritanism." To a certain extent, I am guilty of what Perry Miller described as

---

7. E. Brooks Holifield, "On Toleration in Massachusetts," *Church History* 38 (1969): 188–200.

8. Alan Heimert, *Religion and the American Mind from the Great Awakening to the Revolution* (Cambridge, Mass., 1966).

9. Marvin Meyers, *The Jacksonian Persuasion, Politics and Belief* (New York, 1957), pp. v–xii.

taking my "Puritanism for granted."[10] As a distinct religious movement in sixteenth- and seventeenth-century England and America,
I think that its existence is beyond doubt.[11] But Puritanism is a
weasel word. Ecclesiastical reformers of the Stuart period and historians ever since have haggled over its exact definition, and the
battle continues with little sign of abatement. I sidestep this his-
toriographical conflict simply by assuming, especially in chapter 1,
that men like William Perkins, William Ames, William Gouge,
John Downame, Richard Sibbes, John Preston, Alexander Leighton,
and Samuel Ward were Puritans and that their writings on theological as well as political matters can be taken as a genuine expression
of Puritan beliefs.[12] In the later chapters on New England, I regard
almost all Congregationalists as Puritans. Certainly, no test is applied
to establish whether acceptance of something like the Half-Way
Covenant made a person less a Puritan than someone who rejected
it. I leave it to the historians of religion to distinguish the various
degrees of Puritanism.

Some readers may protest that this is a study not about Puritanism
but about Puritan political ideas, two entirely separate matters.
After all, the historian Charles George has recently declared that
"Puritan political thought is almost as non-existent as puritan
theology but it flourishes in the canon of modern historiography."[13]
George's point is well taken. Many of the ideas which the Puritans
held about the character of the good ruler were shared by the great
majority of seventeenth-century Englishmen. In the first part of
chapter 1 these common notions are discussed at length. But in the

10. Perry Miller, *The New England Mind*, 2 vols. (Boston, 1961), 1:
viii.

11. Charles H. George and Katherine George take the opposite position in *The Protestant Mind of the English Reformation, 1570–1640*
(Princeton, 1961).

12. My discussion of Puritanism relies heavily on William Haller,
The Rise of Puritanism (New York, 1957); Haller, *Liberty and Reformation
in the Puritan Revolution* (New York, 1963); John F. H. New, *Anglican
and Puritan: The Basis of Their Opposition, 1558–1640* (Stanford, 1964);
Perry Miller, *Orthodoxy in Massachusetts, 1630–1650* (Boston, 1933);
Miller, *New England Mind*, and Norman Pettit, *The Heart Prepared:
Grace and Conversion in Puritan Spiritual Life* (New Haven, 1966).

13. C. H. George, "Puritanism as History and Historiography," *Past
and Present*, no. 41 (1968), p. 101.

same chapter I also point out that the Puritans pushed these ideas further than most of their contemporaries were willing to go. The Puritans' political thought was distinct in two respects. First, they demanded something close to perfection in their rulers; and second, they stressed the citizen's moral obligation to replace bad or ineffective magistrates with better ones.

The unique quality of the Puritan political rhetoric may have had its roots in the writings of men like Christopher Goodman, a Marian exile who as early as 1560 declared that the Lord entrusted every Christian with a responsibility to rid the state of ungodly tyrants. Goodman distinguished himself from the other churchmen of his generation by insisting that each individual had to decide for himself whether his ruler merited obedience. If the subject concluded in the negative, he had to remove that ruler from power. Goodman did not appeal to uninstructed conscience, to be sure, but to conscience tempered by its regard for the law. He made it clear that God would punish any nation, especially a favored one like England, whose citizens temporized in the face of evil. Chapter 1 explains how the Puritans altered Goodman's ideas to fit the peculiar conditions of the 1620s.

The Puritans who came to America in order to escape Charles I and Archbishop Laud believed that civil government was established upon a covenant between the ruler and the ruled; and, like Goodman, they insisted that it was the duty of each freeman to judge whether his magistrates fulfilled their obligation to God and the people. The voluntaristic element in Puritan political thought endured while other ideas were altered or discarded. During the late seventeenth and early eighteenth centuries various writers in New England continued to emphasize the people's responsibility to participate in government affairs and to guard against bad magistrates. Men like John Wise, Benjamin Franklin, and Jonathan Mayhew—persons not usually classified as Puritans—carried on the political traditions of the founders by telling the freemen of their own day that it was a matter of conscience, not convenience, whether Massachusetts was governed by good rulers.[14]

14. For a short discussion of the development of Puritan political ideas during the colonial period see the introduction to Edmund S. Morgan, ed.,

Throughout the book, I have tried to avoid what Robert G. McCloskey has described as the compulsion among American political historians "to transmute able statesmen and learned judges into something else."[15] The men who appear in the following chapters—John Winthrop, Samuel Nowell, William Hubbard, Joseph Dudley, John Wise—were not great political theorists. None of them produced any writings which rival the works of their more famous English contemporaries: Thomas Hobbes, James Harrington, Algernon Sidney, and John Locke. What made the Americans interesting was the fact that they did *not* rise above the notions and prejudices of their own generation. They were men intimately involved with the religious, political, and economic problems of their day; and, as such, they offered many insights about the development of Puritan political ideas which more abstract theorists might not have provided.[16]

Barring a few exceptions, I reproduced the spelling and punctuation exactly as they appeared in seventeenth-century sources. Wherever necessary I transposed "i" for "j," "u" for "v," "th" for "y," used a single form of "s," and expanded abbreviations to correspond to modern usage.

Puritan Political Ideas, 1558–1794 (Indianapolis, 1965), pp. xiii–xlvii; also, Morgan, "The Puritan Ethic and the American Revolution," *William and Mary Quarterly,* 3d Ser. 24 (1967): 3–43.

15. Robert G. McCloskey, "American Political Thought and the Study of Politics," *American Political Science Review* 51 (1957): 116.

16. Charles M. Andrews, "Historic Doubts Regarding Early Massachusetts History," *Publications of The Colonial Society of Massachusetts* 28 (1930–33): 292–93.

1

THE ENGLISH BACKGROUND:
THE 1620s

NY Englishman could see that something was wrong. Throughout the kingdom during the 1620s there were signs of the growing polarity. The nobility to which the people traditionally looked for leadership did not seem so worthy of honor and preferment as it once had.[1] Whenever Parliament met the members of Commons engaged the Crown in an ongoing, and increasingly bitter struggle over the limits of royal prerogative. Everywhere one heard rumors of Catholic intrigues at Court, of Spanish alliances, of government corruption.[2] But nowhere were the strains and disagreements over principles of government more visible than in the church, in the clash of words between Anglicans and Puritans.

One Sunday in 1623 an Anglican bishop, Robert Sanderson, lectured his parishioners about the nature of civil government and the selection of good magistrates. It was unusual for Sanderson to preach about such temporal matters. Throughout his life, he had tried to avoid controversy. In fact, his friends regarded him as a "timorous and bashful" person, an individual more happily involved in scholarship than in politics. After graduating from Oxford Sanderson had risen steadily in the ranks of the Church of England. His orthodoxy was unquestioned, his piety greatly respected. The unsettling events of the time, however, forced the bishop to discuss civil affairs. Like most moderate men of the period he hated the

1. Lawrence Stone, *The Crisis of the Aristocracy, 1558–1641* (Oxford, 1965), pp. 65–128.

2. J. H. Hexter, "The English Aristocracy, Its Crisis, and the English Revolution, 1558–1660," *Journal of British Studies* 8 (1968): 62–64.

political contention which the Puritans and their allies in Parliament
had helped to exacerbate.[3]

In his sermon the bishop stressed the distinction between political
theory and practice. While his ideal magistrate was a charitable,
impartial, and courageous person, Sanderson did not expect to find
these abstract standards very often fulfilled in this world. Nor did
this lack seem to bother him very much. "We must not be so dainty
in our choice then," he explained to his audience, "as to find one in
every respect such as hath been characterized. We live not *in Republica Platonis,* but *in faece saeculi;* and it is well if we can find
one in some good mediocrity so qualified." The bishop was irritated
by political perfectionists whose extreme and unrealistic demands
created faction, bitterness, and frustration. Sanderson certainly did not
expect the magistrates of his native Lincolnshire to transform the
country into a New Israel; nor, for that matter, did he believe that the
Lord would punish England if her rulers were not the virtuous leaders
that Moses and Nehemiah had been. "Amid the common corruptions
of mankind," he counseled, "he is to be accounted a tolerable good
man that is not intolerably bad; and among so many infirmities and
defects as I have now reckoned, we may well voice him for a
Magistrate, not that is free from them all, but that hath the fewest
and least."[4]

Thomas Adams, an altogether different sort of man, preached the
Puritan word from his London pulpit; and the people who came to
hear him referred to Adams as the "Shakespeare" of the Puritan movement.[5] In 1625 he delivered an important sermon entitled "The
Holy Choice" at the election of the lord mayor of London. The
fiery minister instructed the city's voters to look to the Lord when
they made their selection. There was no distinction to be made
between a ruler's real and ideal characteristics. The Puritan preacher
had no use whatsoever for "tolerable good" magistrates, men whom
he knew would accept the *"faece saeculi"* of England with little

3. Izaak Walton, *Izaak Walton's Lives; Sir Henry Wotton, Mr. Richard
Hooker, Mr. George Herbert, Dr. Robert Sanderson* (London, 1960),
p. 301; also, *Dictionary of National Biography* (hereafter referred to as
DNB); Works of Robert Sanderson, 6 vols. (Oxford, 1854).

4. Sanderson, *Works,* 2: 202.

5. *DNB.*

more than a stoic shrug of the shoulders. While Adams did not denigrate the possession of wealth or nobility, he did not feel that these attributes alone were enough. He expected the candidate, regardless of social background, to purge the city of wickedness after attaining political office. "To speak morally," the clergyman declared, "active worth is better than passive: this last we have from our ancestors, the first from ourselves. Let me rather see one virtue in a man alive, than all the rest in his pedigree dead." He insisted that "new birth" or spiritual grace, not worldly titles, prepared individuals for the business of government; and, unlike Sanderson, Adams required something near perfection in his rulers. "It is not enough," he warned, "to avoid fault, but even the suspicion." Adams saw no reason to be apologetic for making demands which other persons may well have regarded as unrealistic. England was in imminent danger of moral collapse, and "A Timorous and flexible magistrate is not fit for these corrupt times."[6]

To some extent, the political differences between the Anglicans and Puritans are difficult to understand. Men like Sanderson and Adams shared many fundamental ideas about the nature of the cosmos and about the ideal characteristics of the good ruler.[7] What separated them during the 1620s, what made all the difference, in fact, was the way in which the Anglicans and Puritans related these common beliefs to English political practices. The Anglicans tended to accept the fact that magistrates would err and fail to meet the rhetorical standards of their profession. But the Puritans insisted

6. *The Works of Thomas Adams: Being the Sum of His Sermons, Meditations, and Other Divine and Moral Discourses*, 3 vols. (Edinburgh, 1861–62), 2: 255–60. Another Puritan minister, John Downame, declared, "Let no man . . . boast himselfe of his farre-fetcht pedigree, unless he can prove also a succession of virtues and good parts" (*The Christian Warfare* [London, 1619], pt. 2, p. 330). Michael Walzer's *The Revolution of the Saints* (Cambridge, Mass., 1965) contains a good, although overstated, discussion of the Puritan commitment to active virtues, e.g. pp. 60–65, 264–65.

7. The best treatment of the ideas which the Anglicans and Puritans held in common is Charles H. George and Katherine George, *The Protestant Mind of the English Reformation, 1570–1640* (Princeton, 1961); also see George, "Puritanism as History and Historiography," *Past and Present*, no. 41 (1968), pp. 77–104; Perry Miller and Thomas Johnson, eds., *The Puritans*, 2 vols. (New York, 1963), 1: 1–19.

that rulers fulfill the basic attributes of their calling with unwavering strictness. Only after one studies the areas of agreement, can one begin to see why the Sandersons and the Adamses of England disagreed so intensely.

Anglicans and Puritans: Common Political Ideas

Anglican and Puritan writers of the early 1600s seldom discussed the good ruler without reference to a cosmic scheme which has come to be known as the Elizabethan world picture. They assumed that God had arranged His creatures into hierarchies, so that "even in degree and order . . . one should be above another."[8] All agreed, however, that unity and harmony, not diversity, had been the Lord's ultimate aim. Human society was therefore seen as an organic structure in which all men, regardless of their various ranks and stations in life, cooperated for the greater glorification of God. The rich and the poor, the nobles and the peasants—all were committed to the smooth operation of the community as a whole.[9]

The Elizabethan cosmology had far-reaching political implications, as Englishmen at the time were fond of pointing out. For one thing, the system explained social inequality as both necessary and natural. When Bishop Joseph Hall stated that "Equality hath no place, either in earth or in hell," and then advised his parishioners not to look for it in heaven either, he was merely repeating a conventional piece of wisdom.[10] The hierarchical scheme received its fullest and

8. Edmund S. Morgan, ed., *Puritan Political Ideas, 1558–1794* (Indianapolis, 1965), p. 51, citing William Perkins, "A Treatise of the Vocations or Callings of men, with sorts and kinds of them, and the right use thereof." Also see *The Works of Lancelot Andrewes,* 11 vols. (Oxford, 1854), 7: 174 [From "The Pattern of Catechistical Doctrine"].

9. E. M. W. Tillyard, *Shakespeare's History Plays* (London, 1956); Tillyard, *The Elizabethan World Picture* (New York, n.d.); Wallace Notestein, *The English People on the Eve of Colonization* (New York, 1962), pp. 30–35; Margaret Judson, *The Crisis of the Constitution* (New York, 1964), pp. 17–43, 311–48; John D. Eusden, *Puritans, Lawyers, and Politics in Early Seventeenth-Century England* (New Haven, 1958). For an excellent discussion on cooperation by William Perkins, see Morgan, *Puritan Political Ideas,* p. 50.

10. Philip Wynter, ed., *The Works of the Right Reverend Joseph Hall,* 10 vols. (Oxford, 1863), 8: 366–67; also Sir John Doderidge, *Honors*

most popular expression from a talented Tudor official, Sir Thomas Smith. In his famous book, *De Republica Anglorum,* Smith divided English society into four separate groups—gentlemen, citizens, yeomen artificers, and laborers. The various levels of society corresponded to visible attainments made possible by wealth and good breeding; and each rank carried with it certain distinct prerogatives. The kingdom's highest classes, for example, were granted the right to govern the rest of the population. According to Smith, laborers, poor husbandmen, landless merchants, and all artificers "have no voice nor authoritie in our common wealth, and no account is made of them but onelie to be ruled, not to rule other."[11] Like Smith, most Englishmen who bothered to record their views assumed that the country's "natural rulers" would be drawn from the upper class.[12]

The Elizabethan world picture also sanctified civil obedience; or, put another way, it branded rebellion as an expression of man's sinful nature. The more English writers became aware of the social insecurity around them, of the growing number of vagabonds who wandered from area to area, of the revolutions in countries like Scotland, France, and Holland, the more they stressed the value of civil order.[13] They reminded their readers that God expected each

Pedigree or the Several Fountaines of Gentry (London, 1652); John Ayre, ed., *The Works of John Whitgift,* 3 vols. (Cambridge, Eng., 1851–53), 1: 160.

11. L. Alston, ed., *Sir Thomas Smith's De Republica Anglorum* (Cambridge, Eng., 1906), p. 46; see J. W. Allen, *A History of Political Thought in the Sixteenth Century* (London, 1960), pp. 262–68.

12. Henry Peacham told his readers that "Noble or Gentlemen ought to be preferred in Fees, Honours, Offices, and other dignities of command and government before the common people" *(The Compleat Gentleman* [London, 1643], p. 13). Also see Charles H. McIlwain, ed., *The Political Works of James I* (Cambridge, Mass., 1918), p. 33. McIlwain's long introduction to this work remains one of the finest discussions of early Stuart political theory. John Keble, arr., *The Works of the Learned and Judicious Divine, Mr. Richard Hooker,* 3 vols. (Oxford, 1845), 1: 175.

13. J. G. A. Pocock, " 'The Onely Politician': Machiavelli, Harrington, and Felix Raab," *Historical Studies: Australia and New Zealand* 12 (1966): 255; Winthrop D. Jordan, *White over Black: American Attitudes toward*

person to stay in the place to which he had been assigned. The Lord made some men rulers, others subjects, so that any confusion of these two ranks clearly represented blasphemous disrespect of the divine plan. In an extravagant statement typical of this era, Bishop Lancelot Andrewes proclaimed that "obedience to government ought to be dearer to us than our goods, yea than our lives."[14] In the early decades of the seventeenth century few Englishmen were willing to sacrifice either their lives or goods to the Stuarts, although most of them did believe that obedience was an excellent quality—at least in the abstract.[15]

Much of the discussion about the good ruler drew heavily upon the doctrine of calling, which was but one facet of the Elizabethan cosmology. In simple terms, this doctrine explained why some men became carpenters, others sailors; some ministers, others magistrates. The Lord provided each person with the special skills necessary for his calling or vocation.[16] God's benevolence, however, was more in the nature of a trust or stewardship than an outright grant, for in the final day of judgment He held all men responsible for the manner in which they had used His talents. Richard Sibbes, chaplain at one of the Inns of Court, warned, "We must give a strict account;

the Negro, 1550–1812 (Chapel Hill, 1968), pp. 41–43; and J. H. Elliott, "Revolution and Continuity in Early Modern Europe," Past and Present, no. 42(1969), pp. 35–56.

14. Andrewes, Works, 7: 179; see Downame, Christian Warfare, pt. 2, pp. 344; Robert Bolton, Two Sermons Preached at Northampton at Two Severall Assises {1621 and 1625} (London, 1635), pp. 9–11; Hooker, Works, 2: 227–28; James Ussher, The Whole Works, 17 vols. (Dublin, 1864), 2: 275–76.

15. Seventeenth-century theologians generally discussed civil obedience under the heading of the Fifth Commandment, Honor Thy Father. See e.g. William Ames, Workes (London, 1643), pp. 308–14; Andrewes, Works, 7: 174.

16. William Perkins, Workes, 3 vols. (London, 1608–31), 1: 727–56; John Preston, Life Eternall, Or, A Treatise of the Knowledge of the Divine Essence and Attributes (London, 1631), pt. 1, pp. 146–50; Thomas Taylor, Christs Combate and Conquest . . . (Cambridge, Eng., 1618), p. 150. Also T. H. Breen, "The Non-Existent Controversy: Puritan and Anglican Attitudes on Work and Wealth," Church History 35, no. 3(1966), pp. 273–87.

[for] there is no calling so mean but a man shall find enough to give a good account for."[17] The young lawyers in Sibbes's audience apparently did not need to be reminded that the opposite was also true, that no man, however high or important his calling, was able to escape the Lord's review.

In theory, all callings were equal in the sight of the Lord, since He measured success by attitude, not by monetary achievement. The authors of this period, however, treated the callings of the magistrate and the minister as a special category. They referred to them as "public callings," as distinguished from the thousands of "private callings," given to ordinary men.[18] The differences between the two types were striking. God granted rulers greater, more important responsibilities than he did to wheelwrights, joiners, and masons. Civil leaders, in fact, had to ensure the smooth operation of the entire society, a task which under the best of conditions was extremely difficult. The Elizabethan chronicle, *The Mirror for Magistrates,* summed up the opinions of many men. "The goodnes and badnes of any realme," the author observed, "lyeth in the goodnes or badnes of the rulers. . . . For in dede the welth and quiet of everye common weale, the disorder also and miseries of the same, cum specially through them."[19] It was no wonder that one minister wanted "angels," not humans to serve as England's magistrates.[20]

But since no angels were forthcoming, English writers felt compelled to provide a full description of the attributes that they expected their rulers to possess. They urged prospective governors to consider these qualifications with great care. "There is no trade of life but a peculiar wisdom belongs to it," Thomas Adams ex-

17. Alexander Grosart, ed., *Complete Works of Richard Sibbes,* 7 vols. (Edinburgh, 1862–67), I: 243.

18. See Ames, *Workes,* pp. 313–14, for an excellent discussion of the magisterial and the ministerial callings. Also William Haller, *The Rise of Puritanism* (New York, 1957), pp. 126–27.

19. Lily B. Campbell, ed., *The Mirror for Magistrates* (Cambridge, Eng., 1938), p. 64; also William Gouge, *Gods Three Arrowes . . .* (London, 1631), pp. 122–23.

20. *The Works of Henry Smith,* 2 vols. (Edinburgh, 1866–67), I: 358. Smith wrote, "for want of angels we are fain to make magistrates of men." See Christopher Morris, *Political Thought in England: Tyndale to Hooker* (Oxford, 1953), p. 69.

plained, and then added, "how much more to the highest and busiest vocation, the government of men!"[21] The authors of this period apparently had little confidence in their magistrates' ability to acquire the necessary "wisdom," for their writings were filled with detailed advice about the requirements of the civil calling. The history of their own nation may well have taught them that the ruler who misinterpreted his abilities might later be crushed by the burden of office, or worse, become a tyrant. To some extent, of course, each author emphasized different characteristics and depicted an ideal ruler who conformed to subjective views. Nevertheless, it was possible to perceive five central prerequisites which were repeated throughout the magisterial literature: wealth, piety, moderation, wisdom, and justice. Several of these qualifications were so obvious that they require little explanation. Others, however, were more complex than they might at first appear.

English writers commonly assumed that wealthy men would make the best magistrates Affluence indicated that a person possessed high social status, good political contacts, and perhaps even a title from the king. Samuel Ward, a Puritan preacher whose brother, Nathaniel, later achieved fame by codifying the laws of Massachusetts, observed that in judging a magistrate's potential, "I exclude not birth and blood, which many times conveys spirit and courage with it." Ward also noted that while "money makes not the man, yet it adds some mettle to the man."[22] The letters of John Winthrop provided another example of the importance generally attached to wealth as a characteristic of the good ruler. In 1625 he wrote to a neighbor explaining his plan to find some "eminent" person to run for Parliament. With a little arm twisting, he thought someone as prominent as a deputy lieutenant could be persuaded to enter the race. As a suggestion, Winthrop offered his friend, Sir Nathaniel Barnardiston, who was not only a Puritan, but also one of the richest men in England.[23]

21. Thomas Adams, *Works*, 2: 259.

22. *The Sermons and Treatises of Samuel Ward* (Edinburgh, 1862), pp. 119–20.

23. Massachusetts Historical Society, *The Winthrop Papers*, 5 vols. (Boston, 1929–47), 1: 324–25; for Barnardiston see *DNB*.

The second qualification required for the magisterial calling was piety. One could expect godly rulers to defend the "true" church by punishing sin and by discouraging heretics. In a sermon entitled "A Manuall for Magistrates," Samuel Garey declared, "They who be not religious, and fearing God, what place soever they hold on earth, they are but Cyphers in Gods Account."[24] What Garey preached a thousand others repeated across the land. All explained that pious magistrates could be trusted to exercise civil power honestly; and, under the early Stuarts, such assurance was to mean consideration.

A third characteristic upon which most Englishmen could agree was moderation. No good ruler could afford to indulge himself in fits of melancholy or bursts of temper. The best leaders were "mediocre" men. Strange as it sounds to modern ears, "mediocrity" in this period implied a compliment which one applied to the person who avoided extreme behavior of any type. Unfortunately, magistrates seemed particularly susceptible to excessive ambition, a failing which seventeenth-century writers felt would soon be followed by general civil corruption. Robert Bolton captured the general view when he explained that ambitious rulers "will not sticke to lie, dissemble, breake their words, forsweare, machiavellize, practice any policy or counterpolicy to honesty, reason, religion."[25] Other authors stressed the danger of unbridled ambition by pointing to the Old Testament character, Achitophel, who betrayed his friends and ignored God's laws in an effort to attain political power.[26] Certainly overly aggressive candidates made easy targets for bribes and flattery. In a sermon directed specifically at magistrates, Thomas

24. Samuel Garey, *A Manuell for Magistrates Or, A Lanterne for Lawyers* [an assize sermon delivered at Norwich, 1619] (London, 1623), p. 39. Also Edward O. Smith, Jr., "The Elizabethan Doctrine of the Prince as Reflected in the Sermons of the Episcopacy, 1559–1603," *Huntington Library Quarterly* 28 (1964–65): 15.

25. *The Works of the Reverend Robert Bolton* (London, 1641), p. 187.

26. See Nathanael Carpenter, *Achitophel, Or, The Picture of a Wicked Politician* (London, 1629). Carpenter asked his congregation to imagine Achitophel before them: "Behold here the first and chiefest character of a worldly wise Politician, who cares little how great a rupture he makes through Gods sacred lawes and common equitie to meet with his own advantage, choosing rather to lose his soule than his wicked purpose" (p. 5).

Sutton challenged "the precipitant forwardnesse of some, who boldly intrude into places of eminence . . . though it is well enough knowne that they are as eminent for their imperfections, as they are for their places."[27] In theory, at least, the good ruler had no need to rely on prior promise or platform to gain civil authority.

Wisdom was the fourth general attribute demanded of the seventeenth-century magistrate. But wisdom had to be defined with care, since the mere mention of it in relation to political affairs made many Englishmen very uneasy. The basis of their fear was the fact that wisdom possessed several quite different meanings, some acceptable and some unacceptable. On the one hand, the term referred to honest, Christian policy; on the other, it pertained to clever, atheistic guile. Writers had to make it extremely clear, therefore, just what they meant when they advocated wisdom as a characteristic of the good ruler.

English writers of this period assumed that God gave every individual an understanding of the problems which he might face in his particular calling. They referred to this raw, intuitive comprehension as man's "natural wisdom." John Downame, a leading Puritan divine, explained, "Civill and morall wisdome is a common gift of Gods Spirit bestowed on man, whereby the understanding being enlightened, he is able to judge and discerne, what is truth, and what is falsehood, what good, and what evil, in humane and worldly affairs."[28]

But "civill wisdome" was extremely dangerous, as Downame well knew, for its use tended to inflate man's sense of his own worth. Magistrates frequently grew so proud of their own achievements in office that they forgot that God's gift was responsible for their success.[29] Robert Bolton mirrored the general suspicion of wisdom

27. Thomas Sutton, *Jethroes Counsell to Moses: Or, A Direction for Magistrates* [preached 1621] (London, 1631), p. 18; Ward, *Sermons*, p. 117.

28. Downame, *Christian Warfare*, pt. 2, p. 70.

29. Bolton, *Works*, p. 212 ["A Sermon Preached at Lent Assises"]; Downame, *Christian Warfare*, pt. 2, pp. 70–71, 87–88, 91; Miles Smith, *A Learned and Godly Sermon, Preached at Worcester, at an Assise* (Oxford, 1602); Thomas Fuller, *The Holy State* (Cambridge, Eng., 1642), p. 257; and John Reading, *Moses and Jethro: or the Good Magistrate* [an election sermon delivered at Dover] (London, 1626), p. 15. Reading preached, "This feare of God is the ground of all ability, it is the beginning of wisdome."

when he stated that the "great politicians and jolly wise men of the
world (as they are called) for all their depths and devices, with all
their wit and windings, cannot understand one title [tittle] of the
things of GOD." Bolton added that since these so-called wise leaders
depended upon "their own policy, depths, and turning devices,
GOD justly turnes them loose to follow the swing of their carnall
reason."[30] In other words, the Lord provided clever rulers with just
enough rope to hang themselves. Another minister, Richard Sibbes,
also warned civil magistrates that their wisdom might turn into
sinful pride. He urged the "carnall politicians" in his congregation to
imagine "a politician upon his death-bed, that hath striven so much
for riches, that hath striven to root himself by policy, to attain to
such and such places, to obtain his pleasure and delights in the
world; what glory, what comfort hath he in this?"[31]

This ambivalent attitude toward wisdom probably resulted from
England's general hostility to the ideas of Niccolò Machiavelli.
"That which is commonly called the *policie* of *Machiavel* is here to
be condemned," William Perkins announced in *Cases of Conscience;*
"it is not only against the written law of God, but even against the
law of Nature. And the very foundation thereof standeth in the
practice of lying, swearing, forswearing, in fraud, deceit, and injustice."[32] According to English divines, who possessed very little
reliable information about Machiavelli's teachings, the Italian
theorist had glorified "carnall wisdome" for its own sake and, thereby,
had removed God from the business of state.[33] Machiavelli fell into
this terrible error by separating government policy from the lessons

30. Bolton, *Works,* pp. 210-11.
31. Sibbes, *Works,* 3: 273.
32. Perkins, *Workes,* 2: 117.
33. See Felix Raab, *The English Face of Machiavelli: A Changing
Interpretation* (London, 1964), pp. 69-94. Raab claimed, "The general
tenor, then, of political writing in our period [1600-40] was anti-
Machiavellian in the sense that most men could not accept the basic
assumptions upon which Machiavelli's statecraft was built. Although they
frequently agreed on points of detail and cited Machiavelli as a weighty
authority, there was a point at which his blatant secularism aroused hostility
and rejection. For many, that point was 'politick religion,' the principle of
religion as a political device" (p. 90). Also George L. Mosse, "Puritanism
and Reason of State in Old and New England," *William and Mary Quarterly* 9 (1952): 67-80; and Pocock, " 'The Onely Politician,' " pp. 266-73.

of Scripture. According to Sibbes, it was "an abominable conceit to distinguish religion from policy and government, as if the reasons of religion were one and the reasons of state were another." Only an atheist would claim that the God, who revealed all the mysteries of salvation, did not also explain the mysteries of state.[34] Most of the Englishmen who discussed the character of the good ruler regarded the Bible as the most reliable guide to civil policy; after all, it contained in it "more than all . . . Machiavelli's spider-web."[35]

The fifth, and last quality of the magisterial calling was a capacity to administer justice to all citizens. However, the ability to judge equitably, like the ability to form Christian policy, was regarded as a talent possessed by very few men. English writers of this period expected the ideal ruler to demonstrate complete objectivity and to ignore economic, family, and religious interests when he held court.[36] Henry Smith was one of the many clergymen who insisted that justice should be administered indiscriminately, without thought of either class or wealth, since "our laws have been a long time like to spider's webs, so that the great buzzing bees break through, and the little feeble flies hang fast in them."[37] And the moderate Bishop Sanderson declared with rare vehemence that the good ruler should never "be outdared with the big looks and bug-words of those that do him no harm."[38]

34. Sibbes, *Works*, 3: 279.

35. Ward, *Sermons*, p. 116.

36. McIlwain, *Political Works of James I*, p. 277 [from a speech delivered before Parliament, 1603]; also see Richard Carpenter, *The Conscionable Christian* . . . [Somerset assize sermon, 1620] (London, 1623), pp. 117–18.

37. Henry Smith, *Works*, 2: 73; Robert Bolton was especially critical of lawyers, claiming that they seldom brought Christian equity to England. The Puritan minister pointed out that clients paid lawyers to defend causes which the advocates knew were unjust and immoral *(Two Sermons Preached at Northampton*, p. 98); also see John Squire, *A Sermon Preached at Hartford Assises* (London, 1618).

38. Sanderson, *Works*, 2: 195. The demand for objective treatment before the bar was a fair request in this period, for many of the nation's courts seemed to sanction the worst venality. See Edmund S. Morgan, *The Puritan Dilemma* (Boston, 1958), pp. 25–26; H. E. Bell, *An Introduction to the History and Records of the Court of Wards & Liveries* (Cambridge, Eng., 1953), pp. 133–49.

But courage to stand up to the "big looks" did not in itself make a magistrate a good judge. Justice required intelligence as well as backbone. Certainly, it was no sign of judicial talent to apply the same inflexible decision in every case, regardless of whether the offender was a habitual criminal or an inexperienced youth.[39] William Perkins provided a full description of the magistrate's legal duties in an essay written around the turn of the seventeenth century. Perkins explained that the ruler, in his capacity as judge, had to understand two quite different types of law. The first were the laws of God which were "of such universall righteousnesse, as that at all times, and in all places, they are of equall strength . . . to be executed without dispensation, relaxation, or any mitigation." The second type were man-made. These laws were not inherently equitable for the obvious reason that they lacked divine perfection. Human ordinances were the work of legislators who erred despite intentions to the contrary. Thus, according to Perkins, it was the responsibility of the good ruler to see that citizens were not oppressed by outmoded and ill-conceived statutes.[40]

The best magistrates recognized that true Christian equity lay somewhere between a literal and a loose interpretation of man's imperfect law. "Both *extremitie* and *mitigation* are within the law," Perkins explained, "but it is in the hand principally of the Magistrate . . . to discerne the several circumstances, when the one is to be executed, and when the other." He advised judges to take three separate elements into account, God's law, local statute, and anomalous detail. Perkins regarded this last element as particularly important; for only after a judge understood the irregular and personal factors in a case could he determine whether equity required extremity or mitigation.[41] The theory of Christian equity, therefore, assumed that the ruler possessed broad discretionary power in interpreting the law. Those who subscribed to this theory, however, often had a difficult time. When Governor John Winthrop and

39. Richard Hooker explained, for example, that "Laws are matters of principal consequence; men of common capacity and but ordinary judgment are not able (for how should they?) to discern what things are fittest for each kind and state of regiment" (Hooker, *Works*, 1: 176).

40. Perkins, *Workes*, 2: 436, 439.

41. Ibid., pp. 438–41.

other Massachusetts magistrates later tried to put Perkins's ideas into practice, they ran into stiff opposition; for the members of the lower house in the Puritan colony came to regard discretionary power more as an invitation to arbitrary rule than as a means to achieve Christian equity (see chap. 2).

Almost every discussion about the nature of the ruler's calling during this period contained one or more of these five elements. These were the points on which Anglicans and Puritans could agree—at least, on paper. And there was the rub. Was the insistence on these five qualities merely rhetorical? Was Bishop Sanderson correct in advising his parishioners not to expect perfection in their magistrates? Or was the rhetoric about the good ruler to be taken seriously, as an injunction from the Lord? Was a Puritan like Thomas Adams justified in demanding so much from civil leaders? In the 1620s these were the questions that set Englishmen at odds and ultimately contributed to the founding of a new American commonwealth.

The Puritans: What Is to Be Done?

The Puritans were irritating people. They insisted on exact, legalistic interpretations of Scripture, and they had the audacity to try to live by the standards which they found there. In politics, as in religion, they demanded something close to perfection. If the ruler's calling required piety, then he had better possess it, or else find some vocation more suited to his talents. The Puritans had no sympathy whatsoever with the kind of magistrates which Bishop Sanderson described—magistrates who were tolerably good, but willing to compromise with the wickedness of the world.

But literal-mindedness was not the only element which distinguished Puritan political rhetoric from that of other Englishmen. During the course of the 1620s, the Puritans' ideas about the good ruler underwent an important transformation which separated them even further from their contemporaries. In the early years of the seventeenth century, the Spiritual Brotherhood, as the Puritan clergy is sometimes called, aimed its criticisms directly at England's rulers, hoping in that manner to persuade them to reform their ways.[42]

42. The term "spiritual brotherhood" comes from William Haller's *Rise of Puritanism*, pp. 49–82.

But when magistrates refused to listen and conditions within the country grew progressively worse, the Puritans changed their political tack. Instead of talking to their rulers, they began to talk to the people, reminding them that they bore the ultimate responsibility for the kind of men who exercised civil power. By the end of the 1620s the Puritans had made the character of the good ruler a topic of public concern and given elections new significance. This shift in focus from the magistrates to the people had an impact, not only on English, but also on American politics for years to come. To understand this development, we need to begin our story in the early 1600s; for during that period the Puritans still believed that civil leaders would pay attention to the pleas of the Spiritual Brotherhood.

The Puritans' concern about the good ruler grew out of their even greater concern about the covenant. They insisted that the Lord had made a compact with the English people at some indeterminable time in the past, granting them peace, prosperity, and Protestantism in exchange for obedience to scriptural law. The Puritans regarded this agreement as a real and binding contract for which all men could be held responsible. If a nation failed the Lord by allowing evil to flourish, He punished the entire population, saints and sinners alike. The ruler became a crucial figure for the Puritans, because it was his duty to make Englishmen uphold the terms of their compact whether they wanted to or not. If he was unsuccessful in his calling, there could be no hope of pleasing the Lord.[43]

43. See William Haller, *The Elect Nation* (New York, 1963), pp. 224–50. Thomas Gataker in his *Two Sermons: Tending to Direction for Christian Carriage* . . . (London, 1623) offered one of the better descriptions of the typical Puritan.

If a man live somewhat *more* strictly than the looser sort doe, though not so strictly neither as his Christian profession requireth of him, (for even the best and the forwardest have their failings and come farre short of what they should) he shall not scape to have those opprobrious tearmes and titles fastened on him, of a *Precisian, a Puritane,* and the like. . . . If he be conversant in Gods word, and diligent in frequenting the ministry of it; he is a *Bible-bearer,* and a *gadder* up and downe *after Sermons.* If he *make conscience of an oath,* and will reprove others when they sweare, he is *a superstitious fellow,* too straitlaced, more nice than wise. If hee will not swill and

As the Puritans looked around them in the early 1620s, they saw little that was good and much that was very bad indeed. In fact, England did not seem like a covenanted nation at all. Part of the problem, of course, was historical. In the early days of Elizabeth's reign the Spiritual Brotherhood had convinced itself that England was the New Israel, the Elect Nation of God, and they set about to make it live up to its special charge. Yet, somewhere along the way reform had stalled so that, by 1620, the quality of English life appeared to be corrupt as ever. While the Stuart Puritans complained of many ills in their society, they stressed two grievances far above the rest, the church and the court. It was in these areas that the country's rulers most clearly disappointed the Lord.

The unreformed state of the Anglican church particularly annoyed the Puritans. In theory, at least, England's magistrates were supposed to defend and purify the church. God charged them with the responsibility to punish heretics, to abolish unscriptural ceremonies, and to fight the Antichrist wherever he might appear.[44] In metaphorical language, good rulers served as the Lord's gardeners, keeping "the good plants watered, the weeds and stones throwne out that hinder growth, the hedge kept strong and good about it."[45] Un-

---

swagger, drinke healths and play the goodfellow, goe for company to *a Brothel-house*, or to *a Play-house*, little better, *the very seminaries and nurseries of all filthinesse and prophanenesse;* he is a man altogether unsociable, of a *melancholy disposition*, little better than *a lunaticke*, as they said sometimes of *John the Baptist*. [pp. 118–19]

Gataker remained proud of his own Puritanism despite the opprobrious terms which were used to describe the Spiritual Brotherhood.

44. William Perkins wrote: "Magistrates in townes and corporations carrie and drawe the sword for the maintenance of peace and civill order: it is well done, for it is the work of their calling; yet not the principall, and they commonly faile in this, that they use not the sword for this ende, to urge men to the keeping of the commandments of the first Table, to a practice of pure religion, and the keeping of the Sabbath day. This is the maine dutie of the Magistrate, who beares the sworde specially for the good of mens soules" (*Workes*, 1: 741).

45. John Preston, *Sermons Preached before His Majestie; and upon other speciall occasions . . .* (London, 1630), p. 221. William Ames, one of the most influential theologians among the American Puritans, wrote that "it is required of superiors that they have power, and authority, that

fortunately, many of the English magistrates had been careless gardeners for quite some time. Throughout the countryside, the Puritans found foul, heretical weeds choking God's church and sin flourishing in the open sun.

In 1620 the church problem was already old. Ever since 1558 when Elizabeth rescued the country from Mary's frightful reign, the Puritans had been waiting for ecclesiastical reform. Radical Calvinists, trained in Geneva, assumed the new queen would purify the English church, abolishing the prelacy, removing the vestments, and disavowing all traces of the nation's Catholic past. The Puritans soon learned, however, that Elizabeth did not share their views—at least, not so intensely—for while she listened to their theological debates, she changed her church very little. Under her government most Puritans drifted along, sometimes happy, sometimes angry, reasonably certain that things would get better before they got worse.[46]

When James I became king of England in 1603, Puritan expectations rose. The new monarch agreed to meet with some Puritan ministers at the Hampton Court Conference. James quickly dashed any hope for major reforms, however, and before the conference ended, he warned the clergymen that if they did not conform to the Anglican service, he would "harry them out of the land, or else do worse."[47] Time revealed that the king did not care much for "harrying," and he generally left the Puritans in peace. Nevertheless, the members of the Spiritual Brotherhood were still faced with the same ecclesiastical impurities that had bothered them under Elizabeth. As the years passed, they became increasingly worried that God's patience with England was running out; and, by the 1620s, there

---

they study to further the salvation of inferiors by their authority" (*Workes,* p. 317). See also William Ames, *Conscience with the Power and Cases Thereof* . . . (London, 1643), pp. 164–66.

46. See J. E. Neale, *Elizabeth and Her Parliaments,* 2 vols. (New York, 1966); J. E. Neale, *Queen Elizabeth* (Garden City, 1957); M. M. Knappen, *Tudor Puritanism* (Chicago, 1965); Haller, *Elect Nation,* p. 249.

47. David Hawke, *The Colonial Experience* (Indianapolis, 1966), p. 53; J. R. Tanner, *English Constitutional Conflicts of the Seventeenth Century, 1603–1689* (Cambridge, Eng., 1962), pp. 17–33; also see Roland G. Usher, *The Reconstruction of the English Church* (New York, 1910).

was little about the church that the Puritans found encouraging.

Under James's son ecclesiastical affairs took a turn for the worse. The new king, who assumed the throne in 1625, not only ignored the Puritans' demands, but also supported a heretical doctrine known as Arminianism. This new theology derived its name from Jacobus Arminius, a Dutch religious leader. Some of his English critics claimed, perhaps unfairly, that Arminius believed man could effect his own salvation, an option which Calvin had clearly denied. Orthodox Dutch Calvinists expelled the Arminian faction (or Remonstrants) at the Synod of Dort, but several Anglican leaders carried the new, appealing ideas back to England.[48] Important Anglicans like William Laud, Richard Montagu, and Lancelot Andrewes began to emphasize man's ability to earn God's grace by good works, and they called for the establishment of elaborate ceremonies within the church service itself. The Puritans interpreted this movement as an additional sign of England's corruption, and some even warned Parliament that there was no difference between Arminianism and popery. Alexander Leighton reflected their general attitude when he declared, "wee may be bold to say of religion, & state, as David said of himselfe, there is but a step betweene them & death."[49]

Men who worried about the nation's covenant found the condition of the Stuart court as offensive as that of the English church. Surely, they argued, God must be upset by the monarchs' equivocal policy toward the Catholics. James I, for example, dawdled, while the Catholic Hapsburg army drove Frederick the Elector out of the Palatinate. The Hapsburg victory came as a bitter blow, for the English Puritans had come to regard Frederick, James's Protestant son-in-law, as the last best hope against the Catholic resurgence on the Continent. The anonymous author of a tract entitled *The Practice of Princes* captured the Puritan resentment: "King James

48. John F. H. New, *Anglican and Puritan: The Basis of Their Opposition, 1558–1640* (Stanford, 1964), pp. 13–16; and Paul A. Welsby, *Lancelot Andrewes, 1555–1626* (London, 1958).

49. Alexander Leighton, *An Appeal to the Parliament* . . . (London, 1628), p. A3; William Prynne, *The Church of Englands Old Antithesis to New Arminianisme* (London, 1629); also, H. R. Trevor-Roper, *Archbishop Laud, 1573–1645* (London, 1962).

died in the practice of such papists and popelings, as everyday lulled him asleep with tales, flatteries, jests, songs, and catches, while the Palatinate was loosing."[50] James's favorite, the Duke of Buckingham, increased Puritan fears by begging Spain to provide a Catholic wife for Prince Charles, England's next king. And, although the Spanish negotiations failed, Charles did eventually marry a Catholic, Henrietta Maria of France.[51]

Anxious Puritans also believed that James's statements about the nature of kingship would irritate the Lord. For better or worse, the English monarch stood out as one of the more original political thinkers of his generation. His theory of divine right for which he is remembered grew out of a fight he waged against a group of Catholic intellectuals. His opponents insisted in the early years of the seventeenth century that the pope could relieve English subjects of their allegiance to the king, a doctrine which clearly undermined the ruler's sovereignty. James countered that he had received his authority directly from God and that no "Bishop of Rome" could abrogate this relationship.[52] To the members of Parliament, James once declared, "The State of MONARCHIE is the supremest thing upon earth: For Kings are not onely GODS Lieutenants upon earth, and sit upon GODS throne, but even GOD himselfe they are called GODS."[53] Ordinarily the Puritans would have applauded any attack on the Catholics, but in this case they found the inflated court rhetoric difficult to support. Court preachers, eager for preferment, enthusiastically made "the pulpitt a stage of flattery."[54] Roger Man-

50. A. Ar., *The Practice of Princes* (Amsterdam?, 1630), p. 6.

51. See Christopher Hill, *Puritanism and Revolution* (London, 1958), pp. 249–52; Roger Lockyer, *Tudor and Stuart Britain* (New York, 1964), pp. 234–52; Irvonwy Morgan, *Prince Charles's Puritan Chaplain* [John Preston] (London, 1957), pp. 51–73.

52. See McIlwain, *Political Works of James I,* introduction; Judson, *Crisis of the Constitution,* pp. 171-217.

53. McIlwain, *Political Works of James I,* p. 307 [speech before Parliament, 1609].

54. See "Tom-Tell-Troath: or, a free Discourse touching the Manners of the Time [1621 or 1622]," *Somers Tracts,* 10 vols. (London, 1809), 2: 470–92. The anonymous Puritan author of this political satire described Court ministers: "the preachers of greatest note and creditt will hould themselves bound in duty to praise him [the king] against their con-

waring, for example, titillated his royal patron by observing, *"Kings above all, inferiour to none, to no man, to no multitude* of men, to no *Angell,* to no order of *Angels*."[55]

The Puritans rejected the theory of divine right because it smacked of idolatry, one of the most loathsome sins. The court's political idolatry, its appeal for subjects to worship their king, was clearly an insult to God. As the great Puritan leader, Richard Sibbes, explained, "Due honour must be given unto those who carry God's image, our governors, yea, great respect and honour . . . but to go beyond our bounds herein, is to commit *idolatry*."[56] If monarchs possessed divinity, it was only by analogy, for anyone could see that kings died like all other men.[57] The Stuarts' theory could only serve

---

sciences, and, laying aside divinitie, make the pulpitt a stage of flattery; where you shall have them indue him after a most poeticall manner, with more than all virtues, and paint him so excellently good, as would make all that heare them happy, if they could believe those thinges of princes, as well as those of God, in spite of their sences" (p. 489).

55. Roger Manwaring, *Religion and Allegiance* (London, 1627), p. 8. Also Isaac Bargrave, *A Sermon Preached before King Charles, March 27, 1627* (London, 1627), p. 18; Robert Sibthorpe, *Apostolike Obedience* (London, 1627); Bartholomew Parsons, *The Magistrates Charter Examined* (London, 1616), pp. 13–14; John White, *A Defence of the Way of the True Church* . . . (London, 1624), cited in Judson, *Crisis of the Constitution,* p. 179; Henry Valentine, *God Save the King* (London, 1629). Valentine claimed that *"Kings* are but pictures of God at length, and represent him in such due proportions, that as *God* is our *invisible King,* so the *King* is our *visible God"* (p. 6). See Welsby, *Andrewes,* pp. 203–08.

56. Sibbes, *Works,* 2: 383 [italics added]; Arthur Hildersam, *Lectures upon the Fourth of John* (London, 1629), p. 39; A. Ar., *Practice of Princes,* p. 7; Thomas Gataker, *God's Parley with Princes* (London, 1620), p. 45; Downame, *Christian Warfare,* pt. 2, p. 198.

57. William Sclater, *A Sermon Preached at the Last Generall Assise Holden for the County of Sommerset at Taunton* (London, 1616), p. 8; also see William Sclater, *Funerall Sermon for John Colles, esq., justice of the peace of Somersetshire* (London, 1629); Henry Smith, *Works,* 1: 365. The Puritans were masters of scriptural interpretation, and the Eighty-second Psalm—"I say, 'You are gods, sons of the Most High' "—offered them no trouble. John Downame explained, "whereas it may be alleaged, that Princes are said in the Scriptures to be Gods; to this I answer, that this name is attributed unto them, not in respect of any thing in their persons, but onely in regard of their office and ministry" *(Christian Warfare,* pt. 2, p. 198).

as a temptation to the Lord; and, as one Puritan who had studied
history warned, when Rome became an empire "some of their
emperors were made gods . . . wherein they could not have devised
to have done them greater wrong, for they came most of them to
fearful ends."[58] Charles I and his flattering followers would have
done well to have paid closer attention to this Puritan's advice.

The Spiritual Brotherhood criticized the court for far more than
the king's theory of divine right. During the 1620s, in fact, most
of the Puritans censured court life in general; its manners and
morals, its taste and theology. It seemed to them that the bowing
and scraping of courtier society had no place within a covenanted
commonwealth.[59] Nicholas Breton captured the Puritan sentiment
when he described the typical courtier as "kissing of the hand, as
if hee were licking of his fingers, bending downe the head, as if his
neck were out of joynt; or scratching by the foote, as if he were
a Corne-cutter."[60] Another member of the Spiritual Brotherhood,
John Downame, warned the Englishmen of his "flattering age"
against giving "unto Princes and great personages the highest and
most transcendent titles of virtue and goodnes, as *most* mighty,
most excellent, *most* high, *most* gracious, *most* divine." It worried
Downame to see persons at court employ these phrases *absolutely*,
not *comparatively*, in respect to other men and thus, "leave none that
are higher for God himselfe."[61] The Puritans believed that neither
rulers nor their subjects were supposed to be crawling creatures of
favor and patronage. In Massachusetts and Connecticut more than
half a century later, American Puritans again attacked the quality
of court life; and, like their spiritual predecessors of the 1620s,
they expected their magistrates to embody a different moral and
political standard (see chap. 7).

The corruption in the English church, the king's ambivalence

58. Sibbes, *Works*, 2: 383.

59. See Stone, *Crisis of the Aristocracy*, pp. 61–62, 123, 231–34, 664–68;
Hexter, "The English Aristocracy," pp. 62–64.

60. Nicholas Breton, *The Court and Country* [1618] (Edinburgh, 1868),
p. 180.

61. Downame, *Christian Warfare*, pt. 2, p. 198; Thomas Gataker, *Certaine Sermons* . . . (London, 1637), pt. 1, p. 75; Sibbes, *Works*, 2: 383;
John Dod and Robert Cleaver, *A Plaine and Familiar Exposition of the Ten
Commandments* (London, 1619), p. 221.

toward the Catholic threat, the sycophants at court; all these things were insults to the Lord, gross insults, but during the early 1620s the Puritans thought there might still be time left for reform. God's patience was running thin, however, and the Puritans saw signs that the end might be very near. Only when one understands the Puritans' growing anxiety about England's condition, can one appreciate the dark, fearful tone of their political rhetoric. Edward Bagshawe, for example, concluded, "If ever there was a time for *Righteous Men* that are in authority to shew themselves, the time is now come."[62] Others shared Bagshawe's apprehension. "Wee are those on whom the ends of the world are fallen," Thomas Gataker reported. "This age of ours is the Worlds Old age: That which wee call Antiquity, was indeed the worlds youth. Time is growne gray with us, that was greene with them that then lived."[63] Certainly, if England was to be saved, her magistrates would have to stop winking at "the corruption of the times."[64] The problem for the Puritans, therefore, was to make other men aware of the seriousness of the situation, to make them reform before God withdrew His covenant.

In this atmosphere of crisis the Puritans turned first to their rulers. The Spiritual Brethren recognized that civil leaders could not successfully reform the nation until they had reformed themselves. Thus, the time had arrived for magistrates to display that piety, wisdom, wealth, justice, and moderation which ideal rulers were expected to possess. The threat of a broken covenant made it imperative for English magistrates to fulfill the requirements of their calling; and with rigorous, militant language, the Puritans urged them to be up and doing. Thomas Taylor's *Christ's Combate,*

62. Robert Bolton, *Mr. Bolton's Last and Learned Worke* . . . (London, 1639), dedication by Edward Bagshawe, p. A2.

63. Gataker, *Certaine Sermons,* pt. 2, p. 43.

64. Gouge, *Gods Three Arrowes,* p. 7. See also Preston, *Life Eternall,* pt. 2, pp. 101–02. The Puritan minister, Arthur Hildersam, wondered why the Lord's judgment had not come already. In his *Lectures upon the Fourth of John,* he decided, "There bee many of Gods faithfull servants that pray unto him fervently day and nights, and so stand in the gap, to keepe out Gods judgements from the Land. It is true, fasting and prayer is not so much in use as of old it was: yet still it is used by many: and this hath great force to keepe away Gods judgements" (p. 388).

John Downame's *The Christian Warfare*, Thomas Gataker's "The Spiritual Watch," and Richard Sibbes's "The Soules Conflict" were typical of the Puritan literature of this period. Every borough and shire had become the field for a great moral battle; and the reformers demanded good magistrates to lead the saints into combat against Satan. "For unless the Magistrate use his power," explained John Dod, "and shew his authoritie against sinners, they will be practicing and striving against Gods children."[65]

Whenever the battle against sin seemed to lag, as it often did during the 1620s, the Puritans directed their criticism at their rulers. It was the governors, not the people, who were responsible for these setbacks. John Reading explained that "it commeth to passe that when the Magistrate will not execute justice, nor punish sinne, to remove evill from the land, God entreth for default of justice, and severely punisheth the whole common-wealth."[66] Samuel Ward fully accepted this reasoning and blamed the men in public office for the nation's wickedness. "Whatever swervings or stumbling any part of the body politic makes," he claimed, "the blame lights not upon the gentry or commonalty, the immediate delinquents, but on the principle lights in the magistracy . . . which, being as guardians and tutors of the rest should either prevent or reform their aberrations."[67] The entire thrust of the Puritan appeal at this time was to force magistrates to reassess their talents—to force them, in other words, to decide whether they possessed the necessary characteristics of the good ruler.

Outspoken Puritans did not mince words when they found a magistrate who did not fulfill the requirements of his calling. In fact, several of the Puritans thoroughly enjoyed goading the country's temporizers. Richard Carpenter, for example, labeled such men "*luke-warme neuter-passive* Magistrates," and then went on to ex-

65. Dod and Cleaver, *Ten Commandments*, p. 218; and Bolton, *Two Sermons Preached at Northampton*, p. 62.

66. Reading, *Moses and Jethro*, p. 18. Reading told his audience that he had tried hard to focus his discussion on the subject of godly political behavior. He noted that people had criticized the election sermon he had delivered the previous year because it had been too general and had not described the exact characteristics of the good ruler (p. 19).

67. Ward, *Sermons*, p. 113.

plain how "a good many of our neuter-passive Magistrates, scare-
crow Constables, and meale-mouthed under officers in Towne and
Country, who resembling Ostritches, which have great feathers, but
no flight . . . suffer many heinous and hidious enormities of whore-
dom, blasphemy, drunkennesse, prophaning of the Sabbath."[68] The
Puritans observed with dismay that there were many English leaders
who refused to support reform lest they "bee accounted precise and
pragmaticall."[69] To weak magistrates of his type, Paul Baynes lectured, "Luke-warmenes (though men thinke it a part of prudence)
. . . is odious with God, and will make us be cast up with displeasure."[70] Civil leaders probably did not appreciate being reminded of their failings, especially in insulting terms. But the
Puritans insisted they were doing their rulers an important service.

Samuel Ward's sermon, "Jethro's Justice of Peace," was typical
of the Puritan effort to instruct the nation's rulers. Ward, a moderate
Puritan, spoke before the assembled magistrates of Suffolk County.
"You gentlemen," he began, "complain often of idle shepards, dumb
dogs, &c., in the ministry." The round-faced Suffolk justices must
have nodded, for indeed, many of them over the years had protested
the clergy's lack of training and intelligence. Generally, "dumb dogs"
were ministers who were either too lazy or too ignorant to write
sermons. There may have been some uneasy stirring, therefore, when
Ward asked how many "dumb dogs" were in the magistracy. "Some
in commission," the speaker declared, "never sit on the bench but
for fashion; constables that are but cyphers in their places." He
added that the "strait-buttoned, carpet, and effeminate gentry"
seemed so taken up with games and tobacco that it was "little acquainted with the tediousness of wise and serious business."[71]

68. Richard Carpenter, *The Conscionable Christian,* pp. 30–31. Also
Thomas Taylor, *Christs Combate and Conquest,* p.335. Taylor wrote:
"Alasse, how many Magistrates are of *Gallios* minde, to thinke religion
but a matter of words, as if God made them governours of men onely,
but not of Christians; keepers of the second table to preserve peace and
justice, and not of the first to preserve piety and religion?"

69. Carpenter, *Conscionable Christian,* p. 31; and Bolton, *Works,* p. 217;
Bolton, *Two Sermons Preached at Northampton,* p. 90.

70. Paul Baynes, *The Trial of a Christians's Estate* (London, 1618), p. 18.

71. Ward, *Sermons,* pp. 131, 119. Samuel's brother, Nathaniel, who
came to New England, prefaced "Jethro's Justice of Peace." He noted that he

Since Suffolk was a Puritan stronghold, the county's magistrates were probably good rulers—at least, as far as men like Ward were concerned. But beyond the boundaries of East Anglia the "dumb dogs" were clearly in the majority.

Most Puritan ministers avoided intemperate political statements. They simply, but firmly, reminded their rulers of the requirements of the magisterial calling. "My good Lords," one Puritan declared, "your places of authority, and these exulcerated times of iniquity, require in you *Moses* his spirit, *Phineas* his zeale. . . . Oh, put them all on, as complete armour, suitable to your calling and dignity."[72] Puritans, of course, had always considered diligence necessary in any vocation, public or private, but the rulers of England seemed to have forgotten the Lord's command to be active. Alexander Leighton refreshed the memories of the members of Parliament on this point, telling them that "As God hath set you forth . . . for this great work of Reformation; so your choyce and place requireth you to bee *men of activitie*."[73] There was no room in seventeenth-century England for idle and cowardly rulers who let God's sword lie in disuse. "And so it is with every thing that is made for an end," Preston observed, "as fire, that is made to warme a man, if it doe burne the house, we put it out; a vessell that is made to keep wine and beare, if it doe corrupt it, we lay it aside, and put it into one more wholesome."[74] The Puritans found it difficult to understand why rulers who knew the fundamental attributes of their calling failed to put them into practice.

At some point during the 1620s, it became apparent to various Puritans that their political strategy was not working. The appeals, the counsel, the criticism which they directed at their rulers had done little good, for the majority of English magistrates plainly did not care about the terms of the national covenant. Despite repeated warnings, they continued to drift with the evil currents of the day, placing political prudence before spiritual reform. What could the

---

had studied law and had held several civil offices but was "made weary of the errors I saw" (p. 133).

72. Carpenter, *Conscionable Christian*, p. 72.
73. Leighton, *Appeal to the Parliament*, p. A3 [italics added].
74. Preston, *Life Eternall*, pt. 1, pp. 146–47.

Puritans do? Since rulers throughout the country were "neuter-passives" in their calling, the Spiritual Brotherhood was forced to find some new, more effective plan of action. In essence, the Puritans confronted one of the oldest, most difficult dilemmas known to man: How should the citizen behave when the civil government ignores what he believes to be his just demands? Their answer to this question involved a pragmatic assessment of their own political strength, as well as an intellectual tradition which dated back to the beginnings of the Protestant Reformation.

During the first half of the sixteenth century Protestant reformers found that they had to define the limits of political obedience. Some of the earliest leaders, like Martin Luther and John Calvin, condemned all resistance to civil authority as sinful. Luther, for example, was rudely shocked by the peasant revolt in Germany; and informed the rebels, "If your enterprise were right, then any man might become judge over another, and there would remain in the world neither authority, nor government, nor order, nor land, but there would be only murder and bloodshed."[75] For the most part Calvin agreed with Luther. The spiritual head of Geneva rejected all civil disobedience except that of legally constituted government assemblies. In the *Institutes of the Christian Religion,* he advised private citizens to stay clear of civil business, "that they may not deliberately intrude in public affairs, or pointlessly invade the magistrate's office, or undertake anything at all politically."[76] According to these Protestants, the correct response to tyranny was prayer, not violence.[77]

---

75. *The Works of Martin Luther,* 12 vols. (Philadelphia, 1915–32), 4: 228, cited by Winthrop S. Hudson, ed., *John Ponet: Advocate of Limited Monarchy* (Chicago, 1942), p. 120.

76. John T. McNeill, ed., *Calvin: Institutes of the Christian Religion,* 2 vols. (Philadelphia, 1960), 2: 1511.

77. See A. H. Murray, ed., *Theodore Beza, Concerning the Rights of Rulers over their Subjects and the Duty of Subjects toward Their Rulers* (Cape Town, n.d.). Beza wrote, "What then, will someone say, is there no remedy remaining against the supreme Ruler who abuses his authority and power in violation of all the precepts of divine and human rights? Nay, there doubtless is a remedy remaining derived from human institutions. But when I say this, let no one be of opinion that I wish to favour

Later reformers like John Knox, John Ponet, and Christopher Goodman adopted a more active, and, therefore, a more radical political doctrine. In large measure their thought was influenced by the serious reverses which Protestantism had suffered throughout Europe. In particular, they saw Mary Tudor's reign as a major setback. The Catholic queen set out to eradicate every trace of the English Reformation; and to the exiles who watched the rule of terror from the safety of Geneva, it seemed that God would never demand obedience to such a tyrant. Two English writers, Ponet and Goodman, demonstrated from Scripture that resistance to heretical rulers was a Christian responsibility. They insisted, in fact, that divine law superseded human law and that it was the duty of each person to decide for himself when the commands of God and man clashed.

Christopher Goodman told the English people in 1558 that the Lord demanded rebellion against all ungodly rulers: "if the Magistrates would whollye despice and betraye the justice and Lawes of God, [then] you which are subjectes with them shall be condemned except you mayntayne and defend the same Lawes agaynst them, and all others to the uttermoste of your powers."[78] While Goodman appealed to individual conscience, he did not expect each man to act on different principles. Subjects were to judge their rulers by standards clearly laid out in the Bible. Ponet, too, grounded his theory of resistance on the right of enlightened, individual judgment. He reminded the citizens that they would eventually have to answer to God for their behavior, "and therefore christen men ought well to considre, and weighe mennes commaundements before they be hastie to doo them, to see if they be contrarie or

---

the fanatical Anabaptists or other factious and mutinous men" (p. 29). The responsibility for removing evil rulers lay with government assemblies and not with the citizens (pp. 43–44, 72–75). Also see Robert M. Kingdon, "The First Expression of Theodore Beza's Political Ideas," *Archiv fur Reformationsgeschichte* 44 (1955): 88–99; Pierre Mesnard, *L'Essor de la philosophie politique au XVI siècle* (Paris, 1951), chapters on the Protestant reformers.

78. Morgan, *Puritan Political Ideas*, p. 9 [Christopher Goodman's *How Superior Powers Ought to Be Obeyed of Their Subjects . . .*]; Allen, *Political Thought in the Sixteenth Century*, pp. 116–18.

repugnaunt to Goddes commaundementes and justice: which if they be, they are cruell and evill, and *ought not to* be obeyed."[79] The radicalism of these reformers lay in their willingness to go over the ruler's head and appeal directly to the people. For them, the basis of political participation became the individual's interpretation of scriptural law, a view reaffirmed by the Puritans of the late 1620s. For the citizen confronted with "neuter-passive," rather than outright ungodly rulers, Goodman and Ponet had no advice.

For the most part, Elizabeth's successful administration undermined the relevance of violent resistance or tyrannicide. The great majority of Englishmen regarded her as a vast improvement over Mary; and despite many faults, Elizabeth was not "ungodly." Under her there were Puritans in court as well as in Parliament, and the men who desired church reforms had little reason to talk of civil disobedience. A few, however, reminded their countrymen that "Governors . . . must governe under God. . . . where he hath no acknowledgement of superioritie, there man hath no commission from him to beare rule."[80]

Most of the English Puritans at the turn of the century were reluctant to break with their magistrates, even in so important a matter as ecclesiastical reform. The temptation to go it alone, of course, was always present. Robert Browne, for example, took an extreme path and separated from the English church altogether. In 1582 he stated his position in a little tract entitled *Treatise on Reformation without Tarrying for Anie.* Browne told the reformers that they were foolish to rely on politicians to initiate the Lord's work. The Church of England, he declared, had become so corrupt that it had forfeited any claim to be a true church of God. Since

79. Hudson, *John Ponet,* p. 157 [italics added]. John Knox called upon "the communalitie, my Bretheren" to rebel against ungodly rulers. He wrote in his *The Second Blast of the Trumpet against the Monstrous Regiment of Women,* "Moste justely may the same men depose and punishe him that unadvysedly before they did electe" (cited in Herbert Foster, "The Political Theories of Calvinists before the Puritan Exodus to America," *American Historical Review* 21 [1915]: 487). See also Allen, *Political Thought in the Sixteenth Century,* pp. 106–16, 118–20; *Vindiciae contra Tyrannos* (London, 1689).

80. John Penry, *An Exhortation unto the Governours, and People of Hir Majesties Countrie of Wales* (1588), p. 16.

its very existence insulted the Lord, men could ill afford to tarry for temporizing rulers. Browne advised individual clergymen to institute reform on their own authority. The main body of English Puritans rejected the Separatist solution, since they found elements within the English church still worth saving. The Puritans, especially those who eventually emigrated to Massachusetts, decided to wait for magisterial assistance.[81] Most "tarried" for powerful leaders like Lord Rich, who supported an "abundance of able and faithful ministers in Essex."[82] Local mitigations of the most glaring abuses had to suffice until the Puritans could convince all of the nation's rulers to follow the example of Lord Rich.

But, as the moral condition of England deteriorated and her covenant seemed more in danger, the Puritans once again began to stress the importance of individual conscience in political affairs. Yet they did so in a way which Goodman could not have anticipated. During the 1620s the Puritans appealed specifically to the voters, to the freemen of the various counties and boroughs throughout the country. They did not call for violent rebellion. For one thing, the "neuter-temporizers" of this period were not ungodly tyrants as Queen Mary had been; and, for another, the Puritans were not prepared to wage an all-out revolution against the Stuarts. In addition, the reformers knew from experience that they could not expect to change civil leaders who owed their positions to royal appointment or inheritance. Out of weakness, therefore, the English Puritans focused their political energies upon the few elective offices which they could hope to influence directly. Instead of reminding the ruler what he *should* do, they would remind the citizens what the Lord *expected* their rulers to do. It became the people's responsibility, through the franchise, to find magistrates who fulfilled the ideal standards of the calling and thereby, to assist in maintaining England as the Elect Nation of God.

The membership of Commons was an obvious target; so too were

81. Robert Browne, *A Treatise of Reformation Without Tarrying for Anie* (London, 1903); Leland H. Carlson, ed., *The Writings of Henry Barrow, 1587–1590* (London, 1962), pp. 158–59, 406–11. Also Perry Miller, *Orthodoxy in Massachusetts, 1630–1650* (Boston, 1933).

82. Gouge, *Gods Three Arrowes*, dedication, n.p.

many of the powerful jobs within city and borough governments throughout the kingdom. The Puritans' concentration on elected positions produced interesting results. Ministers found that they had to urge the electorate to overlook the family and economic ties which had traditionally determined the recipients of government power.[83] The covenant took precedence over self-interest, and Christian freeholders had to vote as their consciences dictated. "How grossly is the country wronged and befooled," lamented Samuel Ward, "chiefly in the choice of such as into whose hands they put their lives and lands at parliaments, by a kind of *conge d'elire,* usually sent them by some of the gentry of the shires, persuading (if not prescribing) the very couple they must choose."[84] Religious theories about the Lord's compact forced the Puritans to confront the details of political practice in a way they had never done before.

The Spiritual Brotherhood recognized that there would be little progress until the voters asserted their political independence. John Preston, an influential Puritan preacher, saw. this point, and he carefully instructed citizens about their crucial role within the political process. "I wish I could speake and give this rule to all the kingdom at Parliament times," he wrote, "for it is an errour among men to thinke that in election of Burgesses or any others, they may pleasure their friends, or themselves, by having this or that eye to their owne advantage." Preston wanted them "to keepe their mindes single and free" and to choose those whom in the sight of God and their consciences "they thinke fittest for the place."[85] In another piece, he explained, "There is a time when (it may be) a mans voice or suffrage would have turned the scale of a businesse, that concerned much the Commonwealth or the societie where he lives: but when that opportunity is past, it can be recalled no more."[86]

83. See J. E. Neale, *The Elizabethan House of Commons* (Middlesex, 1963) for examples of local election procedures. Often one family dominated the political life of a county for several generations.

84. Ward, *Sermons,* p. 118. English counties or shires usually sent two men to the House of Commons, hence the word "couple."

85. Preston, *Life Eternall,* pt. 2, p. 67. See Christopher Hill's article, "The Political Sermons of John Preston," in Hill, *Puritanism and Revolution,* pp. 239–72.

86. John Preston, *The New Covenant,* 5th ed. (1630), pp. 602–03, cited in Hill, *Puritanism and Revolution,* p. 261. Also Walzer, *Revolution of the Saints,* pp. 264–65.

Puritan ministers were willing to defy traditional political practice in order to please God; they hoped to persuade the people to follow them while the nation still had time.[87]

The participation of all people was necessary to remove the threat of divine wrath from England. In a sense, the freemen possessed a political calling of their own, a calling to hold magistrates responsible for the moral state of the kingdom. In his "An Appeal to the Parliament," Alexander Leighton stated that it was Parliament's obligation, as the representative body of the English people before God, to remove the prelacy and thus, to remove sin.[88] An anonymous Puritan pamphleteer who wrote "The Lawes of England" carried the idea to its logical extreme, claiming that popular consent was the basis of political authority. He declared, "for the manifestation of the right of the people, and mens more peaceable living, the *assent* of them, who are to be governed, hath alwaies been thought necessary."[89] The citizens fulfilled their political calling by making certain that the ruler fulfilled his. If everything had gone as the Puritan ministers had hoped, England would have returned to God's grace.

In a way, the Puritans of the 1620s retreated from Goodman's revolutionary doctrine. They called for votes, while he had advocated violence, even tyrannicide. Yet this apparent difference was misleading, for the political demands of seventeenth-century Puritans were in fact more rigorous than those of the earlier reformers. Goodman, for example, justified resistance only against ungodly or grossly

87. Thomas Scott, a vituperative Puritan pamphleteer, cried, "let the Ministers prepare the people, and warne them of the worke in hand, and let such as are Freeholders conferre together, and (neglecting both their Landlords, or great neighbours, or the Lord Liftenants themselves) looke upon the wisest, stoutest, and most religious persons" *(The High-ways of God and The King* [London, 1623], p. 37). John Reading in his election sermon, *Moses and Jethro: or the Good Magistrate,* told the voters not to listen dumbly to him, but to obey the will of God at the poll. "Sometimes they [the freemen] will heare a sermon before their elections, or assizes, and therein will heare, and follow [it], as far as may make them seeme religious . . . as farre as the word complieth and agreeth with their desires." Reading warned that such irresponsibility insulted the Lord (p. 12).

88. Leighton, *Appeal to the Parliament,* A3.

89. "The Lawes of England," cited in Judson, *Crisis of the Constitution,* p. 338 [italics added].

heretical rulers. While he may have hated the "neuter-passive" magistrates and civil leaders who were lazy Christians, he said nothing about them. The Stuart Puritans, however, demanded something close to perfection and refused to let these slackers get by. Most of the rulers they attacked were not overtly wicked or ungodly men. Nevertheless, these magistrates were inactive in the face of sin; they did show weakness during England's moral crisis. For these failures, the voters were instructed to remove them from office.

It is difficult to determine with accuracy the degree to which Puritan rhetoric influenced the English electorate, especially on the Parliamentary level. During the late 1620s some members of Parliament were clearly Puritan; others just as surely supported Archbishop Laud and the Arminian group. Most of the men who sat in Commons, however, were neither fish nor fowl—at least, they made no statements which allow the historian to classify them with confidence.[90] It is no easier to identify lay Puritans on the local plane. Suffolk was an exception. In this county, Sir Nathaniel Barnardiston, a respected Puritan gentleman, dominated political affairs; but powerful though he was, Barnardiston always worried about "the opinion of his country neighbors."[91] In Suffolk, the Puritan appeal to the voters seems to have had an important impact.

90. Hexter, "The English Aristocracy," p. 64.
91. BM, Anne Barnardiston to Sir Simonds D'Ewes, Jan. 1641, Harleian MSS, 384, fol. 27, cited in Hexter, "The English Aristocracy," p. 68. See J. H. Plumb, "The Growth of the Electorate in England from 1600 to 1715," *Past and Present,* no. 45(1969), pp. 90–116. Plumb noted that historians have long been aware of Parliament's efforts to regulate election methods, "but what has been totally ignored is the consistency of the pressure by some members of the Commons on matters relating to the electorate, the exceptional vigour of this pressure from 1621 to 1628 and the connection between this pressure and a change of fundamental importance that was taking place in the electorate itself. It was these years which saw parliamentary representation secure a wide social base without which the Stuarts might have had far less difficulty in securing control of the corporations and so reducing the power of Parliament or abolishing it altogether" (pp. 95–96). According to Plumb, "When further research is done, I think that we shall find that the men active in opening the franchise were puritans, often lawyers, sometimes merchants, frequently country gentlemen. Certainly the freemen, and the freeholders and the inhabitants must have been aroused, organized and led by some men of influence" (p. 102).

Fortunately, counting Puritans is not the only way to judge the influence of Puritan ideas on English political practice. During the last years of the 1620s, it became increasingly common for constituents to remind their elected magistrates what was expected of them. Sir Henry Crofts, for example, wanted to support Charles's demands but claimed that he could not do so because such a course of action would offend the electorate.[92] Another member of Commons noted that if Parliament gave money to the king "the countrey will blame us." Other representatives received letters from home complaining of this or that problem.[93] The voters' growing interest in the political process suggests that the Puritan sermons had had an effect. Whatever the cause, Englishmen in this period were less willing than ever before to overlook their magistrates' mistakes.

Another indication of the reformers' political success was the willingness of Commons to support Puritan religious demands. The house may not have gone as far as the Puritans desired, but it did attack the spread of Arminianism. In fact, one of the major crises of the decade occurred when Charles I intervened to save Dr. Richard Montagu, an outspoken Arminian, from Parliament's wrath. And, during the famous session of 1629, Commons once again revealed its concern over religious purity, warning, "Whosoever shall bring innovation in religion . . . or introduce Popery or Arminianism . . . shall be reputed a capital enemy to this Kingdom and Commonwealth."[94] Many Puritans hoped for more—impeachment of offending bishops, abolition of the prelacy, total suppression of Catholicism—but even without these reforms, they could see that a substantial group within the House sympathized with their cause. As long as Parliament met and as long as the voters had an opportunity to determine the character of their elected rulers, there was a chance that Commons might preserve England's place as God's Elect Nation.

Naturally, many Puritans regarded 1629 as the end of their

92. Notestein, *The English People on the Eve of Colonization*, pp. 195–96.
93. Judson, *Crisis of the Constitution*, p. 303.
94. "Protestation of the Commons," 2 March 1629, reproduced in J. P. Kenyon, *The Stuart Constitution, Documents and Commentary* (Cambridge, Eng., 1966), p. 85.

political hopes. Charles dissolved his uncooperative Parliament and decided that henceforth he would govern England without the help of Commons. In one blow the king removed the Puritans' major defense against sin and undermined their efforts to influence local elections. The Stuart monarch was now free to lead the nation straight into Hell, free to defy God's covenant, and there was little that the Puritans or anyone else could do about it. It was in this dark hour that John Winthrop told his wife, "The Lorde hath admonished, threatened, corrected, and astonished us, yet we growe worse and worse . . . I am veryly perswaded, God will bringe some heauye Affliction upon this lande, and that speedylye."[95] In this crisis, two political avenues seemed open, revolution or compliance. Since revolution was out of the question in 1629, most English Puritans chose to watch and wait.

But the Puritans who moved to New England took neither of these options. They retreated to America in order to establish a civil government of their own. These Puritans were a "fragment"[96] of the total English culture, a small group committed to certain political and religious ideas which had developed during the 1620s. From the very beginning, the people with Winthrop assumed that it was their duty to find good rulers. In fact, they insisted that elections were matters of conscience.

The New Israel required a very special electorate, for in a society without appointed rulers, without nobles, and without courtiers, the voters bore complete responsibility for the state of the commonwealth. There were no scapegoats. In America the covenant became every man's concern.

95. Winthrop, *Papers*, 2: 91.
96. For a full discussion of the term "fragment" as a historical concept, see Louis Hartz, *The Founding of New Societies* (New York, 1964), pp. 1–66.

2

A FAMILY QUARREL: 1630–1660

S England's moral condition went from bad to worse, one group of Puritans turned their eyes to the New World. The leaders of this body, stockholders in the Massachusetts Bay Company, received a charter in 1629 from Charles I. As far as the king knew, this grant authorized a business venture to explore the wilderness for "the oare of gould and silver." He certainly did not expect the members of this company to transform their patent into a civil constitution. Such a change was probably inevitable, however, for the Puritans who came to America were convinced that since the mother country had abused the Lord so long, the only hope for reform lay in the establishment of an entirely new commonwealth. For these men, the royal charter offered a chance to fulfill old dreams.[1]

The men and women who emigrated to Massachusetts Bay were by and large a homogeneous group, sharing fundamental beliefs about the character of the true Christian commonwealth. These Puritan settlers conceived of themselves as bound by the terms of a divine covenant. If they pleased the Lord by living according to scriptural law, they knew they could expect to see more of God's "wisdome power goodness and truthe then formerly wee have beene acquainted with."[2] The colonists were on a special mission,

1. For the complete text of the Massachusetts Charter, see Edmund S. Morgan, ed., *The Founding of Massachusetts* (Indianapolis, 1964), pp. 303–24.

2. John Winthrop, "A Modell of Christian Charity," in Edmund S. Morgan, ed., *Puritan Political Ideas, 1558–1794* (Indianapolis, 1965), p. 92.

and each one was personally responsible for its success or failure. Governor Winthrop captured the common sentiment aboard the *Arbella*, warning, "If wee shall deale falsely with our god in this worke . . . wee shall bee made a story and by-word through the world, wee shall open the mouthes of enemies to speake evill of the wayes of god."[3]

But no sooner had the Puritans landed in America than they began bickering among themselves. They fought not about fundamentals, but about details—about how to put commonly held theories into practice. One of the most difficult problems for the early settlers was defining the powers of their civil leaders. The Puritans of New England, with the notable exception of Roger Williams, agreed that their rulers were God's vicegerents on earth, and they expected them to defend the purity of the Congregational churches. The majority of the colonists also believed that the people themselves should decide which persons would exercise magisterial authority. But beyond these general notions, there was dissension. Governor Winthrop, for example, assumed that rulers possessed broad discretionary powers, especially in judicial matters. His political actions elicited an immediate and vociferous response from other Puritans who insisted that magistrates held only those powers specifically delegated to them by the electorate. While both groups wanted to create a New Israel in America, neither side trusted the other to make routine government decisions.

Ironically, and one will see this more than once in the study of the good ruler, the arguments between Winthrop and his opponents took on such a bitter character precisely because all the individuals involved shared common political ideas. Certainly there was much evidence in the first years to support Perry Miller's observation that "the bitterest and most furious combats are generally fought between those who agree on fundamentals, for there is no greater annoyance that a man can suffer than attack from persons who accord with him in the main, but apply his principles to conclusions utterly foreign to his liking."[4] At the end of the century, when New Englanders no longer agreed on fundamental principles, political conflicts tended to

3. Ibid., p. 87.
4. Perry Miller and Thomas H. Johnson, eds., *The Puritans*, 2 vols. (New York, 1963), 1: 41.

be far less acrimonious than those of the first generation (see chaps. 6 and 7).

What also seems clear from the debates about the nature of the magistracy is that New England society was politically flexible. Certainly John Winthrop and his critics in the Massachusetts General Court were Puritans by anyone's standards, yet these men held very different notions about the character of the good ruler. The political arguments of this period can best be described, therefore, as family quarrels, disagreements among fellow Puritans about the proper construction of God's commonwealth.

The Sword of God in New England

About the ruler's relation to the church there was little disagreement. The Puritans who sailed with Winthrop planned from the very beginning to establish the right worship of Christ, shedding the unscriptural ceremonies that had corrupted the Church of England. In 1652 the Reverend John Cotton, early New England's most famous divine, angrily reminded Sir Richard Saltonstall, a colonist who had returned to the mother country, "You know not, if you think we came into this wilderness to practice those courses here which we fled from in England."[5] And Edward Johnson, one of the Bay Colony's first chroniclers, pointed out, "we chose not the place for the Land, but for the government that our Lord Christ might raigne over us."[6] The Puritans had emigrated for God, had covenanted with God, and were sustained by God.

The rulers of New England saw themselves as the keepers of the Lord's covenant, citing Moses as their political ideal.[7] They claimed

5. John Cotton to Sir Richard Saltonstall, 1652, printed in Issac Backus, *A History of New England,* 2 vols. (Newton, Mass., 1871), 1: 200. See Charles J. Hoadly, ed., *Records of the Colony and Plantation of New Haven, From 1638 to 1649,* 2 vols. (Hartford, 1857), 1: 11–13; and J. H. Trumbull, ed., *Public Records of the Colony of Connecticut,* 15 vols. (Hartford, 1850–90), 1: 21, for statements about the original religious goals of these colonies.

6. J. Franklin Jameson, ed., *Johnson's Wonder-Working Providence of Sions Saviour in New England* [1654] (New York, 1910), p. 146.

7. John Cotton, *The Bloudy Tenent, Washed, and Made White in the Bloud of the Lambe* (London, 1647), p. 73.

that God had armed them with a sword to defend the First and Second Tables and to preserve the New Israel from moral decay. Cotton called the magistrates *"The Ministers of God,"* since their principal task was the administration of "things wherein God is most directly and immediately honoured, which is promoting man's Spiritual good."[8] The Reverend Thomas Cobbet agreed, calling the ruler "a political Minister of God."[9] In either case, it was clear that the New Englanders would not tolerate "neuter-temporizers" as people in the mother country had done.

The Puritans of Massachusetts regarded church membership as the essential prerequisite for the magistracy. It seemed to them that any civil leader committed to the Congregational faith would be likely to support the colony's religious goals and, thus, to strengthen the covenant. Cotton informed an influential English peer, for example, that the Americans placed great weight on the condition of the ruler's soul. In the New World even nobles had to fulfill certain spiritual qualifications before the voters would consider them for civil office. "Though we receive them [nobles] with honour," Cotton tactfully explained, "and allow them preeminence and accommodations according to their condition, yet we do not, ordinarily, call them forth to the power of election, or administration of magistracy, until they be received as members into some of our churches."[10] In other writings Cotton demanded a good deal more of rulers than church membership. Indeed, he wanted men "so well accquainted with matters of Religion, as to discerne the Fundamentall Principels [for] . . . their ignorance thereof, is no discharge of their duty before the Lord." Rulers expert in theology could identify heresy with speed, and hopefully, with accuracy.[11]

8. John Cotton, *A Discourse about Civil Government in a New Plantation Whose Design Is Religion* (Cambridge, Mass., 1663), p. 17. This work is sometimes wrongly attributed to John Davenport.

9. Thomas Cobbet, *The Civil Magistrates Power in Matters of Religion Modestly Debated* (London, 1653), p. 25.

10. Thomas Hutchinson, *The History of the Colony and Province of Massachusetts-Bay,* ed. Lawrence S. Mayo, 3 vols. (Boston, 1936), 1: 412 (hereafter referred to as Hutchinson, *History); and Thomas Shepard, "Notes for the Election Sermon, 1638," *New England Historical and Genealogical Register* 24 (1870): 366.

11. Cotton, *Bloudy Tenent,* p. 89.

The Bay colonists argued that church membership was such an essential characteristic in the good ruler because the Lord sometimes gave irreligious men "sundry eminent gifts of wisdom, courage, justice, fit for government." Persons of this description could ruin a godly commonwealth like New England if they gained power, for their Machiavellian policies would surely offend the Lord.[12] Cotton observed in his short essay, *A Discourse about Civil Government,* that where individuals choose to live like pagans "a Heathen man or meer civil worldly Politician, will be good enough to be their Magistrate."[13] Some Puritan leaders were so concerned about preserving the colony's religious character that they rejected the teachings of classical political theorists. Governor Winthrop, for example, criticized an election day speaker simply because that minister had grounded "his propositions much upon the old Roman and Grecian governments, which sure is an error, for if religion and the word of God makes men wiser than their neighbors, [then] . . . these times have the advantage of all that have gone before us in experience and observation." Winthrop thought that the Puritans were fully capable of formulating their own rules of government without any assistance from "those heathen commonwealths."[14]

The Puritans' concern about the magistrate's spiritual character was understandable, since in Massachusetts civil officers were responsible for the protection of God's true church as well as for the exclusion of its rivals. The colonists believed, no doubt because of their experience in England, that the state which tolerated unscriptural worship jeopardized its covenant with God. In his short essay, *The Simple Cobler of Aggawam in America,* Nathaniel Ward insisted that if New England ever permitted a false theology to flourish, then it must also give men complete moral freedom "else the Fiddle will be out of tune, and some of the strings crack."[15]

---

12. Hutchinson, *History,* 1: 413.

13. Cotton, *Discourse about Civil Government,* pp. 12–13.

14. John Winthrop, *The History of New England from 1630–1649,* ed. James Savage, 2d ed. 2 vols. (Boston, 1853), 2: 42 (hereafter referred to as Winthrop, *History*).

15. Nathaniel Ward, *The Simple Cobler of Aggawam in America* (London, 1647), p. 8.

Toleration produced war, bad policy, and depression.[16] Moreover, there was always a danger that unpunished heretics would tempt God's proven saints and lead them into sin. Adopting a common metaphor of this period, Cotton described religious dissenters as weeds which attacked the Lord's pure garden church in the wilderness. When errant seeds blew into that garden, the rulers were expected to root them out, lest they choke "the good herbs." But defensive action against the wicked plants was not enough, for "the keepers of his wildernesse should suffer no venomous weeds to grow *neere* his Garden, and poyson those within the Garden that feed on them."[17] Good Puritan magistrates had to persecute heretics aggressively, or as Winthrop warned, "by indulgence toward them, the whole familye of God in this countrey should be scattered, if not destroyed."[18]

Despite their anxiety about the purity of the church, the Bay colonists were careful to set limits on the magistrate's spiritual authority. No ruler possessed the power to punish a heretic until that dissenter had openly announced his errant beliefs. Sins of the mind were therefore beyond the domain of civil government, and as long as a person paid outward respect to Congregational doctrine, he was safe from state harassment.[19] From time to time, of course, outsiders expressed doubts about the value of the New England system. After he had returned to the mother country, Sir Richard Saltonstall became convinced that intolerance produced hypocrisy, not piety, and he asked Cotton whether the superficial conformity required in Massachusetts did not force men to sin against their consciences. If Saltonstall expected to catch Cotton out on a limb, he was disappointed. "If the worship be lawful in itself," the Bay minister responded, "the magistrate compelling him to come to it, compelleth him not to sin, but the sin is in his will that needs to be compelled to a Christian duty."[20] In other words, magistrates per-

16. Ibid., pp. 21–22; Cobbet, *Civil Magistrates,* pp. 24-25; Cotton, *Bloudy Tenent,* p. 162.

17. Cotton, *Bloudy Tenent,* p. 151.

18. *The Winthrop Papers,* 5 vols. (Boston, 1929–47), p. 475. For Thomas Dudley's attitudes toward heretics see ibid., 4: 85–87.

19. Cobbet, *Civil Magistrates,* pp. 13–16; *The Results of Three Synods* (Boston, 1725), pp. 48–49.

20. Backus, *History of New England,* 1: 198–200.

formed a valuable service by coercing settlers to attend church; and, in any case, pious hypocrites made better citizens than did stubborn nonconformists.

The most famous dissenters from Congregational orthodoxy, Roger Williams and Anne Hutchinson, refused discreet silence, and Puritan rulers expelled them. In 1650 the less renowned William Pynchon, founder of Springfield, decided that he had had enough of hypocrisy and published a book which the Bay leaders labeled as heretical. Governor Endecott complained that Pynchon "might have kept his judgment to himself, as it seems he did above thirty years, most of which time he hath lived amongst us with honour, much respect, and love." But, once the Springfield leader had circulated his mischievous opinions, the Massachusetts magistrates believed that they "were called of God, to proceed against him accordingly."[21]

Even though there was extensive cooperation between church and state in Massachusetts, the colonists insisted that they were separate institutions. According to Bay leaders, in fact, the society that "confounded" civil and spiritual authority risked becoming an Erastian or theocratic form of government, neither of which the Puritans found desirable.[22] When an ecclesiastical synod met in 1648, it assured the people that Congregational churches would not interfere with "the authority of Civil Magistrates in their jurisdictions; nor any whit [weaken] their hands in governing; but rather [strengthen] them, & [further] the people in yielding more

21. Governor John Endecott and the Assistants of Massachusetts to Sir Henry Vane, 20 Oct. 1652, *3 Collections,* Massachusetts Historical Society (hereafter MHS), 1: 35–36. The New Englanders claimed that they had acted "as we believe in concience to God's command we were bound to do" (p. 37). Nathaniel B. Shurtleff, ed., *The Records of the Governor and Company of the Massachusetts Bay in New England,* 5 vols. in 6 (Boston, 1853–54), 3: 215–16, 230 (hereafter referred to as *Mass. Records*). See also Samuel Eliot Morison, *Builders of the Bay Colony* (Boston, 1958), pp. 337–78; Henry M. Burt, *The First Century of the History of Springfield,* 2 vols. (Springfield, 1898–99), contains large portions of Pynchon's heretical work, *The Meritorious Price of Our Redemption,* which the Bay magistrates burned publicly (pp. 89–121).

22. Cotton, *Discourse about Civil Government,* pp. 7–8; Hutchinson, *History,* 1: 414–15. "The Tentative Conclusions of the Cambridge Synod 1646," in Williston Walker, *The Creeds and Platforms of Congregationalism* (Boston, 1960), p. 190.

hearty & conscionable obedience unto them."[23] According to the common theory, the clergy had no right to call rulers to account for their civil decisions since Puritan magistrates were directly responsible to God, not to the churches, for their political errors. After the voters had selected a man for a civil position, no clerical censure, including the loss of church membership, could deprive him of that office.[24] But, by the same token, rulers did not possess any purely ministerial powers and were entitled neither to excommunicate heretics, nor to administer the sacraments. Only with great reservation did New Englanders allow magistrates to summon church synods "to consider of, and clear the truth from the Scriptures, in weighty matters of Religion."[25]

Despite the colonists' apparent effort to maintain strict separation, the distinction between civil and spiritual authority sometimes became fuzzy. The clergy held considerable extralegal or indirect power over matters of state policy.[26] Because their calling commanded popular respect and because they had a regular pulpit from which to speak, the ministers were in a position to influence their parishioners' opinions about many political issues. Moreover, the ministers often acted as advisers or arbitrators in disputes between the members of the two legislative bodies in Massachusetts, the Court of Assistants and the House of Deputies. Winthrop cited an accepted axiom of civil policy when he wrote, "Ministers have great

23. Walker, *Creeds and Platforms*, p. 235.

24. "John Winthrop's Essay Against the Power of the Church to Sit in Judgment on the Civil Magistracy [1637]," *Winthrop Papers*, 3: 505–07. Winthrop declared that if the churches could call magistrates to account for their civil acts it "would confounde those Jurisdictions, which Christ hath made distinct: for as he is Kinge of Kings and Lord of Lords he hath sett up another kingdome in this worlde, wherein magistrates are his officers, and they are to be accountable to him, for their miscarriages in the waye and order of this kingdome" (p. 506). See *Mass. Records*, 3: 3, 5, for case of a deputy who retained his civil office even though he was involved in a serious controversy with the Gloucester church. When the freemen of that town elected a new deputy who was in better ecclesiastical standing, the General Court refused to accept him and, instead, supported the original representative.

25. Walker, *Creeds and Platforms*, pp. 192, 234–237.

26. George L. Haskins, *Law and Authority in Early Massachusetts: A Study in Tradition and Design* (New York, 1960), pp. 60–63.

power with the people, whereby throughe the good correspondency between the magistrates and them, they are the more easly governed."[27] Most Puritans did not protest these seeming violations of the separation of the church and state; and, throughout the colony's early years, they appeared satisfied with the relation that Moses and Aaron—the magistrate and the minister—had achieved in America.

Roger Williams was one Puritan who was not satisfied. He informed his fellow New Englanders that the worship of Christ was none of the ruler's business, for there was no evidence that God had asked civil magistrates to maintain the purity of His church. The Bay colonists were obviously not persuaded by Williams's ideas, for they went right on insisting that their magistrates were the Lord's vicegerents on earth. Had they listened to him, however, they would have had difficulty denying the logic of his position, which was based on careful scriptural study.

Despite his winning personality, Williams never gained intellectual disciples; and only his brilliant, aggressive curiosity has saved him from perpetual obscurity. Throughout his long life, Williams pushed ideas to conclusions which contemporaries could not or would not see. In time, he went beyond the boundaries of accepted political theory and, in so doing, achieved even greater historical importance. This iconoclastic streak has helped scholars to define the limits and character of the Puritan mainstream.

Williams approached the Bible through typology, a method of study which sought to make connections between the two testaments and to demonstrate how Old Testament occurrences were premonitions of New Testament events.[28] The Rhode Island Puritan believed that ancient Israel had covenanted with God and that the Lord had sustained both church and state in that original holy land. But when Canaan fell, the divine covenant dissolved; and since that day the Lord had not seen fit to compact with any modern nation.

27. John Winthrop to the Earl of Warwick, Sept. 1644, *Winthrop Papers,* 4: 493.

28. *The Complete Writings of Roger Williams,* 7 vols. (New York, 1963), 7: 15–21. See Edmund S. Morgan, *Roger Williams: The Church and the State* (New York, 1967); Edmund S. Morgan, "Miller's Williams," *New England Quarterly* 38(1965): 514–23.

In terms of typology, Israel was a "nonesuch." It simply did not serve as a model for anything that had happened in later centuries.[29] For Massachusetts to style itself an "Elect" commonwealth, therefore, was an error, because God had made no special agreement with it.[30] In addition, since the Lord never granted spiritual authority to the leaders of the Bay Colony, none of the Massachusetts magistrates could very well claim to be His vicegerents. The rulers of the Old Testament were the last men whom God had ordained as defenders of the faith. Of course, He could easily have created others if He had wanted the state to protect His worship, "for he that could have legions of Angels, if he so pleased, could easily have been and still be furnished with legions of good and gracious Magistrates to this end and purpose."[31] Williams observed, with tongue in cheek no doubt, that if civil governments were truly intended for some divine role, then the seventeenth century seemed strangely devoid of godly rulers.[32]

The Rhode Island dissenter enjoyed ridiculing the intolerance of Bay leaders, an intolerance which had caused him no little inconvenience. Williams declared that it was unnecessary for magistrates to dash "to the *Cutlers shop, the Armories* and *Magazines*" every time someone blasphemed God, for "a false *Religion* out of the *Church* will not hurt the inclosed *Garden*."[33] The Lord was in no hurry; He could punish evil doers easily enough in the next world. Besides, Williams warned, the ruler who forced men to religious conformity risked a far worse danger than did the ruler who tolerated diverse theological opinions. Authorities who coerced conscience "into a pretended holy fellowship and Communion with *God*" committed "soul-rape," and by Williams's standards hypocrites were sinners.[34]

Williams was well aware that rulers throughout history had seldom, if ever, adopted his own tolerant views. In fact, it was far more usual for each government to proclaim its own particular version of religious truth and then to make war on all dissenters. In their

29. Williams, *Writings,* 7: 159; 3: 311–30.
30. Ibid., 1: 77.
31. Ibid., 3: 121.
32. Ibid., 4: 345.
33. Ibid., 7: 179–80; 3: 198.
34. Ibid., 3: 124–25; 7: 268.

passion to help God, crusading leaders defended erroneous creeds and mistakenly smote the true children of Christ.[35] Unfortunately, the centuries of senseless bloodshed had not impressed the clergy, and they continued to call upon magistrates to protect their own unique biblical interpretations. According to Williams, if history taught any lesson, it was that as long as civil force determined orthodoxy, might would define right, and God's church would remain a subject of the ruler's whim. He observed that the course of the English Reformation pointed up the absurdity of ever trying to establish one true religion. In the years following 1529 each English sovereign had brought a different faith to power; now Catholic, now Calvinist, now Anglican, now in between, until men's consciences were *"tost up and down (even like* Tenis-bals.)" None of this confusion would have occurred if the mother country had kept the boundaries between church and state distinct; for only through strict separation could a state attain its primary goal—civil peace.[36]

Williams's insistence on the secular nature of the state led him to conclude that a ruler could still be a good ruler even though he had never heard of Christ. There was no reason to assume that a person would perform better in his particular calling simply because he was a Christian.[37] In other words, a government like that of Massachusetts which restricted magistracy to church members was foolish, since it overlooked and wasted the political skills of unregenerate men. Williams knew that "there is a *morall vertue,* a *morall fidelitie, abilitie* and *honestie,* which other men (besides Church-members) are, by good *nature* and *education,* by good *Lawes* and good *examples* nourished and trained up in." And, in obvious contrast to Cotton, who denied office to all "carnal" men, Williams declared "that Civill places of *Trust* and *Credit* need not to be *Monopolized* into the hands of *Church-Members* (who sometimes are not fitted for them.)"[38]

In practice, it would have been difficult to distinguish Williams's magistrate from Cotton's, for Williams granted the ruler great

35. Morgan, *Roger Williams,* chap. 4.
36. Williams, *Writings,* 3: 96, 206; 7: 189–90, 201, 218.
37. See discussion of calling in chap. 1; Williams, *Writings,* 3: 398–99.
38. Williams, *Writings,* 4: 365.

authority over public morality. The citizen could worship as he pleased, but he had no right to sin in the streets of Providence. In 1652 Williams wrote, "it is the duty of the *civil sword,* to cut off the *Incivilities* of *our times;*" and proceeded to praise that Roman emperor who had censured "Ovid, for that wanton *Book* of his *De Arte amandi,* as a sparke to immodesty and uncleanness."[39] All governments, Williams insisted, had to punish murder, adultery, thievery, and lying; for without "civil Officers of *Justice* to punish these four sins (especially) it is impossible that men can live (as men, and not as Beasts or worse) together."[40]

Many of Williams's contemporaries regarded him as a political and religious radical. Actually his notions about the character of the magistracy were not as unorthodox as they claimed. Williams rejected the idea that rulers should be removed from office, either by revolution or election, simply because they were ungodly. Certainly the condition of a magistrate's soul did not determine civil obedience.[41] In this view, he broke not only from sixteenth-century figures like Goodman and Ponet, but also from most of the English and American Puritans of his own generation. Against his critics, Williams stubbornly maintained that the citizen's loyalty was due the magistrate because he was a magistrate, not because he was a Christian. Christ himself, after all, had commanded obedience to higher powers in an age when all the rulers in the world were evil tyrants.[42] Williams never speculated whether there was a just cause for revolution beyond religion and appeared content with the Savior's own political conservatism.

Most New England Puritans regarded Williams as a good, but wrongheaded man.[43] Unlike him, they had come to believe that a good ruler wielded the "sword of God" and preserved their special covenant. If he failed in his calling, as Charles I and a host of lesser

39. Ibid., 7: 244.

40. Ibid., 7: 263.

41. Ibid., 3; Morgan, "Miller's Williams," pp. 522–23.

42. Williams, *Writings,* 3: 332–33.

43. I have sometimes used the term "New England" when "Massachusetts" might have done just as well. I did so in the belief that the political ideas of the Bay Puritans were nearly identical to those of Puritans in Connecticut and New Haven, and it seemed rather arbitrary to tie general notions to specific colonies.

English magistrates had failed, then he had to be replaced with someone better. Ultimately it was the freemen in Massachusetts, Connecticut, and New Haven who bore the responsibility for the moral quality of civil government. They were the ones who had to stand guard against ungodly, heretical, and temporizing rulers.

A Vote for God

In Massachusetts the covenant idea proliferated far beyond what it had been in the mother country. The American Puritans felt themselves bound not only by a national covenant made with God, but also by civil and ecclesiastical compacts formed without divine assistance. They spoke of secular government, for example, as a voluntary agreement existing between the ruler and his subjects.[44] On the one hand, the magistrate promised to observe scriptural and colonial laws to the best of his ability; on the other, the people pledged obedience and cooperation. The essential ingredient in this contract was free will. Thomas Hooker, the spiritual leader of Connecticut, explained that the man who desired to enter a social covenant had to *"willingly* binde and ingage himselfe to each member of that society . . . or else a member actually he is not."[45] Al-

44. See Perry Miller, *The New England Mind*, 2 vols. (Boston, 1961), I: 412–13.

45. Thomas Hooker, *A Survey of the Summe of Church Discipline* (London, 1648), pt. 1, p. 47 (italics added). While the formation of the civil compact was a voluntary process, the individual who did not choose to covenant with his neighbors for some sort of public order was being stubborn, if not perverse. Without government man stood in a state of natural liberty—a state which he shared "with beasts and other creatures." Winthrop once declared to the General Court that the "exercise of this liberty makes men grow more evil, and in time to be worse than brute beasts." Puritan magistrates shuddered at the thought of such anarchy and pointed to the sixteenth-century Anabaptist community, Munster, where the New Englanders believed neither women nor property had been safe. Intelligent men gave up their wild, animal freedom and submitted themselves to civil authority. Protected by the powers of government, they gained "civil or federal" liberty. "This liberty is the proper end and object of authority," Winthrop claimed, "and it is a liberty to [do] that only which is good, just, and honest." The state, in other words, granted man the liberty to exercise certain rights; there were no rights apart from the state (Winthrop, *History*, 2: 280–81; also see Stanley Gray, "The Political Thought of John Winthrop," *New England Quarterly* 3[1930]: 681–705.

though the Lord was not a party to this compact, the Bay Puritans agreed that His glorification was their goal.

God, of course, could have created human government on His own, denying man any share in its establishment, but He rejected such an arbitrary path. Instead, the Lord allowed His children to work out the details of their own political organization and to select those persons whom they believed would make the best rulers. "The choice of public magistrates," Hooker preached in 1638, "belongs unto the people by God's own allowance."[46] But there was one important hitch. The Puritans though that the magistrate's office, as opposed to the magistrate himself, was an ordinance of God and as such carried certain duties and prerogatives which He alone determined. Nevertheless, the people still possessed great influence over the affairs of state, and the founders claimed that the formation of any civil government required popular assent. "No common weale," declared Winthrop, "can be founded but by free consent."[47]

The New Haven Colony provided a dramatic example of the voluntaristic nature of civil government in New England. Soon after the main body of settlers had arrived in 1639, the Reverend John Davenport called a meeting of all adult males. He asked these men whether they wanted to bind themselves into "a plantation covenant," that in civil matters "we would all of us be ordered by those rules which the scripture holds forth for us." After the men agreed to form such a covenant, the minister then read several biblical passages describing the character of the good ruler. Scriptural advice was necessary, Davenport claimed, because the New Haveners were about "to cast themselves into thatt mould and forme of common wealth which appeareth best," and they did not want to err. Only after the group had unanimously accepted the covenant did it vote to exclude nonchurch members from participation in civil affairs. In other words, the nonelect voluntarily consented to give up their rights as "Free Burgesses."[48] Davenport recognized, as did the

46. *Collections,* Connecticut Historical Society [hereafter CHS], 1: 20.
47. "A Declaration in Defense of an Order of Court Made in May, 1637," *Winthrop Papers,* 3: 423. Also John Cotton, *An Exposition upon the Thirteenth Chapter of the Revelation* (London, 1655), p. 72.
48. Hoadly, *Records of New Haven,* 1: 11–15, 21.

leaders of Massachusetts and Connecticut, that people will be far more likely to obey a government in which thay have had a voice than one which had been forced upon them.

In the early years of settlement the founders of Massachusetts eased the transition from a chartered company to a civil government by giving the franchise to hundreds of men who could never have afforded stock in the original commercial enterprise. After 1631 every adult male church member could participate in elections; and, because most adults in the Bay Colony belonged to a church, the potential vote was proportionally larger than that of contemporary England.[49] Moreover, frequent elections increased the peoples' political power; for each May they had an opportunity to judge the performance of all major officeholders. Under the Old Charter (1630–84), no person could acquire ruling authority except at the polls. The freemen, as voters were then called, selected at large a governor, a deputy governor, and a group of assistants; and after 1634, the citizens in each town chose representatives to serve as their deputies in the General Court.[50]

Political practices in England clearly influenced the way in which the American Puritans looked at the electoral process. Their frustrating experience in the mother country had underlined the importance of the ballot in ridding the state of "neuter-temporizers" who failed to fulfill the responsibilities of their calling. In theory,

49. Stephen Foster, "The Puritan Social Ethic: Class and Calling in the First Hundred Years of Settlement in New England" (Ph.D. diss., Yale University, 1967), p. 141 and appendix; B. Katherine Brown, "Freemanship in Puritan Massachusetts," *American Historical Review* 59 (1954): 865–83; B. Katherine Brown, "Puritan Democracy in Dedham, Massachusetts: Another Case Study," *William and Mary Quarterly*, 3d ser. 24 (1967): 378–96; Stephen Foster, "The Massachusetts Franchise in the Seventeenth Century," ibid., pp. 613–23; Richard C. Simmons, "Freemanship in Early Massachusetts: Some Suggestions and a Case Study," ibid., 19 (1962): 422–28; Edmund S. Morgan, *Puritan Dilemma* (Boston, 1958), pp. 84–94. For an interesting discussion of the franchise in New Haven, see Hoadly, *Records of New Haven*, 1: 14–15.

50. I have used the terms "assistant" and "magistrate" interchangeably as the people of seventeenth-century Massachusetts did. "Deputy" and "representative" are also employd as synonyms.

at least, the New England electorate voted by conscience, trying at all times to choose rulers who would maintain the colony's special covenant with God. One of the best examples of the impact of the English background on the politics of Massachusetts was the wording of the freeman's oath. Puritan electors swore before their magistrates to "give my vote and suffrage, as I shall judge in *myne owne conscience* may best conduce and tend to the publique weale of the body, without respect of persons, or favor of any man. Soe helpe mee God, in the Lord Jesus Christ."[51] Thomas Adams and John Preston could not have asked for anything more. In fact, when Hooker went to Connecticut, he preached the same political message that these men had preached in the mother country. "The privilege of election, which belongs to the people," he observed, "must not be exercised according to their humours, but according to the blessed will and law of God."[52] The Lord required each Puritan to decide for himself whether his ruler governed according to Scripture. If the people erred by selecting an evil man, they could expect the Lord to punish the entire population, and in the early years of settlement this threat stimulated political vigilance.[53]

Throughout this period the Puritans guarded their electoral rights jealously, resisting any plan which they suspected might lessen their own political power.[54] They were especially adamant in their refusal to allow hereditary authority to develop within the Bay Colony. In 1636 John Cotton explained New England's position to two Puritan peers, Lord Say and Seal and Lord Brooke, two men with ambitious plans for the New World. The colonists accepted the notion of hereditary dignity and honor, Cotton declared, but hereditary authority was quite another matter. Since election was the only path to civil office, the nobles would have to face the voters like any other candidate if they lived in Massachusetts. No doubt

51. *Mass. Records,* 1: 117 (italics added).
52. *Collections,* CHS, 1: 20.
53. See discussion of the Henry Vane affair below.
54. The freemen of Massachusetts were outraged when the magistrates offered several nominations for the Court of Assistants. "This was looked at by the people," Winthrop observed, "as dangerous to their liberty and therefore they would have none of these" (Winthrop, *History,* 2: 419–20).

Cotton's description dampened the peers' enthusiasm, for they never saw fit to join their coreligionists in New Israel.[55]

Despite the freemen's impressive political power both in law and in theory, few of them ever bothered to vote. This apparent apathy can be explained in several ways. In the first place, the people of Massachusetts believed that men like John Winthrop, Thomas Dudley, and John Endecott—all of whom served as governors—bore the essential characteristics of a good ruler. These magistrates seemed to please the Lord, and few citizens felt any compelling need to nominate others to replace them. As long as the "right" men were running there was little incentive to vote. In fact, most of the time it must have been a foregone conclusion who would be chosen to the magistracy. It certainly was not uncommon for a ruler to be elected to the same office for ten or twenty terms. Only rarely did the people rebuke a ruler who disappointed them, a lesson which Winthrop learned in 1634. As governor, Winthrop discouraged the formation of a new legislative body which was to represent the towns, for he thought that the assistants, established by charter and chosen by the voters at large, were capable of ruling the young commonwealth alone. His logic failed to move the freemen, however, and they dropped him from the governorship. Nevertheless, Winthrop continued as an assistant, and within a few years returned once again as the colony's chief magistrate. The 1634 example is noteworthy only because it was so unusual.[56] While they were still alive, governors and assistants were seldom turned out of office.

To some extent the absence of campaigning also discouraged

55. "Certain Proposals made by Lord Say, Lord Brooke, and other Persons of quality as conditions of their removing to New-England, with the answers thereto [1636]" (in Hutchinson, *History*, 1: 410–13); see Winthrop, *History*, 1: 360; 2: 3.

56. Winthrop, *History*, 1: 157. In 1642 Thomas Lechford, a lawyer critical of the Puritan government, questioned whether popular elections would destroy New England, for "to make experiments of governing our selves here by new wayes, wherein (like young Physitians) of necessity we must hurt and spoil one another a great while, before we come to such a setled Commonwealth, or Church-government, as in *England*." Lechford, of course, had not yet heard the unsettling news about the English Civil War. See J. H. Trumbull, ed., *Thomas Lechford's Plain Dealing: Or, Newes from New England* (Boston, 1867), pp. 143–44.

popular political action. The Puritans were suspicious of any man who openly sought office, regarding such efforts as a cover for doubtful intentions.[57] Governor John Haynes, for example, waited until after his election had been confirmed before he announced that he would forego any salary.[58] The leaders of both church and state condemned campaigns in the belief that political competition would divide their commonwealth, and that internal dissension would be a sign that the people who had covenanted with God were no longer united.[59] When Winthrop heard that someone had advocated splitting the magistrates into little factions, he exploded, "If this past for good doctrine, then let us no longer professe the Gospell of Jesus Christ, but take up the rules of Matchiavell, and the Jesuits, for Christ sayeth Love is the bond of perfection and a kingdome or house devided cannot stand: but the others teache (or rather the Devill teacheth them) devide et impera etc."[60] Political parties and

57. Winthrop, *History*, 1: 103.
58. Ibid., 1: 190.
59. See Shepard, "Notes for the Election Sermon, 1638," pp. 361–66. Shepard noted that faction is built upon "a number of vaine (or empty men) & a beggarly crue" p. 365). In 1658 John Davenport was afraid that the factional spirit had invaded the politics of the New Haven colony.

> Concerning our Court matters here; the last election-day was the saddest to me that I ever saw in Newhaven, by our want of him [Theophilus Eaton, a founder and leading magistrate, had just died], whose presence etc. was wont to make it a day of no less contentment, then solemnity. Being weary, after my sermon, I was absent from the Court. The 1st newes that I heard from thence added to my sorrow. For I heard that Mr. Goodyeare was wholly left out in the choyse of magistrates, whereas I had beene secure, thincking they proposed to choose him Governour. But, the day following, upon enquiry into the cause of it, I received such answer as cleared unto me that it came to pass, *not by any plot of men,* but by the overruling providence of God.

At the last moment, the New Haven freemen had decided to choose someone in Goodyear's place, since he was going to England on government business. See John Davenport to John Winthrop, Jr., in Isabel Calder, ed., *Letters of John Davenport, Puritan Divine* (New Haven, 1937), pp. 122–23.

60. "John Winthrop to the Elders of the Massachusetts Churches, Oct. 14, 1642," *Winthrop Papers,* 4: 360. In 1644 Winthrop observed that *"At this court Mr. Saltonstall [a magistrate] moved very earnestly that he*

associations did not flourish so long as the majority of colonists conceived of themselves as knit together in the performance of God's work.

It appears that colonists regarded elections as an emergency safe-guard, as a means, short of revolution, for removing those rulers whom they found unacceptable. The ballot was a constitutional way of easing political discontent without violence. The citizens of Massachusetts remained happy only so long as civil leaders respected the laws of God and the liberties of "free and natuall" Englishmen.[61] Within these limits the magistrate could conduct the routine business of government as he saw fit. But, at the same time, the threat of electoral rebuke contributed to the growth of responsive government, since the Bay rulers could not easily ignore freemen who took conscience as their political guide.

The importance of the vote in the colony's political process should not be underestimated, for it may well have saved Massachusetts from rebellion during the mid-1630s.[62] The immediate cause of unrest was Henry Vane, a young, intemperate man who became

---

might be left out at the next election, and pursued his motion after to the towns. It could not appear what should move him to it." Winthrop decided that Saltonstall, who had sided with the deputies against the magistrates, was angry because his dissenting political views had not prevailed. "Such as were acquainted with the other states in the world," Winthrop noted, "would have concluded such a faction here as hath been usual in the council of England and other states, *who walk by politic principles only*" (Winthrop, *History*, 2: 57 [italics added]).

61. Massachusetts Charter, in Morgan, *Founding of Massachusetts,* p. 318.

62. At the same time the Virginians drove their appointed governor, Sir John Harvey, out of the colony at gunpoint, warning that if he ever returned, he would be "pistoled or shot." Rebellion was the only way to get rid of this petty despot who seemed to have the support of the Stuart court. Certainly the colonists did not have the opportunity to vote him out of office. For interesting comparative material on Virginia politics in the 1630s see, Wesley Frank Craven, *The Southern Colonies in the Seventeenth Century* (Baton Rouge, 1949), pp. 154–55; Bernard Bailyn, "Politics and Social Structure in Virginia," in James M. Smith, ed., *Seventeenth-Century America* (Chapel Hill, 1959), pp. 90–115; Wilcomb Washburn, *Virginia under Charles I and Cromwell, 1625–1660* (Williamsburg, 1957); and Thomas Jefferson Wertenbaker, *The Government of Virginia in the Seventeenth Century* (Williamsburg, 1957).

governor in 1637. Vane was descended from a famous English family, and the Bay settlers naturally regarded his entry into colonial politics with a mixture of pride and excitement. In addition to being the son of a powerful privy councillor, he was also a devout Puritan. When the young Vane left for the New World, someone in England observed, "Sir Henry Vane has as good as lost his eldest son, who is gone to New England for conscience sake; he likes not the discipline of the Church of England."[63] The newcomer's high social status and right religion impressed Governor Winthrop, who noted in his journal when Vane arrived in 1635, that this "gentleman of excellent parts" had forsaken "the honors and preferments of the Court, to enjoy the ordinances of Christ in their purity here."[64] During his first months in America Vane acted as the business agent for Lord Say and Seal. In November he joined the Congregational church in Boston and soon thereafter, increased his growing prestige by arbitrating a dispute between Winthrop and Dudley, the colony's two most respected political leaders.

The New Englanders' love for Vane reached its zenith during the election of 1636. The Puritan freemen selected him as their governor; and, "because he was the son and heir to a privy counsellor in England, the ships congratulated his election with a volley of great shot."[65] John Cotton bragged to English friends about the wisdom of the voters in choosing a "known" gentleman, and everyone seemed to believe that Vane possessed all the attributes required of a good ruler.[66]

They were mistaken. After only a few months in office Vane's popularity began to decline. His support of Anne Hutchinson proved to be his undoing, for she and her Antinomian followers declared—with very little tact—that the majority of Congregational

63. *Calendar of State Papers, Colonial Series, 1574–1660*, pp. 214, 211.
64. Winthrop, *History*, 1: 203; also Hutchinson, *History*, 1: 48.
65. Winthrop, *History*, 1: 222.
66. In "Certain Proposals made by Lord Say, Lord Brooke, and other Persons of quality," the English peers demanded "that the governor shall ever be chosen out of the rank of gentlemen." John Cotton answered, "We never practice otherwise, chusing the governor either out of the assistants, which is our ordinary course, or out of approved known gentlemen, *as this year Mr. Vane*" (Hutchinson, *History*, 1: 411).

ministers in Massachusetts had encouraged good works and thus, had carried Laud's Arminian errors to the New World. According to Mrs. Hutchinson, a justified person—a person predestined for salvation—might find the Holy Ghost within himself. In other words, she seemed to believe in personal revelation, a teaching which would have removed the need for churches, ministers, and even the Bible had it been widely accepted. In November Winthrop noted with great surprise that Vane held "the indwelling of the person of the Holy Ghost in a believer, and went so far beyond the rest, as *to maintain a personal union with the Holy Ghost.*" Vane's unorthodox statements shocked Congregationalists living in the towns surrounding Boston. Certainly no one ever expected a Massachusetts ruler to espouse such heretical ideas. All through the winter of 1636, Vane acted like a child, threatening to quit his position, changing his mind, and then offering his resignation once again. At one point in the melodrama, he burst into tears before the members of the General Court. As the May elections approached, Vane may well have regretted that he had ever heard of New England, and there were a good many Puritans who would have agreed.[67]

The Vane affair ended abruptly at the general election of 1637. The young governor was a proud man; and, though he wanted to leave Massachusetts, he could not bear the embarrassment of public rejection and defeat. Moreover, Vane knew that the Antinomians of Boston counted on his continued support. Under this pressure, he fought his critics, making a noisy effort to win reelection as governor. Many years later, Samuel Sewall's father told his famous son, the diarist, about the 1637 Cambridge election held "upon the Plane in the open Aer." According to the elder Sewall, "Mr. Vane seemed to stand so hard for being chosen again, as to endeavour to confound and frustrate the whole business of Election, rather than that he himself should fail of being chosen." Word of Vane's resistance spread quickly throughout the colony, and for a moment the favorite candidate of the inland towns, John Winthrop, appeared in danger of losing to the Antinomian incumbent. "My father has told me many

67. Winthrop, *History,* 1: 246, 247, 249; see chap. 1 for discussion of Arminianism. Also David D. Hall, ed., *The Antinomian Controversy, 1636–1638: A Documentary History* (Middletown, Conn., 1968).

a time," Sewall recounted, "that he and others went on foot from
Newbury to Cambridge, fourty miles, on purpose to be made free
[freemen], and help to strengthen Govr. Winthrop's Party."[68] The
men of Newbury apparently had never bothered to become freemen
as long as godly Puritan magistrates held office, but in this political
emergency their votes took on special importance. If the Newbury
citizens and many others like them throughout the colony had not
been able to participate in the Cambridge election, they might have
been forced to resort to violence.[69] As Puritans, they knew that God
and conscience demanded the immediate removal of heretical rulers.[70]

Massachusetts escaped political violence, but many people felt
that the events of 1637 had compromised the colony's place as the
"city on a hill." The General Court busily set about assuring everyone that New England would not fail the Lord in the future. It
passed a law requiring a person to live in the colony a full year

68. Samuel Sewall to Edward Calamy, 24 Jan. 1704, 6 *Collections,*
MHS, 1: 295; Winthrop, *History,* 1: 261–63, 267; also see Jameson,
Johnson's Wonder-Working Providence, p. 102, for a tactful poem which
Edward Johnson wrote about Vane.

Thy Parents, Vaine, of worthy fame, in Christ and thou for him
Through Ocean wide in new world tried a while his warrior bin.
With small defeat thou didst retreat [!] to Brittaine ground againe,
There stand thou stout, for Christ hold out, Christs Champion ay
remaine.

69. The threat of violence was real enough. The General Court disarmed
many of Anne Hutchinson's supporters in Boston. The rulers declared,
"Whereas the opinions & revelations of Mr. Wheeleright & Mrs. Hutchinson have seduced & led into dangerous errors many of the people heare
in Newe England, insomuch as there is just cause of suspition that they,
as others in Germany, in former times [the sixteenth-century Anabaptists],
may, upon some revelation, make some suddaine irruption upon those that
differ from them in judgment." The court then required fifty-eight men to
turn in their "guns, pistols, swords, shot, & match" *(Mass. Records,* 1:
211–12).

70. Vane was executed during the Restoration for his part in the trial
and death of Charles I (DNB); Emmanuel Downing, Winthrop's brother-
in-law, wrote from London after Vane had returned, "Mr. Vane's ill be-
haviour there [in Massachusetts] hath lost all his reputation here"
(Winthrop Papers, 3: 512).

before being eligible for the governorship. The legislators apparently hoped that this waiting period would provide the freemen with an opportunity to study an immigrant's true character before making him a magistrate.[71] But, despite this legal safeguard, unpleasant memories of the Vane affair persisted. One man predicted that the 1636 election "will remain a blemish to their judgment who did elect him."[72] Another settler blamed the voters for choosing a governor so "ignorant of the art of government." The errant electors, he claimed, had been "necessitated to undo the work of their own hands, and leave a blemish upon this rash undertaking, for posterity to descant upon, a caveat to us, that all men are not fit for government."[73] If Vane had been appointed by some outside power like the king, the freemen might have been able to rationalize the situation, but after their experience in England during the 1620s, they knew that they had no one to blame but themselves.

Thomas Shepard, who was one of the colony's leading ministers, gave the freemen their severest rebuke for forgetting the characteristics of the good ruler. He had recently been "harried" out of England by Archbishop Laud, and no one in Massachusetts questioned his orthodoxy. The assistants shrewdly decided in 1638 that Shepard was the best man to deliver the annual election sermon. The preacher took the opportunity to explicate the biblical parable about the foolish "Trees" who passed over the honored "Fig and Olive" and selected the lowly "Bramble" to serve as their ruler. This lamentable choice caused corruption in government and general suffering throughout the community of Trees.

Shepard's Puritan audience, of course, knew what he was talking about. The Trees symbolized the freemen of Massachusetts, and the

71. William Hubbard, *A General History of New England* [1680] (Boston, 1848), p. 235; Hutchinson, *History,* 1: 57. After Vane had been voted out of office, he and Winthrop fought over the magistrates' claim that they had the authority to restrict immigration. Winthrop wrote two essays on this subject, Vane one. The documents of this discussion are found in Thomas Hutchinson, *The Hutchinson Papers,* 2 vols. (Albany, 1865), 1: 79–107.

72. Cotton Mather, *Magnalia Christi Americana; or, the Ecclesiastical History of New England* (London, 1702), p. 136.

73. Anonymous ms letter cited in Hutchinson, *History,* 1: 58.

Bramble was Henry Vane. Shepard blasted the colonial citizens for their error, declaring that the Trees "are exceedingly apt to be led by colours like the birds by glasses & larkes by lures, & golden pretences." The Trees should not have been so eager to throw off their old, established leaders for selfish and thoughtless reasons. The Bramble produced faction in God's commonwealth and endangered the true church of Christ. Shepard explained, "a wise people will never submit to them whom they cannot honour; the trees were so hasty to make the bramble [Vane] a governour that they passed by many other trees [Winthrop and Dudley] that were better than the aspiring bramble." Do not be misled, the minister warned, by anyone who comes to America, though "never so nobly descended, never so pious." He closed by asking the freemen to be on guard in the future and to root out any Bramble that tried to creep into the Lord's New England garden.[74]

Fortunately there were few crises in early Massachusetts similar to the Vane affair. Most of the political arguments were fought not over religious fundamentals, but over differences within a commonly shared theory of government. The most important question for the majority of Puritans was not whether good rulers governed the colony, but rather, what the good rulers who did govern should be doing. In other words, what were the specific duties of a Puritan ruler beyond the defense of Congregational orthodoxy? Colonial voters seldom had occasion to rush to elections as Sewall and his neighbors had done. Usually, they remained a silent, but omnipresent, force in civil affairs. At no time, however, could the rulers of New England forget that they were only players before a large electoral audience.

Storm over the Magistracy

In the first years of settlement few Puritans foresaw that the construction of their godly commonwealth would in itself become a source of friction, or that they would disagree over the details of ecclesiastical and civil organization. But disagreements did occur, and

74. Shepard, "Notes for the Election Sermon, 1638," pp. 361–66 (spelling modernized).

during the early decades the founders of New England argued fierce-
ly about the precise forms of church and state.

A battle over the character of magisterial authority began as soon
as the settlers attempted to define the ruler's powers with precision.
One group of Puritans claimed that their civil leaders held broad
discretionary powers and, within obvious scriptural limits, were free
to govern the commonwealth as they alone saw fit. The opposition
responded that the citizens themselves had *delegated* prerogatives to
their magistrates. This faction expected rulers to stay within any constitutional boundaries which the freemen might set. For over fifteen
years the conflict between these two theories dominated the political
life of New England. It should be made clear at the outset, however,
that these groups were not formal parties or associations, but broad
persuasions about the nature of civil power.

Governor Winthrop became the chief spokesman for the discretionary forces. He was a man of strong opinions, and his opinions
about the magistracy were no exception. He regarded the social
covenant between the ruler and the ruled as the essential element
in colonial government, but he interpreted it in a special way. Winthrop stressed the divine nature of the ruler's office, while disparaging
the freemen's active role in political affairs. "It is yourselves who
have called us [the magistrates] to this office," he told the citizens
in 1645, "and being called by you, we have our authority from God,
in way of an ordinance, such as hath the image of God eminently
stamped upon it."[75]

According to the advocates of discretion, the Lord called magistrates the same way He called merchants, farmers, and sailors.
Popular elections merely confirmed the presence of God's gift. In
1629, for example, Winthrop saw the hand of Providence behind
his selection as governor of the Massachusetts Bay Company, explaining to his wife that "I have assurance that my charge is of the
Lorde and that he hath called me to this worke."[76] The freemen's
vote in this case simply corroborated a prior trust which already
existed between Winthrop and God. Throughout his long political
career Winthrop insisted that the ruler's calling was reserved for

75. Winthrop, *History,* 2: 279–80.
76. John Winthrop to his wife, 20 Oct. 1629, *Winthrop Papers,* 2: 161.

a small and select group of persons. In fact, as far as he could determine, only the governor, the deputy governor, and the assistants
were full-fledged magistrates. For these men government service was
a genuine vocation; for others it was an incidental responsibility de-
tracting from some regular calling. The Lord had decided not to
grant special ruling skills to lesser officials like the deputies, so that
by Winthrop's standards they were not real magistrates.

Discretionary spokesmen argued that God created magistrates for
the specific purpose of preserving the common good and defending
the Christian faith. Their unique political skills enabled rulers to
perceive dangers of which other men were not aware. This magisterial insight was vital to the colony's welfare; and as Winthrop
warned, it was imperative for rulers to be given great freedom
in accomplishing the Lord's work. Discretion provided magistrates
with the margin of room they needed in doubtful circumstances when
civil problems did not have simple, clear-cut solutions. Human re-
straints on magisterial power insulted God, since such limitations
implied that man was capable of restricting the divine talents of the
calling. Wise citizens were therefore advised to allow civil leaders
as much flexibility as possible. Winthrop once explained that Scripture was the only valid restriction on the ruler's authority, and that
in those matters about which the Bible was silent the people simply
had to trust that their magistrates would do the right thing.[77]

Persons of the discretionary persuasion regarded the ruler's ability
to judge well as his most important characteristic. Winthrop and
his allies clearly planned to put William Perkin's theory of Christian
equity into practice in the New World; and the governor often explained that the magistrate's chief responsibility was the interpretation of God's law within the colony's courts.[78] Good rulers, he
declared, reflected "the wisdome and mercy of God, (which are his
Attributes) as well as his Justice: as occasion shall require."[79] As
soon as they arrived in New England, the Puritan magistrates asserted their judicial authority and, over the next twenty years, stub-

77. Winthrop, *History*, 2: 280.
78. See discussion of William Perkins's ideas in chap. 1. Also Haskins,
Law and Authority, pp. 56–60.
79. "John Winthrop's Discourse on Arbitrary Government [1644],"
Winthrop Papers, 4: 476.

bornly proclaimed their sovereignty in matters of civil justice,
resisting any attempt to limit what they took to be the rightful
powers of their calling and labeling any restriction on their judicial
discretion as a frustration of God's will. "All punishments," Winthrop wrote, "except such as are made certain in the law of God, or
are not subject to variation by merit of circumstances, ought to be
left *arbitrary* to the wisdom of the judges."[80] Winthrop worried that
voters would not bother to search for those few rulers who possessed
God's special gifts if they thought that all men could judge equally
well.[81]

While most of the colonial magistrates jealously defended their
judicial discretion, they had great difficulty agreeing on how their
power should be employed. Thomas Dudley, for example, attacked
Winthrop's interpretation of equity, even though both men believed that Puritan rulers possessed broad discretionary authority.
Dudley's irritation, no doubt, sprang from personal pique as well
as from genuine intellectual differences. He was a tenacious individual, "one that would not be trodden under foot by any man."
Before coming to America Dudley had been a soldier and had acquired a respect for the rigors of military life. In contrast, Winthrop
had been trained as a common law lawyer, an experience which
convinced him of the need for flexible punishments. In any case,
their feud represented a rift within the discretionary ranks and not
a division between discretion and delegation.

Dudley first challenged what he thought to be Winthrop's judicial

---

80. Winthrop, *History,* 2: 67 (italics added).

81. "John Winthrop to the Elders of the Massachusetts Churches,"
Winthrop Papers, 4: 359. Winthrop explained to the ministers that the
deputies

> in their first institution . . . were appointed, as the representative bodye
> of the Freemen, and therefore, where the people cannot exercise Judica-
> ture in their owne persons, thoughe they have power to substitute
> others, there their deputyes are not Judges in waye of such an Ordinance
> and I feare least this hath been a great Cause of Gods withholding so
> muche of his presence from us, since that Court hathe dealt so frequently
> in judginge private Causes, *to which they have no ordinary callinge,*
> that I know: for our Saviour teaches us, that everye man that shall ex-
> ercise power of Judgement over others, must be able to prove his
> Callinge thereto.

laxity in 1632. The argument continued intermittently until 1636 when Henry Vane, then still in good repute, called a meeting of ministers and magistrates to resolve the differences between these two leaders. When the arbiters asked Winthrop if he had "dealt too remissly in point of justice," he answered "that it was his judgment, that in the infancy of plantation, justice should be administered with more lenity than in a settled state, because people were then more apt to transgress, partly of ignorance of new laws and orders, partly through oppression of business and other straits." Despite Winthrop's able defense, the men at this gathering concluded that his administration had been too moderate. He accepted their findings and promised in the future "(by God's assistance) to take a more strict course."[82] Most of the time, however, men like Winthrop and Dudley stood shoulder to shoulder against those colonists who wanted to limit magisterial discretion.

Whenever someone condemned the discretionary view of government as arbitrary, and such charges were common enough, Winthrop became indignant. By his definition arbitrary government occurred only "where a people have men sett over them without their choyce, or allowance: who have power, to Governe them, and Judge their Causes without a Rule."[83] No such tyranny existed in Massachusetts; and with the large suffrage, none could exist. Winthrop reminded the skeptics that they possessed safeguards against bad rulers of any sort, be they despots or heretics. In the first place, the Bay magistrates had to belong to a church and "by that covenant, are regulated to direct all their wayes by the rule of the gospell." Second, the rulers took an oath as freemen "to direct their aymes to the wellfare of this civill body." And third, the magistrates shared a corporate identity with all the people of the commonwealth; and, therefore, when they sought their own ends, they simultaneously sought the good of the entire society. "Whatsoever sentence the magistrate gives, according to these limitations," Winthrop argued, "the judgment is the Lords, though he do it *not by any rule particularly prescribed by civill authority*."[84] When one group of ministers had the

82. Winthrop, *History*, 1: 88–89, 91, 99–102, 212–214; 2: 65–66.

83. "Discourse on Arbitrary Government," *Winthrop Papers*, 4: 468.

84. "A Reply in Further Defense of an Order of Court Made in May, 1637," *Winthrop Papers*, 3: 466, 474 (italics added).

temerity to ask what would happen if a magistrate became corrupt, Winthrop shrugged the question off. There was no reason to believe that rulers were more prone to go bad than anyone else. Besides, if a magistrate was bad, the people were free to turn him out and to put a better in his place.[85]

Governor Winthrop countered his critics with the reminder that it was possible to restrict the magistrate's discretion too much; or, put another way, to open the way for a tyranny of the people. He called for a balance of "the authority of the magistrates and the liberty of the people" in the belief that a society achieved harmony by granting both the ruler and the ruled full exercise of their just dominions.[86] John Cotton, another champion of the discretionary view, advised the Puritans to limit their rulers, since "what ever transcendent power is given, will certainly over-run those that give it." But Cotton added that civil peace required a blend of popular and magisterial power. "If you pinch the Sea of its liberty," he explained, "though it be walls of stone and brasse, it will beate them downe: So it is with Magistrates, stint them where God hath not stinted them, and if they were walls of brasse, they would beate them downe."[87] In other words, the defenders of discretionary authority accepted controls only so long as those controls did not reduce the divine prerogatives of the ruler's calling.

While discretionary leaders supported the freemen's right to participate in elections, they were clearly afraid that such popular involvement might get out of hand, creating foolish and irrational policies. The Reverend Thomas Shepard, one of Winthrop's closest friends, captured the essence of the discretionary view, explaining that "the temper of the multitude especially in free states where the government depends on popular election" was apt to be unpredictable, uninformed, and shortsighted.[88] Winthrop agreed. In 1638 he warned Thomas Hooker of the danger of having a large body of men determine political questions, since "the best part is always the least, and of that best part the wiser is always the lesser."[89] On an-

85. "Winthrop to the Elders," *Winthrop Papers*, 3: 360.
86. Winthrop, *History*, 2: 280.
87. Cotton, *Thirteenth Chapter of the Revelation*, p. 72.
88. Shepard, "Notes for the Election Sermon 1638," p. 362.
89. *Collections*, CHS, 1: 2; see Winthrop, *History*, 1: 182; *Hutchinson Papers*, 1: 78.

other occasion, after some freemen had challenged a magisterial decision, Winthrop noted sarcastically "how strictly the people would seem to stick to their patent [the charter], where they think it makes for their advantage, but are content to decline it, where it will not warrant such liberties as they have taken up."[90] It was fine for citizens to choose good rulers, but after the ballots had been counted, Winthrop expected them to stay out of routine government affairs.

One of the main problems with popular participation was that the mass of people was interested only in local matters. Discretionary spokesmen like Winthrop condemned this myopic view of politics, insisting that Massachusetts required rulers with a broad outlook, leaders who were not tied to the will of a narrow constituency. During the early years Winthrop reminded various groups of freemen about the magistrates' responsibility to promote the welfare of the entire colony. When the citizens of Roxbury petitioned the General Court to alter a law in 1639, for example, he lost his temper, and wrote, "When the people have chosen men to be their rulers, and to make their laws, and bound themselves by oath to submit thereto, now to combine together (a lesser part of them) in a public petition to have any order repealed, which is not repugnant to the law of God, savors of resisting an ordinance of God." Winthrop added that between elections, the freemen had "no power to make or alter laws, but are to be subject."[91] The deputies of Essex County made the same error in 1644. They caucused before a meeting of the colonial legislature "to prepare business" which favored the particular needs of their own county; and, when the deputies from other shires arrived, the Essex group easily pushed two statutes through the lower house. "But when the two bills came to the magistrates," Winthrop declared triumphantly, "they discerning the plot, and finding them hurtful to the commonwealth, refused to pass them."[92] The discretionary faction regarded the assistants as representatives of the electorate only in the sense that they worked for the common good;

90. Winthrop, *History,* 1: 364.
91. Ibid., 1: 362–63.
92. Ibid., 2: 204.

they never for a minute admitted that anyone had the right to tell
the assistants what that common good was.[93]

Men like Winthrop had sufficient reason to be defensive about the
magistrates' claim to discretionary power. In Massachusetts, where
all the colonists belonged to essentially the same social class, there
was little outward difference between the ruler and the ruled. As
early as 1620 the famous Separatist leader, John Robinson, recognized the difficulty of establishing civil authority upon social equality;
and when the Pilgrims departed for Plymouth, he advised "whereas
you are become a body politic, using amongst yourselves civil government, and are not furnished with any persons of *special eminency
above the rest,* to be chosen by you into office of government; let
your wisdom and godliness appear." He told the settlers to elect men
who would love them and who would promote the common good.
Once these rulers were installed in office, the citizens should yield

---

93. During the 1630s most voters accepted the notion that magistrates
looked after the colony's broader interests; but, at the same time, they apparently thought that every major town should have a magistrate of its own.
Since the assistants were usually wealthy, influential men, their residence
was a source of local pride, and because the magistrates were responsible for
the administration of justice, even on the lowest levels, their proximity became a matter of convenience for litigious Puritans. The settlers in Watertown
regarded their assistant, Isaac Johnson, as "the chefeste stud in the land . . . the
cheiffeste man of estate"(*Winthrop Papers,* 3: 18). When one of the larger
towns lost a magistrate, the citizens reacted emotionally. In 1635, for example,
Nathaniel Ward wrote to John Winthrop, Jr., then an assistant in the Bay
Colony and later the governor of Connecticut, "that your absence hath bredd
us much sorrowe, & your still going from us to Connecticote doth much discourage us. I feare your tye or obligation to this state, & in speciall to this
towne, is more than you did well consider when you engaged your self
another way." Ward added that the people of Ipswich "are in a misery for the
want of you" (Nathaniel Ward to John Winthrop, Jr., *4 Collections,* MHS,
7: 25).
The Massachusetts General Court recognized the magistrates' local ties
and in 1638 ordered "that every towne shall beare the charges of their *owne
magistrates*" (*Mass. Records,* 1: 228; 2: 47). But by the 1640s the assistants
had apparently dropped much of their identification with individual towns;
for the counties, and later the General Court itself, began to pay for their
services (ibid., 2: 140–41; 3: 320). The magistrates' exact obligation to the
towns or to the freemen who elected them was never clearly defined.

"unto them all due honour and obedience in their lawful administrations, not beholding in them the *ordinariness of their persons.*"[94]
Robinson's admonition held as well for Winthrop's Boston as it did
for Bradford's Plymouth. The discretionary magistrates of Massachusetts never liked to be reminded of the "ordinariness of their persons," however, and treated lese majesty with a harshness that can
only be explained as an expression of their sense of social insecurity.
Thomas Hutchinson, the eighteenth-century governor-historian, explained quite correctly that "The generality of the colony being very
near upon a level, more than common provision was necessary to
enforce a due obedience to the laws, and to establish and preserve
the authority of the government, for, although some amongst them
had handsome fortunes, yet in general their estates were small, barely
sufficient to provide them houses and necessary accommodations;
a contempt of authority was therefore next to a capital offense."[95]

How seriously the discretionary magistrates regarded their own
dignity is revealed throughout the colonial records. During the early
decades they insisted that Bay rulers should receive the same defer-
ence from their constituents as English officials received from theirs;
and they reacted angrily whenever anyone questioned their prerogatives or suggested that political leaders did not require a unique
calling for their work. In 1633, when Thomas Dexter rashly declared that the best of governors was "but an atturney," the Court of
Assistants fined, jailed, and disfranchised him for his insult.[96] The
next year, the magistrates fined John Lee for suggesting that the
governor "was but a lawyer's clerke."[97] Nor were the rulers of Massachusetts amused when Captain John Stone called a magistrate,
Roger Ludlow, a "just ass."[98]

The assistants' concern for their own dignity reached absurd
heights when they dealt with Israel Stoughton. This man was clearly
no troublemaker, for he held the rank of captain in the local militia.
In fact, his neighbors thought so highly of Stoughton that in 1634

94. Samuel Eliot Morison, ed., *William Bradford, Of Plymouth Plantation*
(New York, 1952), p. 370 (italics added).
95. Hutchinson, *History,* 1: 370.
96. *Mass. Records,* 1: 103; also p. 97.
97. Ibid., pp. 132–33.
98. Ibid., p. 108.

they proposed electing him to the magistracy. Yet when those same neighbors persuaded him to write a small pamphlet challenging the rationale behind the magistrates' legislative veto, Winthrop exploded with rage. He cried that Stoughton was *"the troubler* of Israel," "a worme," and "an underminer of the State." The court disabled Stoughton from all public office for three years.[99] Although his punishment was clearly disproportionate to his crime, Stoughton accepted it with courage and grace. In a letter which he later wrote to his brother, he noted that the magistrates, especially Winthrop, had overemphasized the importance of their office. Winthrop, he explained, "hath lost much of that aplause that he hath had (for indeed he was highly magnified). . . . He is indeed a man of men: but he is but a man: & some say they have idolized him, & do now confesse their error."[100]

But it would be wrong to assume that the discretionary leaders relied solely on force. Throughout the period they made every effort to persuade their constituents that they deserved the broad powers which they had claimed. Or, put another way, they attempted to make political practice conform to political theory by appearing before the people as God's vicegerents on earth and by emphasizing the full dignity and divinity of their office. One of the best examples of their role playing occurred in 1636 when the assistants met to heal factions which had developed within their membership. In order to create an impression of gravity, harmony, and wisdom, they decided that the magistrates should "ripen their consultations beforehand, that their vote in public might bear (as the voice of God.)" And since the Puritan authorities did not want the electorate to see them fighting or behaving like English politicians, they pledged that in the future they would "frequently" proclaim their mutual "tenderness and love." But perhaps their most significant reform was their promise that *"magistrates shall appear* more solemnly in public, with attendance, apparel, and open notice of their entrance into the court."[101] For men who denigrated the people's involvement in

99. Captain Israel Stoughton to Dr. Stoughton, 1635, *Proceedings,* MHS, 5(1860–62): 137–39; *Mass. Records,* 1: 136; Winthrop, *History,* 1: 185–86.

100. *Proceedings,* MHS, 5: 140.

101. Winthrop, *History,* 1: 213–14 (italics added).

government affairs, the discretionary magistrates went to great lengths to woo the electorate.

Winthrop's group recognized that personal wealth and status contributed to the popular acceptance of magisterial authority. The Puritan colonists, like their English predecessors, seemed more willing to obey rulers who were—or appeared to be—their social betters than they did their own peers. In fact, as soon as an affluent Englishman decided to move to Massachusetts, he stood an excellent chance of being selected as an assistant. In 1636 the freemen elected two gentlemen, John Humphrey and William Coddington, merely "because they were daily expected."[102] Certainly, part of Henry Vane's initial charm had been his noble parentage.

Rulers of discretionary persuasion also assumed honorific titles, the most common being that of esquire. The factors which enabled persons in seventeenth-century New England to take on symbols of rank remain obscure to modern scholars.[103] Nevertheless, the magistrates were usually the esquires, and the coveted abbreviation, "esq.," enhanced their claim to a special power.

While discretionary magistrates understood what behavior would win the voters' respect, they found the trappings of authority expensive. Since most New England rulers did not possess noble fortunes to match their noble dreams, they were sometimes tempted to live beyond their means. In 1634 Winthrop protested that he had never campaigned for office, but "being chosen I furnished my selfe with servants and provisions accordingly in farr greater proporcion than I would have done, hadd I come as a private man or as an Assistant onely."[104] But spending money on public office was often a thankless gesture, as Winthrop learned in 1641 when "Mr. Hathorn [William Hathorne], one of the deputies, and usually one of their speakers, made a motion to some of the deputies on leaving out two of the ancientest magistrates, because they were grown poor, and

---

102. Ibid., p. 91.

103. See Norman H. Dawes, "Titles as Symbols of Prestige in Seventeenth-Century New England," *William and Mary Quarterly* 3d ser., 6 (1949): 69–84.

104. *Winthrop Papers*, 3: 173.

spake reproachfully of them under that motion."[105] Only after John Cotton told the grumblers to honor their political fathers did this criticism stop.

The Other Side: Delegated Authority

The majority of colonists who rejected the discretionary persuasion remain anonymous to the historian. Sometimes government records link an individual to a specific complaint or protest, but more often Winthrop's opponents were simply the deputies. These representatives, elected by the freemen in the towns, were as good Puritans as anyone else in Massachusetts—after all, they had to be church members even to hold office. The deputies and their political allies shared many fundamental beliefs with the discretionary leaders. They all assumed, for instance, that New England Puritans had formed a covenant with the Lord. Where the representatives broke with Winthrop's group was over the nature of the social compact between ruler and ruled. Their interpretation of this civil contract favored an active political role for the citizens, while playing down the concept of divine magisterial authority. The deputies argued that the freemen themselves *delegated* civil power, determining not only which persons gained office but also exactly what prerogatives the office carried with it. But most important of all, the advocates of delegation could not accept the idea that either their happiness or God's required government leaders to possess arbitrary power.

105. Winthrop, *History,* 2: 66–67. Cotton told the deputies "that such as were decayed in their estates by attending to the service of the country ought to be maintained by the country, and not set aside for their poverty, being otherwise so well gifted, and approved by long experience to be faithful." In February 1647 Samuel Symonds, an assistant, told Winthrop that God had brought the Puritans to New England "To exercise the graces of the ritcher sort in a more mixt condiccion, they shall have the liberty of good government in their hands yet with the abatement of their outward estates. And that the poorer sort (held under in Engl:) should have inlargement." In other words, God was responsible for social mobility (*Winthrop Papers,* 5: 126). Emmanuel Downing advised Winthrop in 1639 that it was better to be poor in office, "then if you had gayned riches as other Governours doe, both in Virginea and elsewhere" (*4 Collections,* MHS, 6: 53–54).

The men who shared the delegated persuasion were extremely sensitive about the possible misuse of political authority, for they had grown up in an age when conspiracies were common and had witnessed Parliament's struggle against Stuart despotism. While Winthrop revered the traditional rights of all Englishmen, he seldom made a fuss over them, assuming that good Christian rulers would preserve these ancient liberties in the natural course of their calling. But Winthrop's relaxed attitude did not satisfy his opponents, who demanded specific guarantees that no present or future magistrate would ever duplicate the Stuart tyranny in Massachusetts. Their lives and properties were tender possessions, and no amount of legal protection seemed sufficient to guard them. As early as 1632 a group of inhabitants from Watertown complained that the assistants had taxed them without representation, and "that it was not safe to pay moneys after that sort, for fear of bringing themselves and posterity into bondage." Winthrop convinced the Watertown delegation that the freemen were not slaves, but over the next twenty years various other colonists continued to worry about the dangers of arbitrary government.[106]

The Puritans who rejected the discretionary view seldom attacked Governors Winthrop, Dudley, or Endecott personally; and, even during the fiercest political battles, the freemen never dropped a magistrate from office because his ideas about the nature of civil power conflicted with theirs. New Englanders obviously did not think that Winthrop was another Charles I or Vane, since they elected him either as their governor or assistant as long as he lived. Their goal throughout this period was not the destruction of magisterial discretion but a greater voice in defining the character of the common good. Three case studies, involving William Pynchon, Israel Stoughton, and Thomas Hooker, will help to clarify the delegated persuasion.

William Pynchon was typical of the New Englanders who favored greater controls over the magistrates. He arrived in America with the first wave of Puritan immigrants, but instead of settling in the Boston area, moved west where he founded Springfield. Citizens throughout Massachusetts apparently recognized his political ability, for they

106. Winthrop, *History*, 1: 84.

frequently elected him to the Court of Assistants. During the late 1630s Pynchon became involved in a complex dispute with his southern neighbor, Connecticut. At one point in this controversy, the leaders of Connecticut accused Pynchon of breaking his oath as a magistrate because he had refused to impound a man's canoe for public service. The charge incensed Pynchon. "If magistrates in N.E.," he stormed, "should *ex officio* practice such a power over mens properties, how long would Tyranny be kept out of our habitations: Truly the king might as legaly exact a loan *Ex officio* of his subjects by a distresse on mens properties (because he pleades as greate necessity) as to presse a Cano without legal order." Pynchon rejected any "lawlesse law of discretion." He reminded the Connecticut Puritans, who seemed to have forgotten the lesson of forced loans and ship money, of their parliamentary heritage. "The lawes of England," Pynchon lectured, "count it a tender thing to touch another mans propriety [private property] and therefore many have rather chosen to suffer as in *a good cause* then to yeeld their goods to the king *ex officio:* and to lose the liberty of an English subject in N.E. would bring woefull slaviry to our posterity."[107] In 1646 certain events moved Pynchon to ask Winthrop whether Massachusetts intended to desert the model of English law. He advised the governor that "it should be our care, in thankfulnesse both to God & that state [England], to preserve & adhere to what ever lawes or customes they have, except those that be contrary to God."[108] Pynchon had no sympathy with legal innovation, and he hated autocratic discretion. He believed that a man's property was his own and that no magistrate by virtue of his calling had any right whatsoever to invade that privilege. Not until the Glorious Revolution did New Englanders again have such a stout defender of the "good old cause."

Israel Stoughton, that "underminer of the State," shared the delegated view of magisterial office. When he arrived in Massachusetts, he found the civil government of the Bay Colony disappointing. The assistants possessed full authority to tax, punish, and legislate

107. *Proceedings,* MHS, 48(1914–15): 48.
108. William Pynchon to John Winthrop, 9 Mar. 1646, 4 *Collections,* MHS, 6: 381–83.

"att their discretion," and there was no representative body or lower
house at that time to curb their acts. Later, after the formation of
the deputies in 1634, Stoughton denied that the magistrates' calling
gave them transcendent powers to interpret law as they pleased.
In the little pamphlet that brought his disfranchisement, Stoughton
wrote that the ruler's power "was not so great that they could do
ought [anything], or hinder ought simply according to their owne
wills." Stoughton's effort to control the prerogatives of the assistants
won him favor among the freemen, for they chose him one of the
first speakers of the representatives.[109]

The Reverend Thomas Hooker accepted Stoughton's concept of
magisterial power. In 1638 he warned Winthrop that the notion of
some men in society possessing special discretionary authority "is
a course which wants both safety and warrant." Hooker added, "I
must confess . . . it is a way which leads directly to tyranny, and
so to confusion, and [I] must plainly profess, if it was in my liberty,
I should choose neither to live nor leave my posterity under such
a government." Perhaps Hooker's distaste for discretionary power
explains why he moved to Connecticut.[110] In an election sermon
delivered at Hartford, he told his congregation that "they who
have power, to appoint officers and magistrates, it is in their power,
also, to set the bounds and limitations of the power and place unto
which they call them."[111] Unlike Winthrop, Hooker stressed the
popular side of the social covenant.

Most of the deputies sympathized with the delegated view of
civil power, for their own authority clearly originated with the
freemen. They had little opportunity to quibble about their close
relationship to the colonial voters, since the General Court had
defined the character of the deputy's office in law. On May 14,
1634, the legislature ordered that each town select two or three men
who "shalbe hereafter soe deputed by the ffreemen of [the] severall
plantations, to *deale in their behalfe,* in the publique affayres of the

109. *Proceedings,* MHS, 5: 136–39; *Mass. Records,* 1: 185–86. The deputies chose several speakers at each session, usually a chief speaker and two
assistant speakers.

110. *Collections,* CHS, 1: 11; see Perry Miller, "Thomas Hooker and the
Democracy of Early Connecticut," *New England Quarterly* 4(1931): 663–712.

111. *Collections,* CHS, 1: 20.

commonwealth, [and who] shall have full power and voyces of all the said ffreemen."[112] In other words, the deputies were surrogates for the many citizens who could not easily participate in the routine affairs of colonial government. But, at the same time, the freemen were careful to study their deputies' behavior, especially in time of crisis. The voters in a town would frequently write instructions telling their representatives how to handle specific legislation before the General Court. Since the townspeople watched to see what results their instructions produced, the deputies could not very well ignore them.[113] The freemen also paid the representative's salary and travel expenses, which probably meant in practice that he hesitated before acting contrary to the will of his constituents.[114] Winthrop complained of the deputies' stubborn commitment to local interests and on one occasion noted with disgust that they seemed willing to sacrifice the general good to the narrow demands of their own towns.[115]

Few persons in Massachusetts claimed that these representatives possessed magisterial skills or stood in a special relationship to the Lord by virtue of their office. There is no evidence, however, that the deputies' seemingly inferior status concerned the freemen. In fact, they apparently believed that the representatives more than made up for their lack of divine calling by guarding the people's civil liberties and by limiting the assistants' discretion whenever possible. As will become apparent in the next section, the deputies' effort to protect the traditional rights of Englishmen and their fear of arbitrary executive authority were matters of major importance in the political life of New England, not only in the 1630s, but throughout the entire colonial period.

Discretion versus Delegation: The Legislative Battle

The advocates of *discretion* and *delegation* confronted one another within the Massachusetts General Court. The story of the battle be-

112. *Mass. Records*, 1: 118–19 (italics added). The author of "Good News from New-England [1648]" claimed that "from each town two Deputyes are sent in the name of the Freemen" (*4 Collections*, MHS, 1: 204).

113. Kenneth Colegrove, "New England Town Mandates," *Publications of the Colonial Society of Massachusetts* 21(1919): 411–49.

114. *Mass. Records*, 1: 228; 2: 140; 3: 320.

115. Winthrop, *History*, 2: 140–41.

tween these two groups is complex—far too complex, in fact, to cover fully in this section. Basically, the seeds of political dissension were sown early in the 1630s, in the years before the office of deputy had been created. Leading magistrates, men like Winthrop and Dudley, assumed certain discretionary powers which they felt their calling required. But as time passed, the elected representatives from the towns became increasingly critical of what they regarded as the assistants' arbitrary actions and demanded greater, more explicit restrictions on magisterial authority. It appears that the delegated persuasion developed largely in reaction to the stands taken by Winthrop and his allies. In other words, specific political crises forced the proponents of delegation to work out clearly their own ideas about the nature of civil office. In this discussion we will look at only four issues in detail: the permanent council, the interim governing committee, the magisterial veto, and the codification of Massachusetts law. It should be kept in mind that each of these examples was but a single round in an ongoing fight over the character of the good ruler.

During the late 1630s a debate over life tenure for magistrates exposed deep political divisions within the General Court. The issue first arose in 1636 when the colonial legislature ordered "that a certain number of the magistrates should be chosen for life." The permanent council was to consist of governors and ex-governors "who, during their lives, should assist the governor in managing the chiefest affayres of this little state"; and, while the duties of this new body were not well defined, the legislators seem to have regarded it as a way to entice English noblemen to come to America.[116] Certainly Cotton held out the bait to Lord Say and Seal in 1636, telling him that the colonists had selected "for the present, onely two (Mr. Winthrope and Mr. Dudley) not willing to choose more, till they see what further better choyse the Lord will send over to them." As it turned out, the Lord did not see fit to send over Lord Say and Seal. At first the deputies backed the magisterial council, but within a few years they had second thoughts, declaring that the Massachusetts Bay Charter did not give any person governing author-

116. Ibid., 1: 219–20.

ity "except he were chosen in the annual elections to one of the said places of magistracy established by the patent."[117]

Winthrop and his supporters saw no reason to fight over life tenure, especially since the institution had not developed into an important part of the colonial government. Winthrop himself explained in 1642, "For the Office of C[ouncillor] I am no more in love with the honor, or power of it, then with an olde friese [wool] Coat in a summers daye."[118] The assistants compromised with the deputies by preserving the council in name, but depriving it of all meaningful authority. The General Court, obviously under pressure from the delegated party, announced "that no such counsellor shall have any power as a magistrate, nor shall do any act as a magistrate, etc., except he be annually chosen, etc., according to the patent."[119] What apparently happened was that the assistants had caught the deputies off guard. Only belatedly did the representatives realize that life tenure was an invitation to arbitrary rule; but after their awakening, they eagerly labeled the council a magisterial "plot" to insulate discretionary powers from the vote of the freemen.[120]

A second area of contention involved the powers which magistrates held when the General Court was not in session. The Massachusetts legislature consisted of both assistants and deputies, and until 1644 when it became bicameral, the two groups sat as a single body. The entire General Court convened each year for four short periods, and between meetings it was customary for the assistants to administer civil business alone. Not only did the magistrates act in an executive capacity, they also formed a court of law, hearing cases of both original and appellate jurisdiction. These judicial responsibilities raised serious questions about conflict of interest, since the assistants were ruling on the fairness of decisions which they had made earlier as judges in the colony's lower courts.

The deputies saw this unrestricted interim power as potentially dangerous. It seemed to them that the system gave the magistrates

117. "Copy of a letter from Mr. Cotton to Lord Say and Seal in the year 1636," Hutchinson, *History,* 1: 417; Winthrop, *History,* 1: 363.

118. *Winthrop Papers,* 4: 347. See Ellen Brennan, "The Massachusetts Council of the Magistrates," *New England Quarterly* 4(1931): 54–93.

119. Winthrop, *History,* 1: 364.

120. Ibid., 1: 363.

an opportunity to indulge their arbitrary desires as soon as the representatives had left the capital. To limit the assistants' discretion, they suggested that a specially chosen commission of seven magistrates, three deputies, and Nathaniel Ward handle affairs of state "out of court." The assistants resisted this plan, of course, claiming that it would be a bad precedent for them to accept a commission from the General Court, even a commission assuring them a seven to four majority. Winthrop's discretionary group insisted that rulers "had power of government before we had any written laws or had kept any courts," and, therefore, did not need any grant from the legislature to govern in its "vacancy."

Winthrop's explanation did not satisfy the hotheaded speaker of the representatives, William Hathorne, who warned the assistants to come up with a better answer or "You will not be obeyed."[121] Fortunately cooler men decided that the time was ripe for a group of ministers to arbitrate the dispute, and the assistants and deputies agreed on the format for a conference. Each side would submit a separate list of questions about the interim power. The questions and their answers possess special significance for the historian of political ideas, for they reveal that the real basis of the controversy was not the interim council at all, but the broader issue of the nature of magisterial authority.

The magistrates, representing the discretionary persuasion, asked the consulting elders "Whether the deputies in the general court have judicial and magisterial authority?"—or put another way, whether the deputy's office required special, God-given talents? The arbitrators were in a difficult position, since both sides obviously expected their support. They therefore approached the assistants' question with care, making a distinction before answering. Magisterial authority, they explained, contained three discrete parts—legislative, judicial, and directive. The assistants had no monopoly on the legislative and directive functions, but the judicial power belonged to them alone. Since the Lord granted magistrates unique skills for discerning Christian equity, the deputies could not make judgments without encroaching upon the duties of the ruler's calling. Although the ministers confirmed the assistants' claim to judicial

121. Ibid., 2: 205–06.

authority, they reminded the Bay rulers that the orders of the General
Court were sovereign and that all judges had to determine equity
within restrictions set by civil law. The magistrates possessed discretion, but it was a discretion tempered by the legislature.[122]

On their part, the deputies demanded to know whether the assistants had any right "to dispense justice in the vacancy of the general
court, without some law or order of the same to declare the rule."
The elders responded diplomatically that the General Court should
indeed limit discretionary power as much as possible. No doubt
satisfied with that answer, the deputies then inquired if the legislature could create a commission, presumably consisting of both
deputies and assistants, to administer "all things" between sessions
of the colonial assembly. But here the arbitrators balked. They told
the representatives that if "all things" included judicature, then that
commission was not acceptable, since it would deprive the magistrates of "their principal work."

To their credit, the consulting ministers saw merit on both sides
of the debate between discretion and delegation. Over all, however,
their decisions tended to favor Winthrop's discretionary view of
the magisterial calling. The good Puritan ruler was still the Lord's
vicegerent who brought justice into the world through special God-
given talents. Unfortunately this important conference closed on an
ominous note. Winthrop observed that while most of the deputies
accepted the mediation, "some few leading men (who had drawn on
the rest) were still fixed upon their own opinions. So hard a matter
it is, to draw men (even wise and godly) from the love of the fruit
of their own inventions."[123] The interim commission was a dead
issue, but the discontent with discretionary authority was still very
much alive.

A third major controversy in this period centered on the magistrates' claim to a legislative veto. After the creation of the deputies
in 1634, the representatives and assistants sat together as a unicameral
legislature and voted on civil matters as one group. The majority
voice did not always dominate, however, for the magistrates demanded a right to negate all proposals, even those which had re-

122. Ibid., 2: 251–54.
123. Ibid., 2: 254–56.

ceived the deputies' full support. Their veto power allowed the
assistants, or a majority of them, to control judicial as well as legislative business, because the Massachusetts General Court served the
dual function of supreme court and colonial assembly. The Bay
settlers usually referred to this magisterial check over their representatives as the negative voice; and during the colony's early years,
the assistants regarded it as the crucial element in preserving discretionary authority.

The deputies' irritation over this arrangement was natural. After
1634 it was customary for Massachusetts towns to send one, two,
or three representatives pretty much as they chose.[124] The growth
of the deputies was, therefore, linked to the growth of the number
of towns, and that number expanded rapidly. By the end of the
1630s there were over forty representatives attending sessions of
the colonial legislature.[125] While the deputies continued to prolifer-
ate, the number of assistants remained static. The Massachusetts
Charter, in fact, specifically limited their membership to eighteen,
but the freemen never elected that many until the 1680s; in the
forties, the normal figure ran about ten. As the deputies sat with
the assistants, the disproportion in the size of the two groups apparently
struck the representatives as inequitable, and they certainly failed
to see any logic in the claim that a few magistrates, divinely called
or not, should be able to frustrate the will of the majority merely
by exercising a questionable veto.

The first attack on the assistants' negative voice occurred in 1634.
At that time the contestants became so angry over the issue that
John Cotton felt obliged to deliver a sermon in order to restore
peace. The minister explained that the magistracy by virtue of its
authority, the ministry by virtue of its purity, and the people by
virtue of their liberty possessed a mutual veto over each other.[126]
For the moment, Cotton's words calmed the colonists, but in the
early 1640s the veto again sparked a bitter political battle between
the deputies and the magistrates.

124. *Mass. Records,* 1: 118.
125. *Winthrop Papers,* 4: 387.
126. Winthrop, *History,* 1: 168–69; see *Mass. Records,* 1: 167, 168,
174–75.

The immediate cause of this second, more serious, crisis was a trial which has come to be known as the "sow's case." Goody Sherman, a poor Boston widow, brought criminal action against Captain Robert Keayne for stealing one of her pigs, and when the matter reached the General Court on appeal, the deputies took up her cause. A majority of assistants, however, supported the influential Keayne; and what had begun as a trivial business soon developed into an angry confrontation over the magisterial veto. The representatives made it clear that they were determined to override the assistants' will no matter how long they had to wait. In 1644 after two years of stubborn fighting—fighting which we need not recount here—the colonial legislators agreed to divide the General Court into two separate houses, each possessing veto power over the decisions of the other. From the assistants' point of view the bicameral system represented an important victory, for their opponents had at last accepted the magistrates' claim to a negative voice. While the controversy was still hot two leading discretionary spokesmen, John Winthrop and John Norton, wrote defenses of the veto. These statements are valuable to our discussion because they reveal the crucial role which the concept of magisterial discretion played throughout the dispute.

Winthrop's "Defense of the Negative Vote" was an excellent expression of the discretionary persuasion. The author thought the abolition of the veto would place deputies and magistrates on a par—one man, one vote, and majority rule. According to Winthrop, one of two equally abhorrent possibilities would result from such a scheme. Either the representatives would consider themselves full-fledged magistrates holding the divine talents of that office, or, worse, the magistrates would be reduced to mere deputies. Winthrop dismissed the deputies' pretensions to special calling, noting that since they represented the freemen, they could claim no authority which the average citizen did not also possess. While he equated the deputies with "the common ranke of Freemen," Winthrop insisted that he meant no insult. It was simply a political fact that "before and after the Court he [the deputy] is but another freeman and so cannot be counted in the same ranke with the magistrates."

The second possibility was even less attractive from the discre-

tionary point of view, for as Winthrop pointed out, if magistrates
were no more than freemen, then Massachusetts was "a meere
Democratie," the worst conceivable form of government. The author
assured his readers that the negative voice did not give the magistrates any dangerous or arbitrary power "over the peoples lives and
libertyes." To the contrary, he reasoned, such a check in the hands
of the Lord's vicegerents constituted a positive good for the entire
commonwealth: "I cannot liken it better to any thinge then the
breake of a windmill: which hath no power, to move the runninge
worke: but it is of speciall use, to stoppe any violent motion which
in some extraordinary tempest might otherwise endanger the wholl
fabricke."[127]

The Reverend John Norton's defense of the negative voice contrasted strikingly with Winthrop's. His discussion, in fact, seems
bizarre in early New England, for Norton argued chiefly from reason,
experience, and history, replacing Old Testament political rhetoric
with reflections on "venitian state policy." Massachusetts, he believed, possessed a mixed form of government—part democracy,
part aristocracy. This system suited the colony perfectly, for it gave
fair representation to all social classes, the "gentry" as well as the
"commonalty." If the colonists abolished the assistants' veto, the
more numerous deputies would dominate the aristocratic magistrates,
thus destroying the constitutional balance. Moreover, without the
negative voice, the magistrate elected by all of the freemen at large
would hold exactly the same authority as the representative selected
by only a few voters in a specific town. "Though among the Deputies,"
Norton observed, "there may be found those which doe excell compared with some of the magistrates yet generally the one being
experienced the other lesse experienced wee may judge accordingly."
As Norton developed his political argument, his secular bias became
increasingly apparent. He declared, for example, that the magistrates
deserved judicial discretion, not because they held a divine calling,
but because history taught that they were usually the fittest men available for the job.[128] The importance of Norton's essay should not be

127. "John Winthrop's Defense of the Negative Vote," *Winthrop Papers,*
4: 380–92.
128. *Proceedings,* MHS, 46(1912–13): 279–85.

exaggerated, for, unfortunately, too little survives from this period to tell for certain whether he was a true political innovator.

The fourth, and most successful, step toward restricting the discretion of the Bay rulers came with the codification of the colony's laws in 1648. Historians have described the process which led to this achievement in detail, and the story requires little amplification here.[129] Essentially, the debate over the code was an adjunct to the larger debate over the character of the ruler's calling. As early as 1635 Winthrop noted that the deputies were agitating for a body of positive law by which the magistrates might not "proceed according to their discretions."[130] In 1641 the colony accepted Nathaniel Ward's *Body of Liberties,* but the deputies viewed these general provisions as too ill-defined, too open to interpretation by individual judges. They continued to press their demands until 1648 when the General Court adopted *The Lawes and Liberties of Massachusetts,* which presented the colony's laws in alphabetical order so that every man could see for himself the limits of magisterial authority.[131]

The proponents of discretion resisted the passage of the legal code as best they could. The assistants understandably considered the entire plan a threat to the fundamental prerogatives of their calling. At one critical juncture in the conflict, the magistrates decided to marshal their chief arguments against fixed, written law, and in five points attempted to destroy the logic of the delegated position. First, the assistants noted that the deputies' demands for set, rigid laws would undermine Christian equity because "it would be unjust to inflict the same punishment upon the least as upon the greatest." William Perkins may well have been the source of this idea. Second, discretionary spokesmen observed that God had given some men special "parts or gifts" to be judges. What good were these talents, the magistrates asked, if the law set specific punishments and paid no attention to the mitigating circumstances of each case. Third,

129. The best are Haskins, *Law and Authority,* pp. 113–40, and Morgan, *Puritan Dilemma,* pp. 166–73.

130. Winthrop, *History,* 1: 191.

131. Haskins, *Law and Authority,* pp. 131–32, 136. The "Body of Liberties" is printed in the introduction to W. H. Whitmore, arr., *The Colonial Laws of Massachusetts* (Boston, 1889); Max Farrand, ed., *The Book of the General Lawes and Libertyes* (Cambridge, Mass., 1929).

they felt that law should be flexible throughout time, since there was no evidence that the Lord had granted consummate wisdom to a particular generation which "should set the rules for all others to walk by." Fourth, the magistrates rejected the idea that legislators acting upon "bare theory" could be as fair or as flexible as the judge who faced the accused directly. And last, they claimed that prescript law limited God's Providence, thus intimating that the Lord still preferred to speak through the mouths of His chosen rulers.[132] The deputies did not make a comparable summation of their views; perhaps they felt that they had recorded their opinions forcefully enough by writing the code.

The battle between the forces of discretion and delegation came to a dramatic climax in 1645 when a group of deputies rashly tried to impeach Winthrop for exceeding his magisterial authority. From the very beginning their attack had little chance of success, since the charismatic Winthrop elicited more intellectual and emotional support from the settlers than did all of the representatives combined. Though his acquittal was a virtual certainty, Winthrop insisted on proceeding with the trial, apparently determined to make a stand for the discretionary persuasion. He stepped down from his accustomed place of honor, took off his hat, and sat with embarrassing humility before the bar. After an uneasy General Court had officially vindicated him of any misuse of power, Winthrop arose and, assuming all the dignity of God's vicegerent on earth, delivered a short, caustic speech to the delegated faction. He reviewed familiar discretionary ideas about the ruler's calling:

> Some of the deputies had seriously conceived, that the magistrates affected an arbitrary government, and that they had (or sought to have) an unlimited power to do what they pleased without control. . . . For prevention whereof they judged it not unlawful to use even extrema remedia, as if salus populi had been now the transcendent rule to walk by, and that the magistracy must be no other, in effect, than a ministerial office, and all authority, both legislative, consultative, and judicial, must be exercised by the people in their body representative.[133]

132. Winthrop, *History*, 2: 66–69.
133. Ibid., 2: 282.

The Puritan leader seemed to sweep the field before him. In fact, after 1645 the effort to limit the magistrates' discretionary power waned for almost twenty years, and Winthrop's foes apparently melted in disarray before their divinely called superiors.[134]

The completeness of Winthrop's victory in 1645, however, was more apparent than real. Certainly, it would be difficult to believe that the deputies would capitulate after battling so long and hard. What seems to have occurred was that changes in the colony's political system made the terms of the original debate less relevant. Despite Winthrop's brilliant summation, the choice in 1645 was no longer an either-or proposition between discretion and delegation. By the mid-1640s the deputies' professional self-esteem had risen to such a degree that they were less intimidated by Winthrop's statement than they might have been a decade earlier. Over the years they had come to realize the importance of their own role in Massachusetts politics and now valued themselves as more than freemen whose only official responsibility was carrying town griev- ances to the General Court.

There were several specific practices which help to explain the altera- tion in the deputies' attitude. During the early 1630s vacancies among the assistants were usually filled by prominent individuals recently ar- rived from England. The Vane affair, however, made the freemen wary of such persons; and, after the English Civil War began, no one, not even potential magistrates, was interested in emigrating to Massachu- setts. In the absence of fresh, outside talent, the deputies took on new importance, for the Bay Colony started to recruit assistants from the representatives. The lower house became a training ground where the deputies gained experience for higher office. Even William Hathorne, the speaker who caused Winthrop so much anguish, eventually became a magistrate in his own right.[135] By the 1640s and 1650s, therefore,

134. See Mark Howe and Louis F. Eaton, "The Supreme Judicial Power in the Colony of Masachusetts Bay," *New England Quarterly* 20(1947): 291–316; see also chap. 3.

135. See Robert E. Wall, Jr., "The Membership of the Massachusetts General Court 1634–1686" (Ph. D. diss. Yale University, 1965), pp. 247–54. Wall gives a biographical sketch of every member of the Massachusetts legis- lature during the Old Charter period.

one could justly claim that if the deputies were not full-fledged rulers, they were at least rulers in waiting.

The deputies' growing self-esteem was also in part a reflection of the way in which the magistrates treated them. In 1634 Winthrop regarded the deputies as passive representatives whose main functions were to "revise all laws, etc., and to reform what they found amiss therein; *but not to make any new laws,* but prefer their grievances to the court of assistants."[136] The deputies probably disagreed with Winthrop's 1634 assessment; but, by the end of the decade, even the staunchest advocates of discretionary power would not have questioned the representatives' right to initiate legislation. Moreover, when the elders arbitrated the dispute over who should rule between General Courts, they pointed out that the deputies held two of the three parts of "magisterial authority"—legislative and directive.[137] In a sense, the division of the General Court into two separate houses in 1644 was as much a victory for the deputies as it was for the assistants; for, while the assistants protected their negative voice, the deputies gained an identity. The new bicameral system allowed the members of the lower house to debate issues free from the magistrates' intimidating presence, to keep their own records, and, in short, to build up a corporate pride in their independent role within the colonial legislature.[138]

A third, fortuitous factor contributed to the deputies' heightened dignity. The magistrates had always mainained throughout the battles of the 1630s and 1640s that the essential characteristic of their calling was judicial discretion; but the expansion of the colony both in area and in population undermined that assertion. The Puritan settlers who pushed west to Springfield and north to Maine and New Hampshire demanded that the institutions of justice follow them. At the same time, the more established towns in eastern Massachusetts grew rapidly, and the number of crimes and civil suits requiring court attention increased proportionately. The colony's ten or twelve magistrates simply could not keep up with the judicial

136. Winthrop, *History,* 1: 153 (italics added).

137. Ibid., 2: 251–54.

138. The deputies' corporate spirit can be seen in their decision to eat together every night during sessions of the General Court *(Mass. Records,* 3: 352).

business which they had claimed as their own private domain. As early as 1638, the Court of Assistants complained of its heavy case load and moved that individual magistrates in the towns where they lived could decide disputes involving less than 20 shillings. What was significant about this order was that the assistants made provision for the many communities which had no resident magistrate, directing that there "the Generall Court shall from time to time nominate *three men,* two whereof shall have like power to heare & determine all such actions under 20s."[139] The magistrates no doubt were pleased to be rid of the small cases which cluttered their docket. Yet to achieve this relief, they were forced to sacrifice the unique mark of their calling, for the "3 men" who would act as judges in the small claims were no magistrates. Over the next twenty years the General Court granted judicial powers to more and more men who neither claimed nor possessed a divine calling for that work. In 1642 the legislature created the associates, a new office, whose duty was to aid and supplement the magistrates when they held County Courts. As one might expect, most of the associates were also deputies.[140] In Springfield and Maine, moreover, the General Court appointed persons "to act in their *respective places as any one magistrate may doe.*"[141] By the middle of the 1640s, therefore, it was foolish for the assistants to maintain that their judicial authority distinguished them from all other officeholders in Massachusetts.[142]

During the 1650s there were few political crises comparable to those of the previous two decades. The storm over the magistracy abated in fury as American Puritans turned their eyes towards the

139. Ibid., 1: 239.
140. Ibid., 1: 168, 175, 213, 328; 2: 5, 14; also Wall, "Membership of the General Court," pp. 350–51, 444–45, 461, 477–78, 504, 524.
141. *Mass. Records,* 3: 423, 230.
142. The following deputies served as judicial associates before 1650: Nathaniel Turner, Thomas Scruggs, Richard Saltonstall, Jr., John Spencer, Israel Stoughton, William Hutchinson, William Heath, Edward Howe, Roger Conant, William Hathorne, Daniel Denison, Samuel Appleton, Ralph Sprage, Richard Browne, Joseph Cooke, Samuel Symonds, William Hubbard, John Woodbridge, Emmanuel Downing, Edward Holyoke, Thomas Willis, John Clarke, Thomas Nelson, Robert Bridges. The following associates later became assistants: W. Hathorne, S. Symonds, D. Denison, R. Saltonstall, Jr., I. Stoughton, R. Bridges, R. Dummer. See *Mass. Records,* 1: 2.

mother country, where Englishmen were having difficulties of their own defining the character of the good ruler. The debate over the nature of civil leadership in Massachusetts was by no means complete; it was merely suspended. During the Restoration period new problems brought about by new political conditions would arise, forcing the colonists to reopen discussion about the qualifications of the good ruler. And in the coming period, there would be no more agreement than there had been in the past.

3

THE FRUITS OF DIVERSITY:
1660–1684

BY their own admission, Puritans after 1660 were the worst of men. Their fathers had endured innumerable hardships constructing the New Israel, but they—the members of the "rising generation"—had demonstrated their unworthiness by allowing vice to spread throughout the Holy Commonwealth.[1] As the years passed and as little progress was made toward spiritual reform, Puritans increasingly criticized one another, warning that the growth of worldliness would exhaust God's patience. The Massachusetts legislature reflected the general mood when it reported with unnerving certainty that "after many years of his fatherly tenderness toward us," the Lord had changed his way, "turning our healthinesse into sicklynesse, our sweete union to much disunion."[2]

The loss of "sweet union" particularly disturbed the members of the rising generation, for they believed, as their fathers had believed, that a covenanted people should be bound together by the force of Christian love. Yet wherever these younger Puritans looked after 1660, they found neighbor set against neighbor, minister against parishioner, and magistrate against deputy. Increase Mather, who served as New England's self-appointed conscience, asked rhetorically in 1682, "Have not we been like foolish Birds, pecking at one

1. Many writers in this period used the term "rising generation." A few examples are William Stoughton, *New-Englands True Interest; Not to Lie* (Cambridge, Mass., 1670), pp. 27–28; Increase Mather, *A Discourse Concerning the Danger of Apostasy* (Boston, 1679), pp. 92–93; Increase Mather, "Diary," 2 *Proceedings*, MHS, 13 (1890–1900): 345; Eleazer Mather, *A Serious Exhortation to the Present and Succeeding Generation of New-England* (Cambridge, Mass., 1671), pp. 16–20.

2. *Mass. Records*, 4: pt. 2, p. 44.

another, until the great Kite be ready to come, and devour one as well as another?"[3] A skeptical historian might well question the basis of Mather's fear, for there is no evidence that the dissension in the Puritan colonies was quantitatively larger after 1660 than it had been before that date. Indeed, when the rising generation praised the harmony of Winthrop's time, it conveniently overlooked such divisive events as the Antinomian crisis and the Vane affair. Fortunately, for our purposes it is not necessary to measure the intensity of religious and political contention. What is important, however, is to see the Puritans of this period as they saw themselves—as a people far more divided than their fathers had ever been.

The members of the rising generation fought over a wide range of issues, some of which were new to the period. Between 1660 and 1684 they argued most passionately about New England's relationship to the mother country, about the limits of religious toleration, and about the meaning of certain Congregational doctrines. Inevitably civil leaders were drawn into these battles. Their involvement, however, revealed that earlier notions about the character of the good ruler were no longer relevant and that the Puritans would have to redefine the magisterial calling to fit changing political conditions. The majority of colonists expected civil leaders to unify the commonwealth; but, ironically, New Englanders could not agree on what attributes would best promote social harmony. Some Congregational ministers, known as Jeremiahs, felt that the times required spiritual reformers—rulers who would save New England from its own vice.[4] Other Puritans, however, took an entirely different tack. William Hubbard, Samuel Nowell, and Joseph Dudley, each in his own way urged magistrates to sheathe the sword of God and pay greater attention to their secular responsibilities.

Throughout this period the political rhetoric of New England underwent a slow transformation. Nowhere was the change more apparent than within the General Court. Beginning in the late 1660s the deputies and assistants renewed the old battle over the limits of magisterial power; but, unlike the legislators of Winthrop's

3. Increase Mather, *A Sermon . . . Preached at a Public Fast* (Boston, 1682), pp. 19–20.
4. See Perry Miller, *The New England Mind,* 2 vols. (Boston, 1961), 2: 19–149 passim.

time, these men seldom spoke of the ruler's office in scriptural terms. In fact, on the eve of the Glorious Revolution, there were few Puritan magistrates in New England who still seriously thought of themselves as God's vicegerents on earth.

The Political Environment

Of the many political issues which divided the rising generation, three stood out above the rest. First, the Puritans argued among themselves about the colony's relationship to the government of Restoration England. Second, they disagreed on how best to deal with heretics and religious dissenters. And last, the people fought over the meaning of certain Congregational doctrines, and civil leaders found themselves, often reluctantly, drawn into bitter theological disputes. Without an understanding of these problems and their political ramifications, one cannot fully appreciate the discussion of the good ruler which took place during this period. Clearly, specific events and personalities influenced those Puritans who bothered to record their views about the character of the magisterial calling.

As soon as the Stuarts returned to power in 1660, they reminded the New England colonies that they were indeed colonies and not independent republics. The Puritan commonwealths, of course, had hardly missed Charles II during his exile, developing trade routes and making civil decisions which showed little concern for the economic needs of the mother country. The new royal government aimed to check this freedom by strenghtening the statutes which controlled commerce throughout the empire; and, for the first time since the founding, the king's commissioners crossed the Atlantic to examine conditions in the New World. When visiting officials discovered American practice at variance with English law they told the colonists to get in step.[5] There were some in Massachusetts who did not object to this meddling in local affairs and who were willing to cooperate with the imperial agents; others, however,

5. For the details of the theory, planning, and execution of the English imperial system in this period, see George L. Beer, *The Origins of the English Colonial System, 1578–1660* (New York, 1908); Charles M. Andrews, *The Colonial Period of American History,* 4 vols. (New Haven, 1964), 4.

savored old animosities, remembering that the Stuart family had once harried their fathers out of the land. These unreconciled Puritans were joined by recent Cromwellians such as John Leverett and Francis Willoughby, who were victims of a second harrying out of England.

While royal interference irritated many Puritans, there was little they could do about it. Charles's government was bent on establishing its authority over the American dominions; and though the colonists successfully evaded many imperial orders, they could no longer ignore England altogether. Soon after the king took the throne he instructed the rulers of Massachusetts to drop church membership as the basis of franchise and to put the new Navigation Acts of 1660 and 1663 into immediate operation.[6] Charles even tried to influence colonial elections, ordering his secretary of state to inform the freemen that since Governor John Endecott "is not a person well affected to his Majesty's person or his Government, his Majesty will take it very well if [at] the next election any other person of good reputation bee chosen in that place, and that he may no longer exercise that charge."[7] Before 1684 these regulatory endeavors seldom succeeded as they were intended. Nevertheless, the threat of expanded English control produced factions, each supporting a different view of how best to meet the imperial challenge.[8]

6. 2 *Collections*, MHS, 8: 54. The General Court retained church membership as a qualification for enfranchisement, but it also seemingly complied with the king's demands by granting the vote to non-church members who were orthodox in religion, virtuous in their lives, and owners of estates yielding ten shillings "in a single country rate, after the usuall manner of valluation." Royal investigators soon discovered that the change was not the liberal move that it appeared to be. They protested that "not one church member in a hundred payes so much, and that in a towne of an hundred inhabitants scarse three such men are to be found." The visiting authorities explained with obvious understatement, "wee feare the king will rather finde himselfe deluded then satisfied by your late act" (*Mass. Records*, 4: pt. 2, pp. 118, 205. See also Steven Foster, "The Massachusetts Franchise in the Seventeenth Century," *William and Mary Quarterly*, 3d ser. 24[1967]: 619–22).

7. *Calendar of State Papers, Colonial Series, 1661–1688*, p. 282.

8. The best account of the internal political dissension caused by imperial demands is Paul R. Lucas, "Colony or Commonwealth: Massachusetts Bay, 1661–1666," *William and Mary Quarterly*, 3d ser. 24(1967): 88–107. For a discussion of the merchant community's reaction to English

During the 1670s and 1680s England's relations with the Puritan colonies were further complicated by the work of Edward Randolph, the king's agent in Massachusetts.[9] Royal authorities dispatched Randolph to the New World in order to enforce the Navigation Acts, which they suspected were being disobeyed. But the choice of Randolph for this assignment was particularly unfortunate. The man's officious nature offended nearly everyone; and from the moment he landed in Boston he treated the Puritans with open disdain. Since Randolph allowed his prejudices to color his reports, he contributed substantially to the growth of imperial misunderstanding. In one typical letter he described the rulers of the Bay Colony as "inconsiderable Mechanicks picked by the prevailing party of the factious Ministry who have a fellow feeling both in the Command & profit."[10] After poking around for several months, Randolph decided that the Massachusetts Charter undermined England's regulatory system by allowing the colonists too much civil autonomy. He worked hard to bring about its annulment and in the process angered many Puritans who had grown fond of their independence.

By the 1680s the future of the charter had become a major political question dividing the colonists as well as members of the General Court. The steadily increasing pressure from England forced the rulers of Massachusetts to decide whether they wanted to defend the original patent at all costs, to accept its revocation as a necessary consequence of New England's colonial status, or to steer a moderate

---

trade regulation, see Bernard Bailyn, *The New England Merchants in the Seventeenth Century* (New York, 1964), pp. 112–68 passim. Even the towns were divided over the imperial issue. In 1664 a group in Billerica wrote to the General Court in order "to testify unanimously that we doe Rest Satisfied in the present Government" (Henry Hazen, *History of Billerica* [Boston, 1883], p. 185). In 1666, however, seventy-two Ipswich men protested the legislature's uncooperative stance toward England and warned the rulers not to irritate the king (Thomas F. Waters, *Ipswich in the Massachusetts Bay Colony* [Ipswich, 1905], pp. 136–37).

9. See Michael G. Hall, *Edward Randolph and the American Colonies, 1676–1703* (Chapel Hill, 1960) for a complete, although overly sympathetic, account of Randolph's work in Massachusetts.

10. Robert N. Toppan and Alfred T. S. Goodrick, eds., *Edward Randolph: Including His Letters and Official Papers . . . 1676–1703*, 7 vols. (Boston, 1898–1909), 2: 206; also 3: 158, 214.

course between these two extremes. No matter which of these three paths the magistrates chose they could be certain that many of their constituents would be displeased and that "sweet union" would be less likely than ever before.

Religious intolerance was a second major cause of dissension within the rising generation. The founders had driven heretics like Roger Williams and Anne Hutchinson from their midst, but when the rulers of the 1660s tried to emulate that example by chasing the Quakers out of the colony, the result hardly seemed worth the trouble. Unlike the Antinomians who moved to Rhode Island, the Quakers refused to accept their banishment, returning to Boston as fast as they were sent away. More out of frustration than fanaticism the Puritan authorities finally executed several of them. John Hull, the colonial mint master and a deputy, described the incident in his diary: "These three persons had the sentence of death pronounced against them by the General Court . . . and well they deserved it. Most of the godly have cause to rejoice, and bless the Lord that strengthens our magistrates and deputies to bear witness against such blasphemers."[11]

But Hull's rejoicing seemed somewhat premature when George Bishop, a Quaker, published a graphic account of the persecution and circulated it among Restoration Englishmen, who had little love for the Bible Commonwealth.[12] The General Court realized that such adverse publicity might endanger the Massachusetts Charter, and in 1661 it diplomatically retracted some of the more severe anti-Quaker measures. Various members of the rising generation were shocked by the extreme punishments which had been meted out to the Quakers; and as the years passed, an increasing number came to question the efficacy of government coercion in matters of conscience.[13] When the ranks of the Baptists and Anglicans began to swell during the 1670s and 1680s Puritan rulers were unsure whether

11. "John Hull's Diary of Public Occurrences," *Transactions and Collections of the American Antiquarian Society* 3 (1857): 189, 215.

12. George Bishop, *New-England Judged* (London, 1661); Charles II to Governor John Endecott, 9 Sept. 1661, 5 *Collections,* MHS, 9: 26–27; see 3 *Proceedings,* MHS, 42 (1908–09): 358–76, for a collection of Quaker protests against the Bay magistrates; Miller, *New England Mind,* 2: 123–25.

13. *Mass. Records,* 4: pt. 2, p. 34.

to chastise the religious dissenters with the sword of God or to let them live in peace.

Of all the controversies during this period, those waged over Congregational doctrine seemed the most bitter. Surprisingly, it was the growth of population rather than the presence of religious dissenters that created the knottiest theological problems. The first New Englanders had decided that only those persons who could give evidence of divine election would be accepted as full church members. In other words, only God's visible saints could receive the two Puritan sacraments, baptism and communion, and have a voice in ecclesiastical government. These people apparently took the Lord's injunction to go forth and multiply seriously, but their many children and grandchildren did not always feel the same stirrings of grace that had moved the fathers. As these young Puritans grew to maturity, the Congregational churches had to decide how to treat them. Should the grandchildren of full members be baptized? Should they be allowed to take communion or to vote in church affairs?[14]

In 1662 the clergy tried to answer these questions, but they succeeded only in dividing the rising generation into two factions which attacked each other at every opportunity. At the synod a majority of the ministers decided that the grandchildren of church members could receive the sacrament of baptism even though their parents could not yet prove their salvation. Despite the fact that the elders refused to allow persons in the Half-Way status to take communion or to participate in church government, many Puritans labeled the proposals of 1662 as gross apostasy. The venerable John Davenport, spiritual head of New Haven, assumed leadership of the opposition; and, when the First Church of Boston called him to be its minister in 1667, he carried the fight to the hub of New England.[15]

14. See Edmund S. Morgan, *Visible Saints: History of a Puritan Idea* (Ithaca, 1965); and Williston Walker, *The Creeds and Platform of Congregationalism* (Boston, 1960), pp. 238–339. Also Morgan, "New England Puritanism: Another Approach," *William and Mary Quarterly,* 3d ser. 18(1961): 236–42; Darrett B. Rutman, "God's Bridge Falling Down: 'Another Approach' to New England Puritanism Surveyed," ibid. 19(1962): 408–21; and Morgan, "Letter to the Editor," ibid., pp. 642–44.

15. See John Davenport to John Leverett, June 1665, *The Hutchinson Papers,* 2 vols. (Albany, 1865), 2: 119.

But, to his immense irritation, a large body of First Churchmen were so angered by his decision to move that they resigned and formed a church of their own which adopted the Half-Way Covenant. By the time Davenport arrived in Boston, the two churches were already locked in battle.

The members of the General Court soon found themselves involved in the controversy between the old First Church and the newly established Third Church (often called the Old South Church). When the lower house, which backed Davenport's cause, invited him to deliver the annual election sermon, the minister used the opportunity to rebuke the rulers of New England for accepting the synod's work and to warn them against forcing human judgments upon Christ's true church.[16] Those judgments were especially hazardous, he railed, "when they are such as prevailed in an hour of Temptation, though consented to by the major part of a Topical Synod, yet disliked by some of themselves, and by other godly Ministers, both in this Countrey, and in other Countries, so that they are things Controverted and under Dispute."[17] The content of Davenport's sermon pleased the deputies so much that they passed a formal bill thanking him for his efforts. The assistants, however, balked at the representatives' resolution and declared that they regarded such an expression of gratitude as "altogether unseasonable, many passages in the said sermon being ill-resented by the Reverend Elders of the Churches and many serious persons."[18]

For an entire year the assistants and deputies disputed the ecclesiastical problems of Boston.[19] By May the situation had become so

16. See Bibliographical Essay for a discussion of the election sermon as a source for the political history of colonial New England.

17. Davenport, *A Sermon Preach'd at the Election* . . . 1669 (Boston, 1670), reprinted in *Publications of the Colonial Society of Massachusetts* 10(1907): 13–14; also Miller, *New England Mind,* 2: 107–08.

18. Hamilton A. Hill, *History of the Old South Church,* 2 vols. (Boston, 1890), 1: 94.

19. The members of the Third Church wanted formal letters of dismission from the First Church. When the parent church refused to cooperate, the legislature divided, each house supporting a different ecclesiastical position (ibid., 1: 98–106). The most recent account of the Third Church crisis is in Richard C. Simmons, "The Founding of the Third Church in Boston," *William and Mary Quarterly,* 3d ser. 26(1969): 241–52.

bad that Deputy Governor Francis Willoughby urged the members of the General Court to stop their feuding and to attend to the regular business of government. The old Cromwellian advised the legislators to "contrive some way before you break up the Court, to adjourne with demonstration of oneness and affection, that it may appear you all scope [aim] at the good of the poor Country."[20] The magistrates and representatives reached a semblance of accord in 1671, although probably not in a manner which Willoughby had anticipated. People throughout Massachusetts who supported the Third Church position apparently worked hard to persuade the colonial freemen to drop most of the pro-Davenport deputies and to return individuals who favored the Half-Way Covenant.[21] When the new legislature met the representatives joined with the assistants to sanction the Third Church, but the spirit of harmony was more apparent than real.[22]

Church dissension in New England was by no means restricted to Boston or to the issue of the Half-Way Covenant. During the same period, for example, the people of Newbury, Massachusetts, divided over other theological questions. A long controversy began when a group of church members led by Joshua Woodman accused their minister, Thomas Parker, of repudiating the Congregational polity established by the founders and of substituting an authoritarian system in its place. The laymen specifically charged Parker with ruling on major ecclesiastical concerns before the Newbury congregation had had an opportunity to discuss them. In defense of their views, the protest party declared, "As for our controversy it is whether God hath placed the power in the elder [the minister], or in the whole church, to judge between truth and error, right and wrong, brother and brother, and all things of church concernment."[23] The Newbury quarrel, like that of Boston, eventually came before the civil author-

20. Hill, *Old South Church*, 1: 104–05.
21. Ibid., 1: 107–10; Miller, *New England Mind*, 2: 108.
22. As late as 1673 Urian Oakes was still urging the people of Boston to drop old animosities and to make peace (Hill, *Old South Church*, 1: 192–95); see also Urian Oakes, *New-England Pleaded With . . .* (Cambridge, Mass., 1673).
23. Joshua Coffin, *A Sketch of the History of Newbury, Newburyport, and West Newbury* (Boston, 1845), p. 87.

ities. Most of the men sitting on the Salem Quarterly Court backed
Parker; but two leading magistrates, Samuel Symonds and William
Hathorne, broke with the majority and supported Woodman's definition of Congregational orthodoxy.[24] The Newbury factions never
worked out a formal peace, and the conflict continued sporadically
until the contestants grew tired of the fight.[25]

One of the many members of the rising generation who was confused by the factious spirit which had divided congregations throughout New England was the Reverend John Woodbridge, Jr. As a
minister, he longed for more authority so that he could discipline
the imprudent church members who "are grown so rude." In a series
of letters written between 1669 and 1672 to Richard Baxter, the
most respected Puritan leader in Restoration England, Woodbridge
analyzed the controversies which had shattered the ecclesiastical
harmony of New England. He told Baxter that Massachusetts Congregationalism had broken into "three formes of Disciplinarians [,]
Each one step higher then his fellow: Rigid Independents, moderate
ones, and those that are Presbyterianly addicted." Woodbridge believed that a majority of the ministers shared his own desire for a
stricter type of church government, but he knew that the rank and
file would defend independency against Presbyterianism and would
refuse to let the clergymen "fly their owne course."[26] Many towns
in the Puritan colonies were split so badly over the question of
clerical power that it was difficult "to find a minister such an
Ambidexter as to be Able to please both sides." The great battles
which had taken place within the churches at Hartford, Windsor,
and Stamford gave clergymen of Woodbridge's type additional reason
to lament the disunity of New England.[27]

The dissension in the churches placed an almost unbearable pres-

24. Coffin, *History of Newbury,* pp. 74–76; also *Mass. Records,* 4: pt. 2,
pp. 512, 523–24.

25. Ibid., pp. 101, 109.

26. Raymond P. Stearns, ed., "Correspondence of John Woodbridge, Jr.,
and Richard Baxter," *New England Quarterly* 10(1937): 574, 576.

27. Ibid., p. 576; George L. Walker, *History of the First Church in
Hartford* (Hartford, 1884), pp. 154–62; *Some Early Records and Documents of and Relating to the Town of Windsor Connecticut, 1639–1703*
(Hartford, 1903), pp. 135–36; *Collections,* CHS, 2: 95; also *Mass. Records,*
5: 180–81.

sure on the rulers of the rising generation, for they most certainly were not "Ambidexters" able to please all men. The civil leaders in Winthrop's time had not hesitated to enter theological disputes, for the issues had been reasonably clear-cut. They had arbitrated controversies involving obvious doctrinal errors—Antinomianism, Separatism, and Anabaptism—and in each case they had been able to discern the false beliefs with confidence. But the magistrates of the 1660s and the 1670s found the job of identifying and punishing heresy much more difficult when each side in an ecclesiastical quarrel claimed that it alone preserved the church of Thomas Hooker and John Cotton.

Most people who wrote about the character of the good ruler in this period recognized that the major problem facing magistrates was not dissension over this or that specific issue, but the fact of dissension itself. The Jeremiahs, as well as their many critics, wanted civil leaders who could bring greater order and harmony to New England society. The crucial question that divided these political writers was how the Puritan magistrate should go about ending the contention. Some spokesmen advocated saintly rulers, men who were prepared to use the sword of God. Others like Hubbard and Nowell responded differently to the changing conditions, defining the character of the good ruler in ways which the Jeremiahs could never accept.

The Jeremiahs' Vision

The sermonic literature of this period consisted almost entirely of jeremiads, statements of lamentation for the alleged "declension" of the New American Israel. The Congregational clergymen who delivered these works have been labeled Jeremiahs; and even though some of them, like Increase and Cotton Mather, were not the most lovable figures, they exerted a major influence over the members of the rising generation. Usually, their sermons followed a set formula. The speaker would observe that his contemporaries had deserted the ways of their fathers, succumbing to a myriad of worldly temptations. Lest their audiences be discouraged, however, the Jeremiahs explained that, if the colonists reformed and returned to the pristine manners of the founders, New England might still be saved from God's wrath.

Some colonial historians have dismissed the Jeremiahs as querulous busybodies, concerned solely with turning back the clock.[28] But this interpretation is misleading, if not wholly false, for the Congregational ministers were no fools. It is far more just to consider them as men possessed by a vision. Always before them was the image of an ideal commonwealth in which the people worked together for the glorification of God. What scholars have generally overlooked is that clergymen of Mather's type appreciated the power which a dream or myth can exert over a community. Indeed, the ministers of this period recognized a truth which has been demonstrated many times throughout history: that the thought of achieving perfection in this world can move human beings to endure great personal sacrifice. The Jeremiahs catalogued the sins of their generation not because they were unable to cope with change or because they were unusually perverse individuals, but because they wanted to spur their listeners to action; or, put another way, they wanted to make the colonists aware of the gap between the dream and the reality. If the ministers' rhetoric seems unsophisticated today, it is probably because we are no longer able to share their vision. A large number of Puritans had no such trouble, however, and looked upon spiritual reform as the best means to check the spread of dissension.

Their vision certainly did not impair the Jeremiahs' ability to understand the immediate problems facing New England. They knew as well as any of their contemporaries what elements kept Massachusetts from becoming the ideal holy commonwealth. As early as the 1660s, ministers observed that economic success lay at the root of the colony's troubles, and it seemed to the Jeremiahs that the members of the rising generation were spending too much time in the countinghouse and not enough time thinking about the Lord. The Reverend John Higginson had to remind his parishioners in 1663 that *"New England is originally a plantation of Religion, not a plantation of Trade.* Let merchants and such as are increasing *Cent per Cent*

---

28. E.g. James Truslow Adams, *The Founding of New England* (Boston, 1921), pp. 326–97; Viola F. Barnes, *The Dominion of New England* (New Haven, 1960); and Peter Gay, *A Loss of Mastery: Puritan Historians in Colonial America* (New York, 1968), pp. 65–76. For a more balanced account of one Jeremiah, see Kenneth B. Murdock, *Increase Mather: The Foremost American Puritan* (Cambridge, Mass., 1925).

remember this."[29] And Increase Mather, the most famous minister of this period, noted with remarkable insight that among New Englanders "there hath been . . . an insatiable desire after Land . . . yea, so as to forsake Churches and Ordinances, and to live like Heathen, only so that they might have Elbow-room enough in the world."[30] There were obviously many men in Massachusetts and Connecticut who did not see the abundance of land or the growth of prosperity as difficulties to be overcome. But, for the Jeremiahs and their supporters, worldliness was sinfulness, and they expected good rulers to put New England back on the right road.

Between 1660 and 1684 the attitude of the Jeremiahs toward civil leaders shifted considerably. Early in this period, they urged their rulers to direct the reformation which was necessary in order to create the ideal society. But, over the years, it became increasingly apparent that the magistrates of New England either would not, or could not, carry out all of the clergy's demands. As time passed the discouraged Jeremiahs showed less and less concern about the character of the good ruler; and, instead, began to search for new nonpolitical means to bring about reform. It is important for our story to trace the ministers' changing views in some detail, for their example tells us a good deal about the relation of political theory to political practice. As we have seen before, general notions about the good ruler were often a response to specific magisterial decisions.

The reforming clergy believed, especially in the early years of this period, that the ministers and magistrates would have to work together in order to construct the ideal society. "We doe not read in the Scripture, nor in History," Increase Mather explained, "of any notable general Reformation amongst a People, except the

29. John Higginson, *The Cause of God and His People in New-England* (Cambridge, Mass., 1663), p. 20. In his election sermon of 1670, *Errand into the Wilderness* (Cambridge, Mass.), Samuel Danforth assured the Puritans that their mission in the New World had not been "the expectation of *Courtly Pomp and Delicacy*. We came not *hither to see men clothed like Courtiers*" (p. 17). Also see [Increase Mather], *The Necessity of Reformation with the Expedients Thereunto, Asserted* (Boston, 1679), p. i.

30. Quoted in Sydney E. Ahlstrom, "Studying America and American Studies at Yale," *Ventures* 9(1969): 76.

Magistrates did help forward the work." Mather assured the Puritan rulers that he knew of no example where civil authorities had assisted in the suppression of evil "but there was (at least wise for the present) some good effect thereof."[31] In a sermon delivered at the funeral of Governor John Leverett, Samuel Willard declared "a work of Reformation is set about in vain, and to no purpose, if Rulers do not lead in it."[32] In many ways the ministers of the rising genera- tion were similar to those clergymen who had refused to separate from the Anglican church during the 1620s; both groups chose to "tarry" for the magistrates, hoping that they would lead the Puritan saints into battle. But, at the same time, it should be noted that the Jeremiahs' appeals, even in the 1660s, were somewhat defensive, as if they suspected that the rulers of New England were ambivalent about the cause of reform.[33]

Ministers of Mather's persuasion knew exactly what type of ruler could best save the Puritan colonies from divine destruction. Election day speakers frequently described the ideal magistrates as "hedges," as "walls," or as "repairers of the old breach."[34] Their favorite ex- ample was Nehemiah, an Old Testament leader who had once saved Jerusalem by rebuilding a protective wall which the citizens had allowed to crumble. Nehemiah replaced Moses as the model biblical ruler for the rising generation; Moses had built the "City upon a Hill," now Nehemiah had to preserve it.[35]

31. [Increase Mather], *Necessity of Reformation,* p. iii.

32. Samuel Willard, *A Sermon upon the Death of John Leverett, Esq.* (Boston, 1679), p. 6; also Samuel Torrey, *An Exhortation unto Reformation* (Cambridge, Mass., 1674), p. 30.

33. Frequently the jeremiad rhetoric sounded anxious, shrill, and coaxing. To see the change in tone that had taken place since the 1630s, one need only compare Thomas Shepard's "Notes for the Election Sermon 1638" with Samuel Torrey's election sermon for 1683, *A Plea for the Life of Dying Religion* (Boston, 1683). As we saw in the previous chapter, Shepard berated the freemen like a stern father scolding a child. Torrey, however, lacked Shepard's self-confidence, and his sermon was more a whining supplication than an angry rebuke.

34. All of these terms were common in the sermon literature of the period, e.g. Torrey, *An Exhortation,* p. 30; Willard, *Leverett,* p. 7; Stoughton, *New-Englands True Interest,* p. 35.

35. See Jonathan Mitchell, *Nehemiah on the Wall in Troublesome Times* (Cambridge, Mass., 1671); Willard, *Leverett,* p. 6.

To a certain extent, the Jeremiahs were guilty of manipulating history in the interests of their own vision. They recognized, no doubt, that Winthrop's colony had been divided by bitter political and religious disputes and that the "City upon a Hill" had never existed in fact. The Puritan founders who appeared in the jeremiads, therefore, were largely mythical figures created for the purpose of shaming the rising generation into reform. The real responsibility of the Nehemiahs was not to restore Massachusetts to 1630 conditions, but to take the Puritans farther along the road toward the New Israel.

The ministers told prospective Nehemiahs that there were two things which had to be done in order to protect the founders' heritage. First, rulers of the rising generation had to guard the colony's covenant with God by ensuring that the people did not deal falsely with the Lord; and second, they had to defend the Massachusetts Charter from its enemies, both at home and abroad. In their sermons the clergy frequently combined these two requirements so that the defense of the charter and the preservation of the covenant became one overarching magisterial responsibility.[36]

The reforming clergy advised the Nehemiahs to protect Congregational orthodoxy at all costs; for, as the ministers never tired of explaining, the Lord had smiled on New England when Winthrop and Dudley punished religious dissenters.[37] The Jeremiahs warned that if civil authorities tolerated beliefs which clashed with Congregational doctrine, then men throughout the world would know that the Puritans had deserted the ways of the founders and turned their backs upon God.[38] In 1674 Samuel Torrey spoke to this point in an election sermon, which in many ways was a model jeremiad. The printed edition, in fact, even carried an introduction by Increase

---

36. E.g., Higginson, *Cause of God,* p. 23.

37. Ibid., pp. 11–12; Samuel Willard, *The Only Sure Way to Prevent Threatened Calamity* (Boston, 1684); Mitchell, *Nehemiah,* pp. 27–29.

38. Several clergymen went out of their way to show that the Half-Way Covenant was not part of the general drift away from the principles of the founders. John Higginson explained the synod's work to the General Court, "There are things we have been defective in, and therefore should be reformed in a *practicall* way" (*Cause of God,* p. 14); see also Mitchell, *Nehemiah,* pp. 28–29.

Mather. Torrey told the colonial legislators that the Lord had called them to office in order to maintain Christian liberty, but he added quickly, "This Christian Liberty doth *not* give men leave to believe, Profess and Practice what they will, (as *Libertines* do vainly suppose) and from thence plead for a Licentious Liberty of Conscience."[39] The speaker's emphasis on order revealed his anxiety about the growing dissension within New England. Unfortunately, in his rush to bring about the ideal commonwealth, Torrey failed to inform the Nehemiahs how they should deal with specific heretics.[40] Should they, for example, continue to harass the Quakers when everyone knew in advance that such action would only displease the king? And even more perplexing, what were the rulers of the rising generation supposed to do about the divisions within the Congregational churches themselves?

The Jeremiahs were of little more help when it came to making

39. Torrey, *An Exhortation,* pp. 25–26; James Allen, *New-Englands Choicest Blessing* (Boston, 1679), p. 9. In the election sermon of 1661, John Norton observed, "If you ask what Liberty is? you may look at it as a Power, as to any external restraint, or obstruction on man's part, to walk in the Faith, Worship, Doctrine and Discipline of the Gospel, according to the order of the Gospel" *(Three Choice and Profitable Sermons* [Cambridge, Mass., 1664], p. 7). In other words, the Jeremiahs thought that New Englanders possessed a negative liberty not to sin, but had no positive liberty to choose whatever doctrines they saw fit. Over the next fifty years the meaning of liberty gradually shifted, and eighteenth-century men wrote of it as a defense against unjust government demands. In 1660 liberty protected the community from rash, nonconforming acts by the citizens; in 1730 liberty guarded the citizens from the tyranny of a ruler (see chap. 7).

40. On November 29, 1677, Solomon Stoddard complained to Increase Mather that a Baptist minister, John Miles, had been allowed to preach in Boston: "I fear it will be a means to fill the town, which is allready full of unstable persons, with error: I looke upon it as a great judgment" *(4 Collections,* MHS, 8: 586–87). In 1681 Thomas Cobbet cried that toleration of "Antipedobaptists" would bring about the destruction of Massachusetts (ibid., p. 291). As late as 1682 Samuel Willard was still warning the magistrates against the spirit of "boundless Toleration," but none of these leading divines offered constructive suggestions on how the heretics might be removed without bringing the wrath of the king upon New England (Samuel Willard, *Covenant-Keeping the Way to Blessedness* [Boston, 1682], p. 101).

suggestions about how best to defend the colony's royal charter. They were fully aware that a centralization of the English imperial system represented a threat to the purity of the Congregational churches; for, if the king rescinded their patent, the mother country would gain greater control over the colony's internal affairs, which included the maintenance of religious uniformity. An anonymous correspondent who obviously knew a good deal about New England explained the situation to a Stuart official. The writer pointed out that the Jeremiahs saw the charter as vital to the success of the Puritan commonwealth: "They well knowing that if the wall of Civil Government [the Charter] be pulled down, the wild boar will soon destroy the Lord's vineyard, and that it is impossible for them to keep the waters of the Sanctuary when the Venice glass which holds them is broken in pieces."[41] Increase Mather may well have been one of the ministers described in this letter, for he recognized the close relationship between the charter and the covenant. In one of his sermons he warned the rulers of New England that the people who had deserted Congregationalism were the very same persons who had grown "weary of the Theocracy, or Government which God hath established amongst us."[42]

The difficulty with advice like Mather's was that it left too much unsaid. None of the reforming clergy, in fact, bothered to mention that the defense of the charter called for varied and subtle political skills, or that a successful Nehemiah would have had to petition Parliament, influence the king, and outmaneuver visiting royal com-

41. *Calendar of State Papers, Colonial Series, 1661–1668,* p. 417.
42. Increase Mather's introduction to Urian Oakes, *A Seasonable Discourse* (Cambridge, Mass., 1682), p. ii. In another sermon Oakes wrote that any "change in our Government will *inevitably* introduce a sad change in our Churches. To divide what God hath conjoyned, viz. Civil and Ecclesiastical Liberties, to deliver up Civil, and yet hope to keep spiritual Liberties, is folly in its Exaltation" *(New-England Pleaded with,* p. 50). Mather himself explained, "If the Lord should be provoked to bring a Change upon us as to our Civil State: If that wall of Government [the charter], which hath hitherto been such a mercy to this people, should be removed; there are three Evils, that would quickly follow; *viz. Superstition, Prophaneness, and Persecution.* If the raines of Government should fall into Hands that are enemies to the wayes of Christ, we can in reason expect no better" *(A Sermon . . . Preached at a Public Fast,* p. 19).

missioners. Such responsibilities required colonial magistrates to learn their way around the Stuart court and thus to develop talents which would have been alien to those fictional Winthrops which appeared in the jeremiads. By the mid-1670s it had become almost impossible for a ruler to emulate the mythical founders, while at the same time trying to solve the real problems of the rising generation.

In the years before the Glorious Revolution the rulers of New England patiently and repeatedly assured the ministers that something would be done about the spread of heresy, immorality, and declension. The Jeremiahs waited for legislation to follow these pious proclamations, but none came. With each passing year civil leaders paid less and less attention to the complaints of the churchmen, and the preachers' sense of betrayal grew as their own political pronouncements became increasingly irrelevant to the actual policies of government. In 1667 the Reverend John Wilson stood before a group of Congregational ministers to attack Separatism and Anabaptism; but, even more, to remind his fellow clergymen that the decisions of church synods had recently received very little respect. Wilson found it particularly galling that the magistrates were of no help in reforming these evils, "either not caring for these things, or else not using their power and authority for the maintenance of the truth, gospel and ordinances of our Lord and Saviour Jesus Christ."[43]

During the late 1660s civil authorities in Massachusetts, perhaps under the Jeremiahs' prodding, made several halfhearted attempts to harass Thomas Gould's Baptist settlement at Noodles Island. The Bay rulers soon dropped even these token efforts, however, and in 1674 John Hull noted in his diary that "This summer, the Anabaptists that were wont to meet at Noodles Island met at Boston on the Lord's Day." Hull added with obvious disapproval, "Some of the magistrates will not permit any punishment to be inflicted on heretics as such."[44] The Baptists respected Governor John Leverett, who held office from 1673 to 1678, and regarded him as their supporter. Under his administration, one happy dissenter declared, "the church of the baptised do peaceable enjoy their liberty."[45] Leverett and his deputy

43. Isaac Backus, *A History of New England,* 2 vols. (Newton, Mass., 1871), 1: 308.

44. "Hull's Diary," p. 238.

45. Backus, *History of New England,* 1: 327; Miller, *New England Mind,* 2: 129.

governor, Samuel Symonds, apparently had decided much to the Jeremiahs' disgust, that the common good was better served by tolerating the Baptists than by running them out of the colony.

No clergyman possessed a stronger vision than Increase Mather, and none was more angered by the magistrates' foot dragging in the cause of reform. He interpreted every event, even the most common-place, in terms of New England's supposed fall from standards set by the founders. In 1675 Mather was more depressed than usual about the condition of the colony, for he had convinced himself that the illness in Boston, the Indians' military successes, and the hardness of his own heart were omens that God was preparing to leave the commonwealth. "Reformation," he lamented, "doth not goe forward. Magistrates [are] too slow in that matter."[46] Mather thought that he might stir the rulers to their work by reading them a long list of the Puritans' sins and corruptions, but the members of the General Court gave him a very cool reception. In fact, Governor Leverett specifically criticized Mather for "some passages in my sermon, viz. that strangers said that they had seen more drunkennes in N.E. in halfe a year than in E[ngland] in all their lives."[47] Leverett, who had lived and fought in old England under Oliver Cromwell, knew that Mather's claim was nonsense. The governor had no patience with the notion that Massachusetts was growing progressively more de-praved, and informed the zealous clergyman "that there was more drunknnes in N.E. many years agoe than there is now, yea at the first beginning of this Colony." Leverett ridiculed the ancestor worship which was an essential element in all jeremiads. A sulking Mather wrote in his diary after this encounter, "Magistrates have no Heart to doe what they might in order to Reformation. *esply the Gover-nor.*"[48]

Mather had another opportunity to chastise the errant rulers in 1677 when he was chosen by the representatives to deliver the annual election sermon, *A Discourse Concerning the Danger of Apostasy.* He spoke to the members of the General Court like a military leader

46. *2 Proceedings,* MHS, 13: 357.
47. Ibid., p. 358 (spelling modernized).
48. Ibid., p. 359 (italics added). Edward Randolph wrote, "The present governor Mr. Leverett is the only old soldier in the colony, he served in the late rebellion, under the usurper Oliver Cromwell, as a captain of horse" (*Hutchinson Papers,* 2: 220).

who has discovered that his troops have deserted before the crucial battle. "Alas! our Nehemiahs are gone," he sobbed. The rulers of the rising generation had not listened to the ministers' advice; they had allowed religious toleration and ecclesiastical dissension to spread throughout New England. Mather attempted to shame them by announcing that "if your blessed Fathers, and Predecessors were alive, and in place, it would not be so; If *Winthrop, Dudley, Endicot* were upon the Bench, such profaneness as this would be suppressed."[49] Ironically, there was a Dudley on the bench in 1677— Joseph Dudley, son of the founder and a future governor of Massachusetts. The younger Dudley and his fellow magistrates were so put off by Mather's self-righteous blast that they refused him the traditional courtesy of publishing his election sermon at government expense.[50] Mather's intemperate show before the General Court only widened the rift between the ministers and the magistrates.

Sometime during the late 1670s the Jeremiahs finally began to realize that their magistrates had no intention of leading a moral crusade. The ministers' response to this situation varied from person to person, of course; some calling for greater vigilance by the freemen at election time, others advancing nonpolitical plans for spiritual reform. Superficially, the Jeremiahs' rhetoric about the character of the good ruler did not seem to change, for they still described the ideal magistrate as a pious individual, someone prepared to wield the sword of God against sinners and dissenters alike—the Lord's vicegerent on earth. But these traditional words merely screened a shift in the clergy's thinking. When one gets beyond the platitudes, one discovers that Mather and his associates were reacting to specific social and political conditions and that they were saying some things that ministers had never said before.

As rulers showed less and less interest in reform, some Jeremiahs turned to the freemen, urging them to participate regularly in colonial elections. There was abundant evidence of political apathy throughout New England. Few towns except Boston bothered to instruct their representatives about the issues to be debated before

49. Increase Mather, *Discourse Concerning the Danger of Apostasy,* pp. 66, 78–79.

50. Miller, *New England Mind,* 2: 136–37.

the General Court, and some did not even select deputies at all.[51]
To make matters worse, the annual elections were more like parties
or fairs than occasions for serious business. In 1676 the ministers
of Connecticut complained of "vain Company Keeping, Rioting &
Revelling at Taverns, especially at publique times, *as days of Election*."[52] In 1679 the Reverend James Allen took the voters of New
England to task for their behavior, noting, "I have heard it much
complained of that Freemens meetings are not attended, not halfe
of them appear upon the choice of Deputies in this Town [Boston]
. . . and many that do come, have never prayed for guidance, nor
made enquires of things, or persons; but only do as they are led."
Allen informed his audience that such citizens not only were negli-
gent in the Lord's work, but also broke their oath as Puritan free-

51. *A Report of the Record Commission of the City of Boston* (Boston,
1881), pp. 6, 15, 17, 20, 26, 48, 110–11, 128, 134. I have examined the
printed town records for this period and have found no other instructions
from the freemen to their deputies. In some towns the people gave instructions to selectmen who guided local affairs between town meetings
(Samuel Green, ed., *The Early Records of Groton, 1662–1707* [Groton,
Mass., 1880], pp. 71–72, 75; Hazen, *History of Billerica*, pp. 61, 198).

Many towns, no doubt, decided not to send deputies because the local
freemen had to pay their representatives' travel expenses and salary.
Some towns got around the travel expense by electing Boston men as
their deputies. The number of nonresident representatives before 1690
was surprisingly high. Captain Humphrey Davy, for example, represented Billerica and received "a fat beast" for his troubles. Later, Davy was
a deputy for Woburn (Zachariah Whitman, *The History of the Ancient
and Honorable Artillery Company* [Boston, 1842], pp. 124, 176). John Hull
and his son-in-law, Samuel Sewall, represented several different towns
("Hull's Diary," pp. 158, 160, 161). There were at least thirty-seven nonresident deputies in this period (Robert E. Wall, Jr., "The Membership of
the Massachusetts General Court, 1634–1686," [Ph.D. diss., Yale University,
1965], pp. 6, 247; Hill, *Old South Church*, 1: 197).

The election of nonresident deputies was not illegal. According to colony
law all towns except shire towns had to choose delegates from among
resident freemen. The shire towns or county seats, however, were allowed
to select any freemen in the colony as their representative. Each shire in
Massachusetts had two shire towns, i.e. places where county courts were
held (W. H. Whitmore, arr., *The Colonial Laws of Massachusetts* [Boston,
1889], p. 145).

52. *Collections*, CHS, 21 (Wyllys Papers): 236.

men.[53] The minister seemed to echo the words of Samuel Ward and John Preston, who in another crisis had warned the saints to take advantage of elections.

What the Jeremiahs were attempting to do, in effect, was to shift the responsibility for New England's declension from the rulers to the voters. In his *New-England Freeman Warned and Warmed*, for example, John Oxenbridge told the colonists to show pride in their "free Election," for "there is no such day in other Colonies abroad." The citizens of Massachusetts possessed the privilege to choose either good or evil magistrates. If they selected a poor candidate, their error would reflect their corrupt character as a people, a sign that they had forsaken the Lord's covenant. "Nothing can undo this Country," Oxenbridge declared, "but the mis-making or mis-acting of Freemen." The minister knew that New England would be very unhappy if it allowed *"any luke warm Politicians"* to gain power, for then "Courtier" rulers would not be far behind. The future of the entire Puritan experiment in the New World lay with the voters: "What say ye now ye Freemen of New England?"[54] In the mother country of the 1620s appeals like this one had hit the mark, for the Puritans of that period had thoroughly disliked their rulers (see chap. 1). But in Massachusetts half a century later the rhetoric about lukewarm magistrates seemed a little stale. It was not that the freemen did not appreciate the right to elect civil leaders; rather it was that they had come to look for different characteristics in their rulers than those recommended by the Jeremiahs. The people shared the ministers' vision, but not to the point of voting any magistrates out of office.

Perhaps because of their failure to influence elections, many Jeremiahs turned to nonpolitical means for reforming the society. In the late 1670s the practice of renewing the covenant became fairly common throughout New England.[55] The members of a church would meet, often accompanied by their children, and after a period of fasting and prayer, would pledge as a group to uphold their covenant

53. Allen, *New-Englands Choicest Blessing*, p. 7.

54. John Oxenbridge, *New-England Freemen Warned and Warmed* . . . (Boston, 1673), pp. 8–9, 28, 33, 44. Also see Increase Mather, *Danger of Apostasy*, p. 91.

55. Miller, *New England Mind*, 2: 114–19.

with the Lord. The Jeremiahs hoped that this public display would awaken the people to the value of a scriptural life and thus bring Massachusetts closer to the ideal commonwealth. In 1678 the Reverend Thomas Cobbet explained to Increase Mather that "I know no other externall means left to further our reformation . . . but a solemne renewing of Covenant with God by all & every of our respective churches."[56] What is important to us about this new ceremony was that it did not involve the magistrate in any official capacity. The renewals offered the clergy a method of combating sin, of leading the Puritans back to the piety of the founders, without calling on the rulers for assistance.

Some Jeremiahs proposed using history as a supplement to covenant renewals. Increase Mather suggested that a printed chronicle describing the Lord's special providences in Massachusetts might awaken the people from their moral stupor, for it would demonstrate—almost empirically—that the colonists had a responsibility to please God.[57] In his election sermon of 1679 James Allen supported Mather's idea, counseling his listeners, "Acquaint your selves with the History of the glorious works of God . . . [for] the full story of *this* people to this day would be one of the best of humane Histories."[58] The project was even more appealing because it required no magisterial assistance. According to an enthusiastic John Higginson, a book of this type would even be of benefit to the clergy, uniting them "in the cause of Religion, which is our predominant interest & cause."[59]

The Jeremiahs' reluctant decision to go it alone, to rely on their own devices for bringing about moral reform, had an important impact on Puritan political theory. For decades New Englanders had assumed that rulers were responsible for the religious purity of the

56. *4 Collections*, MHS, 8: 289.

57. Increase Mather, *Danger of Apostasy*, p. 71. Increase's son, Cotton, provided the Puritans with an account of God's work in New England when he wrote *Magnalia Christi Americana*. For more material on Increase Mather's interest in history as a way of reforming New England see Gay, *A Loss of Mastery*, pp. 55–56.

58. Allen, *New-Englands Choicest Blessing*, p. 13.

59. John Higginson to Increase Mather, 5 Feb. 1683, *4 Collections*, MHS, 8: 284.

commonwealth. As everyone knew, Winthrop had harried dissenters out of Massachusetts, but the magistrates of the rising generation would harry no more. In the realm of political theory, at least, it was no longer clear what characteristics the ruler should possess. During the 1680s, how were the freemen to distinguish a good magistrate from a bad one? With religion out of politics, how could the citizen justify civil disobedience? Revolution? These were questions which New England Puritans would soon have to answer.

Three Cases: Prudence, Property, and Appeasement

There were some in New England who regarded the Jeremiahs' lament for a former age as both irresponsible and misdirected. They knew that the character of the magisterial office had changed a good deal since Winthrop's time, and they wanted to bring political theory into line with political fact. William Hubbard, Samuel Nowell, and Joseph Dudley were three members of the rising generation who brought fresh ideas to the ongoing discussion about the nature of civil government; and each attempted in his own way to demonstrate that a person did not have to be a Nehemiah, or even a Moses, to qualify as a good ruler.

To a certain extent, these three men were as different from each other as they were from the Jeremiahs, and each had his own notions about the duties of the magisterial calling. Hubbard, for example, rejected Mather's rigid formulas for moral reformation, arguing instead for a moderate policy toward religious dissenters. Only through prudence and flexibility, he insisted, could the magistrates of the Bay Colony ever construct that ordered community which had been their fathers' dream. But Samuel Nowell showed no particular concern about the purity of the Congregational churches. He analyzed the ruler's relation to private property and concluded that Puritans could justly rebel against any magistrate who seized or threatened the security of their property. And lastly, men of Dudley's persuasion turned their backs on the local bickering in church and state. They were willing to make a separate peace with old England, believing that colonial leaders should accept and enforce the imperial system, especially when they could work that system to their own advantage. What these three individuals held in common was a desire to adapt the theoretical characteristics of the good ruler to the realities of New England politics.

William Hubbard was a Puritan, as much a Puritan, in fact, as Increase Mather. Why he challenged the Jeremiahs' political views is unclear, for in other respects his life certainly seemed a model of conventional behavior. Hubbard graduated with Harvard's first class in 1642, taking up residence later in Ipswich where he became a Congregational minister. The key to Hubbard's intellectual development was perhaps not so much what he did as what he read. His major published works, *The Happiness of a People in the Wisdome of their Rulers* (1676), *The Benefit of a Well-Ordered Conversation* (1684), and *A General History of New-England* (1680), revealed his impressive command of classical and Renaissance literature. He did not hesitate to support his ideas about the character of the good ruler from the writings of the "great *Italian Polititian*" or to cite the military tactics of the Roman general, Fabius.[60] Like Roger Williams, Hubbard probably formed his opinions about government and society upon a lifelong study of theology and history, upon a blend of Puritan and non-Puritan thought.

In one important respect, however, the specific problems of the rising generation influenced Hubbard's political thinking. Over the years he had come to hate dissension, all dissension, whether in church or state, and he reminded his quarrelsome contemporaries that God had purposely created order out of confusion so that man could share the joys of divine harmony. "It was Order," Hubbard preached, "that gave Beauty to this goodly fabrick of the world, which before was but a confused Chaos, without form and void."[61]

Since order assumed such an important place in Hubbard's thought, it is not surprising that he saw the Puritans' gravest sin not as intemperate drinking or gaming as some had claimed, but as petty squabbling over insignificant issues The dispute about the Half-Way Covenant, the argument about the charter, the feud about religious dissenters, all of these disagreements disrupted God's ordered system, shattering man's intended tranquillity. The members of the rising

60. William Hubbard, *The Happiness of a People in the Wisdome of Their Rulers* (Boston, 1676), pp. 13, 33.

61. Ibid., p. 8.

generation had no business fighting when they knew that such behavior only offended the Lord. "It is one great part of the unhappiness of this life, that neither wise nor good men are all of one mind," Hubbard explained, "but yet all due care had need be taken, that differences be made neither more nor greater then they are, or carried on with such Animosity or bitterness, as should prejudice the interest of Religion, or welfare of the Commonwealth."[62] The magistrate's job was not to crush this or that heresy or to rush about waving the sword of God. To the contrary, more than anyone else in the community, he bore the responsibility to see that all citizens lived in peace.

What particularly distinguished Hubbard's political writing from that of other colonial clergymen was his sense of history, for he saw far more clearly than they did that time was a dynamic force in human events and that society was in a continuous state of flux. In his election sermon of 1676 Hubbard relied on a simple analogy to explain to the members of the General Court how the movement of time influenced government affairs. As an individual matures, he takes on new attitudes and responsibilities, and the difficulties of the child are not usually those of the adult. The same was true in the state; for, as the years passed, the ruler found himself confronted with changing and varied conditions. Since each generation faced different problems, the wise magistrate avoided trying to govern the present by the civil policies of the past.[63] Hubbard's ideas about the evolution of the political environment had special relevance for what he called his own "curious Age." It seemed clear enough to him that Massachusetts desperately needed rulers who were "understanding in the times," men not rigidly bound by irrelevant precedents.[64] The Jeremiahs may well have noted the impact of land and trade upon the character of New England, but, according to Hubbard, when they called for intransigent Nehemiahs they simply did not know what they were talking about.

Hubbard's "understanding" rulers possessed a special kind of pru-

62. Ibid., p. A3.
63. Ibid., pp. A2–A3.
64. Ibid., p. A2; William Hubbard, *The Benefit of a Well-Ordered Conversation* (Boston, 1684), pp. 135–36.

dence—not an abstract wisdom, but an ability to achieve a desired end at the most opportune moment.[65] The Ipswich minister had learned, perhaps from personal experience, that "they are not the wisest men that know most, but they that know what is most useful and proper to bring about the designe they have in hand."[66] In other words, the good magistrate had to be as flexible as possible in the formulation of civil policy, recognizing the influence of "time and chance" on government affairs.[67] Another important part of political prudence was self-control; for, as Hubbard observed, impetuosity in office led to erroneous judgments which in turn jeopardized the security of the entire commonwealth.[68] Of course, the magistrate needed to demonstrate a certain zealousness in defending funda-mental truths, but for opinions of less certainty "it can not be part of wisdom to be *too eager or rigorous* about them."[69] Although Hubbard wrote in general terms, it was clear that he would never have condoned the execution of Quakers or the harassment of Bap-tists, for violence in the cause of truth was self-defeating. Not only were the dissenters encouraged by their own martyrdom, but the Bible Commonwealth lost favor in the Stuart court. Adopting a military metaphor Hubbard advised the Bay leaders, "It is better sometimes to march about to gain the wind than to fall directly upon the Enemy."[70]

Hubbard realized that his discussion of the ruler's understanding, prudence, and wisdom might alienate some of the colonists, for the men who listened to his sermons recognized Machiavellian doctrines when they heard them. Most New Englanders retained—at least, rhetorically—the old Puritan fear of the "great *Italian Politician,*" claiming that his Renaissance policies would poison their godly com-munity. Hubbard tried to steer clear of trouble by pointing out that he had only advocated "Christian prudence" and would never coun-tenance evil acts performed for supposedly good ends.[71] Moreover,

65. Hubbard, *Well-Ordered Conversation,* pp. 135–36.
66. Hubbard, *Happiness of a People,* p. 5.
67. Ibid.
68. Hubbard, *Well-Ordered Conversation,* p. 147.
69. Hubbard, *Happiness of a People,* p. 31.
70. Hubbard, *Well-Ordered Conversation,* p. 147.
71. Hubbard, *Happiness of a People,* p. A3.

he had no intention either of putting "God into the Devils service" or of calling "the Devil into Gods service." Both possibilities, the minister tactfully insisted, were abominations.[72]

Hubbard's political ideas also involved another, more serious, difficulty. If the prudent magistrate was able to solve so many government problems through the use of his own wisdom, then what was God's role in civil events? Hubbard responded that all rulers were the Lord's "instruments" no matter how self-reliant they appeared. "The persons of the best, and most prudent men," he explained, "are not in their own power, or at their own disposal; but are guided by a Divine Providence."[73] He added, however, as no Jeremiah would have done, that God sometimes places an "Achitophel" or a "Machiavel" in the world for His own special purposes. These crafty figures seemed hardly reprehensible when Hubbard coupled their names with the Lord's "radiant beams."[74] What the Ipswich minister had done, in effect, was to throw the ball right back to Mather and his friends. If crafty rulers, say Leverett or Dudley, were the Lord's tools, then how could the Jeremiahs maintain that New England had fallen from grace? By Hubbard's standards the magistrates of the rising generation could be as fully God's vice-gerents as Winthrop had been, even though they were reluctant to launch a moral crusade.

Hubbard especially hoped that "radiant beams" would bless the magistrates when they dealt with the question of religious toleration. He realized, as so many of his contemporaries did not, that "hot" and "fiery" defenders of orthodoxy could not maintain the purity of the church nearly so well as men of "sedate" and "composed" tempers.[75] Overzealousness on the magistrate's part revealed a complete lack of "Christian Prudence"; for, as Hubbard noted, one of the major lessons of history was that persecution seldom convinces its victims of their error. Civil dissenters were psychologically no different from those in religion, for both "by *fair* meanes may be gained, but by too much *severity* are apt to run into uncurable op-

72. Hubbard, *Well-Ordered Conversation*, p. 139–40.
73. Ibid., pp. 162, 132.
74. Ibid., p. 150.
75. Ibid., pp. 40–41.

position and obstinacy."[76] Hubbard even criticized Moses for his impolitic fanaticism; since, by calling the Israelites rebels, the biblical leader had been "more like to increase the Rebellion of their wills against God, than any way alter that evill disposition of their minds."[77] The Jeremiahs called for Old Testament intolerance, but common sense counseled moderation in the handling of dissent both in and out of the Congregational churches.

Hubbard ran into some difficulty when it came to defining the specific religious duties of the ruler's calling, for he rejected extreme tolerance as well as intolerance. The minister weakly informed the members of the General Court that "it is scarce possible to give any general rule about Toleration, that will suit with all times and places, but much must be left to the prudence and discretion, and religious care of Civill Rulers."[78] As long as men did not disturb the public peace or question "fundamental" doctrine, then Hubbard could see no value in persecution. Indeed, he was willing to allow freedom of worship to those individuals who could not accept "every thing professed or practiced in the Religion established."[79] Understanding magistrates would show flexibility in their treatment of dissenters by dealing with each case on its own merits. Hubbard felt certain that his own moderate suggestions could eventually end the futile religious fights in Massachusetts and restore harmony to the commonwealth.[80]

Like most Puritans of this period, Hubbard valued very highly the right to hold free civil elections; and in 1676 he told the General Court that "Our Election is the foundation of our Government." Hubbard had no illusions about the wonders of democracy, however, for his study of history had taught him that men usually misused the right to vote, making their privilege "an occasion of the greatest bondage."[81] Unfortunately, other systems of government had been even worse. So, in spite of the danger of electoral abuse, the min-

76. Hubbard, *Happiness of a People*, p. A3.
77. Ibid., p. 20.
78. Ibid., p. 39. Hubbard was willing to tolerate any group that did not openly blaspheme the Lord or disturb the civil peace (ibid., pp. 36–37).
79. Ibid., p. 41.
80. See Daniel Denison, *Irenicon, or a Salve for New-England's Sore*, printed with Hubbard's *Well-Ordered Conversation*.
81. Ibid., pp. 26, 25.

ister was forced to conclude that only civil authority based on a popular franchise could preserve the "common good and publick safety"
over a long period of time.[82]

Despite his emphasis on prudence and tolerance, Hubbard did
not think that he had deserted the Puritans' original goals, for his
ultimate aim was a godly, peaceful, and united commonwealth. He
knew that the Jeremiahs would label his appeal for "understanding"
magistrates as political heresy. Nevertheless, with men like Mather
in mind, he instructed the members of the General Court to ignore
criticism from persons who had no calling for government. Rulers
alone possessed the talents necessary for making civil policy, and no
one else could rightfully usurp that function. In his election sermon
of 1676 he warned the legislators, "it is possible you may be im-
portunately molested with the clamours of these and those, to make
this or that change in your course, to gratifie particular mens
humours, of which you need take no more notice then the skillful
Pilot at the helme use to doe of the cryes of the unskillful, fearful
Passengers that think that course will ruine the vessel, which [ac-
tually] is the only way to preserve it."[83] Hubbard's purpose was clear.
With as much directness as the sermonic rhetoric would allow he was
calling the Jeremiahs shams, men who claimed to have glimpsed
the ultimate truth when, in fact, they were merely speaking from
their own private prejudice.

As Hubbard had predicted, the unskillful and fearful of his generation did attack his political views as apostasy.[84] Yet, at the same
time, several important leaders supported Hubbard, apparently accepting his prudent tactics. He was a close friend of Daniel Denison,
a Massachusetts assistant who adopted a moderate position on the
question of religious intolerance. Denison's own essay, *Irenicon, or
a Salve for New England's Sore,* was a perfect complement to Hub-

82. William Hubbard, *A Narrative of the Troubles with the Indians*
(Boston, 1677), p. A2.
83. Hubbard, *Happiness of a People,* p. A3.
84. Increase Mather's election sermon of 1677, *A Discourse Concerning
the Danger of Apostasy,* attacked all the ideas which Hubbard had advanced
in his 1676 election sermon, *The Happiness of a People;* Miller, *New England Mind,* 2: 136–37.

bard's *Well-Ordered Conversation,* and the two works were published together.

Samuel Nowell differed from Hubbard not only in thought, but also in style. The Ipswich minister called for peace and understanding, and his tone was usually calm. But Nowell was a fire breather whose writings appealed to arms, resistance, and war. Nowell's violent posture thoroughly frightened Edward Randolph, the imperial agent, who informed his superiors that this New Englander was "preaching up rebellion."[85] Like Hubbard, Nowell graduated from Harvard College and then studied for the ministry. He came from a highly respected family; Increase Nowell, his father, had been the colony's secretary and an assistant for twenty-five years. During the Indian uprisings of the mid-1670s, known as King Philip's War, Samuel Nowell served as a chaplain for the troops and, according to Cotton Mather, demonstrated outstanding courage in battle.[86] In 1678 Nowell delivered the artillery election sermon, *Abraham in Arms,* to the militia of Massachusetts. The clerical life, however, did not hold his interest, and he was never ordained in a settled pastorate. In 1680 he decided to change his vocation altogether by allowing the freemen to choose him as one of their magistrates. He continued in that position until 1686 when England imposed a new appointive government upon the Puritan colonies. Apparently the

85. In 1682 Randolph described Nowell as "a late factious preacher and now a magistrate." Two years later, the imperial agent told Samuel Shrimpton that Nowell had preached "up rebellion" in his artillery sermon, *Abraham in Arms.* As late as October 1688, ten years after Nowell had delivered the offensive sermon, Randolph was still complaining that the work was an example of New England's disloyalty to the king (Toppan and Goodrick, *Edward Randolph,* 3: 155, 318; 4: 245). Perhaps the colonists circulated Nowell's sermon as a protest, almost a whispering campaign, against Andros's regime. In any case, *Abraham in Arms* stands with John Wise's *A Vindication of the Government of New England Churches* and Jonathan Mayhew's *A Discourse Concerning Unlimited Submission and Non-Resistance to the Higher Powers: With Some Reflections on the Resistance Made to King Charles I* as one of the most important statements of Puritan political theory.

86. See John Langdon Sibley, *Biographical Sketches of Graduates of Harvard University* (Cambridge, Mass., 1873), 1; James Savage, *A Genealogical Dictionary of the First Settlers of New England,* 4 vols. (Boston, 1860–62).

people of Massachusetts liked Nowell's tough, outspoken opposition to imperial schemes, for in their last general election before the charter fell, they gave him more votes than they did to any other candidate.[87]

Nowell wanted to preserve Massachusetts' royal patent chiefly because it insulated the colony from English influence. While the charter stood the Puritans could administer the Navigation Acts in their own way and treat visiting commissioners as they chose. Like many of his contemporaries, Nowell had come to place great value on the colony's independence; and, as early as 1676, he warned his friend John Bull about the imperial danger: "As for ourselves in New Engld, we are fearing a Generall Governour. How God will deale with us in our present businesse is uncertaine. I suppose you will judge it convenient to remove, if any such thing should happen, as that a Governour should be sent; although if this man live who is Governour at Boston [John Leverett], I believe the country will oppose." But if anything happened to Leverett, Nowell feared that Simon Bradstreet, the man assured of becoming the next chief magistrate, would not "have spirit enough, or interest enough, to withstand the Authority of Old Engld."[88] To see how different Nowell's attitudes were from those of the Jeremiahs, one only has to remember that Bradstreet was one of the original founders of Massachusetts, a man who supposedly understood the colony's godly mission. When Bradstreet actually did attain the governorship in 1679, Nowell joined with seven other magistrates—"like the late Rump in England"—to protect the charter from London's interference.[89] In 1682 he threw Edward Randolph into a fit by asserting

87. Sibley, *Graduates of Harvard*, 1. Nowell was an assistant for six terms, 1680–86.

88. Samuel Nowell to Jonathan Bull, 25 Sept. 1676, *4 Collections*, MHS, 8: 573.

89. Edward Randolph believed that Deputy Governor Thomas Danforth headed the pro-charter "faction" which included magistrates Samuel Appleton, Bartholomew Gedney, John Richards, Humphrey Davy, James Russell, Nathaniel Saltonstall, Daniel Gookin, and Samuel Nowell. The "faction" opposed a party led by Governor Bradstreet which advocated closer ties with England. In November 1682 Randolph wrote, "It's very true here are many sober & loyall Gentlemen & men of estates in this Colony, who were they in power would with all Cheerefulnes Submitt to

that certain acts of Parliament had no legal force within Massa-chusetts.[90] Nowell believed that it was the ruler's responsibility to maintain the colony's autonomy; but, unlike Increase Mather, he seldom mentioned New England's unique religious heritage. His Nehemiahs, if in fact they were Nehemiahs, were politicians who fought external, foreign enemies before they attacked domestic sin.

Abraham in Arms was one of the more innovative discussions of political theory produced by the rising generation. Whereas the Jeremiahs wrote of liberty in terms of the right to restrict religious dissent, Nowell saw it in a broader context, placing greater emphasis on the ruler's responsibility to protect private property. "There is

---

& promote a thro' regulation & a perfect Conformity to his Majesties lawes: but so long as the faction, whereof Mr. Danforth is the Chiefe (like the late Rump in England) beare down all by their numbers of votes in the house of Deputyes at a Generall Court . . . Very few honest men can be admitted into places of trust or creditt, if the matter be left to their ordering" (Toppan and Goodrick, *Edward Randolph*, 1: 159; 3: 129–31, 214).

90. Ibid., 1: 159; 3: 129; 6: 88. In the early 1680s the General Court sent John Richards, a friend of Nowell's, and Joseph Dudley, to England in order to lobby for the Massachusetts Charter. Their mission was probably hopeless from the start, for Stuart authorities had already decided to ask the courts to issue a *Quo Warranto* against the Bay patent. In March 1683 Nowell wrote to Richards, who was depressed by the impossibility of his assignment. "I am heartily sorry," Nowell explained, "for that unavoidable exercise which the only wise God hath been pleased to carve out for you, it being not possible to please the country & the Court too." Then Nowell told Richards what he believed would happen if the charter fell:

By our Pattent we have full & absolute power to rule & governe, pardon & punish, etc.; by which allways hithertoo we have judged ourselves free from appeales, & either we may finally judge of & determine all things, or else appeals be in all cases, wch will make the Governmt here to be a meer cypher, more contemptible than any other Governmt in all the Plantations, in regard we are under an ill aspect; hence every pragmatick pson will refuse to submit to the judgment of our courts, hoping for relief in Engld, or by some com-missioners here, to which our Government must be subordinate; the case in 1664. [5 *Collections,* MHS, 1: 434–35]

Nowell's fears about the loss of the charter are purely political and there-fore, a great contrast to the Jeremiahs' belief that church and patent were one and the same cause.

such a thing as Liberty and Property given to us," he explained, "both by the Laws of God & Men, when these are invaded, we may defend our selves. God hath not given great ones in the world that absolute power over men, to devour them at pleasure, as great Fishes do the little ones; he hath set Rulers their bounds & by his Law hath determined peoples libertyes and prosperity." Nowell stated emphatically that when a citizen owns something, then another person "being stronger" cannot "make our Right Null and void."[91] When he preached the artillery sermon, he did not abandon the Jeremiahs' religious rhetoric; he used it to another purpose. Nowell's importance to Puritan political theory lay in his claim that God cared about men's property as well as their souls. He implied that the Lord would punish magistrates who illegally seized their constituents' estates; and in so doing he modified Christopher Goodman's argument by substituting property for idolatry and by giving divine sanction to rebellion against those who ignored God's will (see chap. 1).

Nowell's message was essentially the same one that William Pynchon had delivered to the government of Connecticut in the 1640s, for the laws of New England still regarded a man's property as a tender thing (see chap. 2). But Nowell's ideas possessed a threatening intensity which Pynchon's letters had lacked. He asserted in *Abraham in Arms* that "it is lawfull by war to defend what we have lawfully obtained and come by, as our possessions, lands and inheritance here, to which we have as fair a title as any ever had, since Israels title to Canaan."[92] Nowell came very close to calling property a natural right, and he may have been familiar with the pamphlet literature of the Exclusion crisis which foreshadowed the political philosophy of John Locke.[93] In any case, Nowell hated the greedy placemen who came across the Atlantic in search of fortune, and he agreed with the anonymous Boston poet who described Randolph's 1679 arrival in Massachusetts:

91. Samuel Nowell, *Abraham in Arms* (Boston, 1678), p. 10.
92. Nowell, *Abraham in Arms*, pp. 3–4.
93. See B. Behrens, "The Whig Theory of the Constitution in the Reign of Charles II," *Cambridge Historical Journal* 8 (1941–43): 44–70; Peter Laslett's introduction to *John Locke: Two Treatises of Government* (New York, 1963), pp. 15–92.

> Soe Royal Charles is now about to prove
> Our Loyalty, Allegiance, and Love,
> In giving Licence to a Publican,
> To Pinch the purse, but not hurt the man.
> Patience raised Job unto the height of fame,
> Lett our obedience doe for us the same.[94]

Nowell's good rulers were warriors, "Lion-like men," who trained their people "to be expert in War" and to defend their rights and property against all possible dangers. "The Law of nature, which teacheth men self-preservation" commanded that citizens understand "the use of arms, or other parts of military exercise." Nowell warned the colonists that if they did not learn the martial arts quickly, they should "resolve to be *vassals*." He did not think that the local Indians were a major threat or that they were going to subjugate New England. Indeed, God had placed the Indians in America as a favor so that the Puritans could study and perfect the methods of war! The minister told the local militia that Massachusetts urgently needed to develop its horse or mounted cavalry, for without this weapon an invader could easily defeat the colonial foot soldiers. Everyone in the 1678 audience must have seen through the speaker's thinly veiled references, for obviously the enslaving enemy was the English government.[95] It was no wonder then that Randolph accused Nowell of "preaching up rebellion."

Nowells' thoughts on revolution were his most significant contribution to Puritan political theory. The founders of New England had arrived in America committed to the idea that the orthodoxy of the ruler's religion determined civil obedience. Roger Williams, of course, rejected that concept; but his criticisms had little influence on most of the Puritans, who insisted that the Lord required the overthrow of all ungodly magistrates as well as "neuter-temporizers." But by the late 1670s, as we have already seen, the Jeremiahs had begun to move away from politics, concentrating their energies more on covenant renewals and history books. These ministers, albeit reluctantly, took an important step toward the separation of religious and civil affairs, and thereby left the Puritans without an intellectual

94. Toppan and Goodrick, *Edward Randolph*, 3: 63–64.
95. Nowell, *Abraham in Arms*, pp. 5, 10, 11, 18.

justification for resisting their rulers. Nowell partially filled that void, for his own forceful assertion of the magistrates' duty to protect private property hinted at a fresh rationalization for civil disobedience. Nowell began to rechannel the revolutionary force always inherent in Puritan political theory toward more worldly concerns; and, together with the pamphleteers of the Glorious Revolution, who we will examine later, prepared the way for John Wise and other eighteenth-century authors. But, more immediately, the men who shared Nowell's ideas sparked the 1689 rebellion in Massachusetts and deposed Sir Edmund Andros. The imperial planners should have paid closer attention in 1678 when Nowell warned, "Let but a Prince never so great, tread upon a worm, and it will turn; they have that instinct in them to defend themselves."[96]

A third body of colonists shared neither Mather's concern about religious declension nor Nowell's fear that the Puritans would become English vassals. On the contrary, the members of this group came to love, respect, and envy England and hoped to partake in the financial and cultural opportunities offered by the mother country. While most New Englanders grumbled about Randolph's meddling in their affairs, the appeasers ingratiated themselves with the royal officials.

Those of the rising generation who began to look to the Stuart court for favor were mostly civil leaders; and, unlike the ministers, they seldom bothered to publish their ideas about the character of the ruler's calling. However, Edward Randolph's correspondence during the 1670s and 1680s indirectly revealed some of their political attitudes. Randolph was particularly candid in his description of Joseph Dudley, an assistant in the Bay Colony. "Major Dudley," he told the Anglican Bishop of London, "is a great opposer of the faction [the extreme procharter group] heere . . . who, if he finds things resolutely manniged, will cringe and bow to anything; *he hath his fortune to make in the world.*" Randolph suggested that if the king gave Dudley some lucrative post like the captaincy of the Boston castle, then "his Majesty will gaine a popular man and obleige the better party."[97] In 1682 the General Court sent Dudley and another

96. Ibid., p. 10.
97. Toppan and Goodrick, *Edward Randolph*, 3: 145.

man to England to defend the colony's patent from possible revocation; and, although their diplomatic mission failed, Dudley did not waste the trip.[98] When James II rescinded the charter and set up an appointive council in 1686, he chose Dudley as the head of the new government.

In many ways William Stoughton's career paralleled Dudley's. Stoughton was a sort of New England Vicar of Bray, who always managed to turn up on the victorious side of every political struggle. He left the Congregational ministry to become an assistant in 1671, and after 1686 he too was appointed to the Royal Council.[99] No doubt other individuals followed Dudley's and Stoughton's accommodating path and made their peace with Stuart authority.

Why men like Dudley grew indifferent to many elements of the New England Puritan heritage is not clear. The desire for money, power, and patronage may have been the major consideration, or perhaps they were simply disenchanted with the petty squabbling both in church and state.[100] Whatever their motives may have been, they represented a new type of ruler in the Bay Colony; for they were the first colonial leaders who bridged the gap between London and Boston society, who charmed Puritan voters as well as royal officials. But their story properly belongs to a subsequent period of Massachusetts history when the Stoughtons and the Dudleys controlled the colony. Their later success in the world of imperial politics, however, showed the degree to which some members of the rising generation had become cultural anglophiles. These new rulers realized that stern and righteous magistrates would not receive Stuart patronage. In fact, the future seemed to belong to those who could best please the king (see chap. 6).

The Politics of Dissension

The rulers of the rising generation were no more successful than were the ministers in defining the nature of magisterial office. In

98. See n. 90; Everett Kimball, *The Public Life of Joseph Dudley* (New York, 1911), pp. 10–14; and chap. 4 and 6.

99. See Sibley, *Graduates of Harvard*, 1: 194–208.

100. Miller, *New England Mind*, 2: 141; Bailyn, *New England Merchants*, pp. 175–76.

fact, they spent a surprising amount of energy quarreling over an issue which some men had believed settled in 1645. In that year, as we have seen, Governor John Winthrop announced that, since God had not granted the representatives special judicial skills, they could not claim to be magistrates. While the deputies may well have disagreed with Winthrop's view, no one at the time bothered to attack his position in public (see chap. 2). The peace within the Massachusetts legislature was short-lived, however, for by the mid-1660s the deputies and assistants were once again squabbling over the powers of the magisterial office, each side claiming that the other had overstepped its proper bounds. What distinguished this debate from that of the earlier period was the type of political argumentation or language which the contestants used. For the most part the younger Puritans spoke of the ruler's calling not in terms of Scripture, but in terms of personal experience, common sense, and charter rights.

The first hint of the dissension that was again brewing within the General Court came in 1667 when the assistants asked the church elders to help them restore a "loving composure" in the legislature.[101] There is no record of the ministers' recommendations; but, whatever their advice may have been, it failed to accomplish any loving end, for relations between the magistrates and deputies deteriorated steadily after this time. Only the savage and costly war against the Indians, King Philip's War, brought a temporary moratorium to the political controversy. As soon as the troops had put down the Indian threat, however, the two houses returned to their quarrel which continued unabated until England forced a new form of government upon Massachusetts in 1686.

A statute concerning judicial appeals, passed in 1652, originally sparked the renewal of controversy. The law stated that "if there fall out any difference betwixt the Magistrates and the Deputyes, in any case of judicature, either civill or criminall, it shall be determined *by the major part of the whole Court*."[102] Why the magistrates consented to the law of 1652 is not clear, for it repudiated the veto in judicial matters which they had fought so hard to preserve during

101. Massachusetts Archives, 48: 80.
102. *Mass. Records,* 4: pt. 1, p. 82 (italics added).

Goody Sherman's "sow case." Confusion seems to have surrounded the passage of the order, and the members of the upper house may well not have explored its full implications.[103] Whatever the case, the 1652 law did not become a public issue for more than fifteen years. Indeed, it was not until the late 1660s that the assistants realized that they had erred, "doubtless through inadvertency."[104] The upper house set out to rectify its mistake by having the obnoxious act either repealed or amended; and over the next two decades the restoration of the negative voice in judicial affairs became an obsession for the magistrates.[105]

Throughout the long legislative controversy, the assistants protested that the words *"by the major part of the whole Court"* deprived them of the special judicial prerogatives to which their calling entitled them. They claimed that when disputed appeals were settled by the majority vote of the entire General Court, a deputy's opinion counted as much as a magistrate's, and such equality was unacceptable to the assistants. To make matters worse, the members of the

103. The 1652 law reads:

> Whereas there is a manifest & inconvenient mistake in the penning of the order, title Generall Court, page the 8th of the last printed booke, that leaves all or most of the case formerly issued in the Generall Court doubtfull & uncertaine, and takes away the negative vote, both of Magistrates and Deputyes, in making lawes, as well in case of judicature, which was not intended, much less consented to, itt is therefore ordered, that for time to come, if there fall out any difference betwixt the Magistrates and Deputyes, in any case of judicature either civill or criminall, it shall be determined by the major part of the whole court, and the forementioned lawe is hereby repealed *(Mass. Records, 4: pt. 1, p. 82)*.

For a good discussion of the history of this controversial act, see Whitmore, *Colonial Laws of Massachusetts,* pp. 110–16. For another example of the confusion over the printed laws at this time, read T. H. Breen, "Who Governs: The Town Franchise in Seventeenth-Century Massachusetts," *William and Mary Quarterly,* 3d ser., 27(1970).

104. Massachusetts Archives, 48: 114. There are no records in the archives which explain why this controversy flared up when it did. I know of no cause célèbre comparable to the Sherman case in this period.

105. My discussion of the judicial veto relies heavily on Mark Howe's and Louis Eaton's excellent article, "The Supreme Judicial Power in the Colony of Massachusetts Bay," *New England Quarterly* 20(1947).

two houses took different oaths of office; and, in an age that treated oaths with great sanctity, this difference was not unimportant. On the one hand, the representatives swore to resolve all judicial questions that came before them by private "judgment & conscience"; in other words, when they acted in a judicial capacity, they formed a court of equity, not being bound to observe the guidelines of positive law.[106] The magistrates' oath, on the other hand, obliged the members of the upper house to confine their decisions to limits established by colonial law and ordinance. The assistants insisted that some reform was necessary to remove the confusion that resulted when the legislature sat as a supreme court of appeals, for it seemed absurd to them that the magistrates and deputies should simultaneously judge the same case by conflicting legal standards. Throughout the dispute the upper house was willing to accept two possible solutions to the problem: either the entire General Court would take the same oath, preferably the deputy's, and thus become a uniform court of chancery; or second, the magistrates would be given veto power over the judgments of *"the major part of the whole Court."* But neither of these suggestions was acceptable to the representatives, and they resisted every attempt to repeal or alter the law of 1652.[107]

Between 1667 and 1673 the dispute over the judicial question upset almost every session of the General Court. Usually, the assistants acting on their own authority would change or revoke the 1652 law and then urge the deputies to follow suit. But each year the representatives would refuse, causing tempers on both sides to rise to an ever higher pitch.[108] In 1672 the frustrated magistrates wrote a detailed brief summarizing their arguments in support of reform. They explained that the 1652 order unjustly stripped them of the governing powers guaranteed to the magistrates by the king's patent. The problem as they defined it was whether "the freemen or their delegates (which we acknowledge) may by their greater number override the conclusion & finally determine any and every case without the consent and against the judgment of any of the magistrates,

106. Massachusetts Archives, 48: 85; Whitmore, *Colonial Laws of Massachusetts*, p. 142.
107. Massachusetts Archives, 48: 114.
108. Ibid., pp. 85, 105, 110, 111, 113.

or whether the consent of some of the magistrates with the d puties be
not absolutely necessary to make any valid act in the General Court."
The assistants felt that their demands were in harmony with "the
plaine literal sense & true meaning of the patent, the foundation of
our government."[109] The men who wrote this brief declared that,
since constitutional guidelines established by charter superseded the
positive laws passed by the Massachusetts legislature, the act of 1652
was illegal and of no effect. The magisterial argument, however, did
not convince the representatives that they had anything to gain by
reform, and the dispute continued.[110]

In May 1673 the General Court formed a committee of ten, consisting of magistrates, ministers, and deputies, to arbitrate the judicial controversy which by this time had become the legislature's major
concern.[111] Unfortunately the committee's actions only pointed up
the difficulty of reaching any agreement about the ruler's proper
authority; for, instead of bringing peace, its members repeated in
exaggerated form opinions already present within the General Court.
The arbitrators were evenly divided; five of them supported the
magistrates' position, while five denied the need for a negative voice
in judicial matters. The two groups ultimately submitted to the
legislature separate reports which helped to clarify the issues at stake,
even though they did little to restore a "loving composure."

The statement written by the committeemen who supported the
lower house revealed how angry some of the representatives had
become; for these five arbitrators not only attacked the idea of a
negative in judicial appeals, but also made a gratuitous blast at the
magisterial veto in all legislative affairs. The authors, Samuel
Symonds, Joshua Hobart, John Oxenbridge, John Richards, and
Henry Bartholomew, declared that it was "irrational" that a small
body of assistants should have the power to override the conclusions
of the majority.[112] They believed that all legislators, even those

109. Ibid., p. 114.
110. Ibid., p. 118; *Hutchinson Papers*, 2: 166–70.
111. Massachusetts Archives, 48: 127; *Mass. Records*, 4: pt. 2, p. 559.
112. Massachusetts Archives, 48: 125. There is no immediately obvious
reason why these five men should have joined together. Samuel Symonds
was an assistant from 1643 to 1673 and deputy governor under John
Leverett from 1673 to 1678. He is known to have resisted the efforts of the

who possessed the trappings of outward success, should be "equal with the meanest." These five men repudiated, albeit only implicitly, the political principles which Winthrop and the discretionary forces had advanced during the colony's first twenty years, for they refused to recognize any difference between the office of the magistrate and that of the deputy.

The pro-deputy committeemen went on to demonstrate that the law of 1652 was in complete harmony with the spirit of the Massachusetts Charter. When he granted the patent, Charles I had not intended for "the governor, or deputy governor, and six of the assistants" to have a negative voice in all actions of the General Court. In fact, the presence of seven magistrates was necessary only as a legislative quorum, and their assent was not required in judicial settlements.[113] The deputies of the rising generation never claimed to possess special powers by virtue of acting as the people's representatives. To the contrary, the committeemen argued that the members of the lower house, because of their legislative office alone, were as truly rulers as were any of the magistrates.

The other five committeemen, Simon Bradstreet, William Stough-

---

so-called moderate party in Massachusetts which wanted closer ties with England. Joshua Hobart was a perennial leader in the lower house and its speaker in 1674. John Richards and Henry Bartholomew were both deputies. Little is known about Bartholomew; but Richards, who became a magistrate in 1680, shared Symonds's views about English-colonial relations. John Oxenbridge was a leading minister. He delivered the election sermon of 1671 at the representatives' request (see n. 16).

Scholars have never satisfactorily explained the political factions or groupings in Massachusetts during the late Old Charter period. In *The New England Merchants in the Seventeenth Century,* Bernard Bailyn suggests that the division was between men who wanted the colony to continue as a semiautonomous commonwealth and those who favored closer economic and cultural ties with the mother country. No doubt the colony's status within the imperial system was a divisive issue, but there were many others which appear to be just as important. Political loyalties were influenced by church affiliation, family connections, and residency. Historians need to work out the intricate patterns of personal relationships before they can fully understand what was happening in the General Court during these years.

113. Massachusetts Archives, 48: 125–26.

ton, Urian Oakes, John Hull, and Samuel Torrey, defended the magisterial veto.[114] Their study of the patent revealed that it had
granted both the deputies and the assistants a negative "in all things."
These arbitrators concluded, therefore, that it was absurd for the
lower house to deny the magistrates' veto simply because there were
more deputies than assistants in the General Court. "What a strange
solecisme in Policy would it be," they declared, "that the freemen
who have so invested & betrusted the magistracy by their general
election, should yet have a power in general court [through their
representatives] to make both the office & power of the magistracy
void & of no effect in action."[115] Surprisingly, the authors of this
report made claims for the magistrates which the assistants themselves had been unwilling to assert even at the height of the controversy. Between 1667 and 1673 the members of the upper house had
accepted the deputies' right to take part in judicial decisions that
came before the General Court and had only insisted upon having
the same powers as those of the representatives. The committeemen,
however, went all the way back to Winthrop's position, stating that
neither the freemen nor their delegates possessed any judicial authority whatsoever.

The pro-magistrate group also warned the colonists that the representatives' oath to conscience exposed the public to arbitrary justice by allowing the members of the lower house discretion to decide
cases in any manner that suited their fancy. It was the magistrates
who could best secure the people's lives and estates because they had
been sworn to uphold the laws of Massachusetts. Ironically, the committeemen were using arguments which the deputies had employed
against the magistrates in the 1630s; for, in essence, Bradstreet and

114. Simon Bradstreet was one of the original founders of the Bay
Company, a longtime magistrate, and last Old Charter governor of Massachusetts. John Hull was a goldsmith who became one of the richest men in the
colony. He served as deputy for several different towns and in 1680 was
elected a magistrate. William Stoughton began his career as a minister
and delivered the election sermon in 1668. He quit the clerical calling,
however, and in 1671 was chosen one of the assistants. Historians have
often labeled Bradstreet and Stoughton as leaders of the pro-English or
moderate party in Massachusetts. Urian Oakes and Samuel Torrey were both
leading ministers in the Bay Colony.

115. Massachusetts Archives, 48: 130.

the others were advising the freemen to restrain their own delegates in the interests of popular rights and liberties.[116]

The contention over the magistrates' judicial authority affected other, seemingly unrelated, government matters; for, during the 1670s, the deputies apparently decided to challenge as many of the assistants' prerogatives as they could, partly out of pique and partly out of genuine constitutional concern. The magistrates in turn resolved to give no ground. One of the first of these confrontations occurred in 1673 when the lower house ordered that henceforth the consent of the governor, or in his absence the deputy governor, was not necessary for the passage of legislative acts. Why the representatives chose to make trouble on this issue is not clear, for the governors of Massachusetts had rarely interfered with the decisions of the General Court.[117] Whatever their motivations, the deputies' move angered the assistants, who not only rejected the bill, but also countered with one of their own, declaring that the governor's assent was vital to all statutes. Perhaps the assistants realized that if they let the lower house limit the governor, they could not very well resist future attempts to control the magistrates. The debate over the governor's office had hardly died down when the representatives put more coal on the fire. On December 19, 1673, they voted "that some gentlemen shall be added to our Honored Council [the assistants] to act in the vacancy of the General Court." Although the bill died in the upper house, the effort to restrict the magistrates' executive actions revealed that the question of interim power, debated so hotly in the 1640s, was still very much alive.[118]

During this period the representatives also tried to gain military authority at the magistrates' expense. By a law of 1669 the General

116. Ibid., p. 132; Howe and Eaton, "Supreme Judicial Power," pp. 313–14.

117. Massachusetts Archives, 48: 135, 136. The governor's powers within the General Court were never clearly defined. The colonial laws state that "the Governor shall have a casting voice whensoever an Equi vote shall fall out in the Court of Assistants, or generall assembly." The law codes of 1648 and 1660 say nothing about the governor having a veto over legislative acts. However, in 1671 Governor Bellingham appears to have rejected a bill which had been passed by both houses (48: 103). I know of no other example of a governor vetoing legislation.

118. Massachusetts Archives, 48: 143; see also chap. 3.

Court sitting as two separate bodies appointed military officers for
the colony's several shires. The deputies apparently were bothered by
the assistants' power to veto their selections, for they repeatedly
urged that military leaders be chosen "by the whole court sitting
together."[119] The magistrates had learned from the fights over the
judicial negative that once they had surrendered the veto, they might
never get it back again; and, therefore, they rejected all of the representatives' bills. The stubbornness of both houses of the legislature
on this issue led to near chaos in the military; for, when the assistants
directed the troops of Massachusetts to support British forces that
intended to recapture New York from the Dutch, the deputies told
the local soldiers to stay at home.[120] By the end of 1673 the normal
operation of government appeared threatened by the continuous
bickering within the General Court. The breakdown of effective rule
was averted, however, when King Philip's War forced the legislators
to cooperate in order to save the colony from destruction.

The temporary harmony in the General Court dissolved as soon as
the Indian danger had been removed. Although the records are in-
complete, it appears that the deputies were the first to renew the
hostility; for during the late 1670s they made several attempts, all
unsuccessful, to reduce the magistrates' income. Often the tone of
the representatives' bills was abrupt, as if intended to increase tensions
within the legislature. When New Hampshire became an independent colony with its own government in 1679, for example, the
deputies moved that the assistants' salary be lowered to twenty pounds
because the magistrates no longer had to travel so far to hold county
courts. Moreover, the deputies pointed out that since Massachusetts
had begun to elect the full eighteen assistants specified by patent, the
work of individual magistrates was much easier than it had ever
been before. The upper house vetoed this proposal without offering
any explanation. No doubt it saw the deputies' bill as part of the
growing rivalry within the General Court and not as a manifestation
of the representatives' concern for the common good.[121]

In 1685 the legislature was once again divided over the question

119. Massachusetts Archives, 67: 59, 59D.
120. Ibid., pp. 194, 194A; also pp. 60, 60B, 124.
121. Ibid., 48: 166, 170; also 153, 157.

of the magistrates' judicial veto. The assistants adopted a much more aggressive stance during this debate than they had in the disputes of the 1660s and 1670s. At one point, they even threatened to walk out of the General Court unless the deputies came to terms.[122] But the lower house apparently was not impressed by this show of force, refusing to repeal, or in any way amend, the law of 1652.[123] After much quarreling the General Court decided to create a separate Court of Chancery which would remove judicial matters from the purview of the legislature; but this reform never had a chance to prove itself, since James II annulled the Massachusetts Charter almost as soon as the order took effect.

In many ways the legislative fights of the 1670s and 1680s appear to be a natural continuation of the controversies that had divided the legislators of Winthrop's generation. To a certain extent this is a correct interpretation, for the deputies of the later period did attempt to limit the magistrates' privilege and discretion in as many ways as they could. What had changed since the 1640s were not the political goals, but the forms of argument employed to gain these goals. During the entire dispute over the magistrates' judicial veto neither the deputies nor the assistants ever mentioned the doctrine of calling or referred to William Perkins's discussion of equity. The magistrates were eager to preserve their special governing powers, but they no longer based their defense on Puritan theology.

An indication of what had happened to political rhetoric since Winthrop's time was the use made of the king's patent. In the 1630s and 1640s rulers had talked of God's Providence and biblical command; they had seen the Lord's revealed will as the chief guide for civil government. The founders rarely argued from statute or from charter alone. In the 1670s, however, rulers had begun to turn away from spiritual language in politics and to search through English and colonial laws for precedents with which they could justify their actions before the public.[124] The leaders of the rising generation spoke of the patent as their constitution and quoted from it to bolster their points. By the 1680s, in fact, many colonists treated the

122. Ibid., p. 180.
123. Ibid., 47: 77, 79, 80–81; 48: 176, 177, 180, 183, 190.
124. E.g., Massachusetts Archives, 48: 115.

charter with the kind of reverence that had previously been reserved only for Scripture.

What was even more surprising about the disputes of the 1670s and 1680s was the debaters' reliance on reason and personal experience. When the magistrates wrote their brief defending the veto in 1672, they insisted that their opinions were backed by "right reason" or "common reason."[125] At one point in their discussion, the assistants supported their case for the negative by pointing out that, because they were elected by all of the freemen at large, they were in a better position to preserve the colony's general welfare than were the deputies chosen by the individual towns. "What privilege or advantage can it be to the freemen," the magistrates asked in 1672, "to have the choice of their governor and magistrates if their lives & estates may be taken away [in case of judicial appeal] without and against their [the magistrates'] consent . . . by the deputies in whose choice not the 100d & in most not the 1000d part of them have concurred." The magistrates were not arguing as God's vicegerents on earth, but as pragmatic politicians. They appealed directly to the voters' most basic instinct, telling them that the assistants could more adequately protect their "lives & estates" than could the members of the lower house. In fact, the assistants claimed to be working for the common good, while the deputies were merely appealing to the "restless and turbulent passions of some particular persons."[126]

Despite their use of new sources and fresh approaches to the problems of government, the political leaders of the rising generation were no more successful than were their fathers in finding a definition of the good ruler which all the members of the General Court could accept. The magistrates and the deputies were as far apart in 1685 as they had been in 1644. One suspects that there may well have been something inherently divisive about the bicameral form of legislature; for, even though the same freemen elected both houses, the magistrates and the deputies took on different characteristics and defended different political points of view. Whatever the case may have been, the establishment of the Dominion of New England and the arrival of Governor Edmund Andros put an end to these problems by putting an end to the General Court.

125. Ibid., pp. 114, 116.
126. Ibid., pp. 115, 116.

4

THE GLORIOUS REVOLUTION:
1684–1691

HE events which occurred in New England between 1684 and 1691 had a crucial impact upon the development of Puritan political ideas, yet this period has seldom received the attention which it deserves. Part of the problem has been the tendency of some historians to side with Stuart administrators, praising English imperial schemes on the one hand, while condemning colonial resistance on the other. Indeed, the standard work on the Glorious Revolution in Massachusetts treats the overthrow of Governor Andros as a major tragedy in the history of Anglo-colonial affairs.[1] From the Imperial viewpoint there was simply no reason to

---

1. The standard work on the Andros regime is Viola F. Barnes's *The Dominion of New England* (New York, 1960). Her book which was originally published in 1923 reflected the biases of her teacher, Charles M. Andrews, the leader of the so-called imperial school of colonial American history. Like Andrews she felt that the English meant well by the Americans; and, if the colonists had not been so shortsighted, both culturally and economically, they would have welcomed the Navigation Acts and the government centralization of 1686.

Perry Miller, in his *The New England Mind: From Colony to Province* (Boston, 1961), offered some tantalizingly brilliant observations on the events of this period, but he did not follow up or systematically explore the evolution of Puritan political ideas (pp. 150–62). The student interested in the Glorious Revolution in Massachusetts can refer to Thomas Hutchinson, *The History of the Colony and Province of Massachusetts-Bay*, ed. Lawrence S. Mayo, 3 vols. (Boston, 1936), 1; Michael G. Hall, *Edward Randolph and the American Colonies, 1676–1703* (Chapel Hill, 1960); Herbert L. Osgood, *The American Colonies in the Seventeenth Century*, 3 vols. (New York, 1904–07), 3: 415–40; and Michael Hall, Lawrence Leder, and Michael Kammen, eds., *The Glorious Revolution in America:*

bother about Puritan political ideas or to examine how Andros influenced attitudes about the character of the good ruler.

During the twenty years preceding Andros's arrival, as we have seen, the colonists advanced various theories about what they should or should not expect their magistrates to do; but none of the ideas had been tested by rulers who were palpably bad. Andros presented the Puritans with a kind of political challenge they had not seen since the days of Sir Henry Vane, for the arbitrary policies of the Dominion governor forced them to reconsider notions about good government and good rulers, and even more important, to translate those notions into action.

The fruit of this political experience was the publication of dozens of pamphlets, essays, and broadsides in the period immediately following Andros's arrest. The New England authors, most of whom remain anonymous, hoped that their writings would justify the revolution and convince William III of the loyalty of the Puritan colonies. One historian, seizing upon the tendentious quality of this political literature, dismissed it as mere "incendiary propaganda," designed only to stir up the people in Massachusetts and to deceive royal officials in London.[2] But the pamphlets were more than a collection of half-truths and exaggerations about the Dominion of New England. They represented the first sustained discussion of political beliefs to take place in the Puritan colonies since Winthrop's death, and this revolutionary literature can be seen as an honest reflection of contemporary thought about the nature of civil government.[3]

Documents on the Colonial Crisis of 1689 (Chapel Hill, 1964), pp. 9–82. However, when one reads all of these volumes, one still comes away with the suspicion that none of these historians has seen the overthrow of Andros as the New Englanders themselves saw it. The one exception is Theodore B. Lewis, Jr., "Massachusetts and the Glorious Revolution, 1660–1692" (Ph.D. diss., University of Wisconsin, 1967).

2. Barnes, *Dominion of New England,* pp. 287–88. Barnes had little sympathy for intellectual history, especially if it had anything to do with Puritanism, and in a bibliographical essay she treated the pamphlets and broadsides which the colonists wrote in defense of their revolution as disingenuous propaganda.

3. Bernard Bailyn's two recent books on eighteenth-century political ideas have pointed out the necessity of reading political rhetoric very care-

The importance of these tracts for the history of Puritan political ideas does not become fully apparent until one has studied Andros's regime in considerable detail. The governor provided New England pamphleteers with plenty of material which they could have used against him, for none of his policies were truly popular. Significantly, however, the writers did not give equal weight to all of Andros's actions. Instead they concentrated their attack on only one aspect of his administration: ignoring things which the founders would not have overlooked.

The revolutionary authors of 1689 insisted that a good ruler had to defend popular rights, especially those associated with private property. The rebels claimed that they had acted upon the dictates of conscience when they locked Andros in jail; but conscience spoke a different language in this period than it had in Winthrop's generation. Religious considerations alone no longer seemed capable of stirring men to civil disobedience; and, according to the New England writers, Andros was unacceptable chiefly because he had seized their personal holdings through illegal and arbitrary procedures. In the early decades of the Puritan commonwealth the foundation of civil power had been godliness, and Puritan freemen made certain that "visible saints" controlled the town as well as the colonial government. But, by the time of the Glorious Revolution, property—more than godliness—served as the basis for political leadership and

---

fully, of seeing it as the product of a specific time and culture. Bailyn discovered that the pamphleteers of the American Revolution wrote of evil conspiracies, of lost Anglo-Saxon virtues, of corruption in the mother country. Until he published his studies, historians had dismissed this seemingly emotional rhetoric, insisting that constitutional precedents and common law niceties were at the core of the colonists' political beliefs. But, as it turned out, the revolutionaries believed what they wrote. Their notions about politics, especially the ones which scholars have regarded as so irrational, grew out of the Americans' ideas about history as well as their own peculiar political experience. By treating the Andros tracts as sincere expressions of political beliefs, no matter how outrageous that may now appear, I was able to establish the importance of the Glorious Revolution in the development of Puritan political ideas. See Bernard Bailyn, *The Ideological Origins of the American Revolution* (Cambridge, Mass., 1967), pp. 94–159; *The Origins of American Politics* (New York, 1968), pp. 3–58.

participation.[4] The pamphleteers eased the transition from an oligarchy of saints to an oligarchy of property holders by assuring the citizens that God supported their attack on the Dominion government. Indeed, the Lord seemed to care as much about the security of the Puritans' rights, liberty, and property as He did about the purity of their church.

The revolutionary experience, including the confusion following Andros's overthrow, divided New Englanders into two camps, each advancing different ideas about the character of the good ruler. Ever since the days of Thomas Adams and John Preston, Puritan leaders in church and state had stressed the importance of the individual in choosing good magistrates; but, when citizens actually banished their leaders in 1689, the spectacle frightened many persons who apparently had considered revolution only as an abstraction. In the years after the Glorious Revolution a small, but influential, group of colonists began to have second thoughts about the value of popular participation in government affairs. While these persons, men like Simon Bradstreet, Samuel Willard, and Gershom Bulkeley, continued to support the citizen's right of election, they emphasized the importance of civil order and obedience. Other New Englanders, however, resisted this reaction, and throughout the revolutionary period proclaimed the people's responsibility to define the common good and to stand vigilant lest their rulers go astray. During the early 1690s the rift between those who glorified executive authority and those who thought that civil virtue resided in the whole populace was hardly discernible amid the general enthusiasm for property rights. Nevertheless, for the next generation of New Englanders this division became a major source of political controversy.

Evils of the Dominion of New England

In the early 1680s the men who formulated English colonial policy, the Lords of Trade, decided to accept Randolph's advice and to terminate New England's political autonomy. For years the citizens of Massachusetts had refused to cooperate with English efforts to make

4. For more on this point, see T. H. Breen, "Who Governs: The Town Franchise in Seventeenth-Century Massachusetts," *William and Mary Quarterly,* 3d ser., 27 (1970).

the American dominions profitable to the mother country, and the Navigation Acts had long been a dead letter in New England ports where no one seemed willing to obey them.[5] The Lords thought that the best way to bring the Puritans into line would be to alter the basis of their governments, allowing royal officials greater control over local affairs. Only the colonial patents issued by the early Stuarts stood in the way of imperial reform. Then in 1684 the Court of Chancery, prodded by the indefatigable Randolph, removed that barrier by annulling the Massachusetts Charter. Similar legal actions were planned against the charters of Connecticut and Rhode Island; and, although in the end these two colonies retained their patents, the Lords went ahead with the reorganization of New England.

The new administrative system, called the Dominion of New England, consolidated the colonies of Connecticut, Massachusetts, Rhode Island, Plymouth, and New Hampshire. Later New York and New Jersey were added, and the entire territory was placed under the control of a single royal governor. This official, acting with the members of an appointed council, held complete executive and legislative authority over the people who lived within his jurisdiction. The Lords of Trade set several general guidelines for the new government to follow. First, ignoring local practices, the imperial planners made no provision for the continuation of elective or representative assemblies. All Dominion rulers were to be appointed either by the king or by the governor. Second, the Lords announced that the new government would guarantee freedom of worship, meaning, no doubt, that the Church of England would be safe from possible Puritan harassment. And last, the planners instructed Dominion rulers to issue land grants in the king's name and to collect a small quitrent upon all acreage in the territory.[6]

The alterations in their government angered most New Englanders. For years they had attempted to forestall the annulment of their original patent, fearing that any change would be for the worse. On the eve of the revocation Increase Mather urged his neighbors to drop any magistrates who failed to resist the threatened political re-

5. See chap. 3 for a discussion of attempted imperial controls over New England during the late Old Charter period.
6. Barnes, *Dominion of New England,* pp. 47–70.

organization, labeling them "Enemies of the Countrey."[7] One such ruler, Joseph Dudley, found his fence smeared with "a virulent Libel" which reportedly was "extreamly abusive, especially to Him."[8] Unfortunately these local protests against moderates like Dudley were counter-productive to the ends which they aimed to achieve, for they only reinforced the belief prevalent among imperial authorities that the Bay colonists were inordinately stubborn men. In fact, one London correspondent warned Mather that the English tended to regard Massachusetts as "whiggish," while they saw the more cooperative Plymouth and Connecticut as "toryish"—a compliment which the leaders of Hartford and Plymouth probably did not treasure.[9] As late as 1686 Randolph found some recalcitrant Bostonians who still believed that "altho his Majestie has obtained a judgment against their charter, yet they have not consented and therefore hope some providence like that of Munmouth's [Monmouth's] Rebellion may fall out wch will restore them to their former priviledges."[10] But in 1686 there was no Duke of Monmouth to lead the citizens of Massachusetts against the powers of the Dominion; and, for the moment, at least, it appeared that the hated Randolph had won his personal controversy with New England.

The Lords of Trade, no doubt, were aware of the popular enmity which the new government would have to overcome, especially in the Bay Colony. Perhaps for this reason they selected Joseph Dudley to be the interim president of Massachusetts, Maine, and New Hampshire until they had worked out the final details for the establishment

7. Robert N. Toppan and Alfred T. S. Goodrick, eds., *Edward Randolph: Including His Letters and Official Papers . . . 1676–1703*, 7 vols. (Boston, 1898–1906), 3: 284.

8. *5 Collections*, MHS (Sewall Diary), 5: 101.

9. *4 Collections*, MHS, 8: 55.

10. Toppan and Goodrick, *Edward Randolph*, 4: 104. In March 1685 Randolph explained to a friend in England that the Puritans, who resisted moderate magistrates like Joseph Dudley and William Stoughton at election, ought to be disbarred from office "being so like our late Sequestrators in zeale & ignorance" (4: 16). It was unfortunate that England's official source of information in Massachusetts, Randolph, was so busy searching for rebels and Cromwellians that he ignored actual conditions within the colony (see n. 85 in chap. 3).

of the complete Dominion.[11] While Dudley's friendliness toward imperial officials made him contemptible to many Puritans, he at least was a native New Englander and a former magistrate knowledgeable in local political practices. He took office on May 25, 1686, and in his first speech calmed some of the Puritans' apprehension by announcing that religious toleration did not mean libertinism since his government would continue to suppress vice and ill manners.[12] In other areas the interim council tactfully avoided policies which might have given the public additional cause to be unhappy. President Dudley did not order new taxes, though he had the legal power to do so; and in a move that was even more diplomatic, he ignored Randolph's counsel, much to the latter's displeasure and surprise. In August 1686 Randolph complained to English authorities that "altho' his Majestie has been graciously pleased to appoint Severall of the members of the late Goverment [sic] to be of his Councill here, yet they retain the Old principles."[13] Randolph called Dudley, whom he had personally recommended for the president's office, "a man of a base, servile, and anti-monarchicall principle."[14] All in all, Dudley guided the Bay Colony with great prudence. He knew from first-hand experience the limits of the New Englanders' patience; and, during the dark days which followed, sought to dissociate himself from the worst features of Dominion policy.[15]

11. The first man proposed to head the Dominion was a professional soldier, Colonel Percy Kirke. On January 9, 1685, Randolph told Dudley that Percy "is a gentleman of very good resolution and I believe, will not faile in any part of his duty to his Majesty nor be wanting to doe all good offices for your distracted colony." A few months later Randolph wrote to Sir Robert Southwell that Kirke was so bad that even the hardships of Bermuda were better than living "under a debauched Atheisticall person who will doe his Majestie in one yeare more disservice than 20 years indulgence can repaire" (Toppan and Goodrick, *Edward Randolph*, 4: 12, 30). Massachusetts was probably fortunate that they did not get Kirke as their ruler, although Randolph may have embellished his description for ulterior reasons.

12. 2 *Proceedings,* MHS, 13: 227.

13. Toppan and Goodrick, *Edward Randolph,* 4: 117, also, 106–07.

14. Ibid., 4: 131.

15. Hutchinson, *History,* 1: 297–99; Everett Kimball, *The Public Life of Joseph Dudley* (New York, 1911), pp. 37–38; Kenneth B. Murdock, *Increase Mather: The Foremost American Puritan* (Cambridge, Mass., 1925), p. 157.

Sir Edmund Andros, Dudley's replacement, took command of the Dominion of New England on December 20, 1686. The people of Massachusetts greeted his arrival with suspicion, for they knew very little about the man.[16] The Reverend John Leverett, later a president of Harvard College, welcomed Andros with the left-handed assurance "that every sinister interpretation of your presence is absent." The minister added that the governor would hold "the place of Caesar" among the citizens.[17]

But many Bostonians must have entertained grave doubts about their "Caesar" from the first time they laid eyes upon him. He dressed like a Stuart courtier, which in itself was enough to provoke Puritans who were used to plainer magistrates. In 1680, for example, two visiting Dutch missionaries had had an interview with the last of the Old Charter governors, Simon Bradstreet, and reported that he "dwelt in only a common house, and that not the most costly. He is an old man, quiet and grave. He was dressed in black silk, but not sumptuously."[18] In contrast, a portrait of Andros depicts him with a flowing, curled wig and a fancy lace cravat.[19] He attended a Harvard commencement in a scarlet coat and a stylish wig.[20] In the

16. Edmund Andros was born in London on December 6, 1637. His first important preferment came in 1660 when he was made Gentleman in the Ordinary to the Queen of Bohemia. During the 1660s he served in the army and in 1674 retired to manage his father's large estates on Guernsey. Almost as soon as he had settled in his new home, the Duke of York called him to be governor of New York. The Duke's proprietary colony was run much more autocratically than were any of the New England colonies. Andros's chief duties were military, and during the Indian wars of the 1670s, he seems to have protected his subjects quite well. When James II, the former Duke of York, chose Andros to head the Dominion of New England, the people of Massachusetts identified Andros with the arbitrary government of New York. They were probably right to be uneasy, for the new governor was a military man in instinct and training and had little sympathy for anyone who questioned his commands (W. H. Whitmore's introduction to *The Andros Tracts,* 3 vols. [Boston, 1868], 1: v–xlix).

17. Samuel Eliot Morison, *Harvard College in the Seventeenth Century,* 2 vols. (Cambridge, Mass., 1936), 2: 480.

18. *Memoirs of the Long Island Historical Society* (Brooklyn, 1867), 1: 378.

19. Morison, *Harvard College,* 2: 479.

20. Ibid., pp. 480–81.

1680s many New Englanders regarded wigs as an outward sign of inward corruption, and Andros's false locks did little to win him Puritan support.[21] As the governor went about his business he must have looked like the fawning, fashionable creature that Samuel Nowell had warned about in his artillery sermon of 1678 (see chap. 3).

Andros's disreputable entourage aroused the Puritans' irritation.[22] Samuel Sewall, a well-meaning gossip, noted in his diary one evening that three dominion officials "come in a Coach from Roxbury about 9 a'clock or past, singing as they come, being inflam'd with Drink. At Justice Morgan's they stop and drink Healths, curse, swear, and talk profanely and baudily, to the great disturbance of the Town and grief of good people." Sewall added indignantly that "Such high-handed wickedness had hardly been heard of before in Boston."[23] Another unreconstructed Puritan, Increase Mather, complained in the spring of 1687 that some men, presumably the governor's followers, had taken to practicing swordplay on a Boston stage immediately after the weekly church lecture "so that the Devil has begun a Lecture in Boston on a Lecture-day which was set up for Christ." And one May soon after Andros's arrival, Mather observed that "A May pole was set up in Charlestown."[24] No further comment was necessary, for Maypoles conjured up the worst images of lechery and debauchery in the New England mind. Mather published a sermon in 1687 significantly entitled *Testimony Against Several Prophane and Superstitious Customs Now Practiced by Some in New-England*. This work apparently did not reform Andros and his friends, for the Puritans had to endure "Healthdrinking, Dicing, Cards, and such like Games" for several more years.[25]

If Andros's only failing had been insulting the Puritans' moral sensibilities, the dominion might have survived. Unfortunately, the policies of the new government intervened in the people's daily lives

21. For Samuel Sewall's opinion of wigs in this period see *Publications of the Colonial Society of Massachusetts* 20 (1918): 109–28.

22. Murdock, *Increase Mather*, p. 160.

23. Cited in Henry W. Foote, *Annals of King's Chapel*, 2 vols. (Boston, 1882), 1: 60.

24. *2 Proceedings*, MHS, 13: 411.

25. Cited in Foote, *Annals of King's Chapel*, 1: 73.

in other ways which they found intolerable. The governor had not been in New England long when he began to exercise the broad constitutional powers that Dudley had wisely ignored. Andros's executive acts over the next few years convinced the Puritans that he was not only an offensive courtier, but also an arbitrary despot. "Nero concealed his tyrannical disposition," Thomas Hutchinson wrote in the eighteenth century, "more years than Sir Edmund and his crea- tures did months."[26] The more Andros insisted on fulfilling the letter of his royal commission, the more he appeared to the New Englanders to be a local or provincial James II, for even in the American colonies men had heard of the king's tyrannous acts.

The Dominion rulers lost any chance whatsover for popular sup- port by taxing people without their consent. As early as June 1, 1686, Edward Rawson submitted a "libelleous paper" to Dudley's council, signed by the deputies of the last Massachusetts General Court, declaring that the new constitution denied citizens their lib- erties as Englishmen, especially "in the matter of legislation and in the Law of Taxes." In their protest the representatives observed that the reorganized government had concentrated all civil power in the hands of a few appointed officials, "there being not the least men- tion of an assembly in the Commission." The deputies asked the councillors to consider whether such an unrepresentative system was "either safe for you or us."[27] As we have seen, Dudley avoided a showdown by not passing any revenue measures, but Andros brought discontent to a head when he and his council ordered the collection of taxes upon certain imports and upon land. Even Dudley, who was serving as one of Andros's advisers, balked at the governor's action, insisting that he had had nothing to do with the arbitrary revenue bills.[28]

26. Hutchinson, *History,* 1: 301.

27. 2 *Proceedings,* MHS, 13: 238. On October 22, 1688, the Old Charter magistrate, Thomas Danforth, wrote to Samuel Nowell in London, claiming that without a "generall assembly . . . our condition is little inferiour to absolute slavery" (Thomas Hutchinson, *The Hutchinson Papers,* 2 vols. [Albany, 1865], 2: 308).

28. On June 5, 1689, Dudley wrote to Cotton Mather explaining that as a Dominion councillor he had done all he could to dissuade Andros from passing arbitrary taxes on land (6 *Collections,* MHS, 3: 504–05). Dudley's

Of all the taxes, the colonists found the one levied on land the most vexing, no doubt because it affected their lives more directly than any of the others. When Andros ordered the towns of Massachusetts to select persons who would assess property values in preparation for the new tax, the citizens of Ipswich resisted. A relatively unknown, but charismatic, Congregational minister, John Wise, reminded his Ipswich neighbors that there were ancient English rights that protected men from taxation without their consent. He advised them that they had "a good God & a good king and Should Do well to stand for or [our] previledges."[29] The people of Ipswich apparently did not require much persuasion, for at a town meeting held on August 23, 1687, they unanimously defied Andros's command. The text of their statement revealed how much they were in harmony with Wise's views.

> The Towne . . . considering that the said act doth infringe their liberty as freeborne English subjects of his majesty, by interfering with the Statute Laws of the Land, by which it is enacted that *no taxes shall be levied on the subjects* without consent of an assembly chosen by the freeholders for assessing the same. They do therefore vote that they are not willing to choose a commissioner for such an end, without said privileges.[30]

No sooner had the Ipswich resistance collapsed than Andros or-

---

protestations of innocence apparently did little good, for in July Danforth noted that "Mr. Dudley in a peculiar manner is the object of the peoples displeasure, even thorow out all the colonies where he hath sat judge, they deeply resent his correspondency with that wicked man Mr. Randolph for the overturning the government, and the manner of his procuring his presidentship, his extream covetousnes, getting to himself so many bags of money, to the ruinating of trade, and since Sir Edmund's arrivall here, hath been his great instrument in the oppression of the people" (*Hutchinson Papers*, 2: 311–12). Dudley's next appearance in the colony was as its appointed royal governor!

29. Thomas F. Waters, *Ipswich in the Massachusetts Bay Colony* [Ipswich, 1905], p. 239. One of the men who listened to Wise and who supported the Ipswich resistance was William Hubbard (see chap. 3).

30. Joseph B. Felt, *History of Ipswich, Essex, and Hamilton* (Cambridge, Mass., 1834), p. 321 (italics added); see Massachusetts Archives, 35: 138.

dered the arrest of Wise and the other men involved.[31] At their trial a Dominion judge informed the rebels that they were mistaken if they believed that their English rights had followed them "to the ends of the Earth." This official added gratuitously that "You have no more Privileges left you, but this, that you are not bought and sold for Slaves."[32] People throughout Massachusetts resented this insult and, judging by some of the bitter comments written after the revolution, they did not forget it. Wise captured the general mood, reporting that Andros had described the citizens of the colony as "but a parcell of ignorant Jacks and Tomes, and that he & his Council had the immediate dispose of our fortunes, and we were told to be put in Bedlam for mad-men as not knowing how to use an Estate when we had gotten it, though with never so much prudence paine & frugalitye."[33] One suspects that Wise himself was the author of the words "prudence paine & frugalitye," for he had experienced firsthand the hardships of working the land. After he had spent several months in jail, Wise begged the governor's pardon. He did not do so because he lacked faith in his political convictions, but, fittingly, because there was an "Indian Harvest" to be brought in and his family needed him.[34] In this moment of defeat other Puritans throughout the colony may well have reflected on Nowell's earlier prophecy. He had warned the New Englanders that without their

31. To understand the Glorious Revolution in Massachusetts, one must realize that the people were genuinely afraid of their governor. The first Redcoats many of them had ever seen were those who landed with Andros in 1686 and who acted as his bodyguard when he traveled throughout the Dominion. The sense of popular fear was captured in a letter which Captain John How, a selectman of Topsfield, wrote on September 16, 1687. Apparently, some of the inhabitants of his town had advocated following their neighbors in Ipswich, but when Wise and the others were arrested, How told Andros, "I fall Downe at your feet humbly baiging your marcy and humbly intreating his excilancy the Governor to pardon me this onc: Promising for time to come to Approve myselfe faithfull in all Respacts to his Excilancy the Governor and Government baring oppen Testimony against all Rabbell that shall anny waies oppose the same" Massachusetts Archives, 127: 109).

32. Massachusetts Archives, 35: 139; Felt, *History of Ipswich,* pp. 124–25.

33. Massachusetts Archives, 35: 168.

34. Massachusetts Archives, 127: 147, 164.

charter their property would be subject to the arbitrary whims of a ruler who would make them "vassals." In Ipswich, Nowell's prediction seemed fulfilled.

Andros apparently learned little from the Wise episode, for he continued to tamper with the colonists' land. The governor stubbornly set out to alter traditional procedures for issuing land titles and to introduce a quitrent into the Puritan colonies. The Old Charter government in Massachusetts had granted land to men in one of two ways: either directly or through town proprietors who in turn parceled out lots to individual settlers. It came as a great surprise, therefore, when Andros announced that the Lords of Trade had found the colony's old land system to be in error. Under English law only corporations possessed the power to issue titles and, since the town proprietors were not validly incorporated, their grants were invalid. To make matters worse for the colonists, the governor announced that he would not honor titles that came from the General Court unless they bore the colony's official seal. Apparently, the Puritan legislators had been lax in the use of the seal, for few of their grants met the rigid new standards. All landholders whose deeds were in doubt had to petition the Dominion government for a legitimate patent to their estates, a requirement which affected almost every family in Massachusetts. As if this reform were not enough, Andros told New Englanders that they would have to start paying quitrents on all of their lands. The innovation shocked colonists who had always assumed that their property was free from tenurial obligations.[35]

Hatred for Andros's land program united New Englanders of different classes and backgrounds, all of whom wanted to secure their

35. Barnes, *Dominion of New England,* pp. 174-211 passim. In March 1689 Governor Andros stopped at the home of the Reverend John Higginson, who lived in Salem. Andros asked the minister if the land in New England belonged to the king. At first Higginson protested that he was a clergyman and had no business advising a ruler about matters of state. However, when Andros insisted upon an answer, the minister explained that the colonists had a clear title to the land through Scripture, charter, and Indian purchase. Hearing this, the governor lost his temper, telling Higginson "either you are Subjects or you are Rebells" (Massachusetts Archives, 35: 145).

property from arbitrary seizure. Some of the richest men in the colony were hardest hit by the order invalidating Old Charter titles and, when they protested, the governor threatened to take their lands through questionable legal procedures. The threat amounted to blackmail; for, even if a man could have beaten Andros in the courts, the cost of trying would have been prohibitive.[36]

Even colonists of modest means protested when they learned that Andros intended to reward his favorites with the property which he had taken from wealthy New Englanders. Samuel Sewall noted with pathetic candor after he had petitioned for a Dominion grant that "the generality of People are very averse from complying with anything that may alter the Tenure of their Lands, and look upon me very sorrowfully that I have given way."[37] Popular irritation increased when the hated Randolph sued for acreage that lay within the commons of Lynn, Watertown, and Cambridge, claiming that these towns had no right to such lands under English law.[38] After watching Andros's venal practices, Increase Mather reported, "The property of his Majesty's loyal subjects . . . has been invaded by their present Rulers. The Governor has taken away the Lands belonging to some particular persons, & given them to his owne creatures."[39] Perhaps the most telling comment about Andros's land policy was a note someone scribbled on the margin of the Dominion land records, no doubt after the governor had departed from New England: Sr. Edmund Andros, Once a Governor, and rascally petty Tyrant, under the King and grand Tyrant of Britain."[40]

New Englanders also lost confidence in Andros's courts, for too often they saw justice sacrificed either to greed or to politics. The colonists collected grisly tales about Dominion judges browbeating

36. Barnes, *Dominion of New England*, p. 199; Hall, *Edward Randolph*, pp. 112-13.
37. *5 Collections*, MHS, 5: 231.
38. Toppan and Goodrick, *Edward Randolph*, 4: 202, 207, 211, 218–20; Hutchinson, *History*, 1: 305–06; Barnes, *Dominion of New England*, pp. 195–99.
39. *4 Collections*, MHS, 8: 115; also Toppan and Goodrick, *Edward Randolph*, 6: 211–12.
40. J. Tuttle, "Land Warrants Issued under Andros, 1687–1688," *Publications of the Colonial Society of Massachusetts* 21(1919): 292.

defendants, letting them languish in jail for long periods without benefit of habeas corpus. The most frequently repeated example of inequity was the case of Major Samuel Appleton, a hero of King Philip's War and a leader of the Ipswich protest, who was denied a hearing for many months after his arrest. During his administration Andros also altered the jury system, allowing men to serve as jurors who would never have qualified under the Old Charter government. The Puritans protested that this change gave non-freemen power over their lives and property. Equally upsetting was the fact that Andros's officials sometimes selected only those jurors who they knew would support the administration. But of all the judicial evils, the New Englanders viewed profiteering as the most contemptible; for, as Cotton Mather later explained, "Foxes were made the Administrators of Justice to the *Poultrey*."[41] One of the most despised Dominion officials, John West, was known throughout the Bay Colony for demanding exorbitant fees in return for the most trivial legal services.[42] While the judicial corruption spread, Andros added to the popular disaffection by ordering citizens to swear oaths upon the Bible. The Puritans had traditionally taken oaths by simply raising a hand, and they regarded the governor's innovation as idolatrous.[43] It did not take the colonists long to realize that their new rulers regarded the law as a means to personal enrichment and as a way for keeping the people subjugated.

Andros's tactless handling of religious affairs gave the Puritans additional cause to be unhappy with his rule. The governor, who was an Anglican, announced as soon as he arrived in Massachusetts that the members of the Church of England would enjoy complete liberty of conscience.[44] The open practice of the Anglican faith was an innovation in Boston, and Increase Mather announced his view on the new policy in a tart sermon entitled *A Brief Discourse Concerning the Unlawfulness of Common Prayer Worship*.[45] Without doubt, enforced toleration by the Dominion irritated many colonists; but in

41. Cotton Mather, "The Life of His Excellency Sir William Phips," *Magnalia Christi Americana* (London, 1702), bk. 2, p. 43.

42. Hall, *Edward Randolph,* p. 110.

43. Barnes, *Dominion of New England,* pp. 111, 115, 116; Felt, *History of Ipswich,* p. 124.

44. Barnes, *Dominion of New England,* pp. 122-34 passim.

45. (Cambridge, 1686).

time they probably could have learned to live with the Church of England in America. Certainly, long before the Lords of Trade established the Dominion government, New Englanders had allowed Baptists to assemble in Boston. The citizens of Massachusetts were most upset by the high-handed manner in which the governor demanded a Congregational meetinghouse for Anglican services. When Andros requested the keys to the Third, or South Church, a committee of deacons went to him and explained that the building and the land upon which it stood were private property belonging to several leading families of the city. They believed that the state had no more right to take their church than it had to seize their homes and businesses. The governor paid scant attention to the deacons' argument, and the Church of England soon began using the meetinghouse.[46]

New Englanders complained of the Dominion's interference with local government and its failure to protect the frontier settlements from Indian attack. Soon after the Ipswich revolt, Andros and his council passed a law restricting town meetings to one a year, and that only for the routine election of local officials.[47] The town meeting was vital to the smooth operation of village affairs, and it is not surprising that the Puritans of Massachusetts regarded the governor's order as another example of Dominion tyranny. In Woburn the citizens ignored the new law and continued to meet as they always had done. Other towns throughout the colony may well have followed Woburn's example.[48] In the last months of Andros's regime there were increasing protests that his government did not adequately defend the scattered villages of western Massachusetts and Maine from Indian harassment. The governor tried to fight the enemy, but somehow the Indians always managed to slip away unharmed. Andros's military failure led to charges that he had supplied the Indians with arms and that he had made a secret covenant with the Catholics in Canada.[49]

One of the chief goals in creating the Dominion had been the

46. Hamilton A. Hill, *History of the Old South Church*, 2. vols. (Boston, 1890), 1: 266.

47. Barnes, *Dominion of New England*, pp. 195–96.

48. Samuel Sewall, *The History of Woburn* (Boston, 1868), pp. 128–30.

49. *Calendar of State Papers, Colonial Series, 1689–1692*, p. 246; Hutchinson, *History*, 1: 314–15; Massachusetts Archives, 35: 164.

enforcement of the Navigation Acts. Andros carried out this responsibility well; so well in fact, that in a matter of months New England's once flourishing trade had all but died. Before 1686 Massachusetts merchants had achieved prosperity by bringing staple goods to Boston from Southern and West Indian colonies without paying the so-called "plantation duty." New Englanders then exchanged these goods directly with European countries, thus breaking the Navigation Acts a second time. When Andros began collecting all of the required duties, local trade collapsed, for merchants found that they could no longer undercut their British competitors. Ironically, under the Old Charter government it had been the merchant community that had advocated greater royal controls over New England, but certainly the shipping interests never expected that the new administration would destroy their livelihood. When commercial leaders deserted Andros he lost a vital source of support. The governor learned what other royal officials would have to relearn during the eighteenth century: it was nearly impossible to please imperial authorities and the colonists at the same time.[50]

In his two years as governor of the Dominion, Andros managed to alienate almost everyone in New England. His economic, religious, and military policies had turned friends into critics and, in the case of Ipswich at least, had transformed critics into rebels. His manner and dress, the greed of his followers, the corruption of his courts— all of these things undermined his position. If Andros had had more time, he might have acquired some of the political skills which he so obviously lacked. Unfortunately time ran out.

Revolution Justified

News of King William's "Protestant" victory did not reach Boston until the spring of 1689; and when it did, Andros tried to suppress the information as long as possible. Despite his efforts, however, the story of James's defeat and subsequent flight to France soon became

50. Barnes, *Dominion of New England,* pp. 135–73 passim; *Calendar of State Papers, Colonial Series, 1689–1692,* p. 60. On the behavior of the merchant community before the revocation of the Old Charter, see Bernard Bailyn, *The New England Merchants in the Seventeenth Century* (New York, 1964), pp. 143–67.

common knowledge throughout New England.[51] The governor's attempted censorship only served to arouse popular suspicion that he was in league with the deposed monarch and part of a Catholic plot. All at once the fears and irritations which had built up over two years exploded.

The Glorious Revolution was over almost as quickly as it had begun, for in a matter of hours New Englanders had imprisoned the major Dominion leaders, Andros, Randolph, and Dudley, and established a provisional government modeled on their old one. The most striking feature of the revolt in Massachusetts was the colonists' unanimity; for, despite differences in class and background, they all agreed that Andros was a bad ruler who had to be removed. No one came to the governor's defense, a fact corroborated by the lack of violence and bloodshed accompanying the events of April 18, 1689. Cotton Mather explained later, with a mixture of pride and disbelief, that the citizens were united by the "most *Unanimous Resolution* perhaps that was ever known to have Inspir'd any People."[52] But even as the Puritans marched Andros and his followers off to jail, they were aware that military victory was only part of revolution and that they would have to justify their actions to England, to the other colonies, and to themselves before they would be secure.

During the months immediately following Andros's overthrow, New Englanders published a number of pamphlets, poems, and broadsides, all attempting to explain why they had rebelled against the Dominion. Most of this political literature, of course, was aimed at William III; for it was in his power to decide whether the colonists' revolution had been an act of patriotism or disloyalty. The titles of some of their appeals, *A Vindication of New England, The Revolution in New England Justified,* and *A Narrative of the Miseries of New-England,* revealed the people's concern that imperial authorities might condemn the events of April 18 and reestablish the Dominion.

A pamphleteer's primary goal was to prove that Andros had indeed been a bad ruler, deserving expulsion by a virtuous people. To

51. Barnes, *Dominion of New England,* pp. 238–41; *Calendar of State Papers, Colonial Series, 1689–1692,* pp. 246.
52. Cotton Mather, "Life of Phips," p. 45; see Council Records, 6: 123.

achieve that end Puritan authors had to describe what they expected of their government and magistrates; or, put another way, they had to set forth clearly the attributes which they demanded in a good ruler. The writers also had to define the conditions which justified revolution against established civil authority. For the historian of political ideas, these pamphlets are an invaluable source, since they represent the first sustained discussion of political theory to take place since the early 1640s and consequently reflect changes which had occurred in popular notions about the character of the good magistrate.[53]

The justification for the overthrow of Andros turned out to be more important to the political and intellectual development of New England than were the actual events of the revolution itself, for local pamphleteers defended their rebellion in language novel to the Bay Commonwealth. For the most part, they dropped the scriptural rhetoric which had permeated much of the political writing in the Old Charter period, and attacked Andros's government for defects which had little or nothing to do with Puritanism. During the Glorious Revolution, in fact, no one echoed the ideas of Christopher Goodman or John Ponet; no one accused Dominion rulers of being idol-

---

53. Viola Barnes and I differ radically on the nature and causes of the revolution. She wrote in 1923,

> To deem it but an echo of the English revolution against James, is to cause it to lose all its significance. The explanation is found in the fanaticism of the Puritan theocrats, who were more Hebrew than English in their thought and ideals and in their government. Like the Jews of the Old Testament, they were the Chosen People and the Andros administration was the period of their captivity, inflicted upon them by a just, stern, and wrathful God. Their holy men had prophesied that this captivity was approaching its end. Therefore, when the revolution occurred in England, the theocrats immediately interpreted it as God's sign that He was about to deliver them from bondage and restore their former judges. [*Dominion of New England,* pp. 250–51].

Barnes's description simply does not fit the facts. The revolt had little or nothing to do with religion, and the colonists justified their actions with arguments that were more constitutional than Puritan. Even the theocrats, if the Mathers can be called theocrats, appealed to the people in terms of life, liberty, and property (infra).

aters whose presence in Boston would bring God's wrath upon the land. According to the revolutionary authors, the people of Massachusetts resisted their governor because he had seized their estates through arbitrary procedures which denied what they believed to be their English rights. What the Puritan pamphleteers were doing in effect was to transform the Moseses and Nehemiahs of former generations into guardians of property. The writers constructed their arguments very carefully, disparaging the importance of certain factors which had angered New Englanders while Andros was still in office.

Nothing better revealed how much the character of the good ruler had changed than the rebels' discussions of the governor's personal behavior. Few of them mentioned Andros's manners, dress, or morals, although the actions of several of his supporters were criticized.[54] A surprised observer informed the Lords of Trade that, "So far as I know there is no complaint or imputation against the person of Sir Edmund Andros."[55] And the imprisoned Randolph wrote with unusual perception that "notwithstanding all the pretensions of grievances mencioned in their papers [the pamphlet literature], and cryes of oppression in the Governours proceedings, it's not the person of Sir Edmund Andros, but the government itself, they designe to have removed."[56] Forgotten, at least in the press, were the scarlet coat, the flowing wig, and the courtier manners. The pamphleteers did not describe the governor as a man guilty of moral indiscretion, but rather used him as a symbol for all of the evils of the Dominion. They held him responsible like the captain of a ship, for the vices and errors of his entire crew.

The colonial writers made no sustained effort to prove that Andros had been a bad ruler because he was ungodly or heretical. A few critics attempted to implicate the governor in a popish conspiracy, but the accusation was a minor theme in the protests agains his administration.[57] Almost no revolutionary author besides Cotton Mather described Andros's regime as a divine punishment for New Eng-

54. *An Appeal to the Men of New-England* (Boston, 1689), p. 4.
55. *Calendar of State Papers, Colonial Series, 1689–1692*, p. 60.
56. Toppan and Goodrick, *Edward Randolph*, 4: 278.
57. E.g., *Andros Tracts*, 2: 122.

land's sins or for the Puritan's loss of religious fervor.[58] The
apologists had little political use for the language of the jeremiad,
finding it much more expedient to explain the colonists' actions in
terms of ancient English liberties. The Puritan pamphleteers, moreover, did not try to relate the events of 1689 to a popular reaction
against the governor's enforced toleration of Anglicanism. "No man
underwent any Confinement," observed the author of *An Account
of the Late Revolution,* "but such as the people counted the Enemies
of the *Prince of Orange,* and of our *English Liberties;* it was not for
any passion for the Service of the *Church of England,* that exposed
any man to hardship; no, even some of that Communion did appear
in their Arms to assist the enterprize; tho' the worship of the Church
of *England* had this disadvantage with us, that most of our Late
Oppressors, were the great and sole Pillars of it there."[59] There is
no way of telling how many Anglicans supported the Glorious Revolution in Massachusetts, but the government records do reveal that
many men who had not been able to become freemen under the old
charter risked their lives and estates to rid the colony of arbitrary
rule.[60] Whatever the case may have been, no one seems to have seen

58. See Miller, *New England Mind,* 2: 179. Miller argues that, "The
tyranny of Andros was . . . a punishment for breach of religious covenant.
An unshakable conviction gripped the New England mind (a conviction
reinvigorated in 1776) that political liberties must be defended on both
religious and political grounds together, largely because the jeremiads for
decades hammered upon this as the moral of the Dominion." I found very
little to support Miller's statement. Certainly men like the Mathers at
times discussed the Glorious Revolution in terms of the jeremiad, but most
New Englanders seemed to have regarded Andros's overthrow as a defense
of political and constitutional rights that dated back to 1215. And after 1690
even the Mathers stopped talking about politics with reference to New
England's covenant with God (infra, chap. 5).

59. A. B., *An Account of the Late Revolution* (Boston, 1689), p. 5.

60. See Massachusetts Archives, 35: 154. In January 1690 a group of
men asked the provisional government to change the franchise law so that
property holders who had risked their lives and estates in the Glorious
Revolution could become voters. The petitioners mentioned that the first
request they had made for expanded freemanship had come as early as May
1689. Also Richard Simmons, "The Massachusetts Revolution of 1689:
Three Early American Political Broadsides," *Journal of American Studies*
2 (1968): 5–6.

the rebellion as a confrontation between the "visible saints" and the rest of New England.

In the months following the revolution colonial writers complained almost exclusively about the threats which Dominion rulers had made against their property. In fact, the pamphleteers believed that the citizens had a responsibility to overthrow a government which arbitrarily seized their personal holdings. One writer explained that the deposed magistrates had "Invaded *Liberty* and *Property* after such a manner, as that no Man could say any thing was *his own.*"[61] Likewise, the author of *The Revolution in New England Justified* expressed hope that England would pay reparations to Andros's victims "whose Properties as well as Liberties have been Invaded."[62] Almost all of this post-1689 political literature contained some discussion of property and the ruler's obligation to protect it. One of the best examples of the new secular attitude was a Boston edition of Bishop Gilbert Burnet's famous *A Sermon Preached before the House of Commons on the 31st of January 1688.* Bishop Burnet had told the English parliamentarians that Commons acted as "the great Fence" defending "two sacred Things, *Liberty* and *Property*"; and according to the preacher neither of these essential elements was secure from illegal assault under King James. At this point in Burnet's sermon, the American printer, Samuel Green, added in the margin—"NEW-ENGLANDS CASE."[63] Andros had broken in upon men's estates and, like James, had to pay the price.[64]

The Puritan writers of 1689 made no attempt to rank Andros's policies by order of their unacceptability; but, if they had, they would probably have placed his seizure of land first on their list. For the most part, seventeenth-century New England was an agrarian society; and consequently, the ruler who threatened to take the colonists' lands also threatened to destroy the livelihood of most of the people. The Old Charter magistrates, whatever their failings may have been, never contemplated confiscating their constituents' farms and pastures; and election day speakers had had no reason to discuss

61. Cotton Mather, "Life of Phips," p. 55; *Andros Tracts,* 2: 273.

62. *Andros Tracts,* 1: 128.

63. Gilbert Burnet, *A Sermon Preached before the House of Commons on the 31st of January 1688* (Boston, 1689), p. 10.

64. *Andros Tracts,* 1: 71–72.

a form of tyranny which existed only in theory. But Andros's corrupt land policies changed theory into fact; and, for the first time since the founding, New Englanders were confronted with rulers who seemed to covet the Puritans' estates. The pamphleteers, often barely able to contain their anger, harped on this point. The anonymous author of *A Vindication of New-England* reminded the people how the Dominion officials had cheated them; for, "altho' King *Charles* (in his Declaration) assured them that no man should be Invaded in his *property,* yet upon the vacating of their Charter their new Masters made bold and did them the *favour* to tell them that they had lost all *Titles to their Lands.*"[65] Another author claimed that without the "happy Revolution" the Puritans might have lost all of their real estate to Andros's grasping council and venal judges.[66] Perhaps the sentiments of the colonists were best captured by a bitter Boston poet:

> All that we counted dear was made a Prize
> To th' raging Lust and hungry Avarice
> Of a few tatter'd Rascals from *New-York,*
> More insolent than ever was *Grand Turk.*
> It would disturb our Fathers' peaceful Graves,
> Saw they their poor Posterity made slaves,
> Or knew our Lives and Liberties betray'd,
> Or knew our Lands for forreign Foes convey'd,
> Yet thus with grief might poor *New-England* cry,
> We our own Lands with our own Coyn must buy.[67]

After the experience of Andros's administration, New Englanders never again neglected to instruct their rulers to protect the people's estates.

The revolutionary pamphleteers frequently coupled liberty with property, revealing that for the Puritans of this period the two were

---

65. *Andros Tracts,* 2: 34–35.
66. *Andros Tracts,* 1: 98.
67. *The Plain Case Stated* (Boston, 1689). Eight of the Dominion councillors came from New York. They were generally the most unpopular group in Andros's government, for they aggressively supported James II and the governor's arbitrary decisions. The popular feeling against the New Yorkers explains the poet's remark in line three.

intimately connected. When the writers complained that Andros destroyed New England's liberties, they referred specifically to those privileges which persons at the time associated with property. One author, for example, claimed that the fact that Andros and his councillors "did make *Laws destructive to the liberty of the Subjects,* is notoriously known, for they made what Laws they pleased *without any consent of the People, either by themselves or representatives,* which is indeed to *destroy the Fundamentals of the English* and to *Erect a French Government.*"[68] Another pamphleteer declared that, in the absence of a General Court, *"Moneys* have been raised by the Government in a most illegal and Arbitrary way, *without any consent of the people."*[69] When New Englanders inquired why the Dominion deprived them of their old privileges, officials supposedly retorted that, *"It was not to His Majesties Interest that we should thrive."*[70]

Irate Puritan writers cited other evidence to prove the relation between their endangered liberties and their property. They pointed out that as soon as the men of Ipswich opposed arbitrary taxation, Andros had curtailed the important right of the colonists to gather freely in their towns for political debate.[71] The loss of the town meeting denied the people of Massachusetts one of the few remaining means by which they could protest the Dominion's revenue policy.

The greed which seemed to motivate Andros and his friends shocked Puritan pamphleteers who believed that good rulers would never use positions of public trust for self-enrichment. Old Charter magistrates had not accepted office for the purpose of gaining wealth, and many of them had lost considerable sums while serving their constituents. But the "base Parasites and Sycophants" who invaded Massachusetts with Randolph and Andros viewed government work as a means to quick money, an attitude they may well have learned at the court of King James.[72] The author of *An Account of the*

68. *Andros Tracts,* 1: 79–80; 2: 5.
69. *Andros Tracts,* 2: 5.
70. *An Appeal to the Men of New-England,* p. 5; *Andros Tracts,* 1: 12–13.
71. *Andros Tracts,* 1: 80.
72. *Andros Tracts,* 2: 78.

Late Revolution in New-England declared that under the governor's rule the state became "a meer *Engine,* a sort of *Machin* contriv'd only to enrich a crew of Abject Strangers, upon the Ruines of a miserable people."[73] A group of Dominion councillors who later turned against the deposed governor: William Stoughton, Thomas Hinckley, Wait Winthrop, Samuel Shrimpton, and Bartholomew Gedney, also reported that the appointed "Strangers" were concerned only for their own immediate profits.[74] The majority of writers who attempted to justify the revolution of 1689 despised the grasping practices of Andros's "Horse-leeches." "Doubtless a Land so ruled as once *New-England* was," one colonist observed, "has not without many fears and sighs beheld the wicked walking on every side, and the vilest Men exalted."[75] The pamphleteers implied that magistrates properly schooled in civil virtue would not have exploited the people's property as Andros had done; for, as one New Englander put it, the Puritans under the Dominion had nearly perished "for the want of such *Super-sober* Councillors."[76]

Andros's government also came under attack from the Puritan pamphleteers for its judicial corruption. One author declared that when the people of New England had attempted to defend their lands from seizure in the courts, Dominion judges had bullied defendants and demanded outrageous fees. "For if men were willing to bring their Titles of their Possessions to a Legal Tryal, they were not only threatened, but fined and prosecuted, and used with barbarous Cruelty. When some Gentlemen in *Boston* resolved in a Legal way to defend their Title to an Island there, Sir *Edmund's Attorney* threatened that it might *cost them all that they are worth, and somehing besides*."[77] A political poem described the same corrupt practice in *The Plain Case Stated:* "Law at a price, and Justice we must buy, / Each small Court-Officer gapes for his fee."[78] The writers of 1689 were claiming, in effect, that the Dominion's judicial system

73. *Andros Tracts,* 2: 192.

74. *Andros Tracts,* 1: 138–40.

75. *Andros Tracts,* 1: 14; also A. B., *An Account of the Late Revolution,* pp. 1–2.

76. *An Appeal to the Men of New-England,* p. 4.

77. *Andros Tracts,* 1: 98.

78. *The Plain Case Stated.*

had perverted the traditional function of law in their society by
failing to protect the colonists from their ruler's illegal acts. The
judges, it was charged, had become Andros's tools, enriching themselves at the Puritans' expense. Moreover, their decisions supported
the governor's arbitrary rule. An anonymous author asserted indignantly that when the citizens of Ipswich protested paying
Dominion taxes one of their most respected leaders "was committed
to prison without any Crimes laid to his Charge, and there kept half
a year without any Fault; and though he petitioned for a *Habeas
Corpus,* it was denied him."[79] The people of Massachusetts naturally
complained to their magistrates about the loss of their judicial
liberties, but the contemptuous authorities informed them "That
the Scabbard of a Red-Coat should quickly signifie as much as the
Commission of the Justice of the Peace."[80] A good ruler, the pamphleteers maintained, would not have tolerated such a situation.

Almost all the writers of this period justified the Glorious Revolution on constitutional grounds, belittling the fact that greed and
dishonesty were primarily moral failings. The pamphleteers explained
—no doubt somewhat defensively—that the New Englanders had
never contemplated radical social and political changes when they
jailed Andros. To the contrary, they declared, it had been the governor
himself who had been the political innovator by denying the colonists
their traditional English rights. His arbitrary demands, like those of
James II, ignored Parliament's courageous defense of England's
ancient constitutional rights against the forces of absolutism. "The
very *Form* of Government imposed upon us," one writer protested,
"was among *the worst of Treasons,* even a Treasonable Invasion of
the Rights which the whole *English* Nation lays claim unto; every
true *English-man* must justifie our Dissatisfaction at it, and believe
that we have not so much *resisted the Ordinance of God,* as we have
resisted an intollerable violation of His *Ordinance.*"[81] Cotton Mather,
who was just becoming a major figure in Massachusetts, announced
with confidence that the events of 1689 had established the Puritans'

79. *Andros Tracts,* 2: 6.
80. *An Appeal to the Men of New-England,* p. 4.
81. A. B., *An Account of the Late Revolution,* p. 1; *An Appeal to the
Men of New-England,* p. 3.

"Title to the Common Rights of Englishmen."[82] Men like Mather and the anonymous pamphleteers were transforming the godly rulers of Winthrop's generation into guardians of popular rights.

It was common for the apologists to describe the Glorious Revolution in America almost solely as a defense of traditional liberties. The author of a piece entitled *The Revolution in New England Justified* explained to his readers that the first Puritan planters had formed *"an Original Contract,"* by which the settlers promised to subdue the wilderness at their own expense in exchange for the enjoyment of English rights. Apparently some Dominion officials had declared the argument about original covenants to be irrelevant, since James II had revoked the Old Charter. To this claim the writer responded hotly, "But he cannot think that Judgment against their Charter made them cease to be *Englishmen.*"[83] Other New Englanders pointed out that Andros had violated rights clearly guaranteed in the Magna Charta.[84] For example, Thomas Danforth, an Old Charter assistant who had fought Randolph's imperial schemes, wrote to Increase Mather soon after the revolution, assuring the minister that Andros's superiors would call the governor to account for acts

82. Cotton Mather, "Life of Phips," p. 45; see Miller, *New England Mind,* 2: 156; *Andros Tracts,* 1: 14, 82.

83. *Andros Tracts,* 1: 126. It is interesting to note that when John Palmer, chief judge under Andros, wrote a pamphlet defending his government, he declared that the formation of the Dominion had meant that men "which for many years had groaned under the severity of a Tyrannical and Arbitrary Constitution, deprived of the Laws and Liberties of *Englishmen,* forced in their Consciences, suffered death for Religion, and denied *Appeals* to the King, were eased of those intolerable Burthens, and allowed the free Exercise of their Religion, and the benefit of the Laws of *England*" (1: 42). Clearly, Palmer and the Bostonians who deposed him defined the laws and liberties of England quite differently. In the eighteenth century the problem of definition became a major source of difficulty. Almost everyone in New England—indeed, almost everyone in the empire—spoke the political language of rights and property; but while the terms were the same, the meanings or values which men attached to these words varied greatly. Part of the shock of the American Revolution was the discovery that people in the mother country thought of rights and property in ways that the colonists rejected or could not understand.

84. See *The Plain Case Stated.*

"contrarie to the magna charta."[85] Another Puritan pamphleteer cited precedents from the reign of Henry VII to prove that Andros's commission had been invalid.[86]

The Puritan writers of 1689 employed secular, legal, and historical evidence to demonstrate that the Dominion governor had been a bad ruler, but they did not push these arguments as far as English contemporaries like John Locke had done.[87] While the colonists dropped much of the Old Testament rhetoric, they refused to go beyond the confines of strict constitutional history or to state their political position in abstract, philosophical terms. That advance had to wait for the next generation.

One tract, far more than the others, reflected the changes which had taken place in notions about the character of the good ruler. Because this anonymous work, *The Humble Address of the Publicans of New-England,* was such an excellent statement of Puritan political ideas, it deserves special analysis. The author, whoever he may have been, was probably a native of Massachusetts; for he knew a great deal about the history of the Bay Colony and about the government of the Dominion.[88] But even more important, he sensed that the Puritans of this period wanted to hear about rights and property, not about moral reformation. *The Humble Address* was filled with Whiggish ideas that were to become commonplace in eighteenth-century America: a constant fear of political conspiracy against popular rights, an obsession with the potential corruption and irresponsibility of all civil power, the necessity for the people to embody certain classical moral virtues if the nation was to avoid despotism, a belief in the superiority of a republic over other forms of government, and a persuasion that only the free participation

85. Thomas Danforth to Increase Mather, 30 July 1689, *Hutchinson Papers,* 2: 312.

86. *Andros Tracts,* 2: 5.

87. See B. Behrens, "The Whig Theory of the Constitution in the Reign of Charles II," *Cambridge Historical Journal* 8 (1941–43): 44–70; Laslett's introduction to *John Locke: Two Treatises of Government* (New York, 1963), pp. 15–92 passim.

88. *Andros Tracts,* 2: 231–69.

of all people in civil affairs could thwart the spread of tyranny.[89]

The author of the essay explained that the Publicans, a debauched group of courtiers, constituted an ever present danger to prosperous and virtuous governments throughout the world. This venal crew was particularly fearsome because it was prepared to use any means, no matter how vile, to gain its ends. The writer noted that the "Publicans *have always had, and will have, a great advantage over other men, by their profound* Abilities in the Arts of *Flattering, Lying, and Cheating;* altho' the rest of Mankind exceed them in every thing else." In their greedy search for riches, the Publicans did not hesitate to use the law as the Devil used Scripture, perverting statutes and constitutions for their own selfish goals. Throughout recorded history one could see how the members of this vicious fraternity had tried to enslave unsuspecting peoples with "Tyrannies, Treacheries, and little Tricks." In the period of the Glorious Revolution, the hero of every Publican was Louis XIV, the master despot of the age.[90]

The anonymous pamphleteer carefully recounted the details of the Publican plot to ravage New England. As early as the 1620s, he revealed, the conspirators had learned to hate the Puritans "because they apprehended some sharp people among the *Puritans* of those days, who were likely to be of some Let [i.e. hindrance] to their Designs." It was in this period that some of the Puritans decided to construct a godly commonwealth in America. The venture, of course, succeeded beyond anyone's hopes, for New England became a community of virtuous people governed by the best of rulers. As the writer put it, *"New-England* had a Sweet, Easie, and Gentle Government, *Made and Constituted by, as well as for the good of the People;* a Government, that knew no interest inconsistent with that of their Country and Charge." On every side the visitor to the Puritan colonies could have seen the wondrous effects of "Religion, Industry, and Sobriety" and fair women free from "Pride, Pomp, and

89. See Caroline Robbins, *The Eighteenth-Century Commonwealthman* (Cambridge, Mass., 1959); Bailyn, *The Ideological Origins of the American Revolution;* and Z. S. Fink, *The Classical Republicans: An Essay in the Recovery of a Pattern of Thought in Seventeenth-Century England* (Evanston, 1945).

90. *Andros Tracts,* 2: 244, 257–59.

Lust." But, unfortunately, New England's prosperity led to its undoing, for the Publicans across the Atlantic envied its wealth almost as much as they hated its virtue. The secret heads of the faction sent Randolph as an advance scout to America to verify the rumors of riches. He not only confirmed the stories, but also persuaded the conspirators to destroy the Puritans' main defense against tyrants, their charter. The conquest of the New Englanders was an easy task for the clever Publicans, because no one in Massachusetts was capable *"of Learning the Arts of Lying, Cheating, and Tricking."* Soon James II appointed "a chargeable [avaricious] Governour, with a sort of an Army, who not only Ruin'd the Countrey, but spent the King's money in the bargain: and this was all brought about, only to bring a few poor Distressed *Publicans* into Imployment: *Thus the King lost by it, and the Countrey lost by it, and none gained, but the Publicans."*[91] Only the Glorious Revolution saved the Bay Colony from complete ruin at the hands of the Dominion rulers.

The author of *The Humble Address* offered some hope, for he claimed that there were several ways to thwart the Publican conspiracy. First of all, the plotters feared republican and commonwealth governments more than anything else because republics were usually a sign of a virtuous and diligent people. "The Publicans make *Common-wealths, as Malefactors make Laws,"* the pamphleteer observed, "for were there no *Malefactors,* there would be no need of Laws: *and were there* no Publicans, *there need be no Republicks."* Second, the classical civil virtues—honesty, frugality, sobriety, perseverance—were the great enemies of Publican plans, and the republic which maintained these values was safe from any of their nefarious schemes. And third, the writer explained that ultimately only the people themselves could be trusted to rise up against tyrants and depose them as the brave patriots of Holland had done to the invading Publicans from Spain. The citizens could never assume that constitutions or mere paper laws would do their work for them. The author advised that *"the hearts of a People are the best, and indeed the only true security to a Prince."*[92] By implication, therefore, the good ruler was a leader who stood constantly vigilant, protecting

91. *Andros Tracts,* 2: 234–35, 242, 243, 253.
92. *Andros Tracts,* 2: 241–42, 245, 246, 247, 249.

his constituents from Publicans both within and outside the government. Such a ruler also maintained and encouraged the people's
virtue so that corrupt moral practices, a sure sign of civil weakness,
would not undermine the strength of the commonwealth. The ideas
in this pamphlet were to be repeated through the eighteenth century
and were to have a profound influence on the politics of the American Revolution.[93]

After the Glorious Revolution, the Puritans' definition of the
good ruler never returned to what it had been before 1686, and the
language of property and liberty became an integral part of the
magisterial calling. In 1689 the colonists set two political goals: first,
to keep Andros from regaining power; and, second, to make certain
that no future ruler of Massachusetts ever had the opportunity of
duplicating the governor's crimes. As it turned out, William III
had little interest in reviving the Dominion of New England; and,
after some haggling with colonial representatives, he granted the
Bay Colony a new charter similar to the one it had lost. The second
goal, however, had to wait until 1692 when a new government, consisting of a governor, council, and lower house, had been established.
One of the first laws which passed the reconstituted General Court
was an act entitled "A Bill for the General Rights and Liberties."
The text of this statute reads like a summary of all the charges which
the people had made against Andros, and that was exactly what the
legislators intended.

One of the first clauses in the bill outlawed arbitrary arrest and
seizure of property: "That no Free man shall be taken and Imprisoned or deprived of his free hold or liberties, or his free customs,
or be outlawed or be Exiled, or in any manner destroyed, nor shall
be passed upon, adjudged or Condemned, but by the Lawfull Judgment of his Peers, or the Law of this Province." The act assured
all defendants that they would be given a fair jury trial by men
living within their neighborhood or shire. Land titles were declared
secure; and bail was guaranteed in all cases except those involving
treason. Perhaps the members of the Massachusetts General Court
had the Ipswich rebels in mind when they ordered that "No aid,

93. See Edmund S. Morgan, "The Puritan Ethic and the American
Revolution," *William and Mary Quarterly,* 3d ser. 24(1967): 3–43.

Tax, Tallage, Assessment Custom Loans, Benevolence or Imposition whatsoever shall be laid, Assessed, Imposed, or Levied on any of their Majesties Subjects, or their Estates, on any Colour or pretence whatsoever, but by the act and Consent of the Governor Councill and Representatives of the People assembled in Generall Court."[94]

The bill for "General Rights and Liberties" is one of the most important, though least known, documents of the seventeenth century and is one of the first bills of rights to be written in America. What gives the act of 1692 special significance for the political historian is the fact that its language and argumentation are essentially English, and it reads as if it belonged to the tradition of The Petition of Right (1628), The Grand Remonstrance (1641), and The Bill of Rights (1689). Without mentioning Andros by name, the Massachusetts statute attacked specific evils which had occurred under his administration, just as Parliament had passed the Declaration of Rights with James II in mind. The colonial legislators made no mention of religion, no call for intolerance, no use of scriptural notation. In fact, their overriding concern was with the security of their rights and liberties as English citizens. To appreciate the great change that had taken place in New England political rhetoric since the 1630s one need only look at Nathaniel Ward's *Body of Liberties* (1641), which was the colony's first bill of rights. Although Ward and Winthrop had fought over the merits of codification, the *Body of Liberties* was still clearly the product of its Puritan environment. It was filled with discussion about the role of the state in church affairs and about ecclesiastical power in civil business. The opening section set the tone for the entire code: "The free fruition of such liberties, Immunities, and priveledges as humanitie, Civilitie, and Christianitie call for, as due every man in his place and proportion without impeachment and Infringement, hath ever bene and ever will

94. The text of this bill can be found in the Massachusetts Archives, 47: 87–88, and in *The Acts and Resolves, Public and Private, of the Province of the Massachusetts Bay*, 21 vols. (Boston, 1869), 1: 40–41. See also Hutchinson, *History*, 2: 48–49. After the act had passed the entire General Court, the Privy Council disallowed it, claiming that the sections dealing with bail and inheritance conflicted with English statutes. The disallowance in no way undermines the importance of this document for New England intellectual and political history.

be the tranquillitie and Stabilitie of Churches and Common-wealths."[95] The legislature of 1692 dropped all notice of Christianity and churches, stating simply "that all and every [one of] the Rights and Liberties of the People in this present act mentioned shall be firmly and strictly held and observed."[96] After the Glorious Revolution some of the problems which had perplexed Ward's society—punishing heretics, settling church disputes, preserving the purity of Congregationalism—no longer seemed so pressing. In fact, the Dominion experience had shown the Puritans that they needed English constitutional rulers, not Christian magistrates.

The differences between the *Body of Liberties* and the 1692 statute should not be overstated, for both acts were passed for the same purpose: limiting the ruler's discretion. As we have seen, the deputies of the 1630s and 1640s thought that Winthrop and his fellow magistrates possessed arbitrary powers, especially in judicial matters. Ward's codification of the laws established clear boundaries within which the assistants had to confine themselves. Winthrop, of course, had never been a tyrant, but Andros was. His brief administration convinced many New Englanders that they had best place controls over their rulers, at least negative ones, so that everyone would know when a magistrate had exceeded his rightful authority. After the Glorious Revolution Puritans looked upon the good ruler as a man who respected the constitutional limitations which the people themselves had set on his office.

There was a certain irony about the literature of the Glorious Revolution which gives it special importance to the historian of political ideas. The pamphleteers knew that the purpose of the Dominion had been to bring the colonists more in line with English practices and that the Puritans had regarded Andros's arbitrary policies as a threat to New England's special heritage. But the writers were also aware that it would be foolish to try to justify their rebellion on the basis of local custom, since William was not apt to be sympathetic with arguments that smacked of independence. In an effort to win the king's support, they stressed the fact that they had

95. Edmund S. Morgan, ed., *Puritan Political Ideas, 1558–1794?* (Indianapolis, 1965), pp. 178–79 (punctuation added).

96. Massachusetts Archives, 47: 87.

defended traditional English liberties. However, what may have been conceived as a clever rhetorical stance or as a form of propaganda soon became an expression of sincere belief, for the New Englanders were convinced by the content of their own appeals. They continued to use the language of rights and property in political discussion long after Massachusetts had appeased the king and acquired a new charter. There can be no doubt that the members of the General Court believed that the bill for "General Rights and Liberties" would please their constituents. The Dominion had attempted unsuccessfully to make the Puritans more English, but the overthrow of that government accomplished the very Anglicization which Andros had been unable to effect.

Aftermath of Revolution

The overthrow of Andros united New Englanders under the banner of liberty and property. But as soon as the governor was safely in jail and men had turned their attentions to the formation of a new government to replace the Dominion, the revolutionary harmony began to break down. While most Puritans regarded the defense of liberty and property as the essence of the magisterial calling, they quarreled over the nature of the ruler's relationship to the freemen. Some of the colonists who had supported the Glorious Revolution simply wanted to be rid of Andros and to establish a government which would protect their estates. They certainly had no desire to encourage popular participation in civil affairs. Other persons, however, felt that the people should have greater control over the formulation of policy. Basically, the question dividing these two groups was whether it was the ruler or his constituents who knew what was best for the common good. The controversy grew more intense as time passed; and, as we will see in following sections, by the beginning of the eighteenth century it had become the major political problem facing New Englanders.

An unexpected result of the Glorious Revolution was the people's heightened sense of their own political importance. Pamphleteer after pamphleteer indicated that New Englanders would never have gotten into such a mess had the colonists been allowed to choose their own rulers. It had been the common people—many of them non-freemen under the Old Charter—who had driven Andros from power; and, in the months following his overthrow, these rebels showed no willingness to withdraw from the political process or to accept leaders who did not represent their views. Of course, New Englanders had long recognized the popular basis of civil government. Winthrop and other Puritan magistrates, however, had encouraged participation only in elections, making it quite clear that the voters had no voice in routine civil decisions. While some men disagreed with this view, it was not until 1689 that colonists assumed an active political role, asserting the right not only to throw out tyrants, but also to criticize specific policies which they found obnoxious.

It was clear from the discussion about a revolutionary government that many colonists would accept no settlement in which they did not have a voice. A group of Old Charter assistants established a provisional administration called the Council of Safety as soon as the Dominion officials had been removed. After a few days this self-appointed body expanded its membership by adding leading citizens such as Wait Winthrop, who had not been magistrates under the former patent. From the very first, the councillors tried to please two different masters: the leaders of the mother country and the people of New England. The interim rulers wanted to avoid any action which might give William III the impression that Massachusetts had set up an independent commonwealth.[97] On the other hand, they knew that the rebels who were in no mood to procrastinate demanded an immediate return to an elective form of government. One pamphleteer reminded the provisional councillors that "an Election or *Free Choice* in *Government* by the People (till special Orders from *England*) was one *main* thing aimed at in the Motion of the Army."[98] Presumably, if the councillors had dragged their feet, they too would have gone the way of Andros and Dudley.

On May 2, 1689, the Council of Safety acceded to popular demands, calling the deputies who had been elected to the last General Court to advise them on what course to follow until the colony heard from England. A week later sixty-six delegates from forty-

97. Hutchinson, *History,* 1: 322–24, 327; Simmons, "Massachusetts Revolution of 1689," pp. 3–4.

98. Simmons, "Massachusetts Revolution of 1689," p. 11.

four towns met in Boston for a special convention and recommended that Massachusetts return to the constitution it had before the Dominion. The council, fearing that such a move might anger the king, told the representatives that it would not adopt any plan until it had heard from the towns; but, when the opinions of the villages had been ascertained, the verdict remained the same. The majority of the colonists wanted the government of the Old Charter restored.[99]

The members of the Council of Safety compromised in late May, agreeing to revive the old system, but at the same time they made it clear that the patent which had been condemned by the Court of Chancery in 1684 was not in force. They declared that their interim government was only an expediency designed to ensure local order until England decided on what to do with Massachusetts. Everyone in the colony seemed reasonably happy with this solution. The men who had been added to the council were dropped from office; and the venerable Simon Bradstreet, an original founder of the colony, was once again the Puritan governor. One writer announced enthusiastically that Bradstreet "tho' he be well toward Ninety Years of Age, has his *Intellectual Force hardly abated,* but retains a vigour and Wisdom that would recommend a younger man to the Government of a greater Colony."[100] Bradstreet, together with his annually elected assistants and deputies, appeared to enjoy broad popular support.

The town instructions which led to Bradstreet's return to power declared almost unanimously that popular consent was the only valid foundation for civil power. Like the founders, the Puritans of 1689 regarded government as a voluntary covenant or contract between the people and their rulers, and the letters which the towns wrote to their representatives revealed that the colonists thought that every

99. Court Records, 6: 11–12, 16–17; Hutchinson, *History,* 1: 327; Barnes, *Dominion of New England,* pp. 244–47. For an excellent collection of documents having to do with the Council of Safety, see Albert Matthews, ed., *Massachusetts Royal Commissions, 1681–1775* (Cambridge, Mass., 1913), pp. 16–28.

100. *Andros Tracts,* 2: 200. Randolph's description of the governor was quite different: "Mr. Bradstreet is very weake and dying: and now Mr. Danforth is sett up for Champion of the peoples Libertyes" (Toppan and Goodrick, *Edward Randolph,* 6: 326).

man's opinion should be heard. The records of Wenham in particular
reflected the colony-wide insistence on popular participation in politics. At a town meeting, "the *freeholders* & *Inhabitants* . . . being
deeply sensible of & thankful to God for his greate mircey in deliv-
ering us from the tyerange & opresion of those Ill men under [whose]
injustice & Cruelty we have so long groaned," called for the return
of the General Court which they had elected in 1686.[101] The people
of Wenham also promised to support the government they had helped
bring into being with their "persons & Estates" and prayed that "all
those who are true friends to the peace & prosperitie of this land
will ridily & hartily Joyne with us herein."[102] At the same time, the
men of Braintree "convened together to give their sentiments &
minds about the present settlement of a Government" and echoed the
spirit of Wenham's resolution.[103] The "free houelders and in-
habetanc" of Boxford likewise moved to terminate "the many in
Conveniencies and hazards of the present unsetelment of our af-
faiers."[104] What is significant about all these local declarations is
that the towns allowed both freemen and inhabitants—in other
words, both church members and nonchurch members—to participate in the formation of the new civil compact. Apparently the
towns believed that all the people affected by the policies of the provisional government should have a voice in its establishment.[105]

While the town instructions were being composed, many people
were also petitioning for an alteration in the colony's franchise law

101. *Wenham Town Records, 1642–1706* (Wenham, 1930), pp. 89–90.
Most of the town instructions have been preserved in the Massachusetts
Archives, 107: 14A, 15, 16, 17A, 19, 20, 36–41, 43–54. For the most part
there is little variation in the form or content of the different letters.

102. *Wenham Town Records,* p. 90.

103. Samuel A. Bates, ed., *Records of the Town of Braintree* (Randolph,
1886), p. 26.

104. *Essex Institute Historical Collections,* 36(1900): 47.

105. During the 1630s only the freemen had been allowed to participate
in either local or colony politics. After the mid–1640s, however, a select
group of non-freemen were given the right to vote in town affairs (see
Massachusetts Archives, 112: 112; Breen, "The Town Franchise"). Thus,
it was a bold step for Boxford and the other villages to let inhabitants
or non-freemen take part in the formation of the provisional government,
a matter that was clearly a colony-wide concern.

so that men who were not church members could legally participate in the choice of rulers. In January 1690 a group informed the General Court that persons who "had been willing to venture their lives and estates for the cause of rights against oppression" should be allowed to vote in Massachusetts elections. Several pamphleteers writing in this period insisted upon an extension of the franchise, at least to include freeholders. One writer asked rhetorically whether the army, "the far greater part of which consits of such as were no free-men in the Old Government," would support the retention of the narrow Old Charter suffrage requirements.[106] The Bradstreet government responded to these demands by changing the franchise laws, giving the vote to any man who paid four shillings in a single country rate, owned a house and/or land valued at six pounds.[107] The new ruling apparently opened the franchise to many people who had been denied freemanship under the former patent, for the Massachusetts Archives show that scores of men took advantage of the act.[108] It was only natural that colonists who had fought a revolution for rights and property should now expect property holders to have a share in the provisional government.

Before many months had passed it became clear that a large number of colonists regarded political participation as more than voting or writing instructions for special constitutional conventions. They demanded a more active role. In fact, the people who had pledged their "persons & Estates" to Bradstreet's government in the spring of 1689 were attacking specific policies by the summer. When the provisional rulers erred there were many persons who refused to overlook the failure or to wait for the next election. In July, for example, the provisional magistrates decided to let Dudley out of jail on bond because he was sick. The move apparently angered a good many Bostonians; for it was not long before a mob of one hundred fifty men, led by George Wells, gathered in front of the governor's house calling him an "old Rogue."[109] Some of the councillors reported that

106. Massachusetts Archives, 107: 94A, cited in Simmons, "Massachusetts Revolution of 1689," p. 6.

107. Massachusetts Archives, 35: 154.

108. Massachusetts Archives, 35: 349–53, 360, 360A; 36: 20, 21–27, 60–62.

109. Lewis, "Massachusetts and the Glorious Revolution," p. 336.

"the tumult in the town is so great and sudden that no reason will be heard or regarded."[110] The popular discontent worried the members of the provisional government, especially those men who had previously served on the Council of Safety. Bradstreet's concern was clearly evident when he wrote to Sir Henry Ashurst, the colony's agent in London, explaining "we are far from willingly doing anything arbitrary; but the long want of directions from England for settlement doth weaken our hands."[111] The governor also begged the local Congregational ministers to call for civil obedience in their sermons; but, whatever the clergy may have done, the people continued to criticize their rulers.[112] A Virginian, Cuthbert Potter, who was traveling in New England at this time, noted widespread unhappiness with Bradstreet's administration; and, in the towns of Cambridge and Charleston, he observed "that many who had been for were now inveterate enemies to the present Government."[113] No doubt the old Puritan governor was a bitter man: the people had insisted on his return to office and then challenged every move he made.

Much of the popular discontent and criticism of the provisional government resulted from New England's military expeditions against the French in Canada. Bradstreet and some of his advisers believed that William III would look more favorably on the colony's request for a new charter if he saw evidence that the Americans supported his efforts to defeat Louis XIV. An attack on the French base at Port Royal, led by Sir William Phips, was a success; but later maneuvers against Quebec proved disastrous.[114] In June Bradstreet's government had trouble getting men to fight the Indians on the Massachusetts and Maine frontier, a problem which had plagued Sir Edmund Andros.[115] And just two months later, Fort Pemaquid, reputedly the strongest position in Maine, fell to the Indians. The people simply refused to back policies which inconvenienced them or struck them as foolish adventures.

110. Ibid.
111. Hutchinson, *History,* 1: 329.
112. Lewis, "Massachusetts and the Glorious Revolution," pp. 336, 339.
113. Newton D. Mereness, ed., *Travels in the American Colonies* (New York, 1916), p. 8.
114. Hutchinson, *History,* 1: 335–41.
115. Lewis, "Massachusetts and the Glorious Revolution," p. 337.

The military campaigns left Massachusetts deeply in debt; and, when the soldiers returned, there was no money to pay them for their service.[116] To avoid a showdown with the troops, the provisional government printed thousands of pounds in paper currency, promising to redeem the notes at full value in specie when taxes came due later in the year. Most of the colonial soldiers needed money immediately and could not afford to wait for deferred redemption. When they tried to spend the new paper currency, however, they found that merchants would not accept it at face value; and a militiaman was fortunate to get twelve or fourteen shillings on the pound.[117] The business community had little confidence in the fiscal stability of Bradstreet's government. When the colony's taxes were finally collected, the disappointment among the troops increased; for speculators who had purchased the currency at reduced rates made sizable profits, while the men who had suffered in Canada received nothing.[118]

Had John Winthrop been alive in 1689 he would have either ignored the critics or informed them that they had no business questioning specific magisterial decisions. But Bradstreet and the other provisional rulers clearly felt the need to justify their policies before the people. Their defense of paper money and increased taxation revealed a growing belief in Massachusetts that magistrates had to answer to their constituents for their official acts. Several pamphleteers who sympathized with the provisional government tried to reason with its critics, urging them to support Bradstreet's policies. The writers maintained that the rulers were not personally responsible for the problems which had beset the colony, and one apologist asked the grumblers "whether it be not better to give a shilling to a publick Account with our own consent in a general Assembly, than

116. Hutchinson, *History,* 1: 335–41.

117. Hutchinson, *History,* 1: 340–41; Andrew M. Davis, "Currency and Banking in the Province of the Massachusetts Bay," *Publications of the American Economic Association,* 3d ser. 1, no. 4(1900), pp. 9–11.

118. Hutchinson, *History,* 1: 341. At the same time that the colony was having difficulty with paper money, the government was raising taxes far above all previous rates, calling for twenty country rates in one year (Massachusetts Archives, 81: 107). Doubtless, the cause of the tax increase was the war against France, but the people were not happy about paying so much for military campaigns that seemed ill-conceived and poorly directed.

to have a penny forced from us without it, *as in the late Arbitrary Government?*"[119] Another felt that the people's lack of support was inexcusable. "Our Present *Rulers,* have no personal benefit by them [the taxes]," he declared. "They spend time and care, and are at cost too, for the Common Weal, and would count themselves well paid for all, in the *Contentment,* of the people."[120]

Defenders of the provisional government also tried to explain why the printing of paper currency had been a sound policy. One anonymous author who wrote *Some Considerations of the Bills of Credit Now Passing in New-England* told the people that their criticism was based on a misunderstanding of the constitution of 1686, the system which they themselves had demanded when Andros had been deposed. The pamphleteer reminded his readers that when they became citizens of the commonwealth they accepted a responsibility to bear the burdens as well as to reap the benefits of the whole society. If the people truly believed that their magistrates had demanded needless revenues or circulated bad money, then they could easily choose better rulers at their next election "if they Know where to find them."[121] The writer thought that the disruption of credit was a sign of the selfish, shortsighted notions that pervaded the commonwealth. He claimed "that the Bill (as *I* have heard) of any *one Magistrate* . . . shall buy any Commodities of any of the Planters; and yet our people (in this pure air) be so sottish as to deny Credit to the Government, when 'tis of their own *Chusing.*" "Is the Security of one Plantation-Magistrate," the author asked sarcastically, "better than that of *All the Massachusetts Representatives?*"[122] He declared that for reasons unknown to himself the people had concluded that there was no lawful government after the overthrow of Andros and that their property was no safer under Bradstreet than it had been under the Dominion. The colonists would gladly have

119. [Anon.], *Further Quaeries upon the Present State of New English Affairs* (1690), p. 10 (italics added).

120. *Some Additional Considerations Addressed* . . . (Boston, 1691), reprinted in Andrew McFarland Davis, *Colonial Currency Reprints,* 4 vols. (Boston, 1910–11), 1: 198–99; Barnes, *Dominion of New England,* p. 257.

121. *Some Considerations on the Bills* . . . (Boston, 1691), in Davis, *Currency Reprints,* 1: 190.

122. Ibid., p. 191.

accepted the government's currency had not their heads been "be-whized with Conceits that we have no *Magistrates*, no *Government*, And by Consequence that we have no *Security* for any thing, which we call our own (a *Consequence* they will be Loth to allow, though they cannot help it, If once we are Reduced to *Hobs* his state of *Nature*, which (says he) is a *state* of War, and then the *strongest* must *sake* all.)"[123] The pamphleteer's bitter comments revealed that the people of Massachusetts were using the same standard of political judgment on the General Court of 1689 that they had used on Andros. Moreover, the popular protests that followed the Glorious Revolution demonstrated that no government, not even one filled with Old Charter magistrates, could win wide support as long as its decisions appeared arbitrary or in conflict with generally held notions about the common good.

The people's active and sudden intervention into the political affairs of this period appalled some New Englanders who had begun to question the worth of popular participation in government. These men did not establish a formal party or association, and they may not have even been aware of each other's existence. It is probably best to view the movement as a spontaneous reaction to specific events. Whatever the case may have been, after the Revolution of 1689 various men throughout Massachusetts and Connecticut con-cluded that the people were as great a threat to the common good as was any despot. Everywhere they saw the need for "prudent and able men" to control the "giddy and enraged mob."[124] Persons of this persuasion felt that the great mass of colonists could never distin-guish the general welfare from their own private interests and that the ruler who followed the will of the people would surely ruin the commonwealth.

One of the best examples of the new spirit was an anonymous essay entitled *Reflections upon the Affairs of New England*. The writer recounted with disgust that "as soon as the hurry of rev-olution was over," the colonists decided that they needed some form of civil authority, and for that purpose "chose the men that had thrown themselves at the head of the action." But when these leaders

123. Ibid., pp. 191–92.
124. *Calendar of State Papers, Colonial Series, 1689–1692*, p. 61.

"could not in all things run with the *mad head strong multitude* they began to be kicked at and when they endeavored a regulation of affaires that the law might have its course it was accounted intollerable."[125] Another pamphleteer in his *Further Quaeries Upon the Present State of New-English Affairs,* probably printed sometime in 1690, felt compelled to remind the people of Massachusetts that "governing is a skill, as great as any of the Liberal Arts." It was, therefore, a gross error to think that the majority or even a large number of men possessed the "experience" necessary to be good rulers. The writer warned against experimenting in the choice of magistrates and instead recommended that the voters select officials "of good Fashion and Quality, and such as maintain the due Grandure of a Government."[126]

Colonists who doubted the worth of popular participation argued that the people had to be brought under control, made to listen to the orders of their superiors. The idea that citizens could do anything they liked simply because they had overturned the Dominion did not sit well with such men as the Reverend Samuel Willard. This leading divine sighed with relief when civil authority was once again securely established upon a new royal charter in 1691. Reflecting on the experience of the Bradstreet administration, Willard explained, "When there was no Governor in *Israel* and every man did what he would, what horrible outrages were then perpetrated . . . and we ourselves have a Specimen of this in the short *Anarchy* accompanying our late *Revolution.*"[127] Persons who shared Willard's beliefs had no intention of standing aside while the people reduced the colony "to *Hobs* his state of *Nature.*" For them anarchy—defined no doubt as constant criticism of government policies—was as bad, if not worse, than tyranny.

Gershom Bulkeley was the most articulate and most extreme spokesman for this group. Surprisingly, historians know very little about Bulkeley's personal life. He was the son of Peter Bulkeley, one

125. *Collections,* CHS, 21: 324–25. The essay was never published, but there is no doubt that the manuscript written in the summer of 1691 circulated publicly.

126. *Further Quaeries,* pp. 4–5.

127. Samuel Willard, *The Character of a Good Ruler* (Boston, 1694), p. 3.

of the leading theologians in Winthrop's generation. After he graduated from Harvard in 1655, Gershom Bulkeley preached in a New London church; but, when he was unable to get along with his parishioners, he moved to Wethersfield where he became a physician. He also accepted a commission from James II as a justice of the peace when Connecticut fell under Andros's jurisdiction. It is likely that scholars would have ignored Bulkeley altogether had he not published two extraordinary pamphlets soon after the people of New England toppled the Dominion: *The Peoples Right to Election* (1689) and *Will and Doom* (1692). Both works bitterly attacked the political leaders of Connecticut for resuming the colony's old charter government in 1689. According to Bulkeley, the local rulers had abrogated their patent by submitting to Andros's authority and therefore had no legal right to reestablish Connecticut's General Assembly as if nothing had happened to the foundation of their government.[128]

Bulkeley's writings challenged the very core of Puritan political theory, the people's right to determine who would be their rulers. He believed that the revolution against Andros had exposed the "levelling, independent, democratical principle and spirit, with a tang of fifth-monarchy" which had infected the populace of his colony. During the Glorious Revolution the New Englanders had acted as if their aim was to create "an Oliverian republic." "Is it not too well known, or can it be forgotten," Bulkeley lamented, "what general . . . satisfaction and rejoicing there was, at the horrid and hellish murder of that excellent prince [Charles I]?" The angry doctor reminded his neighbors that all political authority came from God, not from man. Moreover, the Lord favored monarchy as the best form of government for his children. "We owe no obedience to any man," he declared, "contrary to that obedience we owe to God; and by proportion, we owe no obedience to any inferior governors contrary to that obedience we owe to the king." So that the colonists would not miss his point, Bulkeley added the stinging aphorism, "Rebellion against the King is a mediate rebellion against God." It

128. *The Peoples Right to Election* is printed in *Collections*, CHS, 1; and *Will and Doom* is in *Collections*, CHS, 2. For additional material on Bulkeley and the pamphlets, see Miller, *New England Mind*, 2: 152–53, and *Connecticut Records*, 3: 456.

is impossible to establish how Bulkeley arrived at his political ideas. Whatever the influences may have been, this son of a founding Puritan sounded like one of the creatures who had surrounded James I.

In his *Will and Doom* Bulkeley carried his argument to its logical conclusion: Andros had been the king's lawfully appointed governor; and, try as they would, the Puritans could not justify their revolution against him. The Connecticut writer thought that the politics in his colony following the overthrow of the Dominion was a "tyrannical anarchy" which more than supported his contention that the people had no right to depose or to erect governments on their own authority. "Sovereignty in a king is a sceptre of gold," he wrote in 1692, "but in the hands of a subject it is *a rod* of iron: and so we find it."[129] For Bulkeley, the good ruler obeyed the monarch, enforced the statutes of the realm, and resisted the people's foolish demands.

Other men in Connecticut shared Bulkeley's sentiments about popular political participation, even if they did not fully concur with his royalist beliefs. In September 1693 magistrate Samuel Wyllys wrote to his friend, Fitz-John Winthrop, who was later to become the governor of Connecticut. Wyllys hoped "That their Majestie please to declare that persons of mean & low degree be not improved in the cheifest place of civill & military affairs, to gratifie some little humors, when they are not qualified nor fit for the King's service, which will bring inevitably their Majesties government here into contempt."[130] He thought that "persons of good parintage" would make excellent rulers for the colony, for they would preserve liberty and property as well as maintain the honor of the king. But should William fail them, should Bulkeley's local Oliverians gain the upper hand, then "it is feared *twill be like the waves of a troubled sea.*"[131]

In the period following the Glorious Revolution, New Englanders agreed that the purpose of government was the protection of property and liberty. However, as the years went by it became increasingly apparent that the terms "property" and "liberty" did not mean the same things to all men. As we will discover in later sections, one group of New Englanders, which included John Wise and the author

129. *Will and Doom*, pp. 83, 92, 94, 258.
130. *Collections*, MHS, 3: 17.
131. Ibid.

of the *Humble Address of the Publicans,* regarded rulers as the greatest potential threat to the people's possessions. The colonists who held this view defined the good magistrate as one who listened to the demands of his constituents and who constrained the power of government so that it could never become an instrument for destroying popular liberties. But, at the same time, New Englanders of Bulkeley's persuasion called for strong, upper-class rulers who would guard the rights of the few against the tyranny of the many. Civil order was the magistrate's highest goal. The basic question dividing these two groups was whether civil order was more important than popular rights, a question that would never be answered to everyone's satisfaction.

5

THE POLITICS OF PROPERTY:
1691–1694

N the spring of 1692 Sir William Phips, royal governor of Massachusetts, arrived in Boston bearing the colony's new charter. Many New Englanders, who had grown impatient with Bradstreet's ineffectual administration, welcomed Phips's landing with a sigh of relief. They hoped that their new governor would end the uncertainties of the provisional regime and return the commonwealth to a stable, prosperous course. Unfortunately, he did not fulfill their expectations. Over the next few years Phips and the new constitution he brought with him raised far more problems than they solved; and, instead of establishing political peace in Massachusetts, they sparked a fresh debate about the character of the good ruler and the nature of good government.

After Phips had been in office for only a few months New Englanders decided he was a bad ruler, but they recognized that his failings were of a different sort from those of Andros. The leader of the Dominion had been pompous, overbearing, and arbitrary; while the new charter governor was weak, ineffective, and crude. Phips let other men determine his civil policies for him, which meant that he unwittingly became the voice for a narrow party or faction within the colony. In addition, the governor lacked the personal dignity which Puritans had come to expect their magistrates to possess. People in the early 1690s wanted rulers who would listen to their demands and protect their property without embodying their faults. Unhappily, Phips seemed to mirror their worst qualities, and his presence in New England forced the colonists to refine some of their notions about the magistracy.

Not all the changes in the popular conception of the magisterial

vocation resulted from conscious attempts to show why Phips and
Andros were bad governors. Some beliefs about the calling shifted
undramatically, as accidental by-products of alterations in the colony's relationship to the mother country. After the revolutionary
period, roughly 1684 to 1694, a viable description of the character
of the good ruler had to take into account the fact that England was
determined to bring the American colonies under closer supervision
and control. The days when local magistrates might cavalierly decide
whether they would enforce the Navigation Acts or support religious
toleration were gone. And after 1691 political theorists in Massachusetts had to deal with the new royal charter. This document
turned important civil posts which had been elective under the old
patent into appointive offices. The new charter also separated judicial, legislative, and executive functions, forcing colonial rulers to
become greater specialists than they had ever been before. These and
other changes caused by the reorganization of government contributed to a transformation of the magistracy, making irrelevant much
that had been written before 1684 about the character of the good
ruler.

A New Charter and a Bad Ruler

While Sir Edmund Andros was still in power, Increase Mather
went to London as New England's self-appointed champion. When
the minister heard reports that the citizens of Massachusetts had
jailed the Dominion leaders, he launched an energetic campaign to
convince William III to restore the Bay Colony's Old Charter privileges.[1] While his lobbying at court failed to save the Old Charter,
Mather did win important concessions from the English government;
and the new patent which the king granted in 1691 represented an
impressive diplomatic victory for the Boston divine.[2]

Unfortunately for Mather, there were many men in Massachusetts

1. Cotton Mather, "Life of His Excellency Sir William Phips," *Magnalia Christi Americana* (London, 1702), bk. 2, pp. 37–72.

2. Kenneth B. Murdock, *Increase Mather: The Foremost American
Puritan* (Cambridge, Mass., 1925), pp. 256–61. The text of the new charter
is printed in William Macdonald, ed., *Select Charters and Other Documents
Illustrative of American History, 1606–1775* (New York, 1899), pp. 202–13;
and in *Massachusetts Acts and Resolves*, 1: 1–20.

who were not prepared to accept any changes in Winthrop's charter; and, even before they had seen the new constitution, they concluded that the minister had misrepresented their interests to the king. The leader of these recalcitrant New Englanders was Elisha Cooke, who had been in London with Mather. Cooke was obviously familiar with the complexities of imperial diplomacy, but he made no effort to vindicate Mather's reputation.[3] When Increase returned home in 1692 he expected to receive a hero's welcome, but instead found himself the object of bitter attacks. Much that Increase and Cotton Mather wrote during the 1690s can be read as an apology for the new charter and for the new royal governor, Sir William Phips.[4]

The Mathers were much more attuned to the changes that had taken place in New England than historians sometimes admit. They realized, for example, that the language of politics had been transformed during the Glorious Revolution and that the jeremiad rhetoric would be of little use in selling the new charter to the people of Massachusetts. The ministers appealed directly to Puritan pocketbooks, claiming that the 1691 patent protected both liberties and property. Neither Cotton nor Increase, in fact, missed a chance to remind the colonists of Andros's crimes against their estates. "Is it not *well*," Cotton asked the critics, "that all *Christian Liberties,* and all *English Liberties,* are by Royal Charter effectually Secured unto us? Is it not *well,* That all our *Titles* to our Livings are at once Confirmed, beyond the reach of all *Intruders?*" The clerical defenders called upon their ungrateful neighbors to rejoice that there were no more "Needy, Hungry, Bloody, *Strangers*" to demand quitrents "from them for what they had before possess'd as their *Free-holds* Time out of mind."[5] The Mathers also pointed out that the new charter provided for an elective house of representatives, thus making it impossible for tyrants to impose laws and taxes on the colonists

3. Murdock, *Increase Mather,* p. 315; Robert Calef, *More Wonders of the Invisible World* . . . (London, 1700), p. 95.

4. E.g. Increase Mather, *The Great Blessing, of Primitive Counsellours* (Boston, 1693); Cotton Mather, *Good Men Described* . . . (Boston, 1692); also Viola F. Barnes, *The Dominion of New England* (New York, 1960), pp. 262–73.

5. Cotton Mather, *Good Men Described,* pp. 33, 86.

without the consent of their freely elected delegates.[6] How could Cooke object to a system of government which protected popular rights so well?

Increase and Cotton seemed confident that their arguments about the safety of property and liberty would woo even the most stubborn New Englanders to their side. As part of their campaign, they persuaded a group of Nonconformist English divines to write an open letter supporting the new patent. Significantly, the political language of the London clergymen was no more scriptural than that of the Mathers. The letter assured the Americans that *"Your present* Charter *secures Liberty and Property, the fairest Flowers of the Civil State."*[7] Perhaps if the Mathers had paused to reflect on how much the rhetoric of politics had changed since 1677—the year that Increase delivered his intemperate election sermon—when the fairest flowers of the civil state were piety and intolerance, they might have blushed to think that they were leading the vanguard of change. But the two ministers gave no indication of anxiety as they went about insisting that the charter was New England's "MAGNA CHARTA."[8] The Mathers in effect infused property with a sacred quality and then proceeded to defend it with an evangelistic fervor once reserved only for the church itself.

No doubt the Mathers hoped that their concentration on property rights would obfuscate some of the less popular features of the new charter. The patent of 1691 provided for an upper house consisting of twenty-eight councillors, seven of whom had to reside in the old Plymouth Colony and Maine. These magistrates were not elected by the freemen as the assistants had been, but were chosen by the House of Representatives. The new royal governor not only

6. In his sermon, *Primitive Counsellours,* Increase explained, "By Vertue of this Charter every man is Confirmed in the Peaceable Enjoyment of his *Estate* and *Property,* Nor can any *Taxes* now be imposed on you, or Laws made, without your own consent by such *Representatives* as your selves shall Chuse" (p. 3).

7. *The Andros Tracts,* 3 vols. (Boston, 1868), 2: 298.

8. *Andros Tracts,* 2: 296; see Perry Miller, *The New England Mind,* 2 vols. (Boston, 1961), 2: 169–70 for an excellent discussion of the Mathers in this period. See chap. 3 for an account of Increase Mather's political ideas in the pre-Dominion years.

had veto power over the selection of any councillor but also possessed authority to disallow legislative acts which had been passed by the General Court. Increase Mather admitted somewhat reluctantly that the new charter "makes the Civil Government of *New-England* more *Monarchial* and less *Democratical* than in former Times."[9] The minister hedged, however, by stressing the colonists' control over the ruler's discretionary power. "The People," Cotton explained, "have a Negative upon all the Executive Part of the Civil Government, as well as the Legislative, which is a vast Privilege, enjoyed by no other Plantation in *America,* nor by *Ireland,* no, nor hitherto by *England* itself."[10] The colonists, of course, had not yet discovered what was to become their greatest insurance against a governor's arbitrary schemes: his salary. The new constitution also gave the vote to all men with forty shilling freeholds, the English franchise formula, and thus formally removed church membership as the basis of the colonial electorate.[11] In addition, the patent guaranteed all citizens, except Catholics, the right to worship as they pleased. The Mathers claimed they could not understand why these alterations in the government created such a stir and advised the Puritans to make their peace with the new system before they lost their *"opportunities of becoming* Happy."[12]

In many ways Sir William Phips was the perfect ruler for the property conscious Puritan commonwealth. The robust governor who arrived with Increase Mather in 1692 would have been equally at home in the world of Andrew Carnegie and John D. Rockefeller. Phips was a self-made man who by luck and pluck had fought his way up from obscurity to the very pinnacle of financial and political success. He was born in the rough frontier settlement of Kennebec,

---

9. *Andros Tracts,* 2: 290.

10. Cotton Mather, "Life of Phips," p. 57; Cotton Mather, *Good Men Described,* pp. 86–87.

11. The right to elect the minister was similarly given to all townspeople, not just members in full communion, by a law of 1692. The statute read: "That every minister, being a person of *good* conversation, able, learned and orthodox, that shall be chosen by the major part of the inhabitants in *any* town, at a town meeting duly warned for that purpose . . . shall be the minister of such town" (*Massachusetts Acts and Resolves,* 1: 62–63).

12. Cotton Mather, *Good Men Described,* p. 30.

Maine, and his father is reported to have worked as a gunsmith. While he was still a young man, Phips served as an apprentice to a ship's carpenter; and, after he had mastered the skills of the trade, he moved to Boston to make his fortune. There was never any question about his ambition. Even when he was just getting a start, Phips predicted confidently "That he should yet be *Captain of a King's Ship;* That he should come to have the *Command of better Men* than he was now accounted himself; and, That he should be Owner of a *Fair Brick-House* in the *Green Lane* of *North-Boston.*" Persons who had business dealings with the future governor observed that he possessed a certain "Enterprizing *Genius,*" but they also noted his inability to keep up with "the pleasant and sudden turns of Conversation."[13] The diligent Phips apparently had no time to acquire the social graces of proper Bostonians as he pursued his calling, waiting for the opportunity to join those men who were accounted better than himself.

As was so often the case with Horatio Alger heroes, luck played an important part in Phips's success. First, he married the widow of one of the colony's richer merchants.[14] Soon thereafter, his fondest dream became a reality, for he received the captaincy of an English warship. On one of his early voyages Phips discovered a large Spanish galleon laden with treasure off one of the Caribbean islands. One New Englander hearing of the event commented wryly that the captain's find was "not only sufficient to repair his Fortunes, but to raise him to a considerable figure."[15] When the naval adventurer brought his gold to London in 1687, the needy James II claimed a generous share and in exchange awarded Phips a knighthood. Undoubtedly, the Kennebec carpenter would have given almost anything

13. Cotton Mather, "Life of Phips," p. 39; Murdock, *Increase Mather,* pp. 198–99.

14. Thomas Hutchinson, *The History of the Colony and Province of Massachusetts-Bay,* ed. Lawrence S. Mayo, 3 vols. (Boston, 1936), 1: 336. Phips married the widow of a certain John Hull, but according to James Savage (*A Genealogical Dictionary of the First Settlers of New England,* 4 vols. [Boston, 1861]), this Hull was not the famous mint master and political leader. Viola Barnes mentions that the new charter governor married well without telling who the woman was ("The Rise of William Phips," *New England Quarterly* 1 [1928]: 273).

15. Calef, *More Wonders,* p. 145.

for the chance to call himself Sir William Phips. The wealthy knight soon returned to Boston, where he purchased an impressive home in the city's best section. It is reported that Phips took great pleasure in telling the young men of the area about his climb to fame and fortune so that they could emulate his example.[16]

In 1690 Phips did two things which, coupled with his new wealth, helped to launch his government career. First, he joined one of the Congregational churches in Boston. The Mathers may well have prompted this move, for they seem to have entertained far-reaching plans for the captain. One observer noted in his journal on May 27 that "Sir William Phips was publiquely baptized by young Mr. Mather, made his publication & entered a member, soon after nominated a Magistrate."[17] It is difficult to tell whether there was a causal relationship between this public ceremony and his political nomination, but hints from the Mathers about the colonial governorship may have done much to awaken Phips's spiritual interests. Second, he led a victorious assault on the French position at Port Royal and captured the whole Acadian peninsula for the English. The Mathers may have engineered his selection as commander of the Massachusetts troops, for when a certain "Mr. Nelson" was suggested for the job "the Country Deputies" suddenly rebelled claiming that Nelson was unacceptable because he was a merchant and forced the military responsibility on to Phips.[18] Whether by accident or by design, the former ship's carpenter was thrown into a position where he became the hero of New England, a reputation that was apparently not tarnished by later colonial defeats in Canada and by the failure of the provisional government to pay the troops in hard money. In any case, it was not long after the Port Royal victory that Increase Mather persuaded the king to appoint Sir William as governor of Massachusetts.[19]

Despite the captain's impressive military and naval record, he

16. Barnes, "The Rise of William Phips," pp. 283, 287–88; Murdock, *Increase Mather,* p. 199; Cotton Mather, "Life of Phips," p. 41.

17. *1 Proceedings,* MHS, 16: 105 (Dr. Benjamin Bullivant's Journal); Cotton Mather, "Life of Phips," pp. 46–47.

18. *1 Proceedings,* MHS, 16: 106.

19. Barnes, "The Rise of William Phips," p. 290; Murdock, *Increase Mather,* p. 250.

lacked the essential political skills which were necessary for his new post. Phips was courageous, especially on the field of battle, but he lacked moderation, prudence, and dignity. When some New Englanders suggested that the king might have found a more qualified candidate, Cotton Mather protested that the governor was "the best conditioned gentleman in the world," adding that it was impossible to tell that Phips had been "raised up" simply by talking with the man.[20]

But almost every time Phips opened his mouth he made his clerical patrons look like hypocrites, and it did not take long for the colonists to see that their new ruler was unsuited for his job. The governor had received no formal education and felt extremely uncomfortable in the company of cultured Bostonians.[21] An anonymous pamphleteer quipped, "It was an unlucky thing the want of Education in a Man [Phips] intended for such service, who as they say Learned to read since he was Married, and cannot yet read a Letter, much less write one, and there being no Carpenter's Work in the Government they expect he will not serve them long."[22] Phips was far more at ease among sailors and dock workers than he was among Harvard graduates; and he liked to relax on the wharves "where Noys and Strutt pass for Whitt."[23] Indeed, the governor conducted the affairs of state as if he were still at the helm of an English warship, and his brusque manner often insulted the people with whom he had to deal.

Phips's political position within the colony might have been stronger if he had been able to control his temper. However, the governor seems to have believed that the best way to settle an argument was with his fists or cane. On one occasion a large crowd on the Boston dock was treated to the spectacle of seeing their chief magistrate wrestle an English naval officer who had challenged Phips's judgment on some minor point.[24] "I find great offence taken

20. Cotton Mather, "Life of Phips," pp. 43, 55.

21. Barnes, "The Rise of William Phips," pp. 287–88.

22. "A Letter from New England, 1 November 1694," Gay Transcripts (Phips's Papers), Massachusetts Historical Society.

23. G. B. Warden, "Boston Politics, 1692–1765" (Ph.D. diss., Yale University, 1966), p. 41.

24. Ibid., pp. 41–42.

at your governor Phips, for beating the captain of the man of war there," Sir Nathaniel Rich reported to Increase Mather. The English writer added that it "seems to reflect on the whole plantation, for chusing a governor of no better principles or practices than to forget himself so far as to cane or strike a commission officer."[25] Rich's comments must have been difficult for Mather to bear, for it had been he, not the people of Massachusetts, who had chosen Phips for the governorship. Unfortunately there was little that the minister could say in Phips's defense. The governor's behavior made him look like a foolish bumpkin instead of a responsible civil leader, and his excesses undermined the popular respect which a chief magistrate might have otherwise commanded. While the experiences of the Glorious Revolution had forced Puritans to consider their rulers as guardians of property and liberties, they still insisted on many of the same attributes that election speakers had been demanding since the 1630s. Certainly the colonists expected their rulers to comport themselves in a manner superior to that of the people. No one argued that the magistrate should mirror his constituents' faults, crudities, and weaknesses. In 1692 Americans were still a long way from the age of Jackson when the rugged "alligatormen" of Tennessee would become the political leaders of the nation.[26]

Phips's short temper was the most conspicuous flaw in his character, but New Englanders found other, equally valid, grounds for calling him a bad ruler. From the time of his arrival the governor did as his patrons, the Mathers, beckoned; and, while it is anachronistic to label Phips a "party man," he did favor the interests of a special group. The people of Massachusetts believed that the governor as well as the entire council of twenty-eight owed their positions to the elder Mather's influence with William III and rightly suspected that the new charter magistrates would do the minister's bidding. An entry in Cotton's diary revealed the close relationship between the leaders of government and the Mather family: "We have not the former Charter, but we have a better in the room of it; one

25. Sir Nathaniel Rich to Increase Mather, 25 Jan. 1694, cited in Hutchinson, *History*, 2: 60.
26. See John William Ward, *Andrew Jackson: Symbol for an Age* (New York, 1962), pp. 46–78 passim.

which much better suits our circumstances. And instead of my being made a sacrifice to wicked rulers, all of the counsellors of the Province are of my father's nomination, and my father-in-law [John Phillips], with several related to me, and several brethren of my own church, are among them. The governor of the Province is not my enemy, but one whom I baptised, and one of my flock, and one of my dearest friends."[27]

The list of councillors may have consoled the paranoiac Cotton, but he failed to note that his father had created a political faction by selecting only those men who shared his own views about matters of state. The most striking example of partisanship was the absence of Elisha Cooke on the new council; for Mather was aware, even while he was still in London, that the popular Cooke had assumed the leadership of the group who opposed the 1691 patent.[28] Traditionally, New Englanders had expected their rulers to bring harmony to the commonwealth and to mediate differences that might endanger the Puritans' holy experiment. Under the Old Charter the voters elected men whom they believed possessed magisterial skills. They rarely selected or rejected assistants for policy considerations, and it was not unusual for the freemen simultaneously to support rulers whose views were known to clash. To a great degree, therefore, the breakdown of political cooperation and the rise of a party or factional mentality were Increase Mather's responsibility, for he decided to ignore rival interests rather than to incorporate them into he new charter government. After 1692 the appeals which election day speakers made for political unanimity became progressively more academic.

Not even Phips's piety saved him from popular criticism when he made political blunders or supported a narrow faction. The governor tried, especially in the early days of his short career, to act like God's vicegerent on earth and to take his place among the Winthrops and Leveretts of New England. His arrival, for example, was a carefully staged effort to make him look like an Old Charter ruler, a man who would unite the holy commonwealth. Phips landed

27. Cited in A. P. Marvin, *The Life and Times of Cotton Mather* (Boston, 1892), p. 109.
28. Murdock, *Increase Mather*, pp. 250–54.

on a Saturday; and, according to one visiting English officer, the governor claimed "that God had sent him there to serve his country and that he would not abridge them of their ancient laws and customs, but that all the laws, liberties and privileges that were practicable should be as before and should be maintained and upheld by him. Then he read his commission and letters patent, but when they were about half read he ordered it to cease as the Sabbath was begun, and he would not infringe the Lord's day; and he ordered all firing of guns and acclamations to be put off till Monday morning."[29] Phips's show may well have come at the Mathers' prompting. Whatever the case might have been, the governor's effort to identify himself with the New England past failed to quiet his opponents.

The two Mathers encouraged their hand-picked leaders to stand firm in the face of criticism. "It is true," Cotton told them, "every *Publick Servant* must carry two *Hankerchiefs* about him, one to wipe off *Sweat,* of Travail, another to wipe off the *Spit* of Reproach."[30] And the elder Mather instructed Phips and his council to ignore the malcontents; for "There is such variety and Contrariety in the Opinions of men, that all cannot be pleased; sometimes not a few only, but the major part, take in with the wrong side, and have their unreasonable Dissatisfactions." The minister called upon the rulers to do their duty as conscience demanded—"let the world be pleased or displeased."[31] Edmund Andros would have found it difficult to disagree with such an arbitrary statement; for, in effect, the Mathers were announcing that they alone knew what was the best civil policy for Massachusetts. Since Governor Phips was a weak man, he failed to rise above the animosity stimulated by the Mathers' partisan behavior.

As the colony's first election under the new charter approached in 1693, party feuding became more intense and criticism of Phips more common.[32] The Mathers anticipated that the voters would support Cooke and elect representatives to the lower house who in turn would drop the original councillors appointed by the king. The

29. *Calendar of State Papers, Colonial Series, 1689–1692,* p. 653.
30. Cotton Mather, *Good Men Described,* p. 14.
31. Increase Mather, *Primitive Counsellours,* pp. 13–14.
32. Hutchinson, *History,* 2: 53; Miller, *New England Mind,* 2: 175.

two clergymen also realized that a defeat at the polls not only would be a personal embarrassment but also would diminish their political power in the legislature. In the fall of 1692 Cotton attempted to aid his family's interests by publishing a short satirical pamphlet entitled *Political Fables,* a work which may well have been the first piece of campaign literature published in New England. The young minister portrayed Cooke's backers as ungrateful "sheep" who persisted in hindering the constructive policies of Phips, "the good elephant," and Increase Mather, "the eagle."[33]

If Cotton's heavy-handed effort at political allegory added fuel to the party controversy, his father's election sermon of 1693 brought it to a full blaze. The elder Mather imprudently informed the newly elected representatives that they would be foolish to propose any councillors to the governor "that He cannot Accept of, and so to necessitate him to make use of his Negative Voice." The minister assured the members of the lower house that Phips did not want to employ his veto power, but was prepared to do so if they selected men who were his political enemies. "And you cannot but know," Increase preached, "that no Governour will take those into his Council, who are *Male-contents.*"[34]

The representatives listened to the preacher's threats and then promptly dropped ten of Mather's original nominees. They added insult to injury by choosing Cooke as one of the new magistrates. At this point Phips made one of the greater blunders of his political career by disallowing Cooke's election. This undiplomatic act seemed to confirm what the citizens of Massachusetts already suspected— that their governor represented the Mathers, not the freemen.[35] The veto demonstrated that the popular will expressed through the lower house could be sacrificed at any time to narrow party interests. Suddenly Phips was no better than the "Bramble ruler," Sir Henry Vane, who had used his authority to aid the factious Antinomians, or Sir Edmund Andros, who denied representative government altogether. The Mathers, perhaps more than anyone else in the colony, should have realized that a basic element in Puritan

33. *Andros Tracts,* 2: 325–32.
34. Increase Mather, *Primitive Counsellours,* p. 19.
35. Hutchinson, *History,* 2: 53.

political theory was the participation of the people in the choice of their rulers.

An important legislative battle which took place in 1694 provided the citizens with additional proof of the governor's incompetence. The trouble began when William III ordered Phips to return to London for an inquiry into dockside fights with officers of the royal navy. Since the governor wanted to avoid the embarrassment of censure, he asked the Massachusetts General Court to issue a resolution praising his administration which he could later present to the king in his own defense. But several members of the lower house balked at the proposal, fully convinced that Phips deserved a reprimand. "The opposers," one witness noted, "were gentlemen, principally of Boston, who were too near Sir William to think well of him."[36]

When the governor heard of the legislative resistance, his temper flared. He regarded political opposition as a captain might view mutiny on the high seas. He immediately resolved to purge his critics from the lower house and formulated a plan which he felt certain would catch them all by surprise. Phips had learned from experience that many of his enemies were Bostonians who served as nonresident delegates for other towns and villages throughout the colony. He, therefore, pushed an act through the General Court which declared that a man could represent only the town in which he lived. The bill, which indeed had been unexpected, passed twenty-six to twenty-four after a long, acrimonious debate.[37] Despite the narrowness of his victory, the governor assumed that the next General Court, minus the Bostonians, would cooperate by drawing up a declaration describing him as a good ruler.

When the new legislature convened in May of 1694 the election day speaker, Samuel Willard, delivered a sermon significantly entitled *The Character of a Good Ruler*. The minister, who certainly had never distinguished himself as a champion of the people, tried to persuade Phips to reconsider his actions and to terminate his attack on the House of Representatives. "Laws made to strengthen

36. Letter to London, 1 Nov. 1694, printed in Hutchinson, *History*, 2: 59–60.

37. Ibid., p. 60; 5 *Collections*, MHS (*Sewall Diary*), 5: 386.

a particular separate Interest," Willard warned, "never did Good, but Hurt to a Body-Politick: that which may serve the present turn, may in a little time prove more Mischievous, than ever it was Advantageous."[38]

Unfortunately the stubborn governor ignored the minister's advice, and political tensions within Massachusetts rose as the new delegates came before Phips to be sworn into office. In the group stood Nathaniel Byfield, the representative for Bristol, Captain Davis for Springfield, Samuel Legg for Marblehead, Timothy Clarke for Chelmsford, Captain Dudley for Roxbury, and Ebenezer Thornton for Swansea—all of whom lived in Boston. "On our coming in," Byfield reported, "the Governor said that there were more of the gentlemen of Boston than could serve for that town." Byfield tried to speak out, but "the Governor kept forbidding me to speak, and threatened me if I did not hold my tongue." Samuel Legg boldly announced that he would leave his seat in the house only by order of his legislative peers and that he would never depart from his office at Phips's command. A witness claimed that "the Governor, hearing of this, came down to the Representatives in fury without his hat, said that he had heard that a member, against whom he had objected, had refused to leave the House unless the House put him out, and that he wished he knew who it was. Legg at once came forward, and the Governor said that he had nothing against him and wished he had been returned for Boston . . . but as to the others, if the House did not turn them out he would turn them out himself."[39] Coming from a man who caned naval officers, this threat was no idle gesture.

While they couched their opposition to the nonresidency act in rhetoric about English and charter rights, many delegates had personal reasons for disliking Phips's bill. According to Samuel Sewall

38. Samuel Willard, *The Character of a Good Ruler* (Boston, 1694), p. 27; also pp. 20–24. Nathaniel Byfield told Joseph Dudley, who was in London, that "Mr. J. M. [Joshua Moody or Increase Mather] said a month ago that, but for myself, that law would not have passed; which Mr. Willard well touched on in his election sermon, but as you will see, to no purpose" *Calendar of State Papers, Colonial Series, 1693–1696*, p. 295).

39. *Calendar of State Papers, Colonial Series, 1693–1696*, p. 294; Hutchinson, *History*, 2: 60.

the law hindered the men of "fairest estates" from representing the
towns where their greatest property lay, a custom which the freemen
of Massachusetts had long accepted.[40] Byfield reacted to the situation
dramatically, declaring that if the governor could pack the colonial
assembly whenever he wished, turning out the best representatives,
then "farewell to all good; and I shall find another place to live in."[41]

Few persons in Massachusetts lamented Phips's departure for
London in 1694; and even Increase Mather, who had nominated the
governor, stayed at home the day he left the colony.[42] During his
short administration Phips had managed to exacerbate party divisions
and expose the deficiencies of his own character. The carpenter's
success story ended a few months later on a tragic note when Phips
died without warning. No one in the colonies seemed to care about
the passing of the man who only a few years before had been New
England's greatest military hero. Phips's career had demonstrated
that neither martial courage nor Spanish treasure sufficed to make a
good ruler.

Several years after the governor's death, Cotton Mather attempted
to clear Phips's name, no doubt because Cotton's father had been
responsible for putting Phips in office in the first place. The minister
described "Phippius Maximus" as a "Heroick" man who had been
modest, pious, and generous. "I reckon him to have been really a very
Worthy Man," Mather continued, "that few Men in the world,
rising from so mean an *Original* as he, would have acquitted themselves with a Thousandth Part of his *Capacity* or *Integrity;* that he
left unto the World a notable Example of a Disposition to *do Good,*
and encountered and overcame almost invincible *Temptations* in
doing it."[43] But Robert Calef, who attacked Cotton's role in the
Salem witchcraft trials, could not sit still while the minister re-
worked the facts of history. He protested that the younger Mather
ascribed to Phips "such Achievements, as either were never performed by him, or else unduly aggravated." Calef reminded his
readers of "those miscarrages, wherewith Sir *William* was charge-

40. *5 Collections,* MHS, 5: 386; see n. 51, chap. 3.
41. *Calendar of State Papers, Colonial Series, 1693–1696,* p. 294.
42. *5 Collections,* MHS, 5: 393–94.
43. Cotton Mather, "Life of Phips," pp. 42, 50, 67.

able."[44] Cotton Mather's tendentious appeals failed to salvage Phips's reputation, and he went down in New England history as a bad ruler.

The Good Ruler within the Empire

The revolutionary decade altered the popular conception of the good ruler in ways which were related only indirectly to the misconduct of Andros and Phips. When the English tightened imperial control over Massachusetts in this period, they introduced several important changes into the provincial government which the people in turn incorporated into their political thinking. The new charter of 1691 stripped colonial magistrates of some of the duties which Puritans had traditionally associated with their calling. The royal patent, for example, made the appeal for intolerant Nehemiahs irrelevant; for it granted every individual in the Bay Colony the right to worship as he pleased. Futhermore, imperial authorities reorganized the basic structure of Massachusetts government by transforming elective offices into appointive posts and by allocating executive, legislative, and judicial responsibilities far differently than the Old Charter had done. In fact, the constitutional forms which England imposed upon the colonists influenced their attitudes about government as greatly as did any of the more dramatic confrontations with bad rulers.

In part, new notions about the magisterial calling evolved out of changes in the method of filling civil office and out of the division of government powers. The royal charter of 1691 denied or modified elective rights which the citizens of Massachusetts had enjoyed for almost fifty years. The king now appointed the governor, and the members of the lower house selected the governor's council of twenty-eight. The only colonial officials whom the voters still chose directly were their representatives to the General Court. The constitutional reorganization also separated judicial from legislative authority in the Bay Colony. Judges were no longer the elected assistants or magistrates but were appointed by the governor subject to the council's veto. These alterations in government structure

44. Calef, *More Wonders*, p. 146.

made the task of defining the nature or character of the ruler's vocation very difficult, for each post had its own unique prerogatives and responsibilities. Some men were judges, some legislators, some advisors, some executives.[45] Samuel Willard in his election sermon of 1694, *The Character of a Good Ruler,* decided that the word *ruler* "imports one that hath any Dominion, right, or authority over either Persons or things." But the minister immediately qualified his general statement by explaining that not all civil magistrates "stand in one equal Rank." In a section that revealed Willard's understanding of the political changes which had taken place in Massachusetts, he explained, "There are Supreame and Subordinate Powers and of these there also are some who have a *Legislative,* others an *Executive* Power in their Hands; which two, though they may sometimes meet in the same persons, yet are in themselves things of a different Nature. There are *Superiour Magistrates* in Provinces, and such as are of *Council* with them, and *Assemblymen,* the *Representatives* of the People. There are *Judges* in Courts, *Superiour* and *Inferiours; Justices* of the *Peace* in the several Precincts: and in each of these Orders there Resides a measure of Authority."[46]

Cotton Mather, who felt compelled to defend every aspect of the new charter, viewed the division of governmental powers as potentially beneficial to Massachusetts. Mather suggested that the various ruling branches could check each other so that no one man or body would be able to gain predominant authority over the colony. "If an ill Governor should happen to be imposed on them [the Puritans]," he speculated, "what hurt could he do to them?" According to Mather, the answer was none; for the councillors and the representatives limited the governor's discretion, while the freemen in turn controlled the ambitions of the legislature.[47] Each level of govern-

45. Some men like Samuel Sewall held several different posts at one time. Nevertheless, the practice of multiple officeholding did not undermine the theoretical division of government powers established by the new charter. See Ellen Brennan, *Plural Office-Holding in Massachusetts, 1760–1780* (Chapel Hill, 1945).

46. Willard, *Character of a Good Ruler,* pp. 6, 9.

47. Cotton Mather, "Life of Phips," p. 57; also Cotton Mather, *Good Men Described,* pp. 86–87. Increase followed the same line of argument in his pamphlet, *A Brief Account Concerning Several of the Agents of New*

ment had its own constituency. Mather's theory of balance was extremely sketchy; but his ideas pointed the way to the time when
the colonists would see the existence of distinct and separate ruling
functions as a positive good, as a means, in fact, of thwarting
tyranny.[48]

The charter reform of 1691 gave some rulers new importance
within the colony while it diminished the stature of others. "The
Governor, under the old charter," wrote Thomas Hutchinson,
"altho' he carried great porte (so does the Doge of Venice) yet his
share in the administration was little more than that of any of the
assistants."[49] The new royal patent allowed the chief magistrate of
Massachusetts greater powers than he had ever enjoyed before. The
governor could now call, prorogue, and dissolve the colonial assembly
at will. And, while he took no direct part in General Court debates,
he possessed the right to veto any legislation presented to him. He
also appointed military and judicial officers with the council's consent. All of these privileges transformed the governor into a formidable political figure. As animosity between the representatives and
the royal governors grew during the eighteenth century, the proper
use of these new, expanded prerogatives increasingly became the
subject of popular discussion, and the character of the good governor had to be redefined in light of his enlarged jurisdiction.

While the office of the governor gained importance, the members
of the council never acquired the prominence that the Old Charter
assistants had held. To be sure, affluent men often became councillors
after the 1690s, but the office itself gradually lost its former political
significance. Hutchinson provided the best description of the status
of the upper house in Massachusetts:

> In the royal governments . . . the council can scarcely be con-
> sidered as a distinct branch; frequently they receive their ap-

---

England (1691): "Suppose a Person as bad as *Andros* (and the *New-Eng-
landers* think there can hardly be a worse), should come amongst them,
What can he do? He cannot without the Consent of the Council chosen
by the Representatives of the People, appoint a Sheriff to pack Juries to
serve his turn" (*Andros Tracts,* 2: 290).

48. See introduction to Edmund S. Morgan, ed., *Puritan Political Ideas,
1558–1794* (Indianapolis, 1965), pp. xxxvii–xxxviii.

49. Hutchinson, *History,* 2: 6.

pointment from the recommendation of the governor; they are always liable to be suspended by him, and if it be without sufficient cause, the remoteness of the colonies from the place where redress is to be obtained, and the expence of solliciting it, are very often, sufficient to discourage [them] from applying for it. In Massachusets [*sic*], this branch is dependent both upon the governor and people, and we have seen, at different times, the influence of the one or the other over this branch, according to the degree of spirit and resolution which had respectively prevailed.[50]

For almost fifty years, the Old Charter assistants had jealously guarded their judicial power, insisting that it was a crucial part of the magisterial calling. But the councillors under the new patent had little to do with judicial matters, for most cases were handled in separate courts and appeals were sent to England. The members of the upper house were primarily advisers to the governor, and their position was only as strong or as popular as he was.

As a result of the new constitution of 1691, the representatives became the most popular rulers in Massachusetts. The reason for this change was the fact that the members of the lower house were the only major civil leaders who were still directly accountable to the freemen. At the annual May elections the citizens had an opportunity to judge the competence of their delegates to the General Court; and, although the voters possessed no immediate control over the governor and council, they could instruct their representatives at town meetings. The Puritans had learned from the Andros experience the need for popular participation in government affairs and the importance of having rulers who would defend their liberties and property. Samuel Willard expressed what had been the central political lesson of the Glorious Revolution when he preached, "A People are not made for Rulers, But Rulers for a People."[51] Since the representatives were far more responsive to the demands of the freemen than were the governor and council, it was natural that the voters should come to regard the members of the lower house as the

50. Ibid., p. 7; Richard S. Dunn, *Puritans and Yankees: The Winthrop Dynasty of New England, 1630–1717* (Princeton, 1962), p. 263.

51. Willard, *Character of a Good Ruler*, p. 15; Cotton Mather, *Good Men Described*, p. 49.

special guardians of their rights. The citizens believed that their delegates in the General Court shared their hopes and fears, while they
suspected that the other rulers pursued private aims which conflicted
with the common good.

On their part, the representatives were fully aware of their obligation to support the interests of their constituents. In fact, in the
first sessions of the General Court held under the new charter, they
announced that they held the same "Powers & Privileges here as the
house of comons in England."[52] In March 1694 the aggressive lower
house enacted a bill asserting "That the house of Representatives
of the people of this Province bee and hereby is declared and understood to bee a part of the Great and Generall Court or Assembly
and that they have and, of undoubted right, ought to have a freedom
of Debate and Suffrage in all matters proper to them as the Commons
of the kingdom of England have and use." The declaration claimed
the power to appoint all local officials not specifically mentioned in
the charter. But, more significantly, the delegates demanded to know
exactly how the governor spent the money "raised and Levied of the
People."[53] The *elected* representatives clearly recognized their responsibility to preserve the voters' property from the designs of an
appointed governor.

By removing religion from the magistrates' surveillance, the new
charter altered Puritan political theory in several important ways.
First, enforced toleration meant that it no longer mattered whether
or not orthodox Congregationalists governed Massachusetts. The
ruler's main functions: protecting property, keeping the peace, and
waging war, could be performed equally well by persons from any
Protestant denomination. In effect, the colony had come around
to the position that Roger Williams had advocated forty years earlier
when he claimed that the state of a man's soul has no bearing on
how successful he is in his calling (see chap. 2). Second, toleration
forced the Congregational leaders to stand on their own; for after
1691 ministers could no longer expect any assistance from civil
government. The General Court never again called a church synod and

52. *Massachusetts Acts and Resolves,* 7: 33–34.
53. Ibid., p. 393 (italics added); Massachusetts Archives, 48: 232–33,
398–409.

seldom entered local ecclesiastical disputes as it had done in Boston and Newbury during the 1670s. The magistrates may well have regarded the toleration clause of the new charter with pleasure, for it gave legal sanction to the division between church and state that had begun to be a problem while Governor Leverett was in office.

It took the Congregational ministers in Massachusetts a little time to adjust to the new political system. For sixty years the Jeremiahs had called upon the civil magistrates to defend the purity of the Congregational church, and many of them looked with horror upon any limitation of Nehemiah's spiritual role. After the Andros rebellion, Cotton Mather apparently hoped—no doubt along with many other ministers—that the church-state relations would be returned to pre-Dominion conditions. He begged the members of the General Court in 1690 to remember "That we came into the *Wilderness,* because we would quietly worship God, without *Episcopacy,* that *Common-Prayer,* and those unwarrantable *Ceremonies* which the *Land of our Fathers Sepulchres,* has been defiled with." He announced that he expected the rulers of New England to continue to guard "the pure and full *Dispensations* of the Gospel."[54] But when Increase returned to Massachusetts bearing the new charter, Cotton quickly changed his message. In a sermon delivered before the colonial assembly in 1692, *Optanda, Good Men Described and Good Things Propounded,* the young Mather declared that civil governors should stay out of ecclesiastical matters. "It may be fear'd," Cotton preached with obvious reluctance, "that things will not *go well* when *Haeresies* are not Exterminated. But I pray, when (Except once perhaps, or so, in the case of Donatism) did Fines and Gaols, ever signify any thing for the cure of *Haereticks?*" He even warned the colonial rulers that religious persecution created martyrs, not converts.[55] Ironically the

---

54. Cotton Mather, *The Serviceable Man. Discourse Made unto the General Court* (Boston, 1690), p. 31.

55. Cotton Mather, *Good Men Described,* p. 43. In the same sermon Cotton wrote: "When a man sins in his *Political Capacity,* let Political Societies animadvert upon him; but when he sins only in a *Religious Capacity,* Societies more purely Religious, are the fittest then to deal with him. Indeed, in the Old Testament, the Magistrate was an *Ecclesiastical Officer;* and compliance with the Mosaic Rites was that which Entitled men unto the benefits of *Canaan,* the Typical and Renowned Land. But

content of Cotton's work was almost identical to that of William Hubbard's mildly tolerant *The Happiness of a People in the Wisdome of their Rulers* (1676) which Increase Mather had once labeled as apostasy.

The younger Mather realized in 1692 that whether the Congregational divines liked it or not the Puritan government now had to accept *"Common-Prayer"* books and "unwarrantable *Ceremonies."* He therefore explained that the good magistrate "is most properly, the Officer of *Humane Society;* and a Christian by Non-Conformity to this or that Imposed *Way of Worship,* do's not break the Terms on which he is to enjoy the Benefits of *Humane Society.* A man ha's a Right unto his Life, his Estate, his Liberty, and his Family, altho' he should not come to these and those Blessed *Institutions* of our Lord."[56] In a sense, Cotton's sermon to the General Court summed up the most important lesson of the decade—that the New Englanders of the 1690s expected their rulers to secure the citizen's essential rights of "Life," and "Estate," and "Liberty." The magisterial calling no longer included coercive power over men's consciences, at least, not over Protestant consciences.

In their attempt to adjust to the new charter the Puritan ministers insisted that religious toleration was not a license to sin and that magistrates could still be expected to suppress public vice. According to Cotton Mather, *"Liberty of Conscience* is not to be permitted as a cloak for *Liberty of Profaneness.* To live without any Worship of God, or to Blaspheme and Revile his Blessed Name, is to be chastised, as abominably Criminal." Mather pointed out that the English inflicted strict penalties upon the drunk and the idle, "and yet no *Liberty of Conscience* is invaded in those wholesome Laws."[57] Election preachers in this period continued to demand that the new

---

now these *Figurative* things have *Spiritual* things to answer them" (p. 43). It is interesting to note that Cotton seems to have taken the separation of church and state for granted. In the 1670s the ministers had called for Nehemiahs to run the government; in the 1690s Mather was happy with "Good Men."

56. Cotton Mather, *Good Men Described,* pp. 42–43; see Willard, *Character of a Good Ruler,* pp. 13–16.

57. Cotton Mather, *Good Men Described,* p. 46.

charter rulers be pious men, declaring that the good magistrate would advance the general "truths and ways of God" even if he could not bind the citizen to a particular sect.[58] Willard believed that the mark of the best rulers was their eagerness "to promote *Piety* as well as *Honesty* among men."[59] The ministers may have secretly longed for the old, intolerant community of their fathers; but in its absence they accepted the next best thing, a commonwealth composed of outwardly virtuous men.

After 1691 many clergymen of Massachusetts asked their rulers to consider the moral aspects of state policy, hoping that civil statutes might bolster popular virtue. Cotton Mather, for example, recommended that the government of New England enact prohibitive taxes on vanities and luxuries and thus remove the fuel for lust and sin.[60] But of all the ministers, Willard argued the most persuasively for the magistrates' moral responsibilities within the tolerant commonwealth. He told the members of the General Court in 1694 that the "Liberties and Rights" of the people, the plums of 1689, could never be truly safe from violence and oppression unless rulers promoted virtue throughout the province.[61] The hatred of certain evils —sloth, extravagance, irreligion, slovenliness, pride—remained a vital element in Puritan politics long after the Nehemiahs had been forgotten and property rights had become the business of the state. In fact, political rhetoric in New England grew more secular in the eighteenth century only in the sense that it no longer stressed the doctrines of a specific theology.[62] Men intermixed the language of property and morality, as they did not in England; and because of this blending colonial attitudes about government acquired a unique character. The citizens came to see any invasion of private estates as sinful acts prompted by the magistrate's impiety; and during the American Revolution the mingling of material and spiritual values led Puritans to condemn taxes levied by the idle, sumptuous rulers of Britain as both arbitrary and immoral.

58. Cotton Mather, *Good Men Described*, p. 45; Miller, *The New England Mind*, 2: 176.

59. Willard, *Character of a Good Ruler*, pp. 12–13.

60. Cotton Mather, *Good Men Described*, pp. 61–62.

61. Willard, *Character of a Good Ruler*, p. 16.

62. Miller, *New England Mind*, 2: 171.

6

TWO NEW ENGLANDS: 1695–1730

OLLOWING Phips's sudden departure for London, political controversy in Massachusetts cooled; and, though some men still grumbled about the loss of Winthrop's charter, the colonists appeared more united than they had for nearly twenty years. The two royal governors who succeeded Phips, William Stoughton (1694–99, 1700–01) and Richard Coote, the Earl of Bellomont (1699–1700), were trimmers who above all else wanted to avoid conflict.[1] Fortunately, few civil issues in this period demanded firm executive leadership, and it was relatively easy for these magistrates to drift with the times. To be sure, William III created a Board of Trade in 1696 to oversee American affairs; but, because of a number of complex political problems within England itself, the board had no immediate effect upon the government of Massachusetts.[2]

The short era of good feelings ended abruptly with the arrival of Governor Joseph Dudley in 1702. His administration (1702–14) coincided, albeit accidentally, with a series of internal crises that affected almost everyone in New England. There is no need to describe these problems in detail here. It is enough to know that during the early years of the eighteenth century French and Indian forces harassed frontier outposts in Massachusetts and Maine, sometimes leveling entire towns. Those colonists who were in no im-

1. For an account of Bellomont's political experience in the colony of New York, see John D. Runcie, "The Problem of Anglo-American Politics in Bellomont's New York," *William and Mary Quarterly*, 3d ser. 26(1969): 191–217.

2. See Charles M. Andrews, *The Colonial Period of American History*, 4 vols. (New Haven, 1964), 4: 272–317.

mediate physical danger complained that military operations against the French cost too much and that England had no right to expect so great a sacrifice from the Americans. Foreign trade, the lifeblood of the Massachusetts economy, had not fully recovered following the Glorious Revolution; and, as a result, the Bay Colony sank more and more deeply into debt. As the financial situation grew worse, New Englanders began to print paper money in volume, an expediency which annoyed merchants who were expected to honor the inflated currency.

Governor Dudley and his successors found themselves in an impossible position, torn between conflicting local and English demands.[3] The mother country urged the colonists to support the imperial wars, to obey the Navigation Acts, and to outlaw paper currency; but it did little to promote New England's prosperity. When royal governors tried to follow the instructions which they had received from London, Americans protested that their own interests were being slighted. As the years passed, the citizens of Massachusetts increasingly turned to the members of their lower house for relief. In other words, they expected their *elected* rulers to protect them from the policies of their *appointed* rulers. The Bay representatives seemed to have accepted their new responsibility with enthusiasm, for they challenged the governor's prerogatives at every opportunity. The fierce battles waged within the Massachusetts General Court over the conduct of the war, the printing of paper money, and the limits of executive authority, forced men to consider once again the characteristics of the good ruler. In Connecticut, as well as in the Bay Colony, pamphleteers, clergymen, and civil officers attempted to redefine the magisterial calling in ways which would reflect New England's changing political environment.

Examination of the political rhetoric of this period reveals that New England was divided more deeply than it had ever been before. As we have already seen, the Puritans of Winthrop's generation battled over the limits of magisterial power; but even during their

3. The best general study of the problems facing royal governors in this period remains Leonard Woods Labaree, *Royal Government in America: A Study of the British Colonial System before 1783* (New York, 1930). Also see Bernard Bailyn, *The Origins of American Politics* (New York, 1968), pp. 66–105.

most heated disputes, it was obvious that both sides shared the same notions about the character of civil authority. Persons of Discretionary and Delegated persuasion, for example, agreed that their rulers were responsible for maintaining the colony's covenant with God, for suppressing vice, and for banishing heretics. But by the early decades of the eighteenth century, just fifty years after Winthrop's death, the intellectual consensus had dissolved; and for the first time in the history of New England large groups of colonists openly disagreed on political fundamentals.[4]

To trace the origins of this basic division with any degree of confidence would be difficult. As early as 1689, persons like Gershom Bulkeley broke with their neighbors, angrily denouncing certain elements of Puritan political theory. Yet on the whole, the Glorious Revolution united New Englanders under the banner of property rights; and, if any fundamental split existed at this time, it was obscured by the excitement of overthrowing a governor and receiving a new charter. By 1700, however, the dimensions of the political division had become much more distinct. Indeed, there were now two separate New Englands; and no vision, no ideology, no rhetoric seemed capable of bringing them together again. Religious appeals proved largely ineffective, since many colonists acted as if God had withdrawn from politics; or at the very least, as if He had assumed a role of secondary importance. Regardless of what He may have done it was clear that the threat of a broken covenant or of an angry Lord no longer affected New Englanders as it had in former days.

4. The interpretation of New England politics presented in this and the following chapter differs substantially from the one offered by Robert E. Brown in his *Middle-Class Democracy and the Revolution in Massachusetts, 1691–1780* (Ithaca, 1955). I agree with Brown that the Massachusetts franchise was large. However, I cannot accept his view that there were no significant political divisions within the colony during the eighteenth century, or that the major theme of colonial history was England's effort to suppress American "democracy." Certainly, the imperial regulations influenced the evolution of political ideas in New England, especially in the period after 1763; but other, equally important, factors influenced men's attitudes toward their rulers. The people of Massachusetts did not share common notions about the role of civil government in their society. In this section I have attempted to describe internal, intellectual divisions which Brown ignored.

By the time Governor Dudley left office in 1714, two separate persuasions about the magistracy, the *Court* persuasion and the *Country* persuasion, had clearly become evident in both Massachusetts and Connecticut. Court and Country were not political parties in any modern sense, for they possessed neither formal organization nor specific policy goals. In fact, the terms in the early eighteenth century referred only to loose groupings of New Englanders who shared, perhaps unknowingly, similar notions about the character of the good ruler.

The concept of a Court and Country is by no means peculiar to the American colonies. For many years English historians have found these labels useful in describing the political divisions which existed in their own nation during the seventeenth and eighteenth centuries. The study of Parliament after the restoration of Charles II has revealed that, with the possible exception of Queen Anne's reign, Whig and Tory were almost meaningless categories, since the men who adopted them seldom worked or voted as a body.[5] Early in the eighteenth century Lord Robert Molesworth, himself a member of Parliament, observed how confused political terminology had become: "There has been such chopping and changing both of names and principles that we scarce know who is who."[6] Court and Country are not artificial classifications created by scholars for their own convenience. To the contrary, these words were employed by contemporaries to describe general political attitudes and traditional prejudices as opposed to party ideologies.

Within the context of English history, the Court represented something more than a political persuasion. It was an entire life style. Persons within this group generally owed their positions in government to royal patronage and tended to support the crown regardless of the issues at stake, hoping no doubt that their loyalty would win them larger pensions and more prestigious posts. In so far as the English Court possessed a political ideology, it supported

5. On the politics of Queen Anne's reign, see Geoffrey Holmes, *British Politics in the Age of Anne* (New York, 1967), pp. 13–184 and passim; and J. H. Plumb, *The Origins of Political Stability: England 1675–1725* (Boston, 1967), pp. 129–58.

6. Cited in Archibald Foord, *His Majesty's Opposition, 1714–1830* (Oxford, 1964), p. 20.

the prerogative, insisting that the king held certain powers which Parliament could not touch. During the first half of the eighteenth century, the Court saw no particular benefit in separating the parts of government—King, Lords, and Commons—and it resisted efforts by Country reformers to purge the legislature of all the king's followers.[7] Frequently, Court attitudes toward everything from art to sex and from literature to religion contrasted sharply with those of the plainer, somewhat stuffy Country gentry.

The chief characteristic of the English Country was its "disinterested independence."[8] The Country gentlemen who served in Parliament, especially those who did so during the mid-eighteenth century, were proud of the fact that they did not owe their positions either to the crown or to any faction within Commons. They regarded themselves as impartial jurors, charged by their constituents to judge each bill that came before the legislature solely on its own merits. One English newspaper praised Richard Wilbraham Bootle, a typical Country M.P., because "he attaches himself to no party, but is governed in the votes he gives, by the unbiased suggestions of his judgment, and the fair operation of that influence only which originates in the several arguments he hears."[9] The Country of England warned that no minister should be allowed to grow so powerful that he could dominate Commons simply by passing out patronage. It was largely out of fear, therefore, that Country writers urged their contemporaries to stand vigilant lest some secret cabal destroy England's balanced constitution and establish a tyranny in its place. They also advised those who would listen that no nation which allowed sin to flourish could long expect to maintain its liberty. Indeed, the luxury, indolence, and venality of courtier life seemed to threaten the welfare of the entire kingdom; and Country spokesmen criticized rulers for moral as well as for political failings. Only rarely, however, did Country supporters contemplate seizing

7. See J. G. A. Pocock, "Machiavelli, Harrington, and English Political Ideologies in the Eighteenth Century," *William and Mary Quarterly,* 3d ser. 22(1965): 571.

8. The term comes from Sir Lewis Namier, "Country Gentlemen in Parliament 1750–1784," *Personalities and Powers: Selected Essays* (New York, 1965), p. 60.

9. Ibid., p. 61.

power for themselves. They preferred to remain on the sidelines of the political arena, making certain that the Court did not compromise traditional English rights.[10]

For the most part, the terms Court and Country implied the same characteristics in America as they did in England. In Massachusetts and Connecticut, however, local traditions and unique problems gave the words meaning that they had not possessed in the mother country. The New England Court, for example, consisted of men who for a variety of personal reasons had rejected the voluntaristic elements of Puritan political theory. This group tended to discourage, even to fear, mass participation in government affairs, insisting that most colonial voters were unqualified to judge their magistrates' performance in office. When Court advocates in America described the attributes of the good ruler, they stressed the importance of education, wealth, and breeding. In fact, they defined the magistracy in such a way that only an elite group within the colonies could possibly have met their requirements. Throughout this period, men like Governor Dudley of Massachusetts and Governor Saltonstall of Connecticut complained that traditional political practices in New England allowed demagogues to trick the "giddy People" into choosing mediocre candidates when superior persons were available. But the Court persuasion in the colonies involved more than political attitudes and prejudices. It included cultural values—a distinctive life style—as well. New England Court leaders spurned what they

10. For my understanding of the English Court and Country, I have relied on: Foord, *His Majesty's Opposition,* pp. 20–25; W. R. Fryer, "The Study of British Politics Between the Revolution and the Reform Act," *Renaissance and Modern Studies* 1(1957): 91–114; Namier, "Monarchy and the Party System" and "Country Gentlemen in Parliament," *Personalities and Powers,* pp. 13–38, 59–77; David Ogg, *England in the Reign of Charles II,* 2 vols. (Oxford, 1955), 2: 477, 527; Lawrence Stone, *The Crisis of the Aristocracy 1558–1641* (Oxford, 1965), pp. 61–62, 502, 664–68, 711–12; Robert Walcott, Jr., "English Party Politics [1688–1714]," *Essays in Modern English History in Honor of Wilbur Cortez Abbott* (Cambridge, Mass., 1941), pp. 81–132; P. Zagorin, "The Court and the Country," *English Historical Review* 77(1962): 309; J. G. A. Pocock, "Machiavelli, Harrington, and English Political Ideologies," pp. 549–83; Holmes, *British Politics in the Age of Anne,* pp. 116–47; Hexter, "The English Aristocracy, Its Crisis, and the English Revolution, 1558–1660," *Journal of British Studies* 8(1968): 52–78.

regarded the stifling provincialism of their own society and, in its place, adopted English manners, morals, and dress. The Court's search for a broader cultural identity was an important element in the story of the good ruler; for, by the second decade of the eighteenth century, an influential body of New Englanders had come to assume that the best magistrates were those who seemed most thoroughly Anglicized.

What distinguished the New England Country, a group to be discussed in the next chapter, was its loyalty to basic elements of Puritan political theory. Throughout this period its spokesmen stressed the importance of popular elections, reminding the colonists of their responsibility to choose well. For persons of Country persuasion, it was a self-evident political axiom that civil leaders, even those appointed by the king, were accountable to the people for their public policies. Indeed, Country writers regarded the magistrate as the voters' political agent, possessing only those powers which the citizens had specifically delegated to him. In other words, the good ruler remained close to his constituents, aware of their needs, informed of their grievances. But, while he spoke for their political interests, he did not mirror their faults or weaknesses. A good Country magistrate was often the most articulate, honest, and respected individual in his city or town. Yet even with such men in office, the Country urged New Englanders to be on guard since political power in itself was capable of transforming the best rulers into oppressive tyrants. It is difficult to tell exactly what the Country of Massachusetts and Connecticut thought of the Court's cultural Anglicization; but, on the whole, Country writers defended those provincial customs and values which the Court had come to reject.[11]

11. In this chapter and in the one that follows I do not mean to suggest that New Englanders fell neatly into the categories "Court" and "Country." Many men, no doubt, were moderates who saw virtue on both sides of the debates that were going on in Massachusetts; but such persons did not often publish their political views. For the most part, the spokesmen of Court and Country dominated the colonial press and thus made the division in New England appear more complete than it probably was. I regard "Court" and "Country" as terms defining the outer limits of political thinking in the early eighteenth century and believe that to varying degrees the colonists favored one or the other point of view.

The New England Court

The colonial Court was the child of anxiety. Persons of Court persuasion thought that something had gone awry in New England after the Glorious Revolution, something fundamental, but they did not know who or what was specifically to blame. The malaise seemed to have touched the entire society, and wherever the Court looked the story was the same—confusion had replaced the stability of former generations. Everywhere one found unruly colonists insulting their betters, making demands instead of requests.[12] The Reverend Eliphalet Adams reflected the Court's uneasiness when he preached, "We are fallen into Evil and Tempestuous times." He added with

12. I have relied heavily in this section on sermon literature. The clergymen in New England tended to favor the Court's philosophy. There were many reasons why the ministers were socially more conservative than their parishioners, and I shall do an injustice to the complexities of the problem by mentioning only three. First, some of the leading clergymen were concerned about the waning status or prestige of their profession within colonial society. In a sermon dedicated to Governor Dudley's wife, entitled *The Piety and Duty of Rulers* (Boston, 1708), Benjamin Colman warned somewhat defensively, *"That* the Ministerial Work is not to be levell'd wich [*sic*] *Mechanic* Labours, *Merchandize,* nor other more *Liberal* Imployments neither; the Practice of *Physick,* or the teaching of *Phylosophy,* not excepted" (pp. 13–14). In this period another preacher complained that the talented young men of New England were no longer interested in the ministerial vocation and were becoming lawyers and merchants ([Anon.], *A Plea for the Ministers of the Gospel* [Boston, 1706], p. 27).

Second, the ministers were disturbed by the growing disorder within the churches. Colman asked the magistrates, "to give *Authority* . . . to *Ecclesiastical Councils* in their Determinations; and to make People know *that there must and shall be some End* to their Strifes & Discords, the Parents of every *Confusion & Evil Work,* the *bane* of all Religion" *(Piety and Duty of Rulers,* p. 10; see Solomon Stoddard, *The Way for a People to Live Long in the Land that God Hath Given them* [Boston, 1703], pp. 5–6).

And third, the clergymen generally discouraged the people's demands for an inflated currency, for they were tied to fixed incomes. As the agitation for the paper money grew, many ministers openly opposed the will of their parishioners on this issue (see "A Speech Without-doors Touching the Morality of Emitting More Paper Bills," 6 *Collections,* MHS, 2: 235–38; Ola Winslow, *Meetinghouse Hill, 1630–1783* [New York, 1952], pp. 212–20).

a mixture of apprehension and nostalgia that the task of governing New England "is not so Easie . . . at this Day, as sometimes it hath been, when the People were *few & Tractable.*" The central theme running throughout Adam's discourse was the need for order in society. Like other members of the Court, the minister felt menaced by a nebulous group which he labeled simply the "people." Adams warned his contemporaries that when people "are *increased in their Numbers, grown wanton under Privilege & run almost wild with Liberty,*" it is difficult "*to Maintain a steady Order & keep up the due Honour of Authority.*"[13] The appeal for greater authority was no mere rhetorical flourish. For New Englanders such as Adams popular disorder and disrespect were twin dangers threatening the very foundation of colonial culture.

According to the Court some extremely wrong-headed ideas had gained currency in New England. The colonists, for example, no longer seemed willing to accept the notion that human society was a hierarchical structure. In fact, eighteenth-century Americans appeared to have persuaded themselves that one man was as good as another and, therefore, that all persons had an equal right to voice their opinions whenever they pleased. Court writers, of course, did not look kindly on such egalitarian beliefs. The Reverend Eleazar Williams, a leading Court advocate in Connecticut, observed testily that he had heard of men who "will endure no yoke of Government and Restraint, who are saying, *All men are of the same flesh & Blood, and why should any exercise Government over others?*"[14] In Massachusetts the Court complained that the people were drunk

13. Eliphalet Adams, *A Funeral Discourse* (New London, 1724), pp. 41–42; see also Timothy Cutler, *The Firm Union of a People Represented* (New London, 1717), pp. 32–34; Ebenezer Pemberton, *A Sermon Preached in the Audience of the General Assembly* (Boston, 1708), pp. 25–28. Adams may well have been correct about the sudden growth of population in New England during this period: see Kenneth Lockridge, "The Population of Dedham, Massachusetts, 1636–1736," *Economic History Review* 19(1966).

14. Eleazar Williams, *An Essay to Prove, that When God once Enters upon a Controversie with His Professing People, He will Manage and Issue It* (New London, 1723), p. 16. In much the same tone Eliphalet Adams lamented that so many New Englanders had come to consider their rulers more as the "Creatures of our own making, than as the Ministers of God" *(Funeral Discourse, p. 42).*

with an inflated sense of their own worth. Indeed, Ebenezer Pemberton, one of Boston's more articulate Court ministers, felt it necessary
to remind his parishioners that levelism constituted "an open De-
fiance to GOD, his Wisdom and Will."[15] Despite Pemberton's
spiritual language, it would be a mistake to see the Court as merely
reaffirming older Puritan ideas about social inequality. In 1630
Governor John Winthrop informed the Bay colonists that God
organized mankind so that "in all times some must be rich some
poore, some highe and eminent in power and dignitie; others meane
and in subjection."[16] But a great intellectual gulf separated the first
governor of Massachusetts from the eighteenth-century Court. The
Court was the product of a secular environment, and its commitment
to a rigid social hierarchy was more economic and cultural than
religious.[17]

When New England Court writers discussed the problem of social
unrest, they tended to exaggerate the dangers involved, warning of
anarchy whenever anyone challenged or even questioned government
policy. The Reverend Benjamin Wadsworth, who seemed to have
forgotten how much the colonists despised Andros, assured the
Massachusetts General Court in 1716, "Tho' *Tyranny* is burdensome
and *hateful,* yet it's counted a *smaller evil* than meer *Anarchy,* and
confusion."[18] Other men shared Wadsworth's concern. Samuel

15. Ebenezer Pemberton, *The Divine Original Dignity of Government
Asserted* (Boston, 1710), p. 16. This sermon is one of the clearest statements
of the Court persuasion to come out of this period. Pemberton delivered it
as an election sermon in 1710 and was so concerned that the members of
the General Court would regard his words simply as a ceremonial aspect
of the election that he declared, "I hope there are none so vain as to
imagine, that I appear this Day in this *Awful Desk,* only to beat the Air,
& play the *Orator* in an Artful Address to our *Rulers,* either by way of
Unmannerly Satyr, or fulsome Panegyrick" (p. 4).

16. John Winthrop, "A Modell of Christian Charity," in Edmund S.
Morgan, ed., *Puritan Political Ideas, 1558–1794* (Indianapolis, 1965), p. 76.

17. See Benjamin Colman, *The Religious Regards* (Boston, 1718), pp.
17–18; Ebenezer Pemberton, *A True Servant of His Generation Characterized* (Boston, 1712), pp. 15–16; Cutler, *The Firm Union,* pp. 39–40;
Perry Miller, *The New England Mind,* 2 vols. (Boston, 1961), 2: 397–99.

18. Benjamin Wadsworth, *Rulers Feeding and Guiding Their People*
(Boston, 1716), p. 22; also Gurdon Saltonstall, *A Sermon Preached before
the General Assembly of the Colony of Connecticut* (Boston, 1697), p. 32;

Wyllys, for example, told his friend, Wait Winthrop, that Connecticut was "fallinge into the dreges of a democraticall anarkie."[19] The only defense against such civil chaos was a strong government; for as one Court minister observed, "Such are the Lusts and Corruptions of Mens hearts, that 'tis not to be suppos'd any considerable number of them, should live peaceably and vertuously in Society, without having good Laws and them well Executed."[20] In other words, tough, somewhat autocratic rulers benefited the community by protecting the people from themselves.

Court writers would probably have preferred not to discuss the topic of revolution at all. The historians among them knew that the early settlers had rebelled against the heretical Sir Henry Vane, and all Court supporters were familiar with the events surrounding the overthrow of the Dominion of New England. Nevertheless, they would have just as soon forgotten the Glorious Revolution. The spectacle of popular violence, no matter how just the cause, frightened them, as it had frightened Gershom Bulkeley in the previous decade. In the early years of the eighteenth century, however, it had become impolitic to stress obedience to civil authority too far; for one did not want to be mistaken for a Jacobite, a person who condemned the Revolution of 1688 and supported the claims of James II and his Catholic heirs to the English throne. One Court spokesman, Ebenezer Pemberton, assured the Massachusetts General Court that "GOD has not left a State without a *Regular Remedy* to Save itself, when the Fundamental Constitution of a People is Overturned; their Laws and Liberties, Religion and Properties are openly Invaded, and ready to be made a Publick Sacrifice." But at the same time, the minister had to confess, "It is beyond me to imagine that

---

Joseph Belcher, *The Singular Happiness* (Boston, 1701), p. 31; Nathaniel Stone, *Rulers Are a Terror, not to Good, but Evil-workers* (Boston, 1720), pp. 16–18.

19. *6 Collections,* MHS, 6: 38; also John Bulkley, *The Necessity of Religion in Societies and Its Serviceableness to Promote the Due and Successful Exercise of Government* (Boston, 1713), p. 16; see also Roger Wolcott, *Poetical Meditations* (New London, 1725), p. 78.

20. Wadsworth, *Rulers Feeding,* p. 22; also Samuel Estabrook, *A Sermon Shewing that the Peace and Quietness of a People is a Main Part of the Work of Civil Rulers* (New London, 1719), p. 19.

the *GOD of Order* has ever invested any men of a Private Station, who can with a Nodd inflame and raise the Multitude, with a Lawful Power, on Pretence of Publick Mismanagements, to Embroyl the State, and Overturn the Foundations of Government."[21] There were others in New England who shared Pemberton's confusion. Like him, they admitted that a ruler could go bad but offered no advice to a people actually confronted with a tyrant. Samuel Willard, who had been frightened by the anarchy of Bradstreet's short regime, admitted to his congregation in 1703 that he was unable to judge how much oppression the populace should bear before it rebelled. Willard was certain, however, that the petty grievances of which the people always complained did not warrant civil unrest.[22] To a large extent these eighteenth-century New Englanders disavowed the revolutionary spirit that had inspired men such as Christopher Goodman, Thomas Adams, and Samuel Nowell.

A few Court clergymen carried the rhetoric of political obedience to extremes. While their views did not necessarily reflect the opinions of the whole Court, they did mirror—in exaggerated form—its anxiety over the loss of order. Eleazar Williams, for example, told Connecticut legislators in 1723 that God condemned all popular violence even though there may have been some "just matter of complaint, by Rulers doing that which they ought not, or omitting any Duty, to the prejudice of some or more of the Subjects."[23] And Benjamin Wadsworth, who later became the president of Harvard, announced that the Lord punished "rebellious" peoples no matter how "good or bad" their magistrates had been.[24] Most Court advocates avoided any doctrine which smacked of nonresistance or passive resistance, sensing that such ideas might sound treasonable to men who fought for William III and the Protestant succession. Ebenezer Pemberton understood as well as anyone the danger of

21. Pemberton, *The Divine Original*, p. 86 (italics added).

22. Samuel Willard, *Compleat Body of Divinity* (Boston, 1726), p. 650. For a discussion of some of the intellectual problems associated with political revolution in the eighteenth century, see Richard V. W. Buel, Jr., "Democracy and the American Revolution: A Frame of Reference," *William and Mary Quarterly*, 3d ser. 21(1964): 165–90.

23. Williams, *An Essay to Prove*, p. 20.

24. Wadsworth, *Rulers Feeding*, p. 64.

making order the highest civil and social good. "I am not Ignorant to what an extravagant height the *Doctrine of Submission to Rulers* has been carry'd by some," he explained, "and I wish I could see no danger on the Contrary *Extream* of depressing it to a meer Nullity... the *one* may Expose a People to the *Oppression* of Sullen Tyranny; the *Other* to the Confusions of Lawless *Anarchy*."[25] Even the more temperate Court writers could not overcome their dread that the leveling spirit might somehow get out of hand, destroying what little order remained within their society.

According to the Court, most political unrest in New England could be avoided if the people would only stop trying to second-guess their rulers. Colonists of Court persuasion insisted that magistrates knew what policies were in the best interests of their constituents. When average citizens took it upon themselves to define the common good, they not only overlooked the ruler's expertise, but also tended to adopt shortsighted measures which worked to everyone's disadvantage. The Court showed its contempt for popular political demands most clearly during Massachusetts' long bank controversy. This dispute, which started after 1710 and persisted well into the 1750s, revolved around the colony's chronic shortage of specie. New England's imbalance of trade drained her silver away faster than she brought it in, leaving Americans without hard money for domestic business transactions. In the years following Phips's departure the Bay government printed thousands of poun': in paper currency, but the amounts were never enough to satisfy those who believed that additional bills would bring prosperity. For the most part Court spokesmen opposed paper money and other inflationary measures. They attempted to demonstrate that the colonists them-

---

25. Pemberton, *The Divine Original*, p. 85. When the Reverend Thomas Symmes delivered the Massachusetts artillery sermon, *Good Soldiers* (Boston, 1720), he told the troops to obey the orders of their superiors, but then added a qualification, "INDEED, we don't exhort to *Passive Obedience* and *Non-Resistance* in the utmost Latitude, in which those doctrines have been preach'd up by some who (as the *Pharisees* and *Lawyers* did of old), *bind heavy Burdens* on Men's Shoulders, while they themselves will not *touch them with one of their fingers*" (p. 14). Symmes appears to have taken great pains to avoid being identified with the extremists of the Court party.

selves were to blame when specie left New England; and, throughout the debate, they maintained that if the people had truly understood the economic issues involved and had budgeted their silver wisely, there would have been no need for paper currency.[26] "I might also mention the great Extravagance that People, and especially the Ordinary sort, are fallen into," wrote Paul Dudley, the governor's son. He claimed that men usually went "far beyond their circumstances, in their Purchases, Building, Families, Expences, Apparel, and generally in their whole way of Living: And above all, the excessive Consumption of *Rhum* and *Wine*." The younger Dudley revealed his Court bias, explaining that when frugality and good husbandry replaced the foolish chasing after fashion "there would not be such a Clamour for the want of a *Medium* of Exchange."[27] It seemed ludicrous to Court supporters that men who could not even organize their own lives should be allowed to influence the formation of government policy.

During the 1720s other Court authors echoed the younger Dudley's rhetoric, arguing that the popular cry for paper money was merely an expression of human corruption and political ignorance, not a genuine grievance. One minister, Thomas Foxcroft, recommended shortening the terms of credit in Massachusetts "so that People may not be able to consume more than they earn."[28] And "Philopatria" pointed to the colonists' "unquenchable desire" for rich apparel as the chief cause of their economic hardship.[29] Another clergyman who sympathized with Court ideas declared that the citizens simply did not know what monetary policy was best for them and prayed that strong rulers would direct them back to sound financial principles. If the magistrates discouraged the importation of "gay and costly clothing," "inebriating Drinks," and "Chocolate," he believed "there would

26. See Miller, *New England Mind*, 2: 305–23; Joseph B. Felt, *An Historical Account of Massachusetts Currency* (Boston, 1839).

27. Paul Dudley, "Objections to the Bank of Credit Lately Projected at Boston [1714]," contained in Andrew M. Davis, ed., *Colonial Currency Reprints*, 4 vols. (Boston, 1910–11), 1: 255.

28. Thomas Foxcroft, "A Letter from One in the Country to His Friend in Boston [1720]," in Davis, *Currency Reprints*, 1: 440.

29. Philopatria, "A Discourse [1721]," in Davis, *Currency Reprints*, 2: 283–84.

be no occasion for creating more Bills; and the people would ac-
quiesce in the Conduct; and at length, mightily applaud, and be
thankful for the Steerage."[30] Throughout this period, New England
Court writers advanced a paternalistic view of civil authority, insisting that persons like themselves should be allowed to define the
common good.

The Court's discussion of the character of the good ruler reflected
its fear of social disorder and its belief that most people could not
be trusted to use civil power wisely. These concerns, in fact, caused
New Englanders of Court persuasion to define magisterial attributes
in such a way that only a few persons, a colonial elite, could possibly
meet the standard. To some extent Court writers may have sounded
like Governor Winthrop and his Discretionary allies, but the similarity was only superficial. The eighteenth-century Court seldom
described the ruler as the Lord's vicegerent on earth possessing
special, God-given talents for his vocation. The state of the magistrate's soul was his own business; and, as long as he did not openly
or flagrantly sin, the Court was willing to overlook whether he was
one of the Lord's Elect. Of far greater consequence to the good ruler
were such outwardly visible characteristics as education, wealth, and
breeding. Indeed, a magistrate's entire life style figured in the Court's
assessment of his worth.

To succeed in government one needed years of careful training.
The Court rejected the notion that a farmer could become a good
legislator simply by dropping his plow and riding off to Boston. Part-
time rulers were bad rulers. "It is condemned by the wise *Socrates*,"
declared Pemberton, "as an Error too common in the World, yet
most fatal to the good of it; that while several years are thought little
enough to be spent in acquiring the skill of any Trade, how Mean
and Mechanical so ever it may be; yet in cases of Publick Administrations of Government, which of all Professions has most Difficulty and
Intricacy, every one is ready to think himself abundantly qualified."[31]
Joseph Moss, another minister, informed the Connecticut legislators
that a full understanding of the complexities of civil law was not so

30. [Anon.], "A Speech Without-doors," in 6 *Collections*, MHS, 2:
237–38.
31. Pemberton, *The Divine Original*, p. 31.

easily gained "as some men vainly imagine."[32] Persons such as Moss stressed the great problems which the ruler had to face, hoping no doubt to discourage the common sort from ever seeking political power for themselves.

Court writers in this period specifically demanded two distinct types of knowledge in their magistrates. The first sort, in the words of the Reverend Timothy Cutler, was "a Thorough Penetration, a Deep Sense of things, a *Practical* and *Political Wisdom* and *Prudence*."[33] The second type was an understanding of the liberal arts, of the things that "Civilizeth Men, and Cultivateth *Good Manners,* and the want of it bringeth in Bestiality and Rudeness, Barbarity and Fierceness, and all those Ill and Crooked Dispositions that make Society less Pleasant and Delightful."[34] Ebenezer Pemberton was another Court spokesman who placed high value on the polish and good manners which supposedly came with a liberal education. When he delieved the funeral sermon for John Walley, a Massachusetts councillor and judge, he explained that a ruler's schooling properly involved the study of belles lettres as well as practical affairs, for *"to Promote* Good Literature *among a People,* is to Serve them." Pemberton claimed that many Roman emperors regarded *"perfection* in *Letters"* as highly as they did skill in military matters. The Court minister advised the Bay colonists to follow the classical example by training a generation of civil leaders in the liberal arts. "It was an old Observation," the speaker noted, *"Ubi praeses fuerit Philosophus, ubi Civitas Erit Faelix;* A Learned Ruler makes a happy City. The more of good Literature Civil Rulers are furnished with, the more capable they are to discharge their trust to the honour and safety of their People."[35] Pemberton's words over Whalley's grave represent a new thrust in New England political

32. Joseph Moss, *A Discourse Shewing, that Frequent Reading and Studying the Scriptures . . . is Needful and Profitable for Rulers* (New London, 1715), p. 31.

33. Cutler, *The Firm Union, p.* 8; also Belcher, *Singular Happiness,* p. 39.

34. Cutler, *The Firm Union,* p. 39.

35. Pemberton, *A True Servant,* p. 7; see John Norton, *An Essay Tending to Promote Reformation* (Boston, 1708), p. 24; Benjamin Colman, *Ossa Josephi* (Boston, 1720), p. 37.

theory; for, while some Old Charter ministers such as William Hubbard called for wise and understanding magistrates, no one had
previously felt obliged to defend "Perfection in Letters." The eighteenth-century Court was searching for a way to justify the existence
of a ruling elite, a way to rationalize the exclusion of the populace
from civil office. Education offered a partial answer; for if few
colonists had attended college, fewer still knew anything about
good literature.

The Court also expected rulers to be wealthy men, seemingly a
traditional demand. Yet one must be careful not to be fooled, for
the Court's call for wealth represented more than it might at first
appear. Indeed, the importance of this element in Court rhetoric does
not become fully evident until seen in an historical context. Under
the Old Charter, especially after 1660, few writers had mentioned
wealth as a characteristic of the good magistrate. It may well have
been that members of the rising generation took the ruler's personal
affluence for granted and, therefore, did not bother to discuss the
topic. Whatever the case, after the Glorious Revolution persons of
Court persuasion began to remind New Englanders that civil office
required men of wealth. Few of them stated directly that the magistracy should be restricted to a moneyed elite. Usually Court spokesmen couched their concern about magisterial wealth in terms of
the common good. Joseph Moss, for example, explained that the
ruler who held a large estate could *"afford Time to be spent in
Reading & Study, in order to furnish him with Knowledge in State
Affairs, that he might serve the Publick the better."* The Connecticut
minister told his audience that many men might have made excellent
magistrates if they had possessed comfortable incomes. "But for the
want of this," he declared, "they are not only apt to be of mean and
mercenary Spirits, but are also unable to spend that Time which is
needful in Reading and Study, thereby to Treasure up Knowledge,
and so they are upon this Consideration uncapable of being good
Rulers."[36] Thomas Foxcroft, who also voiced Court opinions, begged
the voters of Massachusetts to ignore the candidacy of "Men in difficult Circumstances, who have insolved themselves by their own
Indescretion." It seemed clear to Foxcroft that "men in a needy

36. Moss, *A Discourse*, pp. 27–28.

Condition will be sure to consider it in the first place how it will affect themselves, and if it be likely to increase their Straitness and Difficulty a little, (tho' but for a time) they had need be Men of great Integrity to give their Consent to it."[37]

While education and wealth were important magisterial attributes, they were not in themselves enough to make a good ruler. The Court also assumed that political leaders would embody a certain life style, an amalgam of tastes and attitudes distinguishing them from the mass of New Englanders. The best way to study the Court view is to examine those persons of Court persuasion who actually attained high civil office. This group tended to look to the mother country for cultural models and copied manners and customs which they associated with genteel English society. Ironically, in the early years of the eighteenth century, Court rulers bore such illustrious surnames as Winthrop, Dudley, and Saltonstall; and one might have expected them to view the "City on a Hill," not Queen Anne's England, as the ideal society. Despite their Puritan background, however, Joseph Dudley, Wait Winthrop, Fitz-John Winthrop, and Gurdon Saltonstall seldom mentioned the founders. All of them, in fact, had difficulty accepting provincial values. As local disorders seemed to grow more acute following the Glorious Revolution, Court magistrates desperately attempted to join the mainstream of English fashion and ideas. It embarrassed them to think that they might stand out like bumpkins, like poor country cousins, in the stylish world of London. Most of all these Court leaders hoped to establish an American gentry commanding as much power and prestige as that of its English counterpart. Governor Dudley expressed the Court's cultural outlook well in a letter to his friend Gurdon Saltonstall: "We are some of us *English gentlemen* and such is your owne family; and we should labor to support such familyes because truly we want them."[38]

Why this trend began is impossible to tell. Perhaps a genuine fear of the masses contributed to its growth; perhaps certain rulers desired greater, more lucrative opportunities than colonial society

37. Foxcroft, "A Letter," p. 441; see *The Boston News-Letter,* Apr. 18, 1720, for the Reverend Edward Wigglesworth's economically oriented description of the good ruler.

38. *6 Collections,* MHS, 5: 170.

could provide. In any case, the movement toward a cultural Anglicization was well rooted by 1700, and Sir Henry Ashurst, who served
as the agent of Massachusetts in London, observed "I perceive that
your young men have little regard to the old cause that brought them
thar, and ar for high church and arbitrary."[39] Fitz-John Winthrop,
the governor of Connecticut (1698–1707), seemed to be the kind of
man that Ashurst had in mind, for Winthrop spent almost as much
of his energies fretting about wigs and apparel as he did in running
the affairs of state.[40] Winthrop's successor was the pompous Gurdon
Saltonstall, whose sense of his own dignity went beyond anything
New England had ever seen before. When the Earl of Bellomont
first met Saltonstall, he declared that the Connecticut leader carried
himself like an English aristocrat, a compliment which meant more
to the American than Bellomont ever realized.[41] When Saltonstall
died the Reverend Eliphalet Adams praised the governor for his
"Illustrious" descent, his "Liberal and Ingenious" education, and his
"Noble" bearing. But most of all Adams respected his ability "to
Encounter Popular humours, to Quell and Calm mutinous and
factious dispositions."[42] Another minister stressed Saltonstall's English origins, declaring to the mourners that the governor "was
Descended, (and no *Degenerate Off spring*) of an Honourable Family

39. Ibid., p. 41; see Everett Kimball, *The Public Life of Joseph Dudley*
(New York, 1911), p. 209.

40. R. S. Dunn, *Puritans and Yankees: The Winthrop Dynasty of New
England, 1630–1717* (Princeton, 1962), pp. 328–29; also Wait Winthrop
to Samuel Reade, Feb. 1718, 6 *Collections,* MHS, 5: 282. Herbert L. Osgood,
in his *American Colonies in the Eighteenth Century,* 4 vols. (New York,
1924), wrote of Wait and Fitz-John Winthrop: "In their love of property,
their aristocratic family instinct, they were thoroughly English, and were ready
even to undermine the economic system of New England in order to gratify
this instinct. . . . In everything that pertained to social status the Winthrops
were English aristocrats" (3: 310). For more on land and colonial politics
see Richard L. Bushman, *From Puritan to Yankee: Character and the Social
Order in Connecticut,1690–1765* (Cambridge, Mass., 1967), pp. 86–97.

41. Benjamin Trumbull, *A Complete History of Connecticut,* 2 vols.
(New London, 1898), 1: 334–35. See Connecticut Archives, "Private
Controversies," 4: 136–46.

42. Adams, *Funeral Discourse,* pp. 35, 43; *Dictionary of American
Biography,* 16: 317.

which Flourished for several Ages in the English *Yorkshire*."[43]
For the Court, at least, Saltonstall possessed all the characteristics
necessary for a good ruler.

The Court disliked popular elections, charging that when New
Englanders cast their ballots, they ignored the candidates who
possessed wealth, education, and breeding. The Reverend Pemberton
complained to the Massachusetts General Court that colonists neglected persons who were qualified to govern "by inward Ability's,
and outward Circumstances."[44] And Samuel Wyllys, a Connecticut
Court advocate, knew of many examples which he could have offered
in support of Pemberton's observation. Wyllys once informed his
friend Fitz-John Winthrop with disgust that the voters had replaced
two respected gentlemen in the legislature with "an eminent syder-
drinker" and "a person risen out of obscurity." The writer added
that the elected deputy governor was "an old Crumwellian" whose
only real talents were "drinkinge flipp & taking tobacco."[45] Even
Saltonstall, who owed his position as governor to the vote of the
freemen, declared that they "consult only their Humours; and choose
for such as they hope will most indulge them." Merit and integrity
were slighted, simply because the colonists felt it "a point of Civility,
to Vote for such as have been civil, kind, and obliging to them."[46]
Confronted with such political practices, the Court doubted that
New England could ever become an ordered, deferential society.

When Court writers grumbled about the power of the people in
politics or protested the injustice of elections, they usually had the
lower house in mind. The representatives, especially those in
Massachusetts, perplexed the Court, for they displayed an annoying
fickleness in dealing with most legislative business. Sometimes the
delegates cooperated with the executive rulers, making no attempt to
challenge the governor's prerogatives; but, on other occasions, they
were stubborn and irascible. In 1717 Saltonstall went before the
Connecticut assembly, complaining of "the Quarrels & Factions, and

43. Cotton Mather, *Decus ac Tutamen* (New London, 1724), p. 27.

44. Pemberton, *The Divine Original*, pp. 76–77.

45. 6 *Collections*, MHS, 3: 31–32.

46. Saltonstall, *A Sermon Preached before the General Assembly*, pp.
42–43; also Wadsworth, *Rulers Feeding*, p. 55.

Bad Temper & Murmurings" within the legislature.[47] Governor
Shute shared Saltonstall's irritation. After a long, frustrating fight
with the Massachusetts lower house, he observed, "This House con-
sists of about one hundred, who by an Act of Assembly must be
persons residing in the respective towns, which they represent;
whereby it happens that the greatest part of them are of *small fortune and mean education;* men of the best sense and circumstances
residing in or near Boston." Although Shute was probably unaware
of the fact, he was condemning the Residency Bill which Phips had
forced through the General Court with such difficulty in 1694.
Whatever its history, Shute thought the act had stripped the House
of wealthy Bostonians who could have assisted him in his fight
against the "people."[48] In all fairness to Phips, however, Shute should
have noted that the political situation had changed in the inter-
vening years, and by 1720 the Court was attacking the Country
representatives who "are easily made to believe, that the House is
bravely supporting the privilege of the *people,* whilst they are invading the undoubted prerogatives of the Crown." Shute believed
the elected delegates were too easily intimidated by the Boston
mob, a group "dispos'd to a levelling spirit."[49]

Court leaders expected the representatives to mind their own
affairs, leaving the governor and his council alone. "It is not the duty
of one Ruler to fulfill the Offices of another," declared the Reverend

47. Connecticut Archives, "Civil Officers," 1: 163. Saltonstall declared
that if his executive decisions "be like to beget an increase in Uneasiness
among the people; if the maintaining of some small Degree of that Respect
due to Government, be n't agreeable with Our Constitution, It will be much
better, I should resign my Charge, and never trouble others or myself,
any further, with what is in my Opinion so necessary."
48. See chap. 5; William Douglass, *Summary Historical and Political . . .
of the British Settlements in North America,* 2 vols. (Boston, 1749–51), for
an attack on the residency requirement of 1693 (1: 507).
49. *Calendar of State Papers, Colonial Series, 1722–1723,* pp. 325–26.
On June 1, 1720, Governor Shute complained to the Board of Trade,
"The common people of this Province are so perverse, that when I remove
any person from the Council, for not behaving himself with duty towards
H.M. or His orders, or for treating me H.M. Govr. ill, that he becomes
their favourite, and is chose a Representative, where he acts as much in
his power, the same part that he did when in Council" *(Calendar of State
Papers, Colonial Series, 1720–1721,* 45).

Solomon Stoddard, "but every one is bound to attend the work of his office. They do not discharge their duty by complaining one of another, but by fulfilling their own work."[50] Other Court supporters such as Dudley and Pemberton argued that the aggressiveness of the lower house threatened to upset the balance of the Massachusetts constitution. The Court view was well expressed by an anonymous pamphleteer who wrote, "It is of dangerous consequence for one part of the Constitution to Usurp the Power of the other Parts, it would be unsafe for the Governor to Engross the Power of the two Houses. So likewise for the Council to Exercise the Power belonging to the Governor and Representative, and it would be equally hazardous for the House of Representatives to wrest the Power out of the Hands of the Governor and Council."[51] In the opinion of eighteenth-century Court spokesmen the governor was the only barrier preventing the province from falling into "democraticall anarkie," and they inundated imperial authorities with reports protesting the delegates' overwhelming influence in colonial political affairs. In 1721 the Board of Trade analyzed the situation in Massachusetts through the eyes of the provincial Court, concluding that "altho' the governmt. of this Province be nominally in the Crown and the Govr. appointed by your Majesty, yet the *unequal ballance* of their Constitution having lodged too great a power in the Assembly, this Province is, and is always likely to continue, in great disorder."[52] Apparently conditions in Massachusetts did not improve, for in 1733 the royal governor of New York complained bitterly that "Boston principles" had contaminated the people of his own colony.[53]

If the colonial historian had to rely on Court complaints alone, he would surmise that the governor and council of Massachusetts were helpless before the attacks of the popularity elected the lower house. But the executive magistrates were not as vulnerable as the

50. Stoddard, *The Way for a People*, p. 5; also Wadsworth, *Rulers Feeding*, p. 9.

51. *Another Letter from One in the Country* (Boston, 1729), p. 3.

52. *Calendar of State Papers, Colonial Series, 1720–1721*, p. 412; see also Jonathan Swift, *A Discourse of the Contests* (Boston, 1728), which was published in New England by order from Governor William Burnett.

53. Cited in Stanley N. Katz, *Newcastle's New York, Anglo-American Politics, 1732–1753* (Cambridge, Mass., 1968), p. 68.

Court sometimes pretended; for they possessed several political wea-
pons which allowed them to redress the constitutional imbalance,
if not to weight it to their own advantage.[54] Patronage, for example,
represented one of the more effective arms in the governors' arsenal;
and with the passing years they learned that special favors and lucrative posts thoughtfully scattered among the representatives could
turn a recalcitrant opponent into a Court supporter.[55] As might be
expected, Dudley and Shute did not leave records explaining how they
won their political friends; but in 1727 William Douglass wrote

54. See Pocock, "Machiavelli, Harrington, and English Political Ideologies," for a discussion of different theories about maintaining a balanced
constitution in England. Pocock noted that the Country wanted strict
independence and condemned the efforts of the executive to win the legislature over to its point of view. The Court, however, contended that the
branches of government should be *interdependent* and condoned the use
of patronage in order to gain political ends (p. 571). Also Foord, *His
Majesty's Opposition*, pp. 17–19.

55. In his "The Origins of American Politics," *Perspectives in American
History*, 1(1967), Bernard Bailyn wrote, "at the beginning of the provincial
period the patronage at the disposal of governors was not negligible. In
the course of half a century, however, it was so ground away by forces at
either extreme of the political spectrum [the king and the local legislative
assemblies] that ultimately the governors were left, in the words of one
highly placed official, lamenting his lack of gifts to bestow, 'without the
means of stopping the mouths of the demagogs' " (p. 56). This account
agrees with Leonard Labaree's older, but extremely valuable study, *Royal
Government in America*, pp. 102–06.

However, when Bailyn discussed Dudley's administration, he shifted his
position, claiming that the governor, "by careful use of *limited patronage*
maintained a *semblance* of discipline in the Assembly; but he never *fully*
controlled the House and could not prevent its accusing him and his con-
federates of complicity with the enemy [the French] and of profiteering"
("Origins of American Politics," p. 88 [italics added]). This second assessment of the patronage power around the turn of the century, in Massachusetts at least, clashed with the well-documented account of Dudley's strength
in the General Court contained in G. M. Waller's *Samuel Vetch, Colonial
Enterpriser* (Chapel Hill, 1960), pp. 83–93. Nor does Bailyn's picture agree
with contemporary descriptions of Dudley's ability to win the "Country
Delegates" to his point of view. The governor failed only to gain a regular
salary and to get money for a fortress at Pemaquid, Maine. In other legislative
matters he was remarkably successful. See my discussion of Dudley's career
below.

from Boston, noting, "We have here numbers of candidates for every place of profit and ambition." Douglass added that whoever the royal governor was, he controlled many coveted appointments: "the naval office," "the captaincy of the castle," "the captaincies of the forts," "the nomination of the sheriffs of the several counties," and "the registers of probates."[56] Court rulers also extended their influence through associations and factions, usually held together by family ties, which contained men from all branches of the General Court.[57] Like patronage, party groupings helped to temper some of the representatives' independent spirit, for those delegates who joined the factions discovered that they held common interests with members of the council, and sometimes even with the governor himself. The Court did not look on these devices as evil or corrupt; but, instead, regarded them as means which were necessary to gain their ultimate goal, civil order.

Dudley and Shute: Two Rulers of the Court

During the Glorious Revolution the colonists arrested Joseph Dudley for conspiring with Andros to destroy the liberties of New England. Dudley reacted to his subsequent imprisonment with bitterness and confusion, believing that his acts as president of the council and later as Dominion councillor did not merit the punishment which the colonists now imposed upon him. In June 1689 he wrote a plaintive letter to Cotton Mather, attempting to justify his behavior over the previous decade. Dudley protested that he had done his best to defend the Old Charter; and, contrary to what some people apparently were saying, he had not bowed and scraped before James II in an effort to gain special favor.[58] But neither Mather nor anyone else in Massachusetts was willing to forgive Dudley, and they sent him off to London to stand trial for his supposed political

56. Dr. William Douglass to Cadwallader Colden, Nov. 20, 1727, 4 *Collections,* MHS, 2: 175–77. Douglass noted, "We have few places of any considerable profit in the governor's gift, but a great many small farms well leased out may be equivalent to a few great estates" (p. 176).

57. See Leonard W. Labaree, *Conservatism in Early American History* (Ithaca, 1962), pp. 1–31.

58. 6 *Collections,* MHS, 3: 502–05.

crimes. Although Dudley was exonerated of any guilt, he was deeply hurt by the treatment which he had received at the hands of his neighbors; and during a self-imposed exile which lasted for thirteen years, he never forgot the injustice which he felt had been done to him.

In England Dudley gained a political and cultural education that altered his entire outlook on society. Through luck, charm, and talent, he achieved entrée into the most influential ruling circles at Court. As he rushed from appointment to appointment, it appeared as if Randolph's assessment of Dudley's character had been correct; *"he hath his fortune to make in the world."*[59] One of the American's most important contacts was Lord Cutts, a soldier adventurer, who later became Lord Marlborough's second-in-command. Although Jonathan Swift described Cutts as "the vainest old fool alive," the Irish peer possessed a keen political sense; and, for more than a decade, he was the recipient of royal gifts and patronage.[60] In Dudley Cutts apparently saw the makings of a capable administrator who could guard his domestic interests while he was out of the country. During the late 1690s Cutts established Dudley in several lucrative posts, asking in exchange only that the American give his first loyalties to his patron. In 1695, soon after Dudley had become deputy governor of the Isle of Wight, Cutts explained with obvious understatement, "You know how you came by it; and you know what promise you made (upon your word and honour) when I gave it to you."[61]

As deputy governor of the Isle of Wight Dudley had to master a form of politics alien to the one he had known in Massachusetts. Lord Cutts apparently regarded Wight as his own territory, to do with as he pleased; and he expected his assistant to rule with an iron hand. It was reported, in fact, that when Cutts first assumed control of the island in 1693 "he was extremely unpopular, interfering improperly with the Corporations, disfranchising several Burgesses of Newtown, and imprisoning a Clergyman for several weeks in Cowes

59. See the discussion of Dudley's relationship to Edward Randolph in chap. 3.
60. *2 Proceedings,* MHS, 2: 193.
61. Ibid., p. 178.

Castle."[62] At one point a group of local gentlemen petitioned Parliament, complaining that the Lord "hath abused the power intrusted in him." Among other things, they accused Cutts of employing regular army units stationed on the island to discourage political opposition.[63] After this protest Cutts wisely curtailed some of his more arbitrary practices, but there was never any doubt who governed the Isle of Wight. Indeed, Lord Cutts once bragged that he could always be trusted to deliver six votes in Parliament to the king.[64] Dudley's responsibilities to his patron meant that he had to manipulate elections so that the "right" men were chosen; and when the voters showed signs of unrest, he found ways to bring them back into line.[65] But, more important for Dudley's later career, he learned to regard civil office chiefly as a vehicle for attaining his own personal goals. If he felt any sense of public service during this period he did not reveal it in his correspondence, and most of his letters were whining pleas for additional income and more prestigious posts.[66]

When Queen Anne appointed Dudley governor of Massachusetts in 1702 he showed how much he had learned from his experiences on the Isle of Wight. Before sailing for the colonies, he made certain that his interests would be well represented in England; for he knew that as soon as he was out of the country, factions would be scheming for his job. Dudley found an able lobbyist in John Chamberlayne, a writer and placeman who made a profession of keeping informed of all that happened at court.[67] Chamberlayne was always aware of what the governor should or should not do

62. Sir Richard Worsley, *History of the Isle of Wight* (London, 1781), p. 141. Also see Robert Walcott, Jr., *English Politics in the Early Eighteenth Century* (Cambridge, Mass., 1956), pp. 36–37.

63. For a full text of the petition see Worsley, *History of Wight*, p. 161.

64. See Lord Cutts, "Reflections upon the Government of the Isle of Wight, with regard to the Civil Power," *H.M.C. Report of the MSS of Mrs. Frankland-Russell-Astley* (London, 1900), p. 77.

65. In March 1695 and October 1698 Cutts ordered Dudley to manipulate local elections so that, in Cutts's words, "my Interests" would gain office (2 *Proceedings*, MHS, 2: 190).

66. E.g., 6 *Collections*, MHS, 3: 520.

67. *DNB*.

to protect his position in Massachusetts. In the fall of 1702, for example, he advised Dudley to write letters to the Lord President, the Lord Bishop of London, Lord Weymouth, Lord Nott, and other powerful men, stating his intention to promote "the interests of the Crown & Church of England." "I doubt not," Chamberlayne noted, "but such a letter will fix you in your Government & render you immoveable against the foaming but impotent billows & surges of tumultuous anarchy & republican fanaticism, of which your Excellency has once felt the dire effects in your own country,—& not only against them but against the vain attempts of all parties of what denomination soever."[68] During Dudley's long term of office New Englanders were often mystified by his ability to weather the most severe government storms. What they never seemed to realize was that he understood the operation of English politics better than they did.

When Dudley arrived in Boston he was determined to maintain the full power and prestige of his office. He expected to have his way all of the time; and, perhaps because of the bitter memory of 1689, looked upon political opposition as a form of treason. Like Lord Cutts, moreover, Dudley used his authority in an arbitrary manner; and, as early as 1702, Chamberlayne warned the colonial governor that his high-handed policies were doing his reputation more harm than good. It was rumored at the Stuart court, in fact, that Dudley "was overturning every thing in America, that he had broke in upon their Constitution, violated the Charter of the Massachusetts Colony, turn'd out all of the old justices, especially such as he suspected were not well enclin'd to Episcopacy, & put in new ones against the consent of the Council." These were serious charges, as Chamberlayne was well aware; but, to make matters worse, there was an embarrassing story about the Massachusetts governor circulating throughout London. English critics reported that Dudley had met a man named Gallop, who had been active in the overthrow of Andros, and that the governor had fallen "upon him with bitter invective and reproaches, & alluding to his name, threatened to make him *gallop* out of the country, &c."[69] This particular tale may well

68. 6 *Collections*, MHS, 3: 531. On June 16, 1703, Chamberlayne advised Dudley that, "all honors & profitable places do for the most part run in the same channel as you believe & wish they should" (p. 538).
69. Ibid., p. 532.

have been apocryphal, but it is true that Dudley did everything possible to preserve his prerogatives without consideration for the traditions and sentiments of the people whom he ruled.

An incident which occurred one winter morning in 1705 taught the governor what the colonists thought of his pretensions. Dudley had just set off on a trip from his home in Roxbury to New Hampshire when his coach encountered two carts loaded with wood on a narrow stretch of road. William Dudley, who was driving his father's coach, commanded the carters to move their wagons aside; but, as he later testified in court, one of the men on the carts shouted that he "would not goe out of the way for the Governour: whereupon the Govr. came out of the Charet [chariot] and told Winchester [one of the carters] he must give way to the Charet. Winchester answered boldly, without any other words, 'I am as good flesh and blood as you; I will not give way; you may goe out of the way.'" The governor, who was never known as a calm person, lost all self-control and sputtered, "Sirrah, you rogue and rascall, I will have that way." He drew his sword and charged Winchester, all the while urging his son, "run the dogs through." In the interest of safety one of the carters broke Dudley's sword, but the governor continued to jump about screaming that the two men who had crossed him were "divells" and "Dogs." A local justice finally arrested both drivers; and, at their trial, Dudley explained that they had not shown him the proper respect—"nor did they once in the Govrs. hearing or sight pull off their hatts or say they would goe out of the way, or in any word excuse the matter, but absolutely stood upon it." The county magistrates listened patiently to the evidence and then decided to Dudley's immense irritation that the carters' actions had been fully justified. The governor's dignity did not count for much when he arbitrarily ordered vehicles off the road.[70] There is no way to know how many men in Massachusetts thought as Winchester did, but the number was probably not small.

Dudley shared the Court's contempt for popular elections, especially when they influenced the composition of the upper house or council. Before he took office, the governor had expected the Bay councillors to support his policies; but these hopes went unfulfilled.

70. *5 Collections*, MHS, 6: 144–46.

Although Dudley vetoed the selection of those men whom he found politically obnoxious, the council never became the loyal ally he had desired. The governor concluded that as long as the councillors were selected by the House of Representatives, as they were under the new charter, there would be no chance for reform. After only three months in Massachusetts, he informed the Board of Trade that "the Council being of the People's Election many of the Most loyall Persons, and of the best Estates are not Imployed, and these that are, so many of them are Commonwealthmen, and all so absolutely Depend for their Station upon the People, that they dare not offend them."[71] The imperial authorities did nothing about Dudley's complaints. Their silence, however, did not discourage his efforts to change the council's character, to make it easier for more gentlemen of Court persuasion to serve. "It is every day now more Apparent," he wrote to England in 1703, "that nothing will proceed well here till Her Ma ty [Queen Anne] will please to name her owne Council, the best men in the province can have no Share in Civil Government till then."[72] In 1708 the governor was still grumbling that the representatives of the people had purposely removed "principal Gentlemen . . . of the best estates" from the upper house.[73] The colonists must have recognized the obvious irony of Dudley's position, for one of the men he vetoed each year, Elisha Cooke, Sr., was far wealthier than the governor himself.[74]

Dudley knew that if he were to survive as governor he would need loyal followers in every branch of the government, persons who would support his policies without hesitation. During his first year in office Cotton Mather gratuitously advised the new chief magistrate, "I am humbly of the Opinion, that it will be your wisdome, to carry an indifferent Hand towards all Parties; if in our case, I may use so Coarse a Word as Parties. And give Occasion unto none to say, that any have monopolized you, that you take your measures

71. Board of Trade, Papers, New England (MSS), cited in Kimball, *Joseph Dudley*, p. 89.

72. Ibid., p. 90.

73. *Calendar of State Papers, Colonial Series, 1708–1709*, p. 235.

74. Thomas Hutchinson, *The History of the Colony and Province of Massachusetts-Bay*, ed. Lawrence S. Mayo, 3 vols. (Boston, 1936), 2: 101.

from them alone."[75] But Dudley had no intention of allowing any faction, especially one associated with the Mathers, to "monopolize" him. In fact, during his first year in office, he so aggressively set about forming a party of his own and crushing rival groups which were competing for the Queen's affection over his head, that his friend Chamberlayne had to remind Dudley that "moderation is a virtue, & that Jehu was known by his furious driving at a very great distance [2 Kings 9]. Tis true your Excellency is much farther off, but tho' we cant see you, we can hear of you! Besides, our European statesmen maintain that *wise governors are of no party.*"[76]

Dudley realized, however, that a governor without a party would not long remain governor. He made his son, Paul, the attorney general of Massachusetts despite the outcry against nepotism.[77] He also plied various councillors and representatives with special favors, thereby assuring their political loyalty. Dudley's procedures clearly perplexed New Englanders who were not of Court persuasion. " 'Tis Unintelligible," Cotton Mather exclaimed, "Why will the *Massachusetts* Counsellors permit themselves to be made the Tools of their Governour's particular Designs? Why will Counsellors that are Chosen by the People, be less Concerned for, less Faithful to the People, than the Counsellors in the other Plantations, who are not by the Choice of the People brought unto the Board."[78] Mather's confusion was obviously a compliment to Dudley's enormous talent as a political tactician, and in 1728, almost a decade after the governor's death, William Douglass reported that the Dudley party remained one of the strongest factions within the Massachusetts General Court.[79]

Dudley did not win followers through what would be termed corrupt practices today. He was a man who knew the value of favor and flattery, and he never had to resort to bribery in order to gain

75. "Diary of Cotton Mather," 7 *Collections,* MHS, 7: 464–65.

76. 6 *Collections,* MHS, 3: 542. For evidence of Dudley's strength, see Wait Winthrop to Sir Henry Ashurst, Sept. 1699, 6 *Collections,* MHS, 5: 49–50.

77. "Samuel Sewall's Letter Book," 6 *Collections,* MHS, 1: 339.

78. [Cotton Mather], "The Deplorable State of New-England," 5 *Collections,* MHS, 6: 113.

79. 4 *Collections,* MHS, 2: 184.

his way. The governor's contemporaries recognized—albeit be-grudgingly—the subtle political devices which he employed to transform opponents into supporters. In 1708 Cotton Mather protested "the Carresses" of Dudley's *Table,* which are enough to Dazzle an Honest Countryman, who Thinks every Body Means what he Speaks."[80] And Wait Winthrop, jealous of Dudley's success, complained of the governor's "studied fair speeches and pretensions upon our honest country representatives."[81] His reputation for amusing and entertaining his associates long outlived the man himself; and as late as 1768 there were New Englanders who remembered Dudley as a talented raconteur who "took great delight in telling stories, and had an extraordinary talent for enlargement and embellishment to make a story agreeable."[82] Clearly, the Court governor had been an able politician.

As one might expect, Governor Dudley distributed patronage with great skill, and the prudent award of army commissions seems to have won him many backers in small country towns throughout the Bay Colony.[83] "The Influence which Preferments and Commissions have upon little men, is inexpressible," Cotton Mather complained in 1707. "It must needs be a Mortal Sin, to Disoblige a Governor, that has Inabled a Man to Command a *Whole Country Town,* and to Strut among his Neighbours, with the Illustrious Titles, of, *Our Major,* and, *The Captain,* or, *His Worship."* Mather lamented that the ambitious Dudley had granted the office of justice of the peace to a lowly "Sow-Gelder." The clergyman observed with great solemnity that New England had never had a "Sow-Gelder" in that position before and noted—one hopes with a sense of humor—that the freemen might find themselves in the sow's place if they did not reform the patronage system in Masachusetts.[84] Despite Mather's warning, however, there always seemed to be a large number of colonists who shared Dudley's opinion that civil office was a vehicle for personal advancement and not an instrument for public service.

80. "The Deplorable State," p. 119.
81. *6 Collections,* MHS, 5: 49.
82. Ezra Stiles, Bound Letter (MSS), 5: 65 (Yale University Library).
83. Kimball, *Joseph Dudley,* p. 179.
84. "The Deplorable State," p. 119.

The most serious crisis of Dudley's administration occurred in 1706 when two of the governor's closest business associates, Samuel Vetch and John Borland, were caught trading in Canada while Massachusetts was at war with the French. Naturally many New Englanders thought such practices amounted to treason. What made them even angrier, however, was the suspicion that the governor himself profited from this evil commerce, which in the words of the General Court, "put knives into the hands of those barbarous infidels to cut the throats of our wives and children."[85] Dudley's political enemies resolved to expose his perfidy, hoping that a major scandal would force England to revoke his commission. But the governor, with the aid of the political organization he had established in the General Court, managed to avoid embarrassment or censure. Dudley's most masterful stroke was the transfer of Vetch's trial from the regular Massachusetts courts to the House of Representatives. The Board of Trade explained with remarkable accuracy that the governor was "highly suspected to be concerned in this illegal trade and (as tis said) he artfully complyed with the Assembly's desire of trying these people. Knowing that several in the Assembly suspected him, he had friends enough in that House to prevent the asking such questions as might touch him; which he could not have done had the prisoners been tried in the ordinary courts where he had not so much influence."[86] Vetch paid a fine and left Massachusetts, happy to escape with his life. Yet Dudley's position as governor was never in danger, despite the many complaints which the colonists had lodged against him. The political devices which he had learned on the Isle of Wight protected the Court ruler from the effects of popular protest.

The two Mathers were appalled at the ease with which Dudley avoided punishment, and in 1707 they launched a personal crusade against him. The impetus for their attack came as much from private pique as from a concern for the general welfare. During this period the Mathers were bitterly resentful that Dudley's candidate, John

85. 6 Collections, MHS, 3: 333. The material for the discussion of the Vetch trial came chiefly from Waller, Samuel Vetch, pp. 80–93 passim.

86. Memorandum of the Board of Trade, Sept. 1707, Webster Papers (New Brunswick Museum), cited in Waller, Samuel Vetch, p. 89.

Leverett, had recently won the presidency of Harvard College, a post long held by Increase Mather.[87] The clergymen focused their criticism on the wickedness of Dudley's character and did not contest his obvious political talents. Cotton admitted that he could "with all the sincerity imaginable, acknowledge your [Dudley's] *abilities* and *accomplishments*."[88] Instead the Mathers insisted that the governor had fallen prey to an assortment of sins and corruptions which, taken together, indicated that Dudley was not a good ruler. "Sir," Cotton wrote imperiously, "your *snare* has been that thing, the *hatred* whereof is most expressly required of the *ruler*, namely *covetousness*."[89] They cried that Dudley had transformed the government of Massachusetts into "an engine to enrich himself" and instituted a "horrid Reign of Bribery."[90] The two ministers couched each of their charges in scriptural terms, trying to avoid any suspicion that their own political interests were at stake. "I am afraid that the Lord is offended with you," Increase observed piously, "in that you ordinarily forsake the worship of God in the holy church to which you are related . . . and after the publick exercise, spend the whole time with some persons reputed very ungodly men. *I am sure your father did not so*."[91] Cotton, too, feared that the governor was "in *ill-terms* with heaven," but he felt confident that God would forgive Dudley if the ruler would only "endeavour in *methods* of *piety*."[92] The Mathers reprimanded Dudley as if politics had not changed in the colonies since Winthrop's death, as if there had been no Glorious Revolution in America, as if the two ministers had not themselves fostered the spirit of party and faction during Phips's administration.

Dudley realized immediately that the Mathers had made a tactical blunder and exploited it with relish. The scriptural language which the ministers had employed to attack him now became his tool

87. See Miller, *New England Mind,* 2: 272–76.

88. Cotton Mather to Joseph Dudley, Jan. 20, 1708, *1 Collections,* MHS, 3: 134.

89. Ibid., p. 130.

90. Ibid., p. 130; also [Cotton Mather], "A Memorial of the Present Deplorable State of New-England," *5 Collections,* MHS, 6: 40.

91. Increase Mather to Joseph Dudley, Jan. 20, 1708, *1 Collections,* MHS, 3: 127 (italics added).

92. Cotton Mather to Dudley, *1 Collections,* MHS, 3: 133.

against them. He accused the Mathers of treating him with an "air of superiority and contempt," declaring that such behavior "is insufferably rude towards one whom divine Province had honoured with the character of your Governor." Dudley argued with confidence, no doubt aware that John Winthrop had once lectured the members of the General Court in similar terms.[93] He claimed that the clergy's so-called "Christian reproof" was merely a cover for "faction and sedition" and advised the Mathers to stay in the place God had assigned them and stop meddling in government.[94] The governor had beaten the two ministers at their own game, demonstrating in the process how irrelevant religion was to politics. But Dudley was not finished with his adversaries yet; for he possessed another, more telling, defense against their criticisms. In an apologetic pamphlet addressed to the colonists he pointed out that he had ended piracy, built up naval stores, and bolstered colonial fortifications. "And though the want of the *Spanish* Trade," he continued, "has put a Check to the Great Increase of Bullion at present; yet *New England* never appear'd more flourishing than at this time."[95] Security and property were the governor's ultimate answers to the Mathers' moralizing.

When Dudley died in 1720 Benjamin Colman delivered a funeral sermon which he later published under the title, *Ossa Josephi.* As Colman spoke, he must have been aware of the difficulty of his assignment. During his long political career Dudley not only had rejected the values and traditions of New England, but also had made a great many enemies. The minister tried his best to justify the governor's behavior, explaining that although Dudley had supported the arbitrary government of the Dominion, he had been innocent of Andros's evil designs. Moreover, through a kind of tortured logic, Colman explained that the governor's attachment to the Anglican Church was not the apostasy which most of the colonists believed it to be. According to the minister Dudley "preferr'd the way of worship in *our Churches,* and was wont frequently to say,

93. See chap. 2 for a discussion of Winthrop's speech.
94. Joseph Dudley to Increase Mather and Cotton Mather, Feb. 1708, *1 Collections,* MHS, 3: 135, 137.
95. [Joseph Dudley], "A Modest Enquiry," *5 Collections,* MHS, 6: 87.

'that he lov'd a great deal of *Ceremony* in the *Government*, but as little as might be in the *Church*.'[96] The clergyman praised the governor's learning and culture which he claimed had been widely respected, especially in England.[97] It is doubtful that Colman's strained attempt to salvage Dudley's reputation in New England was successful. Thomas Hutchinson wrote a more fitting epitaph for the governor when he noted simply that "Mr. Dudley's principles, in government, were too high for the Massachusetts people."[98] Dudley was a good ruler only for the Court. The Country, of course, had other ideas.

Dudley's remarkable career revealed something about the relationship between political events and political theory within the Bay Colony. Certainly, after the Glorious Revolution, it appeared as if Dudley would never again rule New Englanders—at least, not if they could help it. They disliked the man for those attributes which had endeared him first to Edward Randolph and later to Sir Edmund Andros. Yet the arbitrary qualities that had angered the Americans won him preferment in the mother country. In fact, he was able to become the governor of Massachusetts in 1702 precisely because he had disowned Puritan political ideas. He could never have served Lord Cutts on the Isle of Wight had he not been willing to discourage popular participation in civil affairs. Unfortunately for the Bay colonists, their new charter of 1691, calling for an appointed royal governor, allowed Dudley to take power without their assent. Indeed, he returned to Boston comfortably aware that it did not much matter what the people thought of him. He alone would decide what the executive ruler should or should not do in office. Court writers made a virtue out of his insulation from the voters, seeing him as a model of good political behavior. But, if unexpected changes in the Massachusetts Charter brought Court rulers to the governorship, they also made the House of Representatives seem more important than it had ever been before. There could be no doubt in 1710 or 1720, as there had been in 1640, that the members of the lower house were genuine magistrates possessing clear con-

96. Colman, *Ossa Josephi*, p. 35.
97. Ibid., p. 38; see Kimball, *Joseph Dudley*, pp. 204–07.
98. Hutchinson, *History*, 2: 111.

stitutional responsibilities. The Bay freemen knew that while they could not determine the character of their *appointed* rulers, they could always drop an *elected* representative who did not meet their standards.

Samuel Shute, who was appointed governor of Massachusetts in 1716, shared most of Dudley's Court prejudices, but he lacked his predecessor's political skills. When he first came to office, New Englanders praised him for his excellent personal qualities, and Samuel Sewall told William Ashurst that "it was a joyfull Surprise to the Inhabitants of this Province to hear the Report of Col. Shutes' being Appointed our Governour. The character given of his Excellency is exceedingly refreshing to us, *as dew upon the mown Grass*."[99] And Cotton Mather informed Lord Barrington that the new governor was the type of person, "whom if it were left unto their own election, the whole people almost to a man, would chuse for their Governour."[100] But Shute had not been chosen by the colonists; and, because he was not, the citizens of Massachusetts were never free from the suspicion that he was working at cross purposes to their own wishes. At the same time, the governor's inept handling of political affairs convinced Court supporters that he was a weak ruler who would not be able to preserve the royal prerogative against the people's assault.

A series of civil crises in Massachusetts destroyed any hope for peace during Shute's rule. The colony's depressed trade and the agitation for an inflated currency were the chief sources of contention, but there were also many other areas of friction. Thomas Hutchinson explained that by 1720 rumors had begun to circulate "that the governor was a weak man, easily led away, and that he was in the hands of the Dudleys, men of high principles in government, and it behoved the people to be very careful of their liberties."[101] The members of the lower house in particular believed that their privileges were in danger and resisted the governor at every chance. In the atmosphere of mutual distrust which pervaded the General

99. 6 *Collections*, MHS, 2: 56 (italics added).

100. *1 Collections*, MHS, 1: 106; see Cotton Mather to John Winthrop, Jan. 11, 1719, *4 Collections*, MHS, 8: 432.

101. Hutchinson, *History*, 2: 166.

Court, the patronage system which Dudley had used to temper the delegates' independence became unworkable.

Shute thoroughly hated his antagonists in the lower house; but he was not clever enough to realize that, if he had hidden his anger, he might have been able to win them over to his point of view. He continually missed opportunities which a man like Dudley would have turned to his own advantage; and his administration degenerated into a name calling contest. In 1721 Shute informed the Board of Trade that

> the House of Representatives generally consist of persons (better adapted to their farming affairs than to be Representatives of the Province) who are drawn into any measures by the craft and subtilty of a few designing persons who when they are indeavouring to invade the Royal Prerogative make the unthinking part of the Assembly believe, that they only are asserting the just privileges of the people, and by this false guise these men become the favourites of the Populace who believe them to be the only patriots of their country.[102]

The governor clearly had lost control of the constitutional balance in Massachusetts, and the Court worried that his failure had opened a Pandora's box of popular demands. The more the people suspected Shute of endangering their liberties, the more actively they participated in politics. Their intervention into government affairs was what the Court feared most, for it threatened what they regarded as the social order of New England. When Governor Shute stole away to England on a ship one night few in Boston were sorry to see him go.

102. *Calendar of State Papers, Colonial Series, 1720–1721,* p. 329.

7

THE COUNTRY PERSUASION

THE Country in New England possessed no more structure or organization than the Court did. Its members came from diverse backgrounds and callings; yet, despite personal differences, they shared certain beliefs about the nature of government and the character of the good ruler. The Elisha Cookes, father and son, carried the Country philosophy to the Massachusetts General Court during the early years of the eighteenth century. The Reverend John Wise's essays and James Franklin's newspaper, *The New-England Courant,* contained many of the same ideas. But probably the most influential Country writers were a group of anonymous pamphleteers who commented on civil policies and whose works reached a wide audience throughout New England. By 1720, in fact, their publications had replaced the election sermon as the most important vehicle for political discussion.

Men of Country persuasion saw government as a voluntary agreement formed by the citizens within a given geographic area. There was obviously nothing very new about this concept. Indeed, John Winthrop and his contemporaries had described civil authority as a compact or covenant made with the consent of the freemen. During the course of the seventeenth century, many things had changed in New England; but the covenant idea endured.[1] The Country writers who subscribed to the contractual theory of government insisted that the people themselves determined the nature and amount of power which a ruler could lawfully exercise. Although the Court tacitly supported this view, Country spokesmen carried the notion of

1. See chap. 2 for discussion of covenants in early New England; also Edmund S. Morgan, ed., *Puritan Political Ideas, 1558–1794* (Indianapolis, 1965), p. xiv.

contractualism far beyond the Court's position, and throughout this period they stressed the popular basis of civil authority, declaring that magistrates had no interests other than those of their constituents. In a typical Country piece, entitled *The Original Rights of Mankind* (1722), an anonymous author explained that in well-governed commonwealths "there is no difference in the Views and Interests of the Governours and Governed, but each striving to Excel, in promoting one the others happiness."[2]

Yet, for all their talk of covenants and compacts, men of Country persuasion felt extremely uneasy about New England's political future. In fact, much of the Country rhetoric was just as anxious, just as shrill, as that of the Court. Both parties sensed that colonial society had lost its direction. There was always a chance, of course, that Massachusetts could become a city on a hill, a model commonwealth; but the outlook was not bright. In the early years of the eighteenth century it appeared far more likely that New Englanders would destroy their own rights and liberties. The Country writers in particular were haunted by a fear that tyrants, usually vague unnamed conspirators, would overturn the colony's popular government and transform Massachusetts into an arbitrary regime. While the Court harped on the threat of social chaos, the Country worried about the loss of liberty and the slavery which was certain to follow. "Remember (Countrymen)," one author cried, "that LIBERTY is a Jewel of an inestimable Value, which once lost, is seldom recovered again."[3] In 1723 the cover of Nathan Bowen's popular almanac carried a short Country poem which might have been mistaken for a protest against Governor Andros if it had not been clearly dated.

> Tyrants & Tyranny! What can be worse?
> (to all but Slaves) an Everlasting Curse.
> When his wild will constrains you to Obey,
> He then insults you like a Beast of Prey.
> At Fez the Slavish Cant prevails so well,
> That Tyranny doth in perfection dwell.[4]

The next year an anonymous pamphlet entitled *The Madness of the*

---

2. J. M., *The Original Rights of Mankind* (Boston, 1722), pp. i–ii.

3. *English Advice to the Freeholders &c. of the Province of Massachusetts-Bay* (Boston, 1722), p. 4.

4. [Nathan Bowen], *The New-England Diary* (Boston, 1723), p. 1.

Jacobite Party reminded "reasonable" New Englanders "that *Liberty* is one Essential Article of Happiness.—without this, all the other bequests both of Nature and Providence, are render'd precarious, may be the Arbitrary Pleasure of Merciless Tyrants and Oppressors, and to be employ'd by *Them* to our utter Destruction."[5] From the perspective of over two centuries the Country's dread of despotism seems groundless, even irrational. Historians have uncovered no plots or conspiracies against New England; and, for the most part, it appears that imperial administrators in London paid very little attention to the American dominions. Nevertheless, to men such as Nathan Bowen and the anonymous pamphleteer the danger to their liberties was quite real; and, unless one appreciates their anxiety about the state of New England, one cannot fully understand the Country persuasion.[6]

Country spokesmen recognized that in theory, at least, the Massachusetts Charter protected their rights and property from encroachment by arbitrary rulers. In his election sermon of 1729 John Wise's son, Jeremiah, told the members of the General Court that *"Civil Rulers,* can't do what they will, either *de Jure* or *de Facto."*[7] The minister counseled his audience to thank the Lord for "modelling the various Constitutions of Government, and settling the several *Boundaries of Power."* But, while Country writers encouraged the establishment of constitutional limits on magisterial authority, they had little faith that such precautions could effectively stem the growth of tyranny. Many of them had witnessed how easily James II had overridden the original Bay patent when it impeded his plans for the Dominion of New England. Regardless of what their individual experiences may have been, persons of Country persuasion had clearly concluded by the 1720s that, even under the best conditions, political office brought out the worst in man's character. It seemed obvious to them that laws alone could not keep bad rulers from gaining power and that the privileges which they granted

5. *The Madness of the Jacobite Party* (Boston, 1724), p. 1.

6. Cf. Bernard Bailyn, "The Origins of American Politics," *Perspectives in American History* 1(1967): 9–46.

7. Jeremiah Wise, *Rulers the Ministers of God* (Boston, 1729), pp. 19–20; see "My son, Fear Thou the Lord [Boston, 1714?]," *Publications of the Colonial Society of Massachusetts* 10(1904–06): 349.

to today's good magistrate might be abused tomorrow. With such dangers in mind, the Country urged New Englanders to delegate civil power with extreme care. In 1722, for example, the author of *English Advice to the Freeholders* argued that "tho' it be granted, that we have some good *Rulers* now; yet we don't know how long they will continue; and therefore it is essentially necessary, for you to secure your selves against a Time of Change." The anonymous Country pamphleteer noted further that "the Power that is allow'd to good Men, you may be sure will be claim'd and taken by ill ones."[8]

Throughout this period Country writers maintained that the only reliable safeguard against tyranny was the colonists' full and continued participation in politics. In reaching this conclusion, the pamphleteers made several assumptions about human nature and group behavior. They admitted that all men had been tainted by original sin and would probably give in to temptation more times than not. Yet, despite man's obvious weaknesses, the Country believed that there was likely to be greater virtue in the entire populace than in any given individual. When persons gathered in groups or in communities, they seemed naturally to temper the vices of their neighbors and to work for the common good. Or, put another way, civil power was apt to corrupt individual magistrates; but it represented almost no threat to the mass of freemen. The people stood ouside the vitiating influence of civil authority and, therefore, were in a position to assess objectively the wisdom of each government policy. Unfortunately, there was no guarantee that the freemen would do their part; and Country authors thought it necessary to warn their readers repeatedly that despots would seize power the minute New Englanders failed to fulfill their responsibilities as free citizens. For the Country, the character of the people was every bit as imporant as the character of the ruler.

Country pamphleteers assumed that one freeman's opinions about civil matters was as valuable as another's, and they dismissed the Court's contention that wealthy persons possessed greater political wisdom or insight than did their poorer neighbors. The intensity of the Country's "leveling spirit" became apparent in 1714 when

8. *English Advice*, p. 4.

the people of Boston debated whether their city should follow the example of many English towns by incorporating its municipal government. Such a move would have replaced Boston's traditional town meeting with an elected governing council. One Country writer weighed the merits of this change in a dialogue which supposedly had taken place between two Bay colonists. One of the characters in this piece—the straight man—argued that incorporation was a good idea since it would allow "Men of considerable Substance" to run the city. But the other citizen, voicing Country opinions, responded hotly that "a Man may be worth £1000 and yet have neither Grace nor good manners, but be a Covetous Man, that may be a Wolfe among Sheep."9 Another author insisted that wealth in itself did not give a person a preeminent right to political authority— at least, it did not do so in Massachusetts.10 If town meetings ceased, he insisted, then farewell "to the Management of the Town Affairs by the Freeholders, Collectively, Rich and Poor Men, they will no more be jumbled together in Town Offices, as they are in the Grave, no more Mobb Town-Meetings of Freeholders, (as some are pleased to call them:) No, no: Then the Rich will exert that Right of Dominion, which they think they have exclusive of all others . . . then the Great Men will no more have the Dissatisfaction of seeing their Poorer Neighbours stand up for equal Privilege with them, in the highest Acts of Town Government."11 These Country appeals apparently succeeded, for Boston's town meeting continued to be an important part of the colony's political life throughout the remainder of the eighteenth century.12

9. "A Dialogue Between a Boston Man and a Country Man," *Publications of the Colonial Society of Massachusetts* 10 (1904–06): 346–67.

10. The author of the pamphlet "My son, Fear Thou the Lord" observed that *"Great Britain* hath and doth abound with Gentlemen, who tho' they dont, it may be, believe, *Dominion is founded in Grace,* yet, as a great many others, in other parts of the World verily believe, so do they, *That its founded in Money;* which by the way is the true reason why often times we see them so much more Solicitous to become Rich Men, than they are to become Good Men" (p. 351).

11. Ibid., p. 352 (italics added).

12. Cf. "A Letter from a Gentleman Containing Some Remarks . . . [Boston, 1720]," in Andrew M. Davis, *Colonial Currency Reprints,* 4 vols. (Boston, 1910–11), 2: 12.

Often the rhetoric of the Country took on a conspiratorial tone, as if the writers sensed some immediate danger to their rights and property. Significantly, when incorporation threatened Boston's town meeting, it was a Country pamphleteer who first announced that there was a plot afoot. He cautioned the inhabitants "that there are some designing Men setting a Trap for them," adding that he hope they would "not shew themselves to be sillier than a Bird; in suffering themselves to be taken by a Trap, set, in their sight to catch them."[13] The Country party in New England knew that the "TRAP-SETTERS" would succeed the very second that the freemen dropped their guard or became apathetic to the affairs of government. In 1721 another Boston publicist felt obliged to remind his readers of the "Egyptian Bondage" which the colony had suffered under Sir Edmund Andros. "The Oppression, and Grievances," explained the author, "that our Fathers lay under, during that Government are too many and too Gross really (some of them), to recount now: and yet they held out, and surmounted those Innumerable Calamities: And shall *We* of *their Race* and *Posterity* (even before some of them, have their Heads laid in the Grave,) . . . seem in the least to be dismayed for our petty Troubles compared with theirs? Surely no!" He exhorted the citizens of Massachusetts to resist their political enemies with the same energy and courage that their predecessors had shown.[14]

Men such as Wise and Franklin placed great importance on the printing press, recognizing that public vigilance meant little if the people did not know the full extent of their constitutional rights and liberties. Elisha Cooke, Jr., a leader of the Massachusetts House of Representatives, was aware of the problems caused by political

13. "My Son, Fear Thou the Lord," p. 352. In the "Dialogue" the Country man thanks the Boston resident for alerting him "to the Bondage and Difficulties that as you say you are like to be brought under." And the Boston man responds, *"That there is not One among them* [the people of Boston] *shall more Earnestly endeavor the Preservation of Property than My Self"* (p. 343).

14. "A Letter from a Gentleman in Mount Hope, to His Friend in Treamount [Boston, 1721]," in Davis, *Currency Reprints,* 2: 262–63. See Elisha Cooke, Jr., *Mr. Cooke's Just and Seasonable Vindication* (Boston, 1720), pp. 12–14.

ignorance and advised his contemporaries that "the happiness or infelicity of a People entirely depends upon the enjoyment or deprivation of Liberty. It's therefore highly prudent for them to inform themselves of their just Rights, and form a due sense of their inestimable Value, that they may be encouraged to assert them against the Attempts of any in time to come."[15] The Country firmly believed that evil rulers would attempt to suppress any facts which threatened to expose their arbitrary designs and would seize power when the uninformed citizenry had been lulled into a false sense of security.[16]

Popular sources of political information expanded greatly in the early decades of the eighteenth century. In part, this growth was the result of the Country's efforts to persuade the colonists to participate in government affairs. It was during this period, for example, that pamphleteers began to analyze civil policies on a regular basis and to attack those decisions which they disliked. For the first time in New England's history, nonclerical authors counseled the freemen on how to cast their votes; and, by the 1720s, essays like *English Advise to the Freeholders &c. of the Province of Massachusetts* had become fairly common. Another innovation occurred in 1721 when Boston printed its instructions to the representatives of the lower house. Every literate colonist, whether he attended Boston's town meeting or not, now knew what the city expected of its delegates; and the pressure on these representatives to honor their instructions must have been great.[17] After 1715, moreover, the lower house of the Massachusetts General Court began to publish and to distribute its records at the end of every legislative session. This plan allowed the freemen in distant villages to see for themselves how well their elected rulers defended the liberties of the commonwealth. The weekly newspapers which started during these years also supplied the people with vital facts about their government by carrying the texts

15. Cooke, *Just and Seasonable Vindication*, p. 14.

16. See *The New-England Courant*, July 2, 1722; also response of the Massachusetts House of Representatives to Governor Shute's proposed Bill for Censorship in *Calendar of State Papers, Colonial Series, 1720–1721*, p. 330.

17. *Instructions to the Representatives of Boston* (Boston, 1721).

of laws and proclamations and by reproducing political essays which had originally appeared in the journals of London. The increase in the number of publications and their changing character meant that men throughout the colony could judge more accurately than ever before whether their rights and properties were in danger. In the long run the Country's most important contribution to the political life of New England may well have been the way it used the printing press to educate the public.

The Country's definition of the good ruler grew out of its fear of arbitrary government and its faith in the people. The pamphleteers realized that a magistrate required special attributes for his work and that wealth, education, and breeding were important aids. But the Country writers did not regard any of these qualities as essential. Indeed, they insisted that a ruler's political philosophy was of far greater concern to the welfare of the commonwealth than were his manners and dress. While such cultural trappings were not to be discouraged, their presence was no guarantee that a man would be a good magistrate. Authors of Country persuasion explained that no one could govern well unless he possessed "public spirit," which in this period meant that he had to demonstrate his hatred of tyranny and his love of English liberties.[18] Jeremiah Wise paid Charles Frost a high compliment in 1725 when he described this Massachusetts councillor as "a *true* Englishman, [who] had a great and just value for the great and glorious Privileges of this *Nation.*"[19] Other writers might have called Frost a "Patriot" or "a Lover of his Country," for such terms entered the political vocabulary of New England during the early years of the eighteenth century.[20] Country voters did not want their rulers to be average men, embodying the faults of their constituents, and would have been appalled by the suggestion that one individual could have represented their interests as well as any other. Nevertheless, they tried to elect persons who in the words of one Country author would "dare boldly [to] exert themselves for the *Publick Good,* by making Laws that will secure you from any

18. See "A Letter from a Gentleman Containing Some Remarks" p. 16.
19. Jeremiah Wise, *A Funeral Sermon* (Boston, 1725), p. 29.
20. *English Advice,* pp. 1, 3.

attempts that may be form'd to your Prejudice by succeeding Rulers."[21]

The arguments which Country writers advanced during the currency crisis revealed just how important "public spirit" was in their assessment of rulers. These authors rejected the moralistic rhetoric which Paul Dudley, Thomas Foxcroft, and other Court leaders had used to discourage demands for additional paper money. Men such as John Wise knew from their own experience that the Court's paternalistic lectures about frugality did little good for the people who were suffering from a depression that was not of their own making.[22] In 1721 Wise wrote a pamphlet entitled *A Word of Comfort to a Melancholy Country* which supported the movement for an inflated currency. With typical candor, he declared that the talk about cutting back on the importation of English finery was irrelevant to the economic problem at hand. "If we Live upon Ground-Nuts and Clams," he explained with sarcasm, "and Cloath our Backs with the Exuviae, or Pelts of Wild Beasts, we may then lower our Expences a great pace . . . but if we intend to Live in any Garb, or Port, as becomes a People of Religion, Civility, Trade and Industry, then we must still supply our selves from the Great Fountain." Wise was certain that the Lord had not planned for his children to live like squirrels, but had wanted them to enjoy the full bounty of nature. According to the Country minister, civil leaders who did nothing to relieve the colonists' poverty were not only irresponsible to their constituents, but also lacking in political wisdom, since prosperity "animates the Farmer; keeps him to his Plough; Brightens and enlivens all his Rurall schemes; Reconciles him to all his hard Labour, and makes him look Fat and Cheerful."[23] The other Country appeals written during the currency controversy possessed neither Wise's brilliant style nor his sense of humor, but their message was the same. The authors reminded the rulers of Massachusetts that public-spirited men throughout the colony would resist any effort "to bring all the people into a dependency upon the *Court Interests;*

21. *English Advice,* p. 4; also Cooke, *Just and Seasonable Vindication,* p. 14.

22. See Court views on currency discussed in chap. 4.

23. John Wise, "A Word of Comfort to a Melancholy Country [Boston, 1721]," in Davis, *Currency Reprints,* 2: 186, 201–02.

and consequently to render them Abject and Servile, which . . . no Lover of his Country should promote."[24] Whenever they had an opportunity, pamphleteers reaffirmed the popular basis of government and lectured colonial magistrates about the responsibility to serve the people.

A corollary of the Country's demand for public-spirited leaders was its insistence that rulers be "independent" men. The anonymous authors who flourished during these years were especially suspicious of representatives who had received gifts or favors from the royal governor; for they regarded patronage as a form of corruption which, if unchecked, would turn the magistrates away from their constituents' true interests. One Country writer told the freemen of Massachusetts that "it highly Concerns your several Towns: to send Good, Honest and Trusty Men: those who have no Commissions, nor any dependence on the Government are certainly the best men, and so you will find it. Men that will make themselves tools to a party, or are merely passive, and will suffer themselves to be led by the nose, are fit for no publick trust."[25] One pamphleteer urged the electorate not to choose any candidates "who have their Obligations to the Governour, for their Preferments and Employment," because only fully independent delegates could be trusted to defend popular liberties against the threat of executive encroachment.[26] Another Country spokesman rhetorically asked the voters of the Bay Colony whether they should give their support to individuals "who for the sake of *Preferments,* or fear of loosing a *Place* or *Pension,* will Change their former Notes, and *turn Courtiers?*" The author of this piece believed that good representatives would show their worth by selecting good men to the upper house or council, "Gentlemen, who laying aside all *Private Gain* in their Publick Stations, and Administration, will joyn hand in hand with the Representative Body, in serving and advancing the Good, and Prosperity of this People."[27]

24. F. .L B. .T, "A Letter from One in Boston, to His Friend in the Country [Boston, 1714]," in Davis, *Currency Reprints,* 1: 285.

25. "A Letter to an Eminent Clergy-Man [Boston, 1721]," in Davis, *Currency Reprints,* 2: 238.

26. [Cotton Mather], "The Deplorable State of New-England," 5 *Collections,* MHS, 6: 119.

27. "A Letter from a Gentleman in Mount Hope," pp. 262–63.

It is not difficult to understand why the citizens of Massachusetts were shocked by Governor Joseph Dudley's political methods or why the Vetch affair sparked such a major government crisis.[28]

Country advocates had little occasion in the early part of the eighteenth century to discuss revolution. Dudley and Shute may have irritated the colonists, but they were not tyrants in the manner of Sir Edmund Andros. Neither man posed a threat to the representative institutions of Massachusetts; and the lower house, which the Country regarded as the major barrier against arbitrary government, held its own against several royal governors.[29] But Country authors did not disown New England's revolutionary tradition, and they clearly did not stress civil obedience in the way the Court had done (see chap. 6). In 1721, for example, an anonymous pamphlet entitled *A Letter From a Gentleman in Mount Hope, To His Friend in Treamount* praised the colonists for their courage against Andros. The Dominion of New England had been a despotic government, and it fully deserved destruction. *"New England Men,"* the author wrote with obvious understatement, "cannot abide to be drove, or long led by the Nose."[30] The Reverend Jeremiah Shepard, who was chosen by the House of Representatives to deliver the election sermon in 1715, insisted that God himself had backed the Glorious Revolution in America.[31] There was no reason to believe that the Lord would

28. See chap. 6. An anonymous Country pamphleteer who wrote "Reflections upon Reflections, More News from Robinson Cruso's Island . . . [Boston, 1720]," attacked a Court author for claiming that the people of Massachusetts did not treat Governor Shute with enough respect: "he [the Court advocate] begins to utter *grievous Menaces,* and to roar and bellow like the Popes Bull, that we have by a *Train of bad Usages* compelled a good Spirited Governour to such an inflexible Resolution, that *he will make us know he is our Governour:* But with submission to his *Holiness,* We *do know* he is our Governour, (and *as such* wou'd have all due Regards paid him;) But what then? Must we therefore *tamely and quietly* give up all our *Rights and Privileges;* and so render our selves obnoxious to the Curse of succeeding Generations?" (In Davis, *Currency Reprints,* 2: 118).

29. *English Advice,* p. 1.

30. "A Letter from a Gentleman in Mount Hope," p. 261.

31. Jeremiah Shepard, *God's Conduct of His Church Through the Wilderness* (Boston, 1715), pp. 16–19; see also Cotton Mather, *Shaking Dispensations* [sermon preached at the death of Louis XIV] (Boston, 1715), pp. 40–41.

not support a similar rebellion if ever again a tyrant of Andros's proportions gained power over the colonies. The Country substituted property for religion without making any attempt to dilute the revolutionary zeal of men like Christopher Goodman and Samuel Ward. Arbitrary rulers who seized property or dispensed with civil liberties would be certain to meet fierce resistance in New England, and colonists like Samuel Adams proved to later generations that the Country meant what it said.

John Wise: A Country Writer

John Wise was a nuisance. He criticized men and ideas while others in New England kept silent. In 1687, as we have already seen, this fiery minister persuaded the people of Ipswich to resist Andros's attempts to tax them without their consent (see chap. 4). A few years later, he spoke out again. This time he exposed General Walley's ineptitude in leading provincial troops against the French in Canada.[32] After another short silence, Wise attacked the Mathers —certainly formidable opponents for anyone. He was convinced that their so-called *Proposals,* a blueprint for church reform in Massachusetts, had conceded too much to Presbyterian polity. According to Wise, the Mathers were willing to subvert the traditional independence of the Congregational churches in New England. And, finally, during the 1720s, Wise supported the popular demand for an inflated currency. No one knows what this man did or thought between battles. He apparently immersed himself in local politics, preached to his congregation, and tended his crops. He left no letters, no diary; only a few pamphlets remain.[33] In fact, just enough of Wise's writing has survived to convince historians that he was one of the most important figures in colonial America.

Scholars who have examined Wise's works have been impressed

32. Wise's account of the attack on Quebec is in *Proceedings,* MHS, 15 (1902): 285–90. See Perry Miller, *The New England Mind,* 2 vols. (Boston, 1961), 2: 161.

33. The major ones are *The Churches Quarrel Espoused* (New York, 1713), *A Vindication of the Government of New England Churches* (Boston, 1717), and *A Word of Comfort to a Melancholy Country* (1721). For some of the details of Wise's life, see George A. Cooke, *John Wise: Early American Democrat* (New York, 1952).

by their innovative quality. Indeed, in many accounts, the minister
is seen as a man ahead of his times, receptive to ideas which other
New Englanders regarded with suspicion. The basis for this interpretation seems to have been Wise's familiarity with the writings
of Samuel Pufendorf (1632–94), a German philosopher noted for
his treatises on natural law. Perry Miller, one of America's most
respected intellectual historians, thought it quite important that
Wise had utilized Pufendorf's "rational proof" in his essay *A Vindication of the Government of New England Churches* (1717) and,
thus, had dared "to dispense, if only for the moment, with Biblical
and historical evidence." According to Miller, Wise should be
viewed as the foremost leader in a "rationalist revolt" against the
old Puritan order in New England.[34]

The problem with this interpretation is that it emphasizes Wise's
uniqueness at the expense of those ideas which he shared with other
men in his own generation. Wise deserves an honored place in
colonial American history not because he was so very different
from his contemporaries, but because he employed a Country rhetoric
which they all understood. To be sure, he was more articulate and
better read than were most of the other Country writers in Massachusetts; but his opinions were basically the same as theirs. Wise
hated arbitrary power in any form. He assumed that man was a
reasonable animal capable of ameliorating his environment, and he
treated the common people with respect. But, even more significant,
this outspoken Ipswich minister cherished the right of the Bay
citizens to determine voluntarily their own political future. He would
have been an important figure in the history of New England even
if he had never heard of Samuel Pufendorf. In fact, it is probably
safe to assume that the Wise whom the colonists loved and followed
was not the "rationalist," but the angry preacher who stood up to
Governor Andros in 1688.

The majority of Wise's political ideas came not from "rational"
philosophers, but from an odd assortment of English Country authors,
most of whom have long since been forgotten. It is largely because

34. Miller, *New England Mind*, 2: 295–97; Perry Miller and Thomas
Johnson, eds., *The Puritans*, 2 vols. (New York, 1963), 1: 194; Perry
Miller's introduction to *A Vindication of the Government of New England
Churches* [1717] by John Wise (Gainesville, Fla., 1958), p. xiv.

intellectual historians have ignored these sources that they have misconstrued the character of Wise's thought. The Ipswich minister read and cited the writings of Lord Warrington, previously Henry Booth, who served in the House of Commons during the late 1670s. Booth was a fierce, sometimes intemperate, advocate of Country views; and once during the Exclusion crisis surprised the members of Parliament by announcing publicly that he would vote only as his constituents had instructed. The idea that the members of Parliament were bound to observe the will of the freeholders was a novel notion in 1680, and it remained so for another century or more. Despite Booth's extreme statements, he remained a stout defender of the old, balanced constitution and apparently never found much appeal in republicanism.[35]

Wise also mentioned Thomas Gordon's study of Holland.[36] Gordon was a leader of a group of extreme Country theorists who are sometimes labeled the "Commonwealthmen." During the 1720s he co-operated with John Trenchard in writing *Cato's Letters*, a series of iconoclastic political essays which enjoyed wide popularity in the colonies throughout the eighteenth century.[37] During his long literary career Gordon eschewed philosophic abstractions, preferring to discuss contemporary problems in relation to English history and to specific legal precedents.[38]

Wise footnoted a scurrilous little pamphlet entitled *The Secret*

35. A. Gray, ed., *Debates of the House of Commons from the Year 1667 to the Year 1694*, 10 vols. (London, 1769), 8: 316, 326, cited in Behrens, "The Whig Theory of the Constitution in the Reign of Charles II," *Cambridge Historical Journal* 8(1941–43): 58, n. 42; Wise, *Vindication*, p. 33.

36. Wise, *Vindication*, p. 30.

37. See Caroline Robbins, *The Eighteenth-Century Commonwealthman* (Cambridge, Mass., 1959), pp. 115–25; Bailyn, "Origins of American Politics," pp. 33–38; and W. H. Greenleaf, *Order, Empiricism and Politics . . . 1500–1700* (London, 1964), pp. 278–80.

38. For a discussion of the forms of political argumentation during this period, see Greenleaf, *Order, Empiricism and Politics,* pp. 268–69, 272, 276–81; Behrens, "The Whig Theory of the Constitution," pp. 42–71; Peter Laslett, ed., *John Locke: Two Treatises of Government* (New York, 1963), pp. 114–15; J. G. A. Pocock, *The Ancient Constitution and the Feudal Law: A Study of English Historical Thought in the Seventeenth Century* (Cambridge, Eng., 1957), pp. 236–41; Pocock, "Burke and the Ancient Constitution—A Problem in the History of Ideas," *Historical Journal* 3 (1960): 125–43.

History of the Reigns of K. Charles II, K. James II. This anonymous publication, representing the yellow press of its day, purported to expose the lewdness, corruption, and depravity of the Stuart Court.[39] And in another place the Country preacher paraphrased Henry Care's (1646–88) popular constitutional history, *English Liberties.*[40] Care informed his readers that patriotic Englishmen over the centuries had had to rescue their liberties repeatedly from the threat of arbitrary, ambitious, and Catholic rulers.[41] Authors such as Gordon and Care seldom appealed to natural laws, as John Locke and Samuel Pufendorf had done, but spent most of their time searching out potential plots against England's ancient constitution. They reflected the fears and beliefs of the Country party and provided excellent ammunition against any Court, even the provincial Court of Governor Dudley.[42]

Wise's political philosophy began in optimism. He dismissed the Court's bleak statements about human corruption and, instead, emphasized the limitless opportunities which he believed were open to man. In his *Vindication* Wise declared, "I shall wave the Considera-

39. Wise, *Vindication,* p. 52.

40. Ibid., p. 95.

41. Henry Care, *English Liberties* (Boston, 1721), pp. 4, 95–113, 130–40; DNB.

42. In 1961 Raymond P. Stearns wrote an article entitled, "John Wise of Ipswich Was No Democrat in Politics," *Essex Institute Historical Collections* 47: 2–18. Stearns intended to clear up some of the misunderstandings that had grown up among historians about Wise's place in the development of American thought, but he only succeeded in further confusing the discussion. He maintained that Wise was "no democrat in politics," because the minister was concerned with ecclesiastical, not civil affairs (p. 12). Stearns concluded that Wise had no particular political importance (pp. 17–18). That I disagree with Stearns's assessment is demonstrated in my section on Wise. The term "democrat" has long been a red herring in the path of Colonial historians who have looked ahead to the events of the American Revolution and to Jackson's presidency and, therefore, have not seen the issues of the early eighteenth century as Wise and his contemporaries would have. The Ipswich minister may not have been a democrat, but he had much to say about politics, rulers, and civil government. See John M. Murrin, "Anglicizing an American Colony: The Transformation of Provincial Massachusetts" (Ph.D. diss., Yale University, 1966) for an excellent discussion of how historians have treated (or mistreated) this period.

tion of Mans Moral Turpitude, but shall view him Physically as a Creature which God has made and furnished essentially with many Enobling Immunities, which render him the most August Animal in the World, and still, whatever has happened since his Creation, he remained at the upper-end of Nature, and as such is a Creature of a very *Noble Character.*"[43] In the Ipswich meetinghouse Wise probably preached from the Westminster Confession. He apparently left Calvin's dark doctrines about human depravity in the church, however, for in civil maters his attitudes were sanguine. Neither sin nor predestination would keep New Englanders from molding colonial government to suit their needs.

Man's ability to reason separated him from the other animals of God's creation, for he alone possessed the understanding necessary to comprehend the "Laws of Nature." Wise insisted that his own "contemplation of our Natural Condition" revealed three general observations which pertained to all persons. First, man "is a Creature extreamly desirous of his own Preservation" and will defend himself against all threats. Second, Wise discovered that men have an innate tendency toward "Sociableness," a desire to unite with their fellows so that they will not harm him. And last, the minister happily explained, "From the Principles of Sociableness it follows as a fundamental Law of Nature, that Man is not so Wedded to his own Interest, but that he can make the Common good the mark of his Aim."[44] Human beings in the state of nature were not warring beasts who would sooner destroy their neighbors than love them. Wise was no Hobbesian, and he regarded man's reasoning power as a source of virtue and dignity. It allowed people of every type to see for themselves that the Lord intended them to cooperate and build a better world together. According to Wise, when men failed to use their minds they denied their essential human quality and announced, in effect, that they preferred to live like the lower animals.[45]

The Ipswich minister believed that in the absence of civil authority all people were free to do as they pleased. Personal judgment alone

43. Wise, *Vindication,* pp. 37–38. George Cooke claimed that Wise had a higher sense of man's worth and dignity than did Samuel Pufendorf, who he declared was his guide (*Early American Democrat,* p. 213).

44. Wise, *Vindication,* pp. 35–37.

45. See Wise, *Word of Comfort,* pp. 201–02.

determined a man's behavior but at the same time, freedom brought social responsibility. Libertinism and anarchy contradicted the fundamental laws of nature. "Such Licence," Wise wrote, "is disagreeing with the condition and dignity of Man, and would make Man of a lower and meaner Constitution then Bruit Creatures."[46] In a state of nature, humans were not only free, but also equal. Equality, in fact, grew out of freedom. Wise argued that "every Man must be conceived to be perfectly in his own Power and disposal, and not to be controuled by the Authority of any other. And thus every Man, must be acknowledged equal to every Man, since all Subjection and all Command are equally banished on both sides."[47] Even before he considered the formation of civil government, the Country minister attacked the Court's basic assumption. Like the log cutters who blocked Governor Dudley's coach on the road to Roxbury, Wise felt that he was "as good flesh and blood" as anyone in Massachusetts. He would have nothing to do with the hierarchical notions of a Pemberton or Dudley. "It follows as a Command of the Law of Nature," Wise observed, "that every Man Esteem and Treat another as one who is naturally his Equal, or *Who is a Man as well as he*."[48]

In Wise's system political power originated in a voluntary grant from the people. Since no one held natural authority over his neighbors, wealth, education, breeding, and physical strength did not give men the right to coerce others to their point of view. "It would be the greatest absurdity to believe," Wise declared, "that Nature actually Invests the Wise with a Sovereignty over the weak or a Right of forcing them against their Wills."[49] In the ideal state the inhabitants established civil order through a series of covenants or agreements. First, they decided as a group whether they wanted to form a society at all; and, if they voted to join together, as Wise assumed they would, they then selected the type of government which they wanted to rule over them. Only after the citizens had resolved these two major questions could they pick their actual magistrates. The people's choice had to be completely free at every level; for, otherwise, the state was a sham, requiring no obedience from the populace.

46. Wise, *Vindication*, p. 38.
47. Ibid., p. 37.
48. Ibid., p. 40 (italics added).
49. Ibid., p. 42.

In essence the subjects created both the ruler and the ruler's office. He possessed no prerogatives which they did not specifically allocate to him in their original covenants. The good magistrate embodied the majority will of his constituents and held no interests that conflicted with theirs. By the same token, evil rulers or tyrants were those persons who gained political position without the citizens' consent.[50]

Wise expected the good ruler to guard the life, liberty, and property of every person. "The Chief End of Civil Communities," the minister explained, "is, that Men thus conjoyned, may be secured against the Injuries, they are lyable to from their own Kind. For if every Man could secure himself singly; It would be great folly for him, to Renounce his Natural Liberty, in which every Man is his own King and Protector."[51] Government was a matter of public convenience; for, obviously, no group would establish a state merely to enrich its magistrates. Wise claimed that even after a civil society had been formed the citizens continued to enjoy some of their original natural liberties. In fact, it was an important part of the ruler's calling to preserve the people's "Personal Liberty and Equality . . . to the highest degree, as will consist with all *just distinctions* amongst Men of Honour, and shall be agreeable with the publick Good."[52]

The Ipswich minister noted that an ideal government would consist of a mixture of democratic, aristocratic, and monarchic elements. This commonplace observation had little relevance for Massachusetts, however, and Wise knew it. There was no formal aristocracy in the colonies comparable to the English peerage. Like most eighteenth-century Country writers the clergyman believed that the chief constitutional friction occurred between the popular and prerogative interests. In other words, the major division in government took place between the democratic and monarchic parts. These two forces vied for political control, and a good constitution balanced the strength of these two contending parties, assuring that neither side would predominate. Wise advocated a monarchy "settled upon a Noble Democracy" as the best system.[53] When he used the word

50. Ibid., pp. 43–47; also Wise, *Churches Quarrel*, pp. 119–20.
51. Wise, *Vindication*, pp. 47–48.
52. Ibid., p. 39 (italics added).
53. Ibid., pp. 50, 61–62, 89.

democracy, however, he did not refer to some unruly form of government in which every citizen could speak out on each issue or decision. The popular branch of the constitution was the General Assembly composed of elected delegates.[54] The representatives looked after their constituents' legislative needs while the voters stayed at home where they belonged. Nevertheless, the electorate always retained the ultimate power, for the freemen could remove members of the General Court whose behavior was irresponsible or indiscreet. Wise stressed the importance of the democratic element, because he felt it to be the most "reasonable" part of government. Civil authority established on free elections preserved man's natural liberty and equality by allowing him the power of free choice. *"A Democracy in Church or State,"* Wise Wrote, *"is a very honourable and regular Government according to the Dictates of Right Reason."*[55]

It was history, even more than abstract reason, that justified a constitution weighted in favor of democracy. Wise explained that the experiences of other countries and other peoples supported his political observations; and in the *Vindication* he argued that "we may very fairly Infer, where we find Nations flourishing, and their Liberty and Property, with the rest of the great Immunities of Man's Nature nourished, secured, and best guarded from Tyranny, we may venture to pronounce this People to be Subjects of a noble Government . . . whose Constitution *will serve to justifie ours.*"[56] The minister copied the style of many English Country pamphleteers, taking Venice, Holland, and England as his examples. Commonwealthmen, such as Thomas Gordon and John Trenchard, generally regarded the Venetian government as the outstanding model of constitutional balance, of a state free from political corruption.[57] Wise told his readers that because the people of Venice lived under "a

54. Ibid., pp. 49–50.
55. Ibid., p. 67; also pp. 61, 91.
56. Ibid., p. 93.
57. See J. G. A. Pocock, "Machiavelli, Harrington, and English Political Ideologies in the Eighteenth Century," *William and Mary Quarterly,* 3d ser. 22(1965): 568–69; also Z. S. Fink, *The Classical Republicans: An Essay in the Recovery of a Pattern of Thought in Seventeenth-Century England* (Evanston, 1945).

limited Democracy," they were able to raise "themselves into so august and flourishing a Capacity . . . as to bridle and curb the pride and haughtiness of *Turk* or *Pope*." Democracy in Holland, moreover, had been the reason why the Dutch succeeded in throwing off the tyranny of Spain. Significantly, the New England clergyman chose the extreme Country pamphleteer, Thomas Gordon, as his guide to the political development of Holland. Wise made no democratic claims for England but believed its *"Original* happy Form of Government" had preserved the citizens there *"from Arbitrary Violence and Oppression."* He had special praise both for the jury system and for Parliament, because he believed that these institutions had given the English people an important voice in determining civil affairs.[58] All of Wise's research proved to his own satisfaction that the best rulers for any nation were those who remained closest to their constituents. A magistrate who cherished the citizens' rights and liberties as if they were his own would never become a despot. "We in the *Country,"* Wise announced, love a government "which sensibly Clogs Tyranny, Preserves the Subject free from slavery."[59]

Like other men of Country persuasion, Wise feared that conspirators might at any time transform Massachusetts into an arbitrary government. He published the *Vindication* and his less famous *The Churches Quarrel Espoused* almost thirty years after Andros had left Boston; and yet the minister's tone still sounded anxious, as if tyranny remained a real and present danger to the colony. His pamphlets were filled with warnings about despotic rulers and secret intrigues. "The very name of an Arbitrary Government," Wise announced, "is ready to put an English man's Blood into a Fermentation"; and, again, *"English men hate an Arbitrary Power (Politically Considered) as they hate the Devil."*[60] Basically the Ipswich leader shared the Country's suspicion of all political authority and saw the threat of state corruption as ever present. He felt that a democratic constitution offered partial protection because it divided sovereignty among many persons, all of whom had an immediate and personal interest in promoting good government. Democratic rulers who had

58. Wise, *Vindications,* pp. 94–95.
59. Wise, *Churches Quarrel,* pp. 13–14.
60. Ibid., pp. 120, 121.

been elected by the people were less likely "to prey upon each other, or embezzle the common Stock; as some particular Persons may be apt to do when set off, and Intrusted with the same Power."[61] In essence, Wise adopted a pragmatic view that the whole people were less likely than their magistrates to lose their civil virtue; and at no time in his career did he show sympathy for the Court's notion that political power belonged to small, educated, and wealthy elite.

Wise also echoed the Country's call for public vigilance. Like many of the anonymous pamphleteers of this period, he believed that the citizens bore the ultimate responsibility for seeing that their government conformed to the original covenant. The minister advised that any person who endangered the "Pillars of *English* Liberty" should "be prosecuted and punished, with the utmost zeal and vigour. For to poyson all the Springs and Rivers in the Kingdom, could not be a greater mischief; for this would only affect the present Age, but the other would Ruine and Inslave all our Posterity."[62] Wise stood firmly in the tradition of Goodman, Adams, and Nowell; for, like them, he insisted that it was the people's job to find rulers of good character.

The Ipswich minister thought that the right of revolution belonged to a "reasonable" majority in every commonwealth. He explained—perhaps anticipating Court criticism—that a virtuous people would never misuse this privilege to change the constitution or to alter the fundamental laws of the nation. Indeed, good people employed violence only as a last resort to restore a civil covenant which had been corrupted by evil leaders. Wise defined "rebels" not as unruly citizens, but as arbitrary usurpers or innovators who trampled upon the natural "Equality & Liberty of their Fellows."[63] Freemen were required to give allegiance only to those magistrates who stayed within clearly defined legal boundaries. The Country minister cited the abusive pamphlet, *The Secret History of K. Charles II. and K. James II.*, in support of his ideas about revolution. The anonymous author of this piece had claimed that civil obedience depended upon a delicate balance between popular and prerogative

61. Wise, *Vindication*, p. 62.
62. Ibid., pp. 95–96.
63. Ibid., p. 52.

rights. The subjects of a nation, presumably England, could be expected to recognize a monarch's powers only so long as he did not *"deprive them of their lawful and determined Rights and Liberties; then the Prince who strives to subject the Fundamental Laws of the Society, is the Traytor and the Rebel, and not the People, who endeavour to Preserve and Defend their own."*[64]

Wise never mentioned the possibility that the freemen themselves could upset the constitution. Unlike the Court writers of this time, he did not fear the "leveling spirit" or worry about the people's "unreasonable humours." He must have felt that his own political experience proved that rulers, especially appointed ones, posed a greater threat to ancient liberties than the populace ever did. Certainly men of Country persuasion in New England regarded Edmund Andros and his superior, James II, as vile usurpers and innovators. Wise and many others like him had learned their lesson under the Dominion, and they resolved never to allow another Andros to subvert their constitution.

At the time of his death Wise was not a discouraged man. He had lived a full life and he knew it. In his last days Wise told a friend that he had always been "a Man of Contention." The Ipswich leader added that "he had *Fought a good Fight;* and had comfort in reflecting upon the same."[65] He had educated his Country neighbors about the character of a good ruler, reminding them to select magistrates who would defend their "Liberty & Equality," who would listen to their grievances, and who would treat them with respect. But, most important, Wise told the colonists to take an active, ongoing interest in political affairs. In a word, he instructed his Country followers to be nuisances like himself.

The New-England Courant: *Voice of the Country*

On August 7, 1721, James Franklin published the first issue of *The New-England Courant.* His journal represented a fresh, striking departure from the style of the other weekly newspapers in Boston. The *Boston News-Letter,* which John Campbell had founded around the turn of the century, had not altered its colorless format for

64. Ibid., p. 53.
65. John White, *The Gospel in Earthen Vessels* (Boston, 1725), p. 38.

nearly twenty years. Campbell had carried accounts of the political
and military events of Europe, while official proclamations and
shipping reports were his domestic fare. He never enlivened his
stories with editorial comment or stirred up controversy by discussing
the problems which faced the local government. After 1719 a second
paper, the *Boston Gazette,* competed with the *News-Letter* for the
readership of Massachusetts; but the content of the *Gazette* was
little different from that of its rival. Neither journal had much in
common with the witty, satirical papers of eighteenth-century
London. In fact, neither gave any indication that this was the age
of Jonathan Swift and Daniel DeFoe.

Franklin's *Courant* suffered from many faults; but dullness was
not one of them, at least not in the early years of publication. The
editor reproduced lively articles from the British Country press and
boldly, even belligerently, entered local political arguments. Sometimes he started controversies where none had existed before, goading New Englanders into sending indignant letters to the city's
other two newspapers. James's famous brother, Benjamin, helped
greatly to animate the pages of the *Courant.* Benjamin's caustic observations about New England society were a regular feature in the
paper until he decided, probably because he was unable to get along
with James, to move to Philadelphia.[66]

The citizens of Massachusetts were a troubled people when the
Franklins' Country journal made its first appearance. The colony's
economy, never too prosperous after the Glorious Revolution, took
a turn for the worse. In the midst of this recession a severe smallpox
epidemic swept through Boston, killing hundreds—perhaps thousands—in that city. Fear, suspicion, disappointment contributed to
an increase in political tension throughout the province. The General
Court no longer trusted the royal governor, Samuel Shute; and for
nearly two years the chief magistrate and the members of the lower
house traded insults and accusations with such intensity that normal
government business came to a halt. Thomas Hutchinson, who knew
as much as anyone about the history of Massachusetts, claimed that
during the early 1720s "the contests and dissensions in the govern-

66. Leonard Labaree, ed., *The Autobiography of Benjamin Franklin*
(New Haven, 1964), pp. 68–69.

ment rose to a greater height than they had done since the religious
feuds in the year 1636 and 37 [the Antinomian controversy]."[67] In
this uneasy atmosphere the *Courant* proceeded to make many enemies; for, unlike the other Boston papers, it took definite stands.

One of the Franklins' favorite targets was Cotton Mather. They took
particular pleasure in ridiculing the minister's plan to inoculate the
colonists against smallpox. Since neither the Franklins nor Mather
possessed much empirical knowledge about the disease, it was easy
to deride the preacher's scheme as sheer quackery. The supporters
of inoculation, returning an eye for an eye, heaped abuse on the
Courant whenever possible. The critics found many allies who were
more than willing to join in the attack. Almost all clergymen, even
those who had no love for Cotton Mather, hated the Franklins' publication. The *Courant* had earned their contempt through its disrespect for local religious customs and traditions. Indeed, the paper
had regularly carried antiministerial statements, mocking the Congregational preachers of New England as saintly hypocrites.[68] The ranks
of the *Courant's* enemies were swelled when Benjamin, writing as
"Silence Dogood," poked fun at the colony's failure to develop
belles lettres—in other words, to break out of its narrow provincialism
and share in England's cosmopolitan culture. The foes of the *Courant*
fought back with a sputtering self-righteousness that surely must
have tickled the two Country editors. One author described the
journal as the creation of a secret libertine group called "The Hell-
Fire Club of Boston."[69] Another attacker blasted the Franklin newspaper as "full freighted with Nonesense, Unmannerliness, Railery,
Prophaneness, Immorality, Arrogancy, Calumnies, Lyes, Contradic-
tions, and what not, all tending to Quarrels and Divisions, and to
Debauch and Corrupt the Minds and Manners of New England."[70]

As much as the Franklins enjoyed stirring up the clergy, their
major interest was politics, not religion. Almost every issue of the
paper contained a discussion of the colony's constitutional rights
and privileges. The Country editors believed that New Englanders

67. Thomas Hutchinson, *The History of the Colony and Province of
Massachusetts-Bay,* ed. Lawrence S. Mayo, 3 vols. (Boston, 1936), 2: 174.
68. See Miller, *New England Mind,* 2: 333–41.
69. *New-England Courant,* Jan. 15, 1722.
70. *Boston News-Letter,* Aug. 21, 1721.

shared liberties which had a long and glorious history dating back to King Alfred and the distant Anglo-Saxon past. When the Franklins founded the *Courant*, in fact, they announced that a major goal of the journal would be to teach American readers about these immemorial liberties and to help them protect their property from arbitrary seizure. In the summer of 1722 the paper carried the main articles of the Magna Charta, and in other issues it warned the people about plots against the ancient constitution and against the Massachusetts Charter.[71]

The Franklins' defense of popular rights frequently extended beyond the newspaper. In 1721 they published the first American edition of Henry Care's *English Liberties,* the study which John Wise had treated with such respect. The Country printers added a special introduction to Care's work, reminding the colonists of "the many Struggles which the People of this Nation have had [in order] to rescue their almost oppress'd Liberties and Religion."[72] On another occasion, James and Benjamin Franklin published a little pamphlet entitled *English Advice to the Freeholders &c. of the Province of Massachusetts Bay.* This appeal, filled with Country rhetoric, called upon the voters to act like "TRUE ENGLISH FREEMEN" and to choose only "PATRIOTS to sit in the General Assembly."[73]

Many of the Franklins' political ideas came from a British Country newspaper called *The London Journal.* In fact, during the early years of publication, almost every issue of the *Courant* contained a long quotation or essay from this source. *The London Journal* had been founded in 1720 in response to a crisis known as the South Sea Bubble, a stock market crash brought on by a series of complex financial deals made between English officials and the South Sea Company. The editors of *The London Journal* hated the Whig ministry then in power and tried to embarrass it at every opportunity. To aid in its assault upon the administration, the paper hired two experienced "Commonwealth" authors, Thomas Gordon and John Trenchard. These men were veteran polemicists who had made a

71. See *New-England Courant,* Nov. 13, 1721; Nov. 27, 1721; May 21, 1722; and July 23, 1722.
72. *English Liberties,* p. A2.
73. *English Advice,* p. 1.

name for themselves by writing for a radical weekly, *The Independent Whig*. While their earlier articles had concentrated chiefly on problems within the Anglican church, Trenchard and Gordon used the pages of *The London Journal* to comment on a wide range of political topics. Generally, their essays, which they signed "Cato," warned the English people about evil and treacherous designs against their liberties. They had a penchant for spotting danger and conspiracy behind every government act. The only hope of curbing the growing civil corruption, they explained, was for the entire population to emulate the classical republican virtues of Venice and Rome.[74]

Cato's Letters had a great influence upon the colonists. New editions appeared throughout the eighteenth century, and men like John Adams and Thomas Jefferson cited the wisdom of "Cato" with reverence.[75] The *Courant* was one of the first American papers to carry these iconoclastic essays. The Franklins apparently felt that the political philosophy contained in *Cato's Letters* reflected their own beliefs. In any case the *Courant* enthusiastically recommended *The London Journal* to all New Englanders for its insights into the true nature of government. From the very first issue of their newspaper the Franklin brothers seemed determined to expose their readers to Country ideas.

The "Cato" whom the Franklins quoted was much less optimistic about human nature than John Wise had been. The essays in the *Courant* stated that all men possessed an innate desire for power and would do almost anything to gain it. Certainly, no person would work for the common good unless someone forced him to do so. Self-preservation was the basic law of all human behavior. "It is nothing strange," "Cato" wrote, "that Men, who think themselves

74. See C. R. Realey, "The London Journal and Its Authors, 1720–1723," *Bulletin of the University of Kansas* 36, no. 23, (Dec. 1, 1935); Robbins, *Commonwealthman*, pp. 117–20; David L. Jacobson, ed., *The English Libertarian Heritage, From the Writings of John Trenchard and Thomas Gordon in The Independent Whig and Cato's Letters* (Indianapolis, 1965), pp. XVII–LX.

75. Pocock, "Machiavelli, Harrington, and English Political Ideologies," p. 573; Bernard Bailyn, *The Ideological Origins of the American Revolution* (Cambridge, Mass., 1967), pp. 35–37.

unaccountable, should act unaccountably, and all Men would be unaccountable if they could. . . . Hence it is, that if every Man had
his Will, all Men would exercise Dominion, and no Man would
suffer it." Only a few individuals in any given society possessed the
"Degree of Virtue" which was necessary to establish a voluntary
rule of law.[76] Fear, not love, was the emotion that eventually saved
the world from anarchy; and civil government grew out of the compacts or agreements that men formed to protect their rights and
property. Each person gave his word that he would not plunder his
fellows in exchange for the security that no one would sack his be-
longings. "Cato" pointed out that before civil government had been
formed the people as a whole had held all political power and that
they had transferred to their rulers only enough authority to guard
their liberties from attack.[77]

Political power frightened the Franklins; and, like the other
Country authors of the period, they believed that government office
tended to corrupt even the best of men. The *Courant* warned its
readers that magistrates would sooner exploit their constituents than
work for the common good. In fact, it was only the threat of punishment or public embarrassment that made state leaders look after the
general welfare at all. The two Country editors counseled the colonists to keep as much civil authority in their own hands as they
possibly could, since power spread among the whole populace was
less likely to degenerate than power concentrated in a single person.
"I know," "Cato" wrote, "it is a general charge against the People,
that they are turbulent, restless, fickle and unruly . . . [but] there
can be nothing more untrue; for they are only so, when they are
made so."[78] The Franklin brothers seemed obsessed by the possibility
that tyrants would win the public's trust through tricks and lies,
and then proceed to turn the government against the unsuspecting
citizenry. In the pages of the *Courant* they urged New Englanders
to be on the alert at all times for men who appeared virtuous, but
who in fact harbored arbitrary designs. While it was extremely
difficult to identify potential despots, the people were well advised

76. *New-England Courant,* Oct. 16 and 23, 1721.
77. *New-England Courant,* Oct. 23, 1721.
78. *New-England Courant,* Sept. 4, 1721; also May 21, 1722.

to avoid anyone who assumed that the prerogatives of the ruler were more important than the rights of the ruled.[79]

The *Courant* reminded its readers that the people could always hold a magistrate accountable for his public behavior. When some of the more outspoken Court advocates in New England claimed that civil authorities were responsible only to the Lord, the Franklins exploded. They quoted a passage from *The London Journal* which pointed out that "wicked Men, their being accountable to God, whom they do not fear is no Security to us against their Folly and Malice . . . Human Reason says, that there is no Obedience, no regard due to those Rulers who govern by no Rule but their Lust: Such Men are no Rulers, they are Outlaws."[80] James and Benjamin Franklin both had come a long way from John Winthrop. In 1640 godliness was a desirable, indeed a vital, characteristic for the good ruler to possess. The Old Charter freemen had assumed that a man of spiritual grace would naturally work for the general welfare; but the Country editors in 1721 were skeptical. They wanted to see tangible results from their magistrates, especially in economic areas, and observed that piety meant very little if the ruler did not promote the people's immediate worldly needs.

Early in 1723 the Massachusetts General Court censured James Franklin for insulting religion and mocking the representatives of His Majesty's government in the colony. The *Courant* responded to these charges with a remarkable tongue in cheek essay. The paper asked its readers what would have to be done in order to restore its good name throughout New England. The author of this piece, probably Benjamin, warned the men who published the *Courant*: "when you abuse and villify Rulers, you do in some sense resist a Divine *Ordinance,* and *he that resisteth it shall receive to himself Damnation.* Princes, Magistrates, and Grandees, can by no means endure their Conduct should be scann'd by the meanest of their Subjects; and such may justly be offended when private Men, of as private parts, presume to intermeddle with their *Arcana,* and fault their administration."[81] Any colonist who had ever sat through a

79. *New-England Courant*, Sept. 4, 1721; also Oct. 9, 1721; Mar. 26, 1722; Apr. 23, 1722.

80. *New-England Courant*, Oct. 23, 1721.

81. *New-England Courant*, Jan. 28, 1723.

long, dreary election sermon quickly caught the gist of Franklin's satire.. The *Courant's* regular readers knew that the article was bombast, since most of the time the paper had counseled resistance, even revolution, when magistrates did not listen to their constituents. In 1722, for example, the journal had instructed the Massachusetts electorate to ignore those candidates "who have discovered [disclosed] their Enmity to the People by Words, Writing, or promoting bad Laws."[82] The entire thrust of this Country newspaper had been the involvement of the freemen in provincial politics and the criticism of all rulers who lacked the essential characteristics of their calling.

According to the *Courant,* strict public vigilance was the only reliable barrier against tyranny. The Franklins observed that "political Jealousy . . . in the People, is a necessary and laudable Passion."[83] On July 2, 1722, the paper made the same point with even greater force, quoting an article from *The London Journal* which had stated, "The Administration of Government is nothing else but the Attendance of the *Trustees of the People* upon the Interests and Affairs of the People . . . [and] it is the Part and Business of the People; for whose sake alone all publick Matters are, or ought to be transacted, to see whether they be well or ill transacted." The "Cato" which appeared in the Franklins' journal observed that "honest" magistrates would never be afraid to have the public examine their official policies: "Only the *wicked Governours of Men* dread what is said of them."[84]

Like *The London Journal,* the *Courant* tried to expose local political corruption. Soon after the May elections of 1722, the Franklins published a curious story about Roxbury. The report explained that a leading—but unnamed—citizen of that town had recently donated a beautiful and expensive piece of silver plate to the First Church. The *Courant* added cryptically that no one in Roxbury knew the motive behind this unexpected generosity. Below this article was a note that the freemen of Roxbury had chosen William Dudley as their representative to the General Court. The Franklins then

82. *New-England Courant,* May 21, 1722.

83. *New-England Courant,* Oct. 23, 1721.

84. *New-England Courant,* July 2, 1722; also Sept. 4, 1721; Nov. 13, 1721; Apr. 30, 1722.

rhetorically asked their readers to "consider how it will be with us, if a haughty, covetous, revengeful Man should get in Power . . . by a specious Pretence of Piety, in giving a Piece of Plate to the Church, and making large Promises of doing Justice to all." The Country editors declared—as Trenchard and Gordon would have done—that benevolence at election time was generally a sign of evil intent. The *Courant* claimed, "*No covetous Person will use more Water to fetch the Pump, than he designs to pump out again.*"[85] Dudley was furious that anyone would question his integrity; and in a public letter published in the *Gazette,* he denied that political considerations had in any way influenced his philanthropy. The *Courant* responded indignantly, protesting that it had not directly charged Dudley with any wrong. The Franklins speculated that Dudley might have read one of "Cato's" general essays about the importance of civil virtue and mistakenly assumed that it had been aimed only at him.[86] As usual, the editors had a good laugh.

The *Courant* died a slow death. Benjamin left Boston in 1723 and with him, no doubt, went most of the paper's wit. James struggled along for several years, but each issue was a little duller than the last. After a time "Cato's" essays no longer appeared, and the *Courant* gradually turned away from political discussion altogether. By the middle of the decade, the once satirical journal was virtually indistinguishable from its old rivals, *The Boston News-Letter* and *The Boston Gazette.* The Franklins' experiment, however, had not been a failure. For several years, at least, the *Courant* kept the colonists in touch with the latest, most radical political rhetoric of England. The journal appealed to the Country, stressing participation, vigilance, and liberty. James Franklin and his contemporary, John Wise, reminded their neighbors of the responsibility to pick good rulers, and even more important, of the duty to keep rulers good once they reached office. The *Courant* passed away, but the Country ideas which it had championed remained. *Cato's Letters* achieved a new popularity later in the eighteenth century; and, whenever men feared the Court, the messages of Wise, Franklin, and the anonymous pamphleteers continued to have relevance.

85. *New-England Courant,* May 7, 1722; also Dec. 25, 1721; Jan. 8, 1722; Apr. 30, 1722.
86. *New-England Courant,* May 21, 1722.

EPILOGUE

NEW ENGLAND PURITANS did not usually observe anniversaries, fearing that commemoration of past events could lead to superstition and idolatry. The year 1730, however, was an exception, for it marked the centennial of the founding of Massachusetts. Several ministers used the occasion to reflect upon the colonists' errand into the wilderness; and one of them, Thomas Prince, was pleased with what he saw. In an election sermon entitled *The People of New-England Put in Mind of the Righteous Acts of the Lord* he explained, "We the Ministers and People account it happy that we see so many in Place of Public Power, descending from the Founders of these Towns and Churches." He hoped the future would bring more magistrates such as Joseph Dudley, Gurdon Saltonstall, and William Stoughton, who would uphold the standards of their fathers by ruling in the "Fear of GOD."[1]

But Reverend Prince, like many other election speakers before him, was so taken with the vision of what New England should be, that he overlooked what it had become. He seemed oblivious to the fact that men such as Dudley and Saltonstall had deserted traditions established by the founders. If Prince had been more observant he might have seen that an unbridgeable intellectual gulf separated the eighteenth-century Court rulers from the leaders of the first generation; for, while some of Dudley's political views resembled those of Winthrop, the two men governed by wholly different principles.

The political battles of the 1630s and 1640s were as hotly con-

1. Thomas Prince, *The People of New-England* . . . (Boston, 1730), pp. 40, 47.

tested as any of those that followed; but beneath the dissension was unity. Winthrop and his opponents fought over two different interpretations of the same political theory. The advocates of Discretion and Delegation agreed that God intended Massachusetts to become a "city on a hill;" that civil authority was founded on a voluntary covenant between ruler and ruled; that the citizen had a right, indeed a duty, to participate in political affairs; and that magistrates were the Lord's vicegerents on earth. Most important, the supporters of both persuasions insisted that the state had religious responsibilities which, if not performed, would bring God's wrath upon the land. Tempers flared only when men differed over the way to put these commonly held ideas into practice; or, more specifically, how to place precise limits on magisterial power.

By the beginning of the eighteenth century the consensus which underlay the earlier political conflicts had dissolved. The spokesmen for Court and Country, unlike those for Discretion and Delegation, divided on fundamentals, making it far more difficult for Wise to communicate with Dudley and Shute than it had been for Winthrop to understand Hathorne and Ward. In the years that followed the Glorious Revolution, Court and Country in New England split irrevocably, appealing to different ideas, sources, and traditions. Each side viewed the other with a mixture of suspicion and contempt, and each side felt that the other was bent on destroying the commonwealth. To appreciate the changes that had taken place since the founding one only has to imagine what would have happened during the Vetch crisis if Joseph Dudley had attempted to duplicate Winthrop's famous speech of 1645 (see chap. 2). The members of the lower house, no doubt, would have regarded the words of the royal governor as a cover for conspiracy against their liberties and property. They would have interpreted the call for order and obedience as special pleading for the narrow interests of a class or party and not as an expression of God's will.

During the fifty years following Shute's departure from Boston, Court and Country drifted further apart. The religious revivals called the Great Awakening, the midcentury controversies over taxes and currency, and eventually the American Revolution itself exacerbated tensions that already existed between these groups. At each crisis Court advocates discouraged broad participation in government affairs, telling rulers to discount popular demands as a factor in formulating civil policy. In 1757 one Court author urged the members of the General Court to "consult not the present Humour of the major Part of your Constituents, but the real Interests of the Public and govern your Votes accordingly."[2] In each case Country writers countered that good magistrates were those who listened to the demands and grievances of the freemen. Throughout the eighteenth century, in fact, Country pamphleteers repeatedly advised the voters to choose civil leaders "whose Interests are the same with your own, and likely to continue the same; Representatives who are not already pre-engaged in a contrary Interest, nor from their Circumstances, Education, Profession, or Manner of Life, are likely to be so engaged."[3] While the Court called for peace and order in society, the Country insisted on public vigilance, even revolution, as essential for the preservation of liberty and property.[4]

2. *The Boston Weekly News-Letter,* Mar. 31, 1757.

3. Phileleutheros, *An Address to the Freeholders and Inhabitants of the Province of Massachusetts-Bay* (Boston, 1751), p. 4.

4. Cf. Alan Heimert, *Religion and the American Mind from the Great Awakening to the Revolution* (Cambridge, Mass., 1966) and Bernard Bailyn, *The Ideological Origins of the American Revolution* (Cambridge, Mass., 1967). Both Heimert and Bailyn regard the mid-eighteenth century as the crucial period in the development of ideas which men eventually used to justify the American Revolution. Heimert explained on the first page of his book, "To comprehend the nature of Americans' intellectual differences in the years of Revolution it is necessary to explore the progress of the American mind in the preceding generation." His massive study demonstrated how the Great Awakening divided the colonists into two camps; on one side stood the evangelical or postmillennial group which welcomed the events of 1776, and on the other side was the rational or premillennial group which aspired to keep the common people in their place. Bailyn traced the Americans' obsession with tyranny, corruption, and conspiracy to the radical Whig rhetoric (the "Commonwealth" tradition), which the colonists employed during the eighteenth century to attack the policies of their royal governors.

I do not take major issue with either Heimert or Bailyn, for I believe that Jonathan Edwards's sermons as well as *Cato's Letters* are important for an understanding of the colonists' response to arbitrary taxation. I would maintain, however, that neither historian has given adequate attention to the development of political ideas before 1730. Certainly the events which occurred at mid-century spawned attitudes which in turn contributed to

Although many of the men who supported Country views were not Puritans in a strictly religious sense, they echoed Christopher Goodman's notion that the individual citizen had to judge in his own conscience whether his rulers were good or evil. For such persons, ridding the state of bad magistrates was not a matter of political convenience, but a moral imperative. At midcentury Daniel Fowle, a Country pamphleteer, explained, "The Rights of the People are *certainly divine* as well as the Rights of Magistrates; and I hope no one will dispute, but the Rights of the People are *more divine* than the Rights of their Representatives, as the latter have no more than a *delegated* Power from . . . the People; and they receive and hold that Power only *from* them, and *by* them."[5] Fowle's statement is important because it shows that the Country was beginning to transfer the divine attributes which had once been associated with the magisterial office to the whole body of the people.

In the years before the outbreak of the Revolution, Thomas Hutchinson came closest to the Court's ideal of the good ruler. Early in his political career he angered the people who had elected him to the Massachusetts House of Representatives by declaring that he would not observe their instructions and would vote in the legislature as he alone saw fit.[6] When he was appointed governor of the Bay Colony in 1770, he tried to calm the "enthusiasm" of the populace and in the process earned the enmity of the Country party. In 1771 "Versus" defended the governor in *The Massachusetts Gazette*, claiming that though the mob called Hutchinson a man of "bad

---

the coming of the American Revolution. Yet to appreciate how the Great Awakening influenced colonial politics or to comprehend why Americans read Commonwealth writers so avidly, one has to know what went on in the years before Bailyn and Heimert began their accounts—one should realize, in fact, that New England was deeply divided long before George Whitefield crossed the Atlantic.

5. Daniel Fowle, *An Appendix to the Late Total Eclipse of Liberty* (Boston, 1756), p. 5; see also Paul S. Boyer, "Borrowed Rhetoric: The Massachusetts Excise Controversy of 1754," *William and Mary Quarterly*, 3d ser. 21 (1964), pp. 328–51; Robert M. Zemski, "The Massachusetts Assembly, 1730–1755" (Ph.D. diss., Yale University, 1967), pp. 278–300.

6. Malcolm Freiberg, "Thomas Hutchinson: The First Fifty Years (1711–1761)," *William and Mary Quarterly*, 3d ser., 15 (1958), p. 47.

Principles" and an "Enemy to Liberty," he deserved praise for refusing "to comply with the inclination and voice of the People,
which is the Rule for all Governors to observe."[7] Later in the same
journal, "Lenitas" wrote, "I would have Men of Candor, Sense, Integrity and Influence chosen to Conduct these [civil] affairs, and
not submit them to a giddy multitude, nor ignorant and imprudent
Men."[8] "Lenitas," no doubt, reflected Hutchinson's own view that
political authority was best placed in the hands of an elite group—
preferably wealthy, genteel merchants who had attended Harvard.
When discontent with the governor's policies mounted in the summer
of 1773, the *Gazette* printed the text of John Winthrop's 1645
speech, hoping that revolutionary Bostonians would respect the
founder's appeal for social order. What the editors of this Court
newspaper overlooked was that Winthrop had been selected by the
freemen, as Hutchinson had not been, and that obedience in 1645
grew out of a voluntary covenant, not arbitrary appointment.[9]

The most articulate Country writer in the period between Wise's
death and the Battle of Lexington was the Reverend Jonathan
Mayhew. In his most famous sermon, *A Discourse Concerning Unlimited Submission and Non-Resistance to the Higher Powers* (1750),
he told the people of Massachusetts that government authority was
a "trust" and that it was the citizens' responsibility to ensure that
rulers fulfilled the obligations of that agreement. Like John Wise,
Mayhew urged the colonists to be on guard for tyrants who would try
to destroy their liberties and lead them into political bondage. The
Country minister explained, "To say that subjects in general are
not proper judges when their governors oppress them, and play the
Tyrant . . . is as great *treason* as ever man uttered;—'tis treason,—not
against one *single* man, but the state—against the whole body
politic;—'tis treason against God. . . . The people know for what
end they set up, and maintain their governors; and they are the

7. *The Massachusetts Gazette,* May 16, 1771.

8. *The Massachusetts Gazette,* Apr. 9, 1772. On July 9, 1772, the
editors of the *Gazette* declared that their journal "is esteemed a very good
Paper by those who are *really* the better sort of people in the Province."

9. *The Massachusetts Gazette,* June 24, 1773.

proper judges when they execute their *trust* as they ought to do it."[10]
According to Mayhew, the best rulers were those who remained
closest to their constituents; for, like other Country advocates, he believed that if there was virtue in the commonwealth it was most
likely to be found in the people.[11]

On the eve of the Revolution the *Essex Gazette* presented Country
ideas in their most radical form. One essayist in the fall of 1770
asked his readers to consider for whom civil government had been
established: "Was it instituted solely for the agrandisement of those
few, who by some fortunate accident have been bred in a manner
which the world calls genteel?—Or to guard and secure the lives,
liberty and property of the industrious husbandmen, the careful
merchants, the diligent mechanics and laborious poor, who compose
the body of the people, and are the basis of society."[12] During the
early decades of the eighteenth century Country authors had not
challenged the idea that rulers should come from the "better sort."
They had only asked that such magistrates respond to the demands of
their constituents. But the writer in the *Essex Gazette* carried Country
thought another step, advising the freemen to choose rulers who
were socially, culturally, and economically like themselves. He warned
New Englanders that tyrants "in all ages and nations, almost in-

10. Jonathan Mayhew, *A Discourse Concerning Unlimited Submission
and Non-Resistance To The Higher Powers: With Some Reflections on the
Resistance Made to King Charles I* (Boston, 1750), p. 39; see also Mayhew,
*A Discourse Occasioned by the Death of the Honorable Stephen Sewall,
Esq. . . .* (Boston, 1760); *A Sermon Preached . . . Occasioned by the Much-
Lamented Death of His Royal Highness Frederick, Prince of Wales* (Boston,
1751); *A Sermon Preach'd . . . May 29th, 1754 Being the Anniversary For the
Election* (Boston, 1754); Charles W. Akers, *Called Unto Liberty: A Life
of Jonathan Mayhew, 1720–1766* (Cambridge, Mass., 1964).

11. In the election sermon of 1754 Mayhew told the members of the
lower house, "As You, honoured Gentlemen, are delegated immediately by
the good people of the Province to represent, and act for, them: You are,
if possible, under a nearer and stricter obligation, to regard their welfare,
than other branches of the legislature. You are more *particularly* the guardians of their rights and privileges" *(A Sermon Preach'd,* p. 43).

12. *The Essex Gazette,* Oct. 23, 1770.

variably [have] sprung from that class among the people called the better sort, and *nobility* and *gentry*."[13]

In October 1770 "America" told the readers of the *Essex Gazette* that "Revolutions are not so dangerous to the people, as to the rulers, for the people remain through all changes, but the rulers often sink to rise no more."[14] The events of the Revolution bore out "America's" observation, for after 1780 a new breed of rulers sat in the Massachusetts General Court. The freemen apparently decided that it was no longer necessary to have magistrates who were wealthier and better educated than themselves, and increasingly they called upon men of modest means and humble occupations to represent their interests in the state government.[15] To a great extent the Revolution removed the Court from New England politics; and, during the Confederation period and the early years of the nineteenth century, the good ruler was one who embodied Country characteristics.

The Revolution and the formation of a new country made the local magistrate less important than he had been in the colonial period. After 1789 the citizens of Massachusetts, along with those of the other states, turned their attentions to the federal government and to the problem of what attributes national leaders should possess.[16] Within this broader context the debate about the character of the good ruler has continued and is not likely to stop.

13. *The Essex Gazette,* Oct. 23, 1770. See Gordon S. Wood, *The Creation of the American Republic, 1776–1787* (Chapel Hill, 1969), pp. 180, 282–83.

14. *The Essex Gazette,* Oct. 30, 1770.

15. Richard V. W. Buel, Jr., "Democracy and the American Revolution: A Frame of Reference," *William and Mary Quarterly,* 3d. ser. 21(1964): 189–90; Jackson Turner Main, "Government by the People: The American Revolution and the Democratization of the Legislature," *William and Mary Quarterly* 23 (1966): 391–405.

16. See Max Farrand, ed., *The Records of the Federal Convention of 1787,* 3 vols. (New Haven, 1927), I: 421–23.

BIBLIOGRAPHICAL ESSAY

SINCE my book deals with such a long period of time, 1600–1730, I have been forced for the most part to use completely different sources for each chapter. I have, therefore, decided to divide my bibliography by chapters and within each section to comment on the materials which I felt were most valuable for my research in that period. With the exception of chapter 3, I have relied almost exclusively on printed collections of government records, private letters, and political pamphlets. In this bibliography I have made no attempt to mention every source which appeared in my footnotes, but only those which I regarded as essential to my understanding of the character of the good ruler. Moreover, I did not attempt to discuss all the secondary sources. Those which I used extensively are treated in the footnotes, where I have tried to give a critical analysis of major secondary works, explaining how they bear on the themes of the book.

Chapter 1

Four books were particularly helpful in guiding me to the political writings of the English Puritans in the period before 1630: William Haller, *The Rise of Puritanism* (New York, 1957); Michael Walzer, *The Revolution of the Saints* (Cambridge, Mass., 1965); Margaret Judson, *The Crisis of the Constitution* (New York, 1964); and Charles H. George and Katherine George, *The Protestant Mind of the English Reformation, 1570–1640* (Princeton, 1961). The Georges' book contains an extensive bibliography of Anglican and Puritan writings; and the footnotes in Judson's extremely valuable work led me to many important sermons that I did not know existed.

I was fortunate to be able to do much of my research for this chapter in the Beinecke Rare Book and Manuscript Library at Yale University. During the late nineteenth century Franklin Bowditch Dexter, Yale's librarian, saw the value of many Puritan tracts which are not now available anywhere else in the United States. It was at Beinecke Library that I read the following materials: William Ames, *Workes* (London, 1643); William Perkins, *Workes,* 3 vols. (London, 1608–31); John Preston, *Life Eternall Or, A Treatise of the Knowledge of the Divine Essence and Attributes* (London, 1631); John Preston, *Sermons Preached before His Majestie* . . . (London, 1630); John Downame, *The Christian Warfare* (London, 1619); Thomas Taylor, *Christs Combate and Conquest* . . . (Cambridge, Eng., 1618); William Gouge, *Gods Three Arrowes* . . . (London, 1631); Robert Cleaver, *A Godly Forme of Householde Government* (London, 1612).

There were a number of single sermons which helped me to understand Puritan attitudes about civil government before colonization. Alexander Leighton's *An Appeal to the Parliament* . . . (Amsterdam, 1628) was one of the clearest expressions of the Puritans' belief in a national covenant. Other important statements about the good ruler were John Reading, *Moses and Jethro: or the Good Magistrate* . . . (London, 1626); Nathanael Carpenter, *Achitophel, Or, The Picture of a Wicked Politician* (London, 1629); Thomas Sutton, *Jethroes Counsell to Moses: Or, A Direction for Magistrates* (London, 1631); A. Ar., *The Practise of Princes* (Amsterdam?, 1630); and Thomas Gataker, *Gods Parley with Princes* (London, 1620).

It apparently was common for ministers, both Anglican and Puritan, to deliver assize sermons before the opening of sessions of county courts or before local elections. The clergymen who delivered the assize sermons usually discussed some aspect of the magisterial calling, and many catalogued the attributes of the good ruler. These sermons may well have been the forerunners of the New England election sermon, which I describe in the bibliography for chapter 3. Some of the assize sermons that I used were included in the collected works of the various ministers, but a few were printed separately. The most important ones for my study were: Robert Bolton, *Two Sermons Preached at Northampton at Two Severall Assises* [1621 and 1625] (London, 1635); Robert Bolton, "A Sermon Preached at Lent Assises," *The Workes of the Reverend Robert Bolton* (London, 1641);

Samuel Garey, *A Manuell for Magistrates Or, A Lanterne for Lawyers* [an assize sermon delivered at Norwich, 1619] (London, 1623); Miles Smith, *A Learned and Godly Sermon, Preached at Worcester, at an Assise* (Oxford, 1602); Richard Carpenter, *The Conscionable Christian . . .* [Somerset assize, 1620] (London, 1623); John Squire, *A Sermon Preached at Hartford Assises* [March 1616] (London, 1618); William Sclater, *A Sermon Preached at the Last Generall Assise Holden for the County of Sommerset at Taunton* (London, 1616).

Some of the most valuable sermons of both Anglican and Puritan clergymen were reprinted in massive, multivolume collections during the last half of the nineteenth cenuty. These sets are usually well indexed, and many contain important biographical notes. For my chapter I found five collections particularly helpful: *The Works of Robert Sanderson*, 6 vols. (Oxford, 1854); *The Works of Thomas Adams: Being the Sum of His Sermons, Meditations, and Other Divine and Moral Discourses*, 3 vols. (Edinburgh, 1861–62); *The Works of Lancelot Andrewes*, 11 vols. (Oxford, 1854); Alexander Grosart, ed., *The Complete Works of Richard Sibbes,* 7 vols. (Edinburgh, 1862–67); *Sermons and Treatises of Samuel Ward* (Edinburgh, 1862).

There were several books that helped me understand English social and political thought in the late sixteenth and early seventeenth centuries. One of the most important guides to this period is L. Alston, ed., *Sir Thomas Smith's De Republica Anglorum* (Cambridge, Eng., 1906). William Haller's *The Elect Nation* (New York, 1963) discusses how Englishmen came to see their country as God's chosen nation, the New Israel. Haller's study is vital background for any investigation of Puritan political ideas. Christopher Morris's *Political Thought in England: Tyndale to Hooker* (Oxford, 1953) offers a short, but valuable survey of sixteenth-century political thought. I found Morris's work far more useful than the more famous, J. W. Allen, *A History of Political Thought in the Sixteenth Century* (London, 1960). Winthrop S. Hudson, ed., *John Ponet, Advocate of Limited Monarchy* (Chicago, 1942) contains a long introduction which is the best treatment of the Marian exiles and their political beliefs. The essay at the beginning of Charles H. McIlwain, ed., *The Political Works of James I* (Cambridge, Mass., 1918) remains the best account of early Stuart political theory.

Chapter 2

During the early years of this century Charles Evans compiled a list of every book, sermon, newspaper, pamphlet, broadside, magazine, and almanac printed in America between 1640 and 1800. Evans omitted a few pieces and sometimes included titles that turned out to be "ghosts"—works that were advertised, but in fact never published. But, by and large, Evans's *American Bibliography,* 14 vols. (Chicago, 1903–59) is a reliable guide to the printed source materials of the colonial period. Recently, Clifford K. Shipton of the American Antiquarian Society at Worcester, Massachusetts, reproduced all the works (except newspapers and magazines) mentioned in Evans's bibliography on Microcards. This collection which contains thousands of titles is usually referred to as *Early American Imprints.* Almost every sermon and pamphlet which I cite in the footnotes for chapters 2 through 7 is easily accessible in this form.

The writings and papers of seventeenth- and eighteenth-century colonists are scattered through the following publications: the *Collections* and *Proceedings* of the Massachusetts Historical Society, the *Publications* of the Colonial Society of Massachusetts, the *Collections* of the Connecticut Historical Society, the *Proceedings* of the American Antiquarian Society, the *New England Quarterly,* the *Collections* of the Essex Institute.

Of particular value in writing chapter 2 was N. B. Shurtleff, ed., *The Records of the Governor and Company of the Massachusetts Bay in New England,* 5 vols. in 6 (Boston, 1853–54). Some of the best material on the character of the good ruler in this period is in *The Winthrop Papers,* 5 vols. (Boston, 1929–47). This collection contains not only John Winthrop's personal correspondence, but also his political essays. The volumes are well indexed and most of the pieces are carefully annotated. I also relied on James Savage's edition of Winthrop's *History of New England from 1630–1649,* 2 vols. (Boston, 1853). I prefer Savage's edition to the one of James K. Hosmer which appeared in 1908 because Savage included useful genealogical comments in his footnotes. Savage was also the author of the pioneer genealogical reference work, *A Genealogical Dictionary of . . . New England,* 4 vols. (Boston, 1860–62), which traces the development of every colonial family in the period between

1630 and 1700. Also useful were *The Hutchinson Papers*, 2 vols. (Albany, 1865) and Thomas Hutchinson's *The History of the Colony and Province of Massachusetts-Bay*, ed. Lawrence S. Mayo, 3 vols. (Boston, 1936). Hutchinson's history was written in the last half of the eighteenth century, but in my estimation, his account is still better than James Truslow Adams, *The Founding of New England* (Boston, 1921); Herbert L. Osgood, *The American Colonies in the Seventeenth Century* (New York, 1904–07); John G. Palfrey, *A Compendious History of New England*, 5 vols. (Boston, 1858–90); or William B. Weeden, *Economic and Social History of New England, 1620–1789*, 2 vols. (Boston, 1890). Mayo's edition of the Hutchinson *History* is especially valuable because it contains several early documents that are difficult to find elsewhere.

There have been more articles and books written about the founding of Massachusetts than about any other period in its history, with the possible exception of the American Revolution. In my footnotes I mention many of the most important accounts, but there are three sources that require special recognition. I have gained more from Perry Miller's *The New England Mind*, 2 vols. (Boston, 1961) than I can ever hope to acknowledge. The second volume, *The New England Mind: From Colony to Province*, stands head and shoulders above any other treatment of seventeenth-century New England. I regard my study as a complement, not a criticism of Miller's work. I have found the introduction to Edmund S. Morgan, ed., *Puritan Political Ideas* (Indianapolis, 1965), extremely helpful in understanding the political implication of the doctrine of calling and the belief in covenant. Stephen Foster's discussion of the political battles of the first generation is one of the best written accounts available, "The Puritan Social Ethic: Class and Calling in the First Hundred Years of Settlement in New England" (Ph.D. diss., Yale University, 1966), pp. 125–85.

Chapter 3

Much of the material for this chapter came from the Massachusetts Archives, a manuscript collection of records located in the basement of the Massachusetts State Capitol Building in Boston. The archives comprise over three hundred reels of microfilm and cover every phase

of colonial life from the year 1630 to 1780. The rolls which I used
in this section were entitled "legislative" and "military." The archives
were organized during the late nineteenth century into such arbitrary
categories as "land," "religion," "private letters," and "judicial."
Often the title of a roll of microfilm has little to do with its content,
and any student working with the Massachusetts Archives would be
well advised to search through reels that would seem to have no bearing on his topic of research.

Of the many different sources I used for this chapter I want to
mention three which were particularly valuable. Robert N. Toppan
and Alfred T. S. Goodrick, eds., *Edward Randolph: Including His
Letters and Official Papers . . . 1676–1703*, 7 vols. (Boston, 1898–
1909), contains a wealth of papers and letters which describe Massachusetts society through the unfriendly eyes of an English official.
Many of Randolph's comments shed light on Joseph Dudley's early
career. For an understanding of English policy in New England, I
found the *Calendar of State Papers, Colonial Series,* helpful. Also the
first volume of Hamilton Hill's *History of the Old South Church,*
2 vols. (Boston, 1890), reproduces some important ecclesiastical documents that are not printed elsewhere.

Since I have cited election sermons extensively in this and succeeding chapters, I thought it essential to comment on their value
as a source for the political history of New England. The election
sermons of Massachusetts are a rich and easily accessible repository
of Puritan political ideas. Historians have usually treated these
sermons as intellectual essays divorced from contemporary and
anomalous events. Such an approach is not wrong, but a deeper
understanding of the election sermons can be gained when one knows
the circumstances surrounding their delivery: Who chose the election speakers, to whom did they speak, and what ends did they hope
to achieve?

The Massachusetts election sermon was probably a modification
of the English assize sermon, although its inspiration may have come
from Calvin's Geneva (see discussion in chapter 1; William Monter,
Calvin's Geneva [New York, 1967], p. 162). During the 1630s
election speakers were chosen by the governor with advice from the
assistants. The deputies were skeptical of this practice, however, for
they did not believe that the ruler's calling included the right to

select election preachers. In 1641 and 1643 the representatives defied
the assistants by inviting clergymen of their own. Winthrop and the
Discretionary forces regarded the deputies' act as an unwarranted
encroachment upon the magisterial office but avoided a showdown,
since the colony was already divided over other, more serious political
issues. Winthrop noted with regret in 1645 that "The governour and
assistants had used for ten or eleven years at least to appoint one to
preach on the day of election, but about three or four years since,
the deputies challenged it as their right and accordingly had twice
made the choice (the magistrates still professing it to be a mere
intrusion &c)." The two houses forged an enduring compromise
when they decided to alternate the selection of the election speaker
between the deputies and the assistants (Winthrop, *History*, 2: 42,
119, 268–69; *Mass. Records*, 3: 80).

The election sermons delivered during the 1660s and 1670s become more meaningful when one realizes that the two houses took
turns picking the minister. The deputies had the choice on odd-
numbered years; the magistrates on the even-numbered ones. Knowledge of this convention helps the intellectual historian to discover
that many seemingly commonplace remarks were actually comments
on contemporary problems. Superficially, for example, the election
sermons of 1669, 1670, and 1671 appear to be quite similar, calling
for the reign of pious rulers and lamenting New England's loss of
virtue. Closer examination, however, reveals that the content of
these sermons is very different. In 1669 Reverend John Davenport
spoke the deputies' mind when he attacked the rulers, presumably
the assistants, for allowing the adoption of the Half-Way Covenant.
The next year, Samuel Danforth delivered a platitudinous sermon,
no doubt designed to sooth the ill feeling which Davenport had
created. The rhetorical dust had hardly settled when the representatives called upon the Reverend John Oxenbridge in 1671. Oxenbridge
more than compensated for Danforth's perfunctory performance and
managed to anger a good part of the colony in the process. He noted
specifically in the printed version that the deputies had asked him to
talk before the General Court, and it was only with the greatest
reluctance that the magistrates agreed to allow its publication. Other
election sermons from this period, especially those of 1676 and 1677,
reflected the differences between the two branches of the legislature

(John Davenport, *A Sermon Preach'd at the Election* . . . 1669
[Boston, 1670], reprinted in *Publications of the Colonial Society of
Massachusetts* 10 [1907]: 1–6; Samuel Danforth, *A Brief Recogni-
tion of New-Englands Errand into the Wilderness* [Cambridge, Mass.,
1671]; John Oxenbridge, *New-England Freemen Warned and
Warmed* . . . [Boston, 1673], p. A3; *Mass. Records,* 4: pt. 2, p. 540).

It is very difficult to tell when and to whom the election sermons
were given. In 1634 John Cotton thought that his sermon could influence the outcome of the election and, therefore, he must have
spoken before a majority of the freemen had cast their ballots
(Winthrop, *History,* 1: 104). As the colony's population grew, an
increasing number of men voted by proxy and, therefore, never
heard the election sermon. The evidence is scant, but it appears that
until the 1670s the ministers preached before the Boston freemen
had voted and before the proxy returns had been counted (see John
Higginson, *The Cause of God and His People in New-England*
[Cambridge, Mass., 1663], p. 23). It is not clear when this practice
changed, but in 1677 Increase Mather noted that, since his words
could not alter the results of the present election, the people should
reflect on his message for future years *(A Discourse Concerning the
Danger of Apostasy,* p. 91).

Although the sermons gradually lost their relevance to specific elections, the colonists probably read, discussed, and circulated them
throughout Massachusetts long after they had been delivered. Only
after the turn of the century did election sermons become dull,
ritualistic performances. In May 1700 Cotton Mather noted in his
diary that the lower house had tried to abolish the practice altogether.
Mather explained:

> Our Governour, the Earl of *Bellomont* . . . proposed, that (tho'
> the Representatives of the Province, had at their last Session
> desired, that instead of a Sermon on the Day of the Anniversary
> Election, there might be only the usual weekly Lecture held on
> the day following, and preached by the Minister, to whom the
> Lecture fell in Course), there might be a Sermon according to
> the ancient Custome at the Opening of the General Court, and
> that such a Minister, as hee then (upon a particular Fancy)
> named, might preach it *(7 Collections,* MHS, 7, pt. 1, p. 349).

Despite the representatives' action, the election sermons continued to be a regular part of the election celebration; and, as far as I can tell, the old practice of alternating the selection of the speaker between houses of the legislature was preserved.

Many eighteenth-century election day speakers avoided discussion of political issues and used the occasion of preaching before the General Court as an excuse to advance their own special interests; in other words, they talked more about their own professional good than they did about the colony's general political good. John Norton's election sermon of 1708, *An Essay Tending to Promote Reformation*, reflected the inanition of the custom. "I shall not take upon me to teach, or prescribe to the Great and General Court in Civil Political Affairs," Norton declared; and Samuel Sewall labeled the performance, "Flattering . . . as to the Governour" *(5 Collections,* MHS, 6: 224). The purely ceremonial character of most election sermons irritated the Reverend Ebenezer Pemberton; for, when his time arrived to speak, he wanted the magistrates to pay close attention to what he had to say. "I hope there are none so vain," he preached in 1710, "as to imagine, that I appear this Day in this *Awful Desk,* only to beat the Air, & play the *Orator* in an Artful Address to our Rulers" *(The Divine Original and Dignity of Government Asserted* [Boston, 1710], p. 4).

The following material is useful in understanding the development of the election sermon: Lindsay Swift, "The Massachusetts Election Sermons," *Publications of the Colonial Society of Massachusetts* 1 (1865): 388–451; Robert W. G. Vail, "A Check List of New England Election Sermons," *Proceedings of the American Antiquarian Society* 45 (1935): 233–66; Martha Louise Counts, "The Political Views of the Eighteenth-Century New England Clergy as Expressed in Their Election Sermons" (Ph.D. diss., Columbia University, 1956); A. W. Plumstead, ed., *The Wall and the Garden; Selected Massachusetts Election Sermons, 1670–1775* (Minneapolis, 1968), pp. 3–37.

Chapter 4

The single most important source for my study of the Glorious Revolution was William H. Whitmore, ed., *The Andros Tracts,* 3 vols. (Boston, 1868). Other valuable pamphlets were published in

Andrew M. Davis, ed., *Colonial Currency Reprints,* 4 vols. (Boston, 1910–11). I used the Massachusetts Archives for this chapter and found that reels 35, 107, 126–29 contained the best material on the period. Also located at the Public Archives of Massachusetts are the Council Records and the Court Records, 6, which contain reports and records of both the Dudley and the Andros administrations. I have commented on Viola F. Barnes's study of the Glorious Revolution, *The Dominion of New England: A Study in British Colonial Policy* (New York, 1960), in n. 1, chap. 4. I want to point out, however, the need for a new investigation of the Andros government and the Bradstreet administration. The manuscript materials in Boston represent a wealth of facts about the day-to-day work of the Dominion authorities, and a statistically minded historian could analyze this material to see if there had been a moderate party in the colony and to find out if the political factions in the period 1685 to 1691 were religiously based as Barnes believed.

Chapter 5

Some of the most valuable material for my discussion of Phips's government came from Cotton Mather's "The Life of His Excellency Sir William Phips," printed in Mather's *Magnalia Christi Americana* (London, 1702). *The Calendar of State Papers, Colonial Series,* and the Massachusetts Archives were also helpful. There are no satisfactory studies of the politics of the 1690s in Massachusetts. Many authors comment on Increase Mather's efforts to win the hearts of the Puritans with the new charter and describe Elisha Cooke's opposition to the change. However, no historian has explained why Cooke attacked the new patent—was it for religious, economic, or political reasons (or all three)? How was the lower house divided in this period? Why did Joseph Dudley think that he could return as governor as early as 1693? These are difficult questions, but I think they can be answered.

Chapters 6 and 7

For my discussion of the Court and Country I relied on pamphlets and sermons that are available in the *Early American Imprint* series and in the *Collections* of the Massachusetts Historical Society. I found Davis's *Currency Reprints* extremely helpful for understanding the battle over banking and paper money. I have mentioned all the books and articles that I used on the English Court and Country in n. 10, chap. 6. The three newspapers which were published in Massachusetts during the period, *The Boston Weekly News-Letter, The Boston Gazette,* and *The New-England Courant,* have been reproduced on Microcard by the Micro Research Corporation in conjunction with the American Antiquarian Society in Worcester, Massachusetts.

INDEX

T. H. Breen is associate professor of history at Northwestern University.